THE NIGHT WILL END

THE NIGHT WILL END

HENRI FRENAY

TRANSLATED FROM THE FRENCH BY
DAN HOFSTADTER

McGRAW-HILL BOOK COMPANY · NEW YORK · ST. LOUIS · SAN FRANCISCO · DÜSSELDORF · MEXICO

Book design by Paulette Nenner.

123456789KPKP798765

Library of Congress Cataloging in Publication Data

Frenay, Henri.
    The night will end.

    Translation of La nuit finira.
    Includes index.
    1. World War, 1939–1945—Underground movements—France. 2. France—History—German occupation, 1940–1945. I. Title.
D802.F8F8613   940.53'44   75–11807
ISBN 0–07–022135–9

Originally published in French under the title *La Nuit Finira,* © 1973 by Opera Mundi.

CONTENTS

MAJOR
PERSONALITIES IN THE M.U.R.

Albrecht, Berty. The author's closest friend and the founder of Combat's Social Service.

d'Astier de la Vigerie, Emmanuel. Leader of Libération, a labor-oriented Resistance group in the M.U.R. umbrella organization.

de Bénouville, Pierre. Ex-member of the right-wing Action Française and the director of Combat's foreign relations.

Bernard, Jacqueline. Headed Combat's propaganda department with René Cerf-Ferrière.

Bernard, Jean-Guy. Combat's staff secretary. Jacqueline's brother.

Bidault, Georges. Left-wing Catholic journalist and director (in association with Jean Moulin) of the underground B.I.P. (Information and Press Bureau). Later Foreign Minister in De Gaulle's Provisional Government and a major figure in postwar French politics.

Bollier, André. Head of printing and distribution for Combat's underground press.

Bourdet, Claude. Initially director of the N.A.P. (Infiltration of Public Administrations). Took over leadership of Combat in Vichy zone after the author's appointment as minister in De Gaulle's Provisional Government.

Brault, Michel. Head of Combat's maquis.

Capitant, René. Law professor and chief figure in Combat's semi-autonomous Algerian branch. Later Minister of National Education in De Gaulle's Provisional Government.

Cerf-"Ferrière," René. Socialist director of Combat's propaganda department (with Jacqueline Bernard).

Chevance, Maurice. Career officer and coordinator of Combat's military arm.

Delestraint, General. Titular head of Secret Army until his arrest by the Gestapo in June 1943.

Dhont, Jacques. Top man (with André Hauriou) of Combat's Toulouse branch.

Guédon, Robert. Career officer who unsuccessfully attempted to organize a Combat branch in the occupied (northern) zone.

Gemahling, Jean. Head of Combat's S.R. (Intelligence Service).

Hauriou, André. Law professor and Combat's chief (with Jacques Dhont) in Toulouse.

Hardy, René. Head of Resistance-Rail. Later suspected of collusion with the Gestapo.

Lévy, Jean-Pierre. Founder of the Lyons-based Resistance group Franc-Tireur within the M.U.R. front.

de Menthon, François. Law professor in Lyons, founder of the Resistance group Liberté, which merged with Combat.

Michelet, Edmond. Militant Catholic and Combat's chief in the Limoges area.

The Night Will End

Monod, Philippe. Combat's representative in Switzerland.

Moulin, Jean. De Gaulle's delegate to the metropolitan Resistance until his arrest in June 1943. Responsible for the allotment of Free French funds to the various Resistance groups.

Peck, Marcel. Combat's chief in Lyons.

Petit, Claudius. Jean-Pierre Lévy's successor as director of Franc-Tireur.

Rabattet, Georges. An organizer of maquis in the Vichy zone.

Renouvin, Jacques. Ex-member of the right-wing Action Française and founder of the Groupes Francs, Combat's shock troops.

Teitgen, Pierre-Henri. A law professor and Combat's chief in Montpellier.

Major Personalities in the M.U.R.

INTRODUCTION

When I decided to
write this book in the spring of
1971, twenty-six years had gone by since
the victory of the Allies in World War II. On
several occasions I had already been urged to set
down my memories of the war, when fate had honored me with a highly unusual experience. Present at the
very birth of the Resistance, before it even bore that name,
I was both a participant in and a witness to its development,
and thereafter I devoted all my energies to the growth of this
fledgling movement.

Stone by stone my comrades and I constructed "Combat" and
each of its clandestine branches: its propaganda, its newspapers, its
Groupes Francs, its Secret Army and its many other specialized
services—an ever vaster and denser spider's web that the Vichy
police and later the Gestapo were to attack relentlessly.

After I had spent three years in the underground, De Gaulle
summoned me to serve in the National Liberation Committee
and then in the provisional government. From November 1943 to November 1945, first in Algiers and then in
Paris, I was involved both in the prologue to the Liberation and in the many controversies and intrigues that were to give the French Republic its new face.

It was an exceptionally fascinating period, and I held several posts in which I could observe what few others were able to see. I was tempted to write my memoirs at the time, and yet as late as 1971 I had not done so. Here is why, as I explained to my friend Colonel Passy when in 1951 I broke my self-imposed silence and agreed to add an appendix of several pages to Volume III of Colonel Passy's memoirs, *Missions en France:*

. . . Heroism and cowardice, ambition and selflessness, mediocrity and greatness are intimately entwined in my memories. Although history did sometimes carry us above and beyond ourselves, we were still only men of flesh and blood with our characteristic weaknesses and flaws.

Must I submit to a pitiless microscopic examination of those wartime deeds which, though forming an epic whole, contained details which were sometimes shabby and common? Must I reveal that some men, as brave in facing death as they had been during our clandestine life, were unable to rise to certain great occasions? No, I have not the heart. Indeed, perhaps I should do ill to speak plainly of those days, for the strength of peoples is often in their legends. It would give me no pleasure even partially to dispel the legendary quality of that marvelous epic which I witnessed and in which I participated. Moreover, the Resistance—the real Resistance of the early years—was experienced by only a handful of people, and it remains for me a secret garden which, alone, I still sometimes enter. I could hardly be reproached for not wanting a holiday crowd to dog me through the garden gate! I have never been fond of profanations.

After offering my opinion of certain passages in Passy's book, I concluded:

One day, perhaps, if my memory is still unclouded, I shall set down for my son alone the story of those great years which I and others experienced so intensely.

This book is that story, for an odd combination of circumstances that to others might seem quite fortuitous has succeeded in changing my mind.

Many studies have been devoted to the Resistance, but for years

The Night Will End

I read almost nothing about it. Although everyone's horizon shrinks as one grows older, I am inclined to look ahead rather than back. That is why I have never been able to join in the activities of veterans' groups. Parades beneath the tricolor and commemorative fanfares, though they command my respect, have never much appealed to me. Yet, favored in the last few years by the leisure of retirement and nagged by a curiosity to which I had previously been immune, I began to read, and I read widely.

I discovered some excellent accounts, straightforward chronicles in which the various political personalities of the day were placed in the camps where I myself judged them to belong. But above all, as the days went by, I realized that my secret garden was no longer secret, that it had, in fact, been desecrated. Here and there, scattered about in these many narratives, were events I myself had experienced, and men whom I had known and about whom I had held my tongue were often portrayed unrecognizably. It was a very trying experience for me.

It was then, by chance, that my friend Charles Ronsac, the editor-in-chief of *Opera Mundi*, urged me to write my memoirs. This apparent coincidence intrigued me. Yet perhaps I still would have resisted his offer if, several days later, a reunion had not taken place—the first since 1945—of those who, like myself, had once been militants in Combat. Many of us had not seen one another for many years, some of us not since the end of the war. We had markedly different opinions and opposing political positions. Yet within a short time it seemed that nothing, neither the intervening years nor our divergent opinions, had ever separated us. Words like *friendship* and *comradeship* can only hint at the depth of our emotions. What passed between us was so utterly direct, so simple and harmonious, that it seemed like a form of religious communion. We were still the great family we had once been, and, for most of them, I was still "the boss."

As I said farewell to them, my mind was already made up: I would write a book that would be theirs as much as mine, even though each one of them had had his own unique experiences in the course of our common struggle and suffered his own ordeals.

My will was reinforced by the thought that, to my knowledge, no clandestine leader had yet told the story of a resistance move-

Introduction

ment—I mean a real movement, not just an undercover ring. Nobody had ever told how, and under what instigation, our movement had been born or how by degrees it had fashioned its own structures and methods, sought out and found the means for effective action. This phenomenon, even in the rich annals of French history, was entirely new. We had no precedent to guide our thoughts and actions.

In writing this book, I told myself, I would perhaps be satisfying a curiosity on the part of many people which the years had not managed to blunt. I would also be offering a well-deserved homage to all my underground companions, not only to the living but above all to those who had fallen in battle and who justly deserved to be rescued from oblivion.

Problems arose. How much should I recount—the clandestine period alone or that which followed as well? How far should I take my narrative? How could I intelligibly describe all our ideas, actions, hopes and disappointments? Must I try to retrace the history of Combat in all its complexity, or should I limit myself to telling what I had personally seen, heard or initiated?

There was also something else that made me quite apprehensive. Though I clearly remembered many events, nearly thirty years had passed, and my memory had surely not retained many things worthy of relating. How could I faithfully assemble this vast puzzle when so many of its pieces were missing?

On the day that Marshal Pétain begged the enemy for an armistice, France's ordeal began. Here, then, my book would also begin. Three years later, to the very day, I left France. My account might well have ended there, but I decided to take it further. The resistance movements were spurred not only by the need to fight Nazism through propaganda, irregular warfare and subterfuge; they were also informed by a deep desire to overhaul the civic traditions and the political, economic and social structures of our nation. We were highly aware of the flaws in the regime that had led France to her downfall and to the humiliating experience of Vichy. It was toward a strong and a pure republic, *une république pure et dure,* as we used to say, that we aspired. We were at once soldiers in mufti and citizens in revolt against the established

The Night Will End

authorities, and we yearned for a social revolution whose contours, little by little, we struggled to block out.

Only a chain of little-known and seemingly minor historical events—events which, I believe, have not hitherto been linked together—can explain why and how this revolution that we bore within us eventually miscarried, why and how the feeble new government of the Fourth Republic buried our hopes forever. I lived through or at least closely followed these events, which took place simultaneously in Algiers and France, during my stint (through which I remained in close touch with my clandestine friends) as *commissaire* and then as cabinet minister. These events are worth the telling, and I have not shied from stressing the responsibility of those who instigated them or had a hand in bringing them about, including General Charles de Gaulle. This is why the first session of the Constituent Assembly marks the end of my narrative, for it was then that the die was cast. It was at that point that I resigned from the government.

What the reader will find in the following pages, then, is not a history of the Resistance or even the history of Combat—which, by the way, has already been excellently done*—but simply my own memories. Likewise, it was impossible for me to devote as much attention to the actions of my comrades as their heroism warrants. What sharpens my regret is that without them, without their warmhearted and loyal teamwork, none of our plans could ever have been brought to fruition. Without them the mad endeavor into which I threw myself in 1940 would have remained only a dream, only a passing fancy. I hope that they will understand and forgive me.

Even less could I have described every courageous operation carried out by our Groupes Francs or by the men of Résistance-Rail. For I myself never blew up a collaborationist den, I myself never derailed a train, I myself never slew a German officer or Gestapo agent with my own hand. Others were so employed. I can report only my own recollections.

These recollections required many an outside aid, especially

Combat, by Marie Granet and Henri Michel, Presses Universitaires de France, 1957.

Introduction

since underground activity precludes the keeping of logbooks. In such cases I had recourse to the numerous testimonials collected after the war by official agencies who interviewed my comrades and myself. Many of my friends, in the course of sometimes multisession interviews, willingly submitted to my probing interrogations. Some of them placed at my disposal original documents which by some miracle they had retained. I take this opportunity to thank them.

And so I wove an ever denser tapestry of facts, which in their turn caused still more facts to emerge from my memory. Little by little I felt myself transported thirty years into the past, and I soon found myself feeling once again the emotions that had animated me long ago—my aspirations, illusions, fears, rages and blighted hopes.

And so I have relived our long-past days, with their joys, their sorrows and often even their dramas—our profound differences with De Gaulle, our desperate efforts in the hope that victory in war might not be followed by defeat in peace.

Those days I have tried faithfully to retrace in this book. Its writing has caused me great pleasure, a pleasure I would very much enjoy sharing with my readers, though sundered from the melancholy which, for me, invariably accompanied it.

The Night Will End

THE NIGHT WILL END

There we were,
three officers at the side of the
road, hunched intently over our crack-
ling field radio. Three miles to the north, on the
canal linking the Marne to the Rhine, a battle was
raging. Our 43rd Army Corps was trying to stem the onslaught of the German troops that had been pursuing us
closely since June 13. Only three days ago, we, the defenders
of the Maginot Line, had received the incredible order to retreat.
Nothing had prepared us for such a move, neither our individual equipment, nor our permanent armored emplacements, least
of all our garrisons' standing order to hold the line at all costs.
In the distance, tall columns of black smoke rose into the air.
Before our withdrawal we were burning our gasoline depots. The
smoke did not altogether hide a clear springtime sky, for the
weather was lovely and Hitler's air force was using it to advantage.
It was not battle news we were so eagerly awaiting but news from
France. We had already guessed that German armor had effectively cut us off from the hinterland. The day before,
General Lescanne, who commanded our army corps, had
called together several of his general staff officers, including myself. "Gentlemen," he had announced,
"the situation is critical, but there's still hope:
Marshal Pétain has just taken charge

of the government."

We already knew that the government had declared Paris an open city to avert its devastation and that three days ago German troops had occupied the capital. We also knew that the government, retreating before the withering enemy advance, had moved to Bordeaux. Bordeaux was an open door to our overseas empire, fresh troops could still be committed, and the enemy's rapid advance imperiled his own columns. In short, as my two companions and I told one another, there was plenty of reason to keep on hoping. Suddenly, through the static on the radio, we heard the words "Marshal Pétain speaks."

Pétain's radio-address is known to all Frenchmen of my generation, but perhaps only those who like myself heard it through the thunder of artillery can still recall the sorrowful gravity of those words: "I offer the gift of my person to France that I may ease her sorrow. It is with a heavy heart that I tell you that we must stop fighting. Tonight I have addressed myself to the adversary to ask him if he is ready to seek with us, in honor, as soldiers after a battle, some way to put an end to the hostilities."

For what seemed like endless moments we remained speechless. With clenched jaws I averted my eyes from those of the others, knowing that I would see tears like those I felt on my own cheeks.

Not far off we could still hear the rattling of the machine guns. Fortunately our gun crews as yet knew nothing—but tomorrow?

"It's impossible. Impossible!" repeated Captain X dazedly. "In one month we cannot have been totally beaten."

"I can't understand it," muttered Lieutenant Y. "Well, at least the Marshal is there. He'll demand respect from the Germans. After all, he is Marshal Pétain!"

For me too Pétain was a great name. And yet . . .

The enemy pressed us from the north, then from the west, forcing us to withdraw into the mountains. Soon the German Army crossed the Rhine. Encircled, we formed the "Redoubt of the Vosges," as the newspapers called it.

First our ammunition started to disappear, then our food. The end was near; by the wish of General Lescanne, it was to be dignified. Bank notes were burned, calculating machines put out of commission, the destruction of artillery pieces prepared. The

The Night Will End

headquarters of the army corps was set up in the Donon pass, a few kilometers from Strasbourg, where, in 1937–1938, after my graduation from the Ecole de Guerre, I had spent a year at the Centre d'Etudes Germaniques. In those days we often came, young men and women together, to the same inn where I was now stationed, the Hotel Vélléda, to enjoy a *truite au bleu* and to go huckleberry-picking in the forest.

Nothing seemed changed. The little cemetery of the Alpine light infantry fallen in the First World War was still there, tucked away unobtrusively, silent save for the sound of spades. Soldiers were digging new graves, for it was fitting that the sons be laid to rest beside their fathers. The men were naked to the waist, and one could almost imagine them singing, so blue was the sky, so sweet-scented the woods, so fine would it have been to dwell here in peace.

Our flags must not fall into enemy hands. This too we had been taught. So they were collected and a fire was lighted. As the name of each unit was called out, an officer would step forward and throw its colors into the flames. Once again we struggled vainly to keep back our tears.

It was all over. There was nothing to do but stand fast and await the armistice. We wondered when it would be signed.

The general staff, who were quartered in some old blockhouses, prepared to fight like infantrymen. We armed about fifty secretaries, orderlies and telephone operators, who doubtless had never even held a rifle. A volunteer was needed to take command of this improvised detachment. I stepped forward, for the old casemates hardly filled me with trust. I have always preferred the open air.

I deployed my men along the edge of the forest directly facing the Donon pass. My job was to cover our command post, to hold the line as best I could. I rather liked the vagueness of these orders. Oddly enough, my men's morale was excellent.

We discovered a chalet with a wine cellar that attested to its owner's good taste. A few bottles passed around in my outfit were greatly appreciated. Like a good Lyonnais, I reserved a bottle of Fleury for myself.

The night passed in utter silence. The attack would surely come at dawn. But it did not come. Shortly after eight o'clock an

The Night Will End

automobile drove through the pass and came within range of our automatic rifles. The car was driven by German officers bearing white flags. They had come to announce that the Armistice had been signed and that we should hold our fire. They were escorted to General Lescanne.

We began to negotiate. Since I knew German I served from time to time as interpreter. General Lescanne was a courageous old fellow and proved himself equal to this dramatic moment. Sixteen German divisions confronted us. Their demands were stiff, so stiff that we almost broke off the talks. I distinctly recall the scene.

The German officer: "General, our conditions must be accepted as a whole. They are not subject to discussion."

Lescanne: "Without a written order from the Fifth Army, I cannot accept them as they stand."

"If you refuse them, we shall resume our attack tomorrow morning, and here is a summary of the strength, condition and stations of the forces which will storm your positions." (An impressive enumeration followed.)

"Sir, as you know, my means are greatly inferior to yours, but I shall still kill a great many of your men."

At this the German mollified his position somewhat, but he was well aware that the armistice convention required, purely and simply, the surrender of our army corps. Nonetheless, Lescanne did obtain fairly honorable conditions: Each officer would remain armed and in command of his unit. The latter would retain its regulation equipment and part of its field gear.

The date was June 5, 1940. News that the accord had been signed spread like wildfire. It was then that I saw our men, who had fought so well right up to the last minute, throw down their arms, abandon their field packs and organize folk dances on the road and in forest clearings. Forgotten were the disaster, the surrender, self-respect, the dignity of the vanquished before the victor. No, I was not mistaken: In the faces of the young German soldiers who passed by, I read astonishment and contempt.

On the following day, June 26, General Lescanne read general order No. 91 to his troops. It rang out like a clarion call:

"During these days of mourning, the 43rd Army Corps has stood fast as a rock in the midst of a raging flood. . . . Deaf to rumors of

The Night Will End

an armistice, it has held out though encircled by sixteen German divisions, until the exhaustion of its resources and its ammunition.

"The 43rd Army Corps has fallen here at Donon. This is symbolic: The 43rd has held until June 24 the last corner of Alsace, the northernmost point of the French front. It fired the last cannon shot.

"Be proud! Be confident! Be loyal to one another! The days of mourning shall come to an end."

So now I was a prisoner! Our troops were rounded up and they surrendered their arms. Along a wide perimeter around the pass, at intervals of 100 meters, a cordon of German sentries was established. Our field radios we also surrendered; about France we no longer knew anything.

What would become of us? The general view leaned toward an early release from captivity; it was corroborated by the German officers with whom we talked.

"In a few days you'll be returned to your government. What could we do with millions of French prisoners whom we couldn't even feed? . . . England will soon be beaten and the war over. Why should we bother to imprison you for so short a time?"

This apparently logical reasoning failed to convince me. I decided to escape, but—sign of the times!—I found not a single officer willing to join me. All accepted the word of the victor.

It was a noncom, Adjutant Bourguet, who became my companion.

The following day the general was informed that the army corps would be marched to Strasbourg on the morning of the 29th. This route eastward, toward the Rhine, did not strike me as likely to lead to a restoration of our freedom. I was not mistaken. Those Bourguet and I left behind on that day were indeed departing into captivity. And in captivity they remained, for five long years.

First we had to slip out of the circle that enclosed us. At dusk, after several unsuccessful attempts, we jumped off the road between two sentries. Soon afterward we were sound asleep under some thick bushes.

At dawn I awakened my companion. "Bourguet, *mon vieux*, we . must choose between two risky courses—to escape notice by

The Night Will End

5

marching only at night, which in this season means six hours at best, or to march due south during the day, which means more like fifteen or sixteen hours. I prefer to march by day. How about you?"

"Let's try it, *mon capitaine*. We'll see what happens."

And so for two weeks we forged ahead, still in uniform, avoiding all roads and paths in order to avoid undesirable encounters.

In any other circumstances it would have been a magnificent excursion. I wonder if France has since seen a summer as splendid as the summer of 1940. We covered the entire Vosges range from north to south, with only a Michelin map and a compass to guide us through the woods. For a long time we followed the line of the crest, passing from knoll to knoll, always on the lookout, for the region was infested with Germans. Often we eluded them only by the skin of our teeth.

I remember as if it were yesterday my wonderment when we arrived at sunset by the shores of the Lac Noir, which lay like a gem gleaming in a casket. Here peace still reigned. The trout were leaping at flies, and I promised myself to come back after the war to fly cast for them. I never did.

Often, in the windings of a hollow or a mountain trail, we came across the debris of recent skirmishes: abandoned materiel, ruined weapons, overturned and charred vehicles, German and French corpses over which flies buzzed.

Our meager provisions soon were exhausted. "Bourguet," I said, "we must eat, and that means we must live off the land. But every hamlet and village is occupied, and many farms are too. What shall we do?"

"Let's divide the risks, *mon capitaine,* so that if one of us is caught, the other will still have a chance. To begin, let's check out that farm at the edge of the woods. There's laundry drying in the garden, so obviously someone lives there. It could also harbor the Fritz. Let's watch it for two hours. If nothing looks suspect, I'll knock on the door. You stay here. Next time it'll be your turn. If all goes well, I'll be back with some food. If not, go on without me."

Not longer afterward he returned, chuckling softly. "Those people were terrified when they saw me come in," he said. "I got the message and explained to them that the sooner I was served the sooner I'd be off. I didn't need to be too graphic. Judge for

The Night Will End

yourself. They were quite generous." And he held up two big sausages, a whole cheese and a long loaf of bread.

We had no lack of adventures. Between Gérardmer and Retournemer, the commander-in-chief of the German 25th Army Corps had condemned to death any escaped prisoner caught after June 30. It was in early July that we first saw his statement posted on a big fir in the forest. Apparently he had lost a lot of POWs on account of some Poles who, arms in hand, were cleaving their way toward Switzerland by main force. The region was unsafe, and we were soon elsewhere.

It is not unlikely that, farther on, one of our hosts "fingered" us, for the directions he gave led straight to an ambush. Hard pressed by three German soldiers, we barely escaped. What saved us was a violent mountain storm. That storm had everything—thunder, lightning, fog and a torrential downpour that no doubt discouraged our pursuers. I'd never realized how fast I could run!

Soon after, thank God, a friendly farm family took us in. Dressed only in our long underwear before a glowing hearth, we dried our uniforms and rested while a ten-year-old boy kept watch by the window.

Our marches were exhausting. From dawn to dusk we cut through thicket after thicket, far from any worn trail. It was only at night that we would stop in some glade, near a spring if possible, where, stretched out on our backs, gazing at the myriad stars, we'd enjoy a moment of peace and security. Often the wind carried the sounds of a German encampment in some faraway valley. Sometimes we would hear young voices raised together in song, expressing a pride born of power and victory, and, closer to us, the thousand nocturnal whisperings of the forest creatures. And so we would fall asleep, pressed against each other, for even in July the nights were chill.

Two days later, on the banks of the Lanterne River, a fisherman and his wife took us in. But it almost cost them dear, for soon we heard the sound of boots outside the door. We hid in a back room, under the beds of their six sleeping children, and it was those children who saved our lives, along with the compassion of the German patrol leader. At the fisherman's request he agreed not to

The Night Will End

wake the children. There was no doubt that he had been looking for us.

As we approached the Saône, the copses became scarcer, the chances of being spotted greater. Before reaching the river we had one last adventure.

"Bourguet, look! In front of us. It's a wolfhound."

The animal disappeared. Several seconds later he returned, lay down and began to stare fixedly at us. I started toward him, and he retreated, growling and baring his fangs.

"He's a military dog, *mon capitaine*. His masters are not far off. We'd better be going, quick."

We dashed through the bushes and brambles. Suddenly a stream appeared before us. No doubt remembering American Western movies, we leaped into the stream and waded along its slimy bottom until at last the dog was gone.

Exhausted, we halted for a moment.

"Bourguet, my friend, we can't go on like this. I'm dead tired, and, judging by your face, so are you. We must rest a bit and get some civilian clothes before going on. But whom can we ask?"

An old peasant, leaning on his spade in a field, gave us the answer. In the next town, Conflandrey, lived a businessman who'd been called up for service in the reserves. His family would surely take us in.

It must have been quite a shock for the maid and her mistress to open their door to two skinny tramps with fifteen-day beards and mud up to their chins. A scale revealed that Bourguet had lost six pounds and I seven.

Our hostess told us the latest news. It was heart-rending. A major French fleet, anchored off Algeria in the roadsteads of Mers el-Kébir, had been attacked by the British Royal Navy. Every single vessel had been sunk. More than a thousand officers and sailors were dead, hundreds more wounded. The radio, she said, had railed against this "cowardly aggression." The government had moved from Bordeaux to Vichy, and Marshal Pétain had addressed the country several times, exhorting it to re-examine its conscience and perform an act of contrition.

France was now partitioned into two zones: a northern—and larger—zone, which was occupied by German troops, and a

The Night Will End

southern zone, where the government was and where the French Army was to be reorganized. Dividing the two was a "line of demarcation" that passed through Châlon-sur-Saône and Arbois, not far, in fact, from where we were. We decided to head south.

The next day an opportunity arose for us to gain our freedom: to hitch a ride in a delivery truck leaving for Lyons. The driver, who had a border pass from the German command, argued that we should go with him. He insisted that the German inspection was a mere formality.

It was a big chance to take. I could already picture our being apprehended in that mousetrap of a truck. But in the end sheer fatigue won out. Discarding our uniforms and donning civilian clothes given to us by the businessman's wife, we hid in the vehicle, ready at the slightest alert to bury ourselves under its cargo.

Endless columns of German infantry were marching northward, probably as part of a massive evacuation of the southern zone. After a night at Vésoul we headed toward Arbois. Soon we were waiting in the vehicle inspection line. Buried under a mound of boxes, terrified, we held our breath. A German noncom was examining the driver's pass. God, how slow he was! At last we heard the motor start up again, and we were on the road. Several hundred yards farther on, our driver turned and said simply, "*Voilà!* You're there."

Freedom! I took Bourguet by the shoulders and we held each other in a long and silent embrace.

As we drove toward Lyons the driver said, "You know, Captain, the battles in this area were fierce. The Senegalese fought like lions. They slaughtered the Bosch, but they paid for it. The Germans executed all Senegalese prisoners. Since then, however, the Germans have conducted themselves properly. The war is over, and now they're helping our people. We're not afraid of them any more. After all, they're human beings like us."

Need I tell this man what I knew about Hitler's Germany and the "new order" these handsome young Germans were serving? I hadn't the heart. We were free, and that was enough.

Lyons was my birthplace, and as we approached it the countryside became more and more familiar: Bourg-en-Bresse, Mâcon,

The Night Will End

the hills of Beaujolais, the meandering Saône, the gently pitched roofs whose Roman tiles already heralded Provence.

Lyons! Our driver stopped at the Place Carnot. How could we thank him for his services, for the risks he had undertaken on our behalf? To offer money would be insulting, we could see that already. I thanked him with all my heart. He smiled, and in a moment he was gone.

The Place Carnot had grown smaller since the days when, as a child, I used to play here under Maman's watchful eye. Ahead of us stood the General Headquarters building. Before 1914 I often came here to wait for my father, a captain in the XIVth Region. Now we entered the building to regularize our military status and to announce our escape.

We were still in mufti. An officer, lost in a mass of papers, greeted us absently and rather coolly. "Aha! So you escaped. What was your regiment? Why did you not remain with it?" (What a question!) "Here, take this slip. You can fill it out in the adjoining room. Tomorrow you'll be reassigned to a new unit."

The suspicious little pencil-pusher was putting us down! Well, he never saw us again. By telegram I notified my mother in Sainte-Maxime that I would be arriving on the following day, and Bourguet did likewise. That evening we dined together but hardly spoke. After dinner we parted quickly.

"Goodbye, Bourguet, and good luck. The next months will be pretty tough."

"And good luck to you, *mon capitaine*."

Our paths never crossed again.

The train that left the Gare Perrache for the Midi was jammed. Luckily I had a reserved seat. Hardly had we left Lyons than an old gentleman, his lapel adorned with the rosette of the Legion of Honor, began telling the passenger across from him that, as far as he was concerned, the French had fully deserved their fate. According to him it was all the fault of the Republic, the Jews, the Freemasons, the schoolteachers, the parliamentary deputies. It was a crying shame that Colonel La Rocque, the head of the Croix-de-Feu, had not been put in power on February 6, 1934.

Past the window slipped the towns of the Rhône valley: Vienne,

The Night Will End

Valence, Montélimar, Orange. Everywhere the platforms were jammed with people, refugees trying to return to their homes in Belgium, Paris and the north.

I learned much during this trip. A flood of refugees, in effect the northern half of the country swept back onto the southern half, had fled wildly from the advancing German columns. And then came Mussolini's "stab in the back," his rush for the "spoils of a dying France," as the rosetted gentleman put it.

In the compartment the conversation struck up again, but I did not join in. I wanted simply to listen and, if possible, to understand. Oddly enough, the retired officer—for that was his profession—met with no opposition. Though I am sure his conversation partners had wept as bitterly as I over our defeat, by now they thought only of exonerating themselves from any responsibility in our national disaster. They wanted a scapegoat.

I even discerned that our defeat had secretly pleased the old military man, confirming, no doubt, some old resentment he had nourished. He flaunted his satisfaction so insistently that I would have been utterly exasperated had I allowed myself to get involved.

A gulf separated me from my fellow travelers. I still lived in the prewar world, when France was strong, respected for her 1918 victory. I had not assimilated defeat. I could not even understand it; it was utterly foreign to me. Somehow I had evaded defeat when I escaped from Donon. I was free, but they, my neighbors, were not. They were defeated; I was undefeated.

At Marseilles the man with the rosette got off, and the conversation died. I did not regret having heard it. I now realized that there were Frenchmen, perhaps many Frenchmen, who thought as he did.

Cassis, La Ciotat . . . Soon I smelled the familiar fragrance of the umbrella pines. We were at Fréjus. At Saint-Raphael my brother Robert and his wife were waiting for me on the platform. A half hour later I was at Sainte-Maxime. My mother—Maman, as I still called her—opened the door. "*Mon petit*, you're back! But how thin you are! And why are you in civilian clothes?"

As I told her my story I glanced out the window at the palm in the courtyard, at the families in swimsuits coming home from the beach. I saw Boniface the fisherman rearranging his nets. Nothing

The Night Will End

had changed; everything was as before. My story seemed oddly unreal, as if from a person from another planet.

Later, meditating on the contrast between the war I'd just left and the peace that reigned at home, I better understood why, when I'd expressed some of my gravest fears to De Gaulle, he'd replied, "No, Frenay, no. France abides."

It was in the Café de France, on the Place des Platanes, before a glass of *pastis,* that I heard that De Gaulle was now in London. On June 18, on the BBC, he had appealed to the French people to join him and fight on. Since June no one knew what had become of him.

For me De Gaulle was more than a name; he was also a profile, a face, a thought. I had met him twice in the Army of the Rhine in 1927. Both my army corps and the batallion of light infantry that he commanded at Trier were part of the same division. Then, during the 1939–40 "phony war," he had commanded the tanks of the Fifth Army, to which I also belonged. He was elegant, distant, self-confident. His fellow officers were not especially fond of him. His peers found him haughty; his subordinates, patronizing. But his speeches were much discussed. In 1939 he was regarded as one of the Army's young lions.

My family was fervently devoted to Marshal Pétain, and I shared their devotion. His victories, his prestige, his advanced age were all guarantees of his courage and the rectitude of his conduct at the head of the new French state that had almost invisibly replaced the Republic.

"Pétain," said Maman, "is a father to France." And so he seemed.

I wrote to the Army in Marseilles for further orders. While awaiting their reply, I talked, I listened and I questioned.

Those about me accepted defeat as irrevocable. They believed that the Germans would first bomb England into ruins and then easily land troops in the absence of an army to oppose them. For many, besides, this would be the just reward for the "cowardly attack" on Mers el-Kébir that had taken the lives of so many French sailors.

The Night Will End

However, I could not believe that Marshal Pétain would accept the downfall of France. France had fallen not before an ordinary adversary but before Adolf Hitler and the *deutsche Weltanschauung* with which he had imbued his people. Our defeat was not confined to loss of life and material wealth. The very soul of France was in mortal danger; our very reasons for living were at stake.

At the Centre d'Etudes Germaniques in Strasbourg, professors like René Capitant (who later became a friend of De Gaulle and a cabinet minister under him) had enlightened me as to the true nature of National Socialism. I had read *Mein Kampf* and Rosenberg's *Myth of the Twentieth Century*. I understood the import of the cult of race and blood, of the doctrine of the supremacy of the "Aryans" over the "slave races."

I remembered the lecture on the German Army I had given at Toulouse less than two years earlier, in September, 1938, before several hundred reserve officers:

A man, or a people, is exceptionally strong when he enters the lists armed with a myth. National Socialism has inculcated the German people with a whole complex of myths: the myth of race, the myth of the political soldier, the myth of German socialism, all of which stir profound echoes in the popular soul. . . .

The German Army is imbued with a mystique which has potentially dangerous consequences. Tomorrow this army will set out, not on a "lovely war," but on a holy war, its chieftains and its soldiers inflamed with a quasi-religious faith.

Listen to one of the Führer's speeches on the radio. When you hear the cries, the frenetic tumult, the collective hysteria of the masses, you will have a true foretaste of the spirit of the Germany Army of tomorrow. . . .

The entire Reich ferments on the edge of the civilized world.

There could be no question of simply resigning oneself to defeat. As long as the war continued, as long as England held fast, there was still hope.

The Night Will End

And then a miracle happened! The July 27 newspapers announced that Churchill had rejected a German proposal for negotiations. He would accept no compromise with Hitler.

Marshal Pétain was hindered by the Armistice convention. He could not act openly against Germany, but his intentions were clear. That which he could not do, *we* would do; I had made up my mind.

That evening, alone in my room, I drew up a manifesto. It stated why we could not and should not accept defeat or succumb to a defeatist mentality. Our struggle was by no means over. It was first and foremost the struggle of the human spirit against barbarism and paganism while we prepared for the day of our armed liberation.

I remember only my final sentence: "May Marshal Pétain live long enough to see the day when success crowns our efforts."

I worked furiously into the night. Troubled, my mother knocked at my door. "What are you doing up so late, *mon petit?*"

"I'm thinking about what's happening to France, Maman. I'm trying to organize my thoughts."

I had concealed my decision from her. Why? I didn't know. My answer had been spontaneous; it was my first clandestine act.

Lying on my bed, still fully dressed, I looked through my window at the stars, while ideas floated about in my head and collided. I was anxious yet happy about the decision I had reached. Defeat had plunged us into night, but tomorrow the night would end.

The Night Will End

FIRST MILITANTS

A notice from the XVth Military Region assigned me to the Marseilles garrison headquarters. My new office was located in the Fort Saint-Nicholas, at the entrance to the Vieux-Port. Colonel Kühnmünch, whose adjunct I was to become, was a tall, thin Alsatian, a refined and rather cool-looking man. Though we got along excellently, I preferred to keep my new project secret from him.

The windows of our vast, light-filled offices gave on the entirety of the Vieux-Port, with a sweeping view of the Canebière. Behind us were the Bassin des Catalans, the Corniche and the Prado, bathing establishments whose habitués we were soon to become.

Marseilles is usually a busy, gay and noisy city, but in early August 1940 it was very different indeed. A substantial portion of the French people seemed to have sought refuge in the old Phocian port, where they mingled with groups of all origins and all classes—Czechs, Poles, Belgians, Dutch and, among all these, numerous Jews fleeing Nazi persecution.

67, Rue de Rome, second floor: I was knocking on the door of Dr. Marcel Recordier. We fell into each other's arms. He, his wife and his daughter Renée had been close friends of mine since the days when, as a reserve surgeon-lieutenant,

2

Recordier had been called up to serve in the Third Alpine Infantry Regiment, in which I commanded a company. Together we had taken part in the summer maneuvers in the Alpes-Maritimes: L'Authion, La Cime du Diable, and Pëïra-Cava, where his family had joined him. A solid friendship had sprung up between us, and until the outbreak of the war we had paid each other numerous visits.

As tall and as typically Provençal as the actor Raimu, whom he strongly resembled, the good doctor had a heart of gold. His predilection for the race track in the Parc Borély probably took front seat to his own profession, which, however, he practiced scrupulously.

"Henri! When did you get in? What are you doing in Marseilles?"

At the family table before a hastily prepared meal, I recounted to them my experiences on the Maginot Line, my escape and my return to Sainte-Maxime.

"That's a fine kettle of fish," said Marcel sadly. "Well, what are you going to do now, Henri?"

I didn't waste a second. Out of my pocket came the manifesto, which nobody had yet seen.

"Here, read this. It'll answer your question."

Slowly, Marcel read the manifesto aloud to his wife and daughter; then he looked at me and said simply, "You are right. If you need us, you know you can count on us."

The first militant had just been recruited, and what a militant! No, he never handled any explosives, but his house, his table, his letterbox, his time, his money were entirely at our disposal. Often when the Gestapo was after me I spent the night on the Rue de Rome. Always the Recordier family was by my side, pretending to ignore the growing dangers, ever smiling, affectionate and available.

That evening and during the following days I mulled over the various ways in which I might recruit more militants. I preferred to leave my family out of the whole business. It was not that the risks seemed great already but rather that they seemed inevitable. All anti-German activity was forbidden by the Armistice Convention. The government, though perhaps secretly approving of such

The Night Will End

activity, was still officially obligated to condemn it and perhaps to stamp it out. One day I might well find myself in the position of the H.C.'s of the French intelligence service.* If captured, they are simply abandoned to the enemy, and they know it—it's one of the rules of the game. Was this the same dangerous game that I would soon be playing?

In England the blitzkrieg had started. Night and day her cities were being bombed. Hitler notified the great powers that he had blockaded Great Britain. Food-supply convoys were relentlessly attacked by submarines, and they suffered enormous losses. German troops stationed in France were now performing embarkation and landing exercises so close to the actual thing that several soldiers had been drowned. Everything pointed to a forthcoming invasion of England.

It was during those dark days, however, that—thanks to a chance meeting in a train, a restaurant or a friend's home—I recruited my first comrades. My most important encounter took place shortly after August 15 in the soldiers' club of Marseilles.

Beside me at the bar was a young man in his early thirties. He introduced himself: "Maurice Chevance, lieutenant in the colonial infantry, presently on armistice leave."

"Henri Frenay."

"My respects, Captain."

We talked, and he told me something about himself. Born to a family of modest means, he had worked in a milliner's shop before joining the army. He stayed on in the service, prepared for the Saint-Maixent officers' training school, and was accepted. After several years in black Africa, where he served as a lieutenant in the camel corps, he had decided to devote his life to what was then called "the Empire."

Talkative and flamboyant, he spoke of the Empire like a lover and a visionary. The French people had understood, so he believed, the opportunity that black Africa represented for France, as well as the opportunity that France represented for black Africa. Immense efforts must be undertaken to weld metropolitan France to her territories. He was certain that he could make his fortune

*"Honorable Correspondents" is the name given in official reports to the informants of the French intelligence service.

First Militants

with a travel and baggage-transport agency he planned to open in Marseilles. The three months' advance salary he had just received would be sufficient to launch the venture. His future fortune would be entirely devoted to his ideals, which were the most important thing in his life.

I realized that the man who was addressing me was a profoundly decent human being. Though utterly selfless, he was nonetheless driven by great ambition. With his broad shoulders and his thick neck, he was also a powerful force of nature. His vigorous mind seemed only barely able to confine his sheer vitality. I decided to put the question to him:

"Chevance, what if the Germans win the war? What would then become of your fine plan?"

"They won't win!"

"Well, they're on the high road to victory right now. Do you realize what a German victory would mean, not only for our colonies but for France herself—for the entire world?"

I spoke to him at length about this possibility. He knew nothing of National Socialism. He had never read *Mein Kampf*. For him, Hitler was only a highly energetic leader, not the dangerous visionary that he really was, the lord of the "master race" that was one day to reign over the "races of slaves."

"As you can see," I concluded, "the stakes are high indeed. Nobody can stay on the sidelines. As for me, I'm in the game already, my mind is made up. Read this." He read my manifesto with his head tilted back. I could already sense that he was one of us. Indeed, he was to become a dear friend and a courageous militant.

Still overwhelmed by their ordeal, many Alsatians and Lorrainers were arriving in Marseilles and in the Midi. Tens of thousands of them, men, women and children, had been torn from their homes with only a pitifully small sum of money. They told how, in the following days, German families had occupied their homes. In Alsace, as in Lorraine, it was the day of the *Gauleiter*.

What was our government doing? What had been Pétain's reaction? The annexation of Alsace-Lorraine was a clear violation

The Night Will End

of the armistice convention. Though our press was muzzled, France must know the truth. She must know that the Battle of Britain was not proceeding as the Wehrmacht communiqués seemed to indicate, for hundreds of German planes had already been shot out of the skies. The need for information, for intelligence-gathering, for propaganda began slowly to impress itself on me.

At the same time I was beginning to wonder just how to organize and put to work the men and women we had already recruited. Gradually I invented the organizational structure I was soon to apply.

What were our big requirements at the end of that summer of 1940? First, to be really well informed—that is, to go out and get the information we needed. Next, to use this information to our own best advantage and, if possible, to transmit to the English such military intelligence as they were in a position to use. Then to broadcast as widely as possible any information that might counteract Vichy's propaganda organs, which were under Nazi control. We also needed men, for the day would come, no matter how distant, when we would finally resort to armed attacks, and at that time we would have need of shock troops. Lastly, our organization had to be strictly cellular, not only for security's sake but also to effect a useful division of labor.

Thus was born the R.O.P.,* a sort of induction service through which each new rookie had to pass, either to remain there and devote himself to Recruitment, Organization and Propaganda or, in accordance with his aptitude and desires, to be transferred to our intelligence service or to Choc (our paramilitary cadres).

The R.O.P. and Choc were further divided into six-man and thirty-man cells. Each chief of a six-man cell knew only his five subordinates and his immediate supervisor in the larger, thirty-man cell. In turn, the latter knew only the leaders of the five six-man cells placed under his orders. Above the thirty-man cells was the clandestine administrative superstructure, with its cantons, arrondissements and departments. Later we were to have

*R.O.P.: *Recrutement, Organisation, Propagande.*

First Militants

_____

_____

_____

complete regional administrations as well. But it was only hesitantly, arduously and unevenly that we turned this organizational idea into a reality.

The idea of a secretly circulated bulletin was also forming in my mind. As yet I could picture neither what it would look like nor how it would be distributed, but the need for such a bulletin seemed more and more pressing. We would put out a paper that would speak directly to the heart and soul of the average Frenchman.

What we really needed was money—money to expand, to push into more French departments. Where and how was I to find the necessary funds?

There was only one solution: to put the bite on each and every friend, every militant, every sympathizer. I had no inclination for this business, but it was necessary, and I decided to accept the risk.

Whenever I met someone I would start the same conversation. I would sound out his feelings about England and Hitler's Germany. I would acquaint him with my personal conviction that Germany would lose the war. I would point out that Britain was fiercely resisting the Nazi onslaught and that sooner or later America would intervene in the conflict as surely as she had done in 1917. France could not remain outside the coming battle. She must gird herself for action. I would then pause to get my interlocutor's reaction. If it seemed sympathetic, I would go still further.

"Men are already gathering in the shadows. Will you join them?"

If the answer was yes, I would pursue the matter in these terms: "I'm delighted by your reply. You must try to bring in any friends of yours who share our views. You'll receive the organization's specific directives from a friend I'll put you in contact with and who's responsible for the city of Marseilles. Perhaps you'd also like to donate a sum to our treasury."

And thus, as the month's went by, my friends and I harvested our funds. A dinner, a drink with a friend, a chance meeting in a railway coach, all these would afford us the opportunity to obtain financial support. It wasn't easy, agreeable, or safe, but at that time real danger was still far off, for the Gestapo had not yet arrived, nor had the Vichy police yet received the order to hunt us down.

The Night Will End

When I left Marseilles in mid-December I realized that my "war treasury" had already climbed to 14,000 francs.

The general drift of French public opinion was profoundly disappointing. Aside from the few friends whom we recruited, there was not a hint of the spirit of revolt. People had made themselves comfortable in defeat just as they would have done in victory. Their principal and sometimes exclusive worry was food, and it was true that supplies were rapidly dwindling. At the end of September rationing cards for bread and meat were issued. Every family got along in its own way, some in genuine hope for a national resurgence but almost all with the conviction that the war would be over before the end of the year.

On the morning of October 25 I bought, as usual, a paper to read over my breakfast in the Café du Mont-Ventoux. I opened it on the café table. Pétain, it said, had just met Hitler in a little town called Montoire. What did this mean? What new concessions had been exacted from our chief of state? The coverage was cursory, as if the paper's editorial staff was vaguely apprehensive about something. Readers were simply informed that the meeting would prove beneficial for France. In any case, the Marshal was shortly to deliver a radio address.

On October 30, in the large vestibule that served him as a sitting room, Recordier and I heard these words: "It is in a spirit of honor, and to maintain the unity of France . . . that I enter today upon the path of collaboration. . . . This collaboration must be sincere. . . . Up to now, I have spoken to you as a father; now I must speak to you as a leader. Follow me. . . . It is I alone whom history will judge."

Collaboration with Hitler's Germany! Only yesterday the Marshal had said that honor required us to refrain from harming our ex-allies. Today honor seemed to require that we collaborate with the enemy! More dejected than disgusted, I could not fathom this new turn. Why the sudden change of tone, the gravity, the solemnity in the old soldier's voice? The next day the newspapers published a photo of the Marshal shaking Hitler's hand. What, I wondered, was the true meaning of this handshake?

First Militants

Several days after Montoire, our Marseilles garrison bureau received notice that the chief of state was preparing to make an official visit to the city, set for December 3. It was our task to prepare all ceremonies involving the army. In concert with the prefecture, the municipal authorities and the general staff, we worked out the specific details of the program. A formal review of the troops was also arranged.

On the morning of December 3 I opened the shutters of my hotel room at the Bellevue. The weather was splendid. The church of Notre-Dame-de-la Garde on the far side of the Vieux-Port stood out against a limpid, cloudless sky. At the entrance to La Canebière, where the procession was to start, traffic was already at a virtual standstill. Two hours before the ceremony all Marseilles had thronged toward the Vieux-Port, until the balconies, windows and rooftops were all jammed with people.

Presently a cry arose and spread through the streets like a gathering storm. *"Vive le Maréchal!"* Waving makeshift banners, the crowds applauded wildly.

Grave and dignified in his uniform, the chief of state stepped out of his motorcar. Unsmiling he gazed at the frenzied crowd, then saluted it with his cane. His snow-white hair, his light-blue eyes and his tranquil bearing were impressive indeed. But just what lay behind that impassive look? After all, had not the hand holding that cane just shaken the hand of Hitler? Had not Pétain said that our collaboration with Hitler must be sincere? And yet, was he himself sincere? Or was he merely trying to deceive the Führer? What were the real designs of this old man who held in his hands the destiny of France?

The parade started. I saw Pétain standing firmly at attention, but already my mind was elsewhere. I questioned the propriety of this military parade in a vanquished and half-occupied land whose army had been forced to throw down its arms in six short weeks. Would it not have been more dignified to leave the soldiers in their barracks and secretly prepare them for the real day of reckoning, the day of the unsheathed sword?

Who in the world could possibly have been impressed by those mounted artillerymen, those companies of bicycle troops, those outmoded, horse-drawn caissons? Certainly not the German ob-

The Night Will End

servers concealed in the crowd. The Marshal himself? Perhaps. But, most of all, the tens of thousands of men and women who were so wildly cheering the troops, and perhaps even the troops themselves, swollen with their own martial dignity.

A thunderous ovation marked the end of the review. The onlookers broke through the police barriers and mobbed the chief of state. I watched in fascination as an elderly man kissed the Marshal's hand, while a fishwife in a well-filled skirt piously brought the hem of his cloak to her lips. I had never before witnessed this kind of quasi-religious fervor, never suspected its emotional power.

Chevance had by now launched his baggage-transport firm and was exhilarated by its hard-earned but modest success. Recordier had provided us with excellent informants in Marseilles and the surrounding region. Solid information had started to reach me, and to it I added the results of our constant monitoring of the BBC. How satisfying it was to learn on September 15 that 115 German planes had already been shot out of the London skies and, toward the end of October, that the enemy's raids had finally ceased! The threat of an invasion had receded.

In November a chance meeting on a train provided me with a contact in Toulouse. The man's name was Jean-Paul Lien. He was a refugee Alsatian railwayman whom we shall meet again in this narrative, though not always on the right side.

In November and December still more recruits joined us. One was Jean Gemahling, a chemical engineer. He became the chief of our intelligence service, which, under his leadership, began to expand considerably. Another was Pierre de Froment, whose role in the occupied zone was later to be decisive.

One evening—it was the fifth or sixth of December—I met with several friends in Recordier's apartment. I had just heard of my nomination to the Deuxième Bureau* of the Army General Staff at Vichy. I felt that I had best take stock of the situation in the company of a few close friends before departing for the capital. I entrusted the Marseilles region to Chevance, leaving him with

*Deuxième Bureau—Army Intelligence.

First Militants

several addresses, a working knowledge of our organizational schema (which was still more theoretical than real) and the urgent task of recruiting more cadres and organizing them into six- and thirty-man cells. He accepted the responsibility, despite the already heavy burden of his baggage agency.

After listening to the BBC broadcast entitled *"Les Français parlent aux Français,"* to which we were all by now addicted, we began to discuss the outcome of the war. Our native optimism triumphed. After all, the Italian invasion of Greece had already met with serious setbacks, and Churchill was still doggedly insisting that the English would never surrender. The winter would render any German landing on the English coasts highly problematical. In the skies over London the RAF had won a decisive battle against the Luftwaffe. Roosevelt had just been re-elected President of the United States, and his determination to aid the United Kingdom was unquestionable. He had already sent a personal friend, Admiral William Leahy, as ambassador to Vichy. The only explanation for this move was that Roosevelt wanted Leahy to counterbalance Pierre Laval, Vichy's minister of foreign affairs, who had already aroused the suspicions of many Frenchmen that he was betting on a German victory. Most of all, every day that passed without some dire catastrophe tended to reinforce our hopes.

It was about this time that one of my comrades gave me a copy of a new newspaper. Actually it was a newspaper in reduced format, a glorified pamphlet. Its title was *Liberté.* It had been slipped into my friend's business mail, and he had no idea where it had come from. We decided to find out who had written it, for its tone was remarkably similar to that of our own views. We were beginning to realize that we were not alone, that others, though still faceless, were working alongside us in the shadows. One day soon we would meet.

Morning, December 14, a thunderbolt: Laval had been arrested! The embarrassed official press gave almost no information. Only Pétain could have ordered the arrest of the cabinet chief, yet the Marshal remained silent. Obviously, if Laval had fallen it was because the clique around Pétain was hostile to his pro-German position. But how would the Germans react?

The Night Will End

It was in this atmosphere of crisis that I left Marseilles on December 16 to undertake my new job. I wondered what Vichy would be like. What was France's true policy now? Had Laval's arrest altered the course that Montoire had initiated? Full of curiosity, anxiety and hope, I soon found myself on the arrival platform of the Vichy station.

First Militants

PÉTAIN IS FRANCE, FRANCE IS PÉTAIN

After a night in an unheated hotel—for coal was running short already—I presented myself at the Deuxième Bureau. Its chief, Colonel Louis Baril, questioned me at some length.

He was a tall, thin, refined gentleman approaching fifty. He had obviously already checked my dossier and was well acquainted with my history: Saint-Cyr, three years in the Army of the Rhine, three more in the Levant, then the Third Alpine Regiment at Hyères, the Ecole de Guerre and finally the Centre d'Etudes Germaniques at Strasbourg. The latter particularly interested him.

"Frenay," he said, "tell me about the Strasbourg Center. What did you get out of it?"

"Colonel, I can answer you in two sentences. First, a broader knowledge of the German language. Second, a greater familiarity with Germany herself—both her history and her philosophy."

"Tell me what you think of her current philosophy," he said, gazing at me with a penetrating but benevolent expression.

"That would take me a long time, Colonel. In brief, I regard it as the greatest monstrosity of the twentieth century, the negation of every spiritual and religious value I hold dear."

He gave me a long, intense look.

3

"It's a pity your view is not shared by France as a whole—especially by Vichy."

I was transfixed. Baril was anti-German, hence anti-collaborationist! But his reference to Vichy was ambiguous. Whom did he mean to criticize? The government? The Marshal? The Marshal's entourage? In any case, the Deuxième Bureau was apparently in good hands.

I left this interview in a better frame of mind. I also had an interesting new job, consisting of daily liaison duties with the minister of foreign affairs. Each day I was to present myself at the Hôtel du Parc, which was the new location of the government and Foreign Ministry.

On the third floor was Marshal Pétain; on the second was the vice-president of the Council of Ministers, a position that Pierre Laval had occupied prior to his arrest. On the first floor was the Ministry of Foreign Affairs, which Pierre-Etienne Flandin had taken over several days earlier. It was my duty to give the Foreign Ministry the intelligence analyses prepared by Colonel Baril and his officers. In exchange, I often received useful intelligence the Ministry itself had obtained. Concurrently I served in a small group that worked alongside Colonel Rivet's intelligence service. With fresh optimism I plunged into my new tasks.

Several days later my friend Berty Albrecht arrived at Vichy. She had lost some weight but was otherwise unchanged. She had the same determined mouth, light-blue eyes and severe hair style in which white hairs mingled with blond. She was still soberly elegant. Her facial expressions, like her words, reflected goodness mixed with firmness. Born Berty Wild to Protestant parents of Swiss origin, she had been brought up in the Marseilles area and had married in England, where her husband, a financier in the City of London, still lived. They had two children, Freddy and Mireille, respectively nineteen and sixteen years old. Desperately homesick for France, she had returned in 1934.

I owed much to her, especially my political education. My family was from Lyons, and in 1934 it was still as typically Lyonnais as it had been in the old days when we had lived in the Perrache district under the shadow of the Abbey of Ainay. My father's

Pétain Is France, France Is Pétain

origins—he himself had been born only sixteen miles from Lyons—had hardly broadened my youthful horizons. A Saint-Cyrien and the son of an army officer, I had absorbed a military way of life since my earliest years. In short, I belonged unconsciously to the traditional French right, with its poverty, patriotism and paternalism.

Before 1914, Socialists, singing the "Internationale" under a panoply of red flags, would sometimes parade on the Quai Gailleton, only a few yards from the Rue Duhamel where we lived. My mother would quickly close the windows, as if a thunderstorm were brewing. At the family table my parents would bemoan the specter of rising revolution.

In Paris in her apartment on the Avenue Victor-Emmanuel (later on the Rue de l'Université), Berty Albrecht often entertained French intellectuals and leftists. The Spanish Civil War had just broken out, and countless rallies were held in support of the Republic. A frequent participant, I became more and more uneasy over Hitler's growing military aid to Franco. Spain might well become a new bastion of European fascism, the final link with the Reich and the Duce's Italy, in the encirclement of France.

At that time numerous German refugees were arriving in Paris, most of them Jews fleeing Nazi persecution. We spent entire evenings listening to them at Berty's, at first skeptical of the horrifying stories they told, then of the barbarism of Hitler's regime. I've forgotten their names, but I do remember that some of them were experts in their fields. I was eager to know more about Germany, and, one year later, when I had finished the Ecole de Guerre, I asked to be transferred to the Centre d'Etudes Germaniques.

In Paris I divided my time between the war college, studying in my apartment at 25, Avenue de Tourville, and completing my political education by a close reading of the entire press, from *L'Humanité* to Léon Bailby's *Le Jour.* My family and friends were aware of my uneasy voyages into these unknown and troubling political waters. The Spanish Civil War, the Third Reich, the Popular Front—all the subjects that then divided French public

The Night Will End

opinion—erected an almost insurmountable barrier between myself and my old social milieu.

And now I was seeing Berty again, on this evening in December 1940. I could tell even before she spoke that we were of a single mind. I explained my plans to her, as well as the organizational form I envisaged and my projects for propaganda and intelligence-gathering.

"Henri," she said, "nothing in the world could please me more than what you've said. I was still uncertain of your feelings. Since the Armistice I've seen so much apathy and so much cowardice, so many fine and brave people utterly misled by propaganda, that I feared that you too might be infected. I'm happy to see that you're a rebel!"

Then, after a moment's hesitation: "But, Henri, you're younger in character than your age would suggest. Do you realize just how dangerous your position is? War is not a game. *Jetzt,*" she said in German, "*ist es kein Kriegspiel aber ein grausamer Krieg.*"*

"I know what I'm doing, Berty. I'm not a child any more. I can't shirk a battle as decisive as this. The government's freedom of action has been severely restricted. But what it cannot do, we can—we rebels, to use your own expression. Our efforts may amount to no more than a drop of water in the ocean of war. But at least we will have taken a stand! To live in peace with one's conscience has its price, you know; but isn't it worth it to be able to look at oneself in the mirror?"

She smiled. Then with a clownish expression she asked, "Want me to join you?"

And so began—in and through the Resistance—the story of our unflinching and loyal cooperation, which lasted until Berty was carried off to prison and gave her life for our cause.

At Christmas time, in the Hôtel du Parc, I learned that Admiral Darlan, the minister of national defense, had recently met with Hitler to appease the Führer's anger over the arrest of Pierre Laval. Thereafter the line of demarcation was to be sealed tight; nobody and nothing could cross it, not even cabinet ministers. But sweet

*"This is no war game, but real war in all its cruelty."

Pétain Is France, France Is Pétain

words alone could not satisfy Hitler. He evidently required a guarantee of sincere collaboration. Would Darlan provide this guarantee? Had he the authority? The Marshal was still in office, and he had just created a triumvirate composed of Darlan, P.-E. Flandin and General Huntziger. These three were empowered to make important decisions. Darlan could hardly buck both the Marshal and his own two colleagues. My anxiety was intense, all the more so because on that day and increasingly thereafter I observed a marked official reticence and embarrassment over the Hitler–Darlan meeting. The whole business smelled bad.

I think it was on December 28 that Colonel Baril informed me that a certain Lieutenant de Froment, passing through Vichy direct from the occupied zone, wanted to talk with me. Baril added with a wink, "I think you two have some interests in common."

Froment? But I had already met him in Marseilles! I had even asked him to "work" the occupied zone. Believing himself too young, he had declined. What did he want now?

One evening soon after he told me in his own words. Relying on his personal means, he had, like myself, initiated a program for information, propaganda and the recruitment of action groups. Curiously, his organizational structure matched our own. With Denise Cerbeau, André Beits and Jean Monmusseau, he had written a number of detachable inserts and pasted them in books. He had also distributed pamphlets and organized crossings of the line of demarcation. His way of going about this was quite original. It appeared that Monmusseau owned vineyards in Touraine, at Montrichard. It was part of his business to ship wine casks throughout France, and in these casks he also stowed men, including Froment himself, as well as materiel and dispatches.

Recalling our conversation in Marseilles, he had come to look me up for instruction and new addresses. He also wanted to know to whom he should give his intelligence reports. It turned out that Baril had a ready answer to that question. The colonel gave him a Swiss contact, another in the British consulate and a third in the American embassy in Vichy. I had not guessed wrong about the chief of the Deuxième Bureau.

As for Froment, this blond and blue-eyed officer of twenty-six,

The Night Will End

who seemed much older than he was, gave proof of an even temperament and a sharp sense of detail in developing his organization. Soon Berty joined us. We talked shop together: cellular cadres, security and how to cross the demarcation line. Armed with new information, as well as his own modesty and courage, Froment re-entered the occupied zone in early January 1941.

My daily liaison duties with the Foreign Ministry and my meetings with intelligence officers and their chief, Colonel Rivet, rapidly assumed great importance for my clandestine work. Not only did I tap an abundant source of information in them but I also formed solid friendships. Often we would exchange information and discuss the latest news in an atmosphere of cordiality and relaxation.

At the Chanteclerc, the restaurant where all Vichy seemed to congregate, my new friends vividly recounted to me the story of the December 13 coup and its aftermath. Laval, still vice-president of the Council of Ministers, had been arrested on that day by Mondanel, the police commissioner. Subsequently, Otto Abetz, the Reich's ambassador to Paris, had actually rescued him from prison with the aid of several armored vehicles. Laval had been spirited to Paris under S.S. protection. That he was Hitler's man was now a proven fact.

The situation was so serious that for a while we feared an overt occupation by the Nazis, who had concentrated columns of elite troops at the line of demarcation. The reaction of General Huntziger, our secretary of state for war, plunged me into utter consternation. Our general staffs and their subsidiary services had been given the order to let themselves be taken prisoners without resisting! I couldn't believe my ears. Even more amazing was that my new friends, whose patriotism was beyond question, informed me of this without betraying the slightest indignation. Orders were orders, and one didn't discuss them. But, in God's name, what kind of man could give such an order, and what kind of government could ratify it?

One evening in my hotel Berty and I were collating intelligence reports. Their quantity was already impressive.

"About that information bulletin you're considering," she said.

Pétain Is France, France Is Pétain

"I suggest we design it like a prewar French house organ—lots of raw news with a minimum of editorializing. I'll type it myself, with several carbons. But to whom should we mail it?"

"Let's send it to a limited number of people we already know. We'll keep our authorship secret and sit back and observe their reactions. They'll be our guinea pigs."

The very next day I selected and classified all our intelligence under different rubrics: war news, the behavior of German troops, early signs of resistance, the situation in annexed Alsace-Lorraine, the pillage of France by Germany and so forth. Berty typed our information bulletin No. 1 with eighteen copies. It wasn't much, but it gave us deep pleasure. It was our first manifesto that was both clandestine and public. Deposited directly in letterboxes, or inserted in the pages of a magazine, ten copies were addressed to people living in Vichy whom we knew well. The others were sent to our friends in the provinces—including Chevance in Marseilles—to elicit their reactions. And their reactions were positive indeed. Our only problem was to satisfy the ever-increasing number of queries we received.

Our bulletins exploded like bombshells. "Where do they come from?" people asked. "Too bad we can't get hold of more. Such and such a powerful figure must read this!"

These modest newsletters, which came out twice weekly, received an astounding reception simply because they brought a breath of freedom. Day after day new addresses were added to our lists, not only in Vichy but in many other French cities as well.

About January 7 or 8 all the occupants of the Hôtel du Parc were in a state of great expectancy. The new ambassador from the United States, Admiral Leahy, was about to present his credentials to the chief of state. For two days I had been unable to meet with my usual informants, but all Vichy was editorializing on the event.

Leahy was no run-of-the-mill State Department official. A personal friend of Roosevelt, he had been appointed to his new post after FDR's 1940 re-election. The act was symbolic. It showed how important France's role in the European war was to the United States. The new ambassador might be able to counterbalance German pressure on Vichy; such, at any rate, was my hope, and that of my comrades in the intelligence service.

The Night Will End

In Vichy and in the surrounding region our organization was slowly taking shape. We were lucky to have the cooperation of the municipal police inspector, Robert Mouzillat, of Raisin, who owned and managed a hotel in the center of town, and, a bit later, of François Bourlier, a trilingual radio operator of twenty-two. He put his German and English to good use at the telegraph- and radio-monitoring station where each day he collected vital information.

Information and propaganda constituted our most salient activities, to the detriment of Choc, our paramilitary outfit, which was not to see action for some time to come. We were not yet on the eve of those Sicilian Vespers that already troubled our dreams.

One day in mid-January the door to my office opened and, before I had time to look up, a voice exclaimed, "Frenay! I'm so happy to see you!"

Before me was a little man in mufti, with tortoise-shell glasses and disheveled hair. It took me several seconds to recognize Robert Guédon, a captain like myself and an old classmate at the Ecole de Guerre.

"Robert, what're you up to here? Where'd you come from?"

For two years at military school we had been part of the same work group—that is, we had spent most of our time together. He had attracted attention for an intellectual agility all the more remarkable in that it was served by uncommon oratorical fluency.

"I'd be happy to tell you what I'm up to, old man, but I'd need a little time. I'm utterly delighted to see you again. There are so many things I want to talk to you about. Why don't we lunch together? We could speak more openly than we can here in your office. Come on, let's escape the telephone and your secretaries."

In the restaurant we had a long conversation. He told me how he had fought in the north of France and in Belgium, how he had been seriously wounded and how he had escaped from captivity. He also related the story of his arduous return home to Granville, where he had received secret medical attention. Since the end of his convalescence he had been passing himself off as a math teacher on the Normandy coast. Meanwhile, in secret, he had laid the foundation for an intelligence network. He already had a

Pétain Is France, France Is Pétain

considerable number of operatives, and his reports were transmitted to London by some agents whom he believed belonged to French intelligence. He wanted to get back home and continue his task as soon as possible. Colonel Baril had told him of my recent assignment to the Deuxième Bureau here, so he had come to see me.

"Robert," I said, "I've never really believed in blind fate. Our meeting here today is no accident. It's a good omen. You see, you too never accepted the finality of our defeat. You are simply continuing the war by other than the conventional means. I hope you realize that I share your view, a view that is unfortunately rather uncommon in the free zone. You'll find out for yourself how resigned and self-serving people here are. Their state of mind is still our number-one enemy. That's why, though I'm involved in intelligence work and the preparation for an eventual armed uprising, I devote much of my energy to propaganda."

Then I recounted to him the details of our accomplishments and our plans.

"Once again, Robert, our paths have crossed. When you return to Granville, why don't you take charge of our movement in the occupied zone? We'll organize a communication line between us. I'll come and see you as often as necessary, unless of course you prefer to come here. Think it over carefully, because it's a serious responsibility. We'll talk about it more tomorrow."

We met again next day at the same restaurant. This time Berty was with us. Guédon was glowing. For the first time since the beginning of the war the British had pulled off an important military success. They had forced the Italians to surrender at Tobruk and taken tens of thousands of prisoners.

"Well, Robert, what do you think of my proposal?"

"Henri, we've worked well together in the past, so why not now? One thing, though. You'd better tell me a little more about your organizational schema and your propaganda methods. After all, we've got to keep our orchestra playing in key. I'll get to work as soon as I return. Please visit me as soon as possible to inspect my operation."

Berty said, "Robert, your current field of operations is Normandy, but Paris is still our capital and your movement will naturally

The Night Will End

34

cover it. You'll need some reliable help. I can give you a name and address that are worth a hundred others: Jeanne Sivadon, director of the Factory Superintendents' School,* 1, Rue Princesse, in the sixth arrondissement. I was her student," she said, smiling. "If she shares our opinions, as I believe she does, her help will be priceless. Just think of the hundreds of social workers she's trained. Today they're all over France, usually in factories. She's a Protestant heathen like me, so she'll probably join us. When you leave, let me give you a message for her."

"Robert," I added, "let me follow Berty's example and give you a single name worth its weight in gold: Lieutenant Pierre de Froment."

I told him about my interview with Froment several weeks earlier.

The rest of the dinner was gay indeed. We overflowed with optimism. I was certain Guédon was going to get cracking as soon as he returned home. Berty told me about Jeanne Sivadon. I didn't know her, but her eventual support seemed both probable and reliable. I had the exhilarating feeling that we had already won a battle. Of course we hadn't, but we certainly had crack troops. Subsequent events were to prove it.

In our mess hall, toward mid-January, I lunched with an officer who was passing through Vichy and whom I had seen haunting the corridors of the Deuxième Bureau. His name was Gouyou. Before the war he had served in the French military mission to Prague. He had been there during Hitler's invasion of Czechoslovakia and had been deeply humiliated by France's hands-off attitude. He was forever giving vent to his hatred for the Nazi regime. He roundly cursed out the collaborators as well, but a little less openly, for already the voice of the stoolpigeon was heard in the land.

I felt emboldened to confide in him, and rarely have I seen a man respond so spontaneously. Right away he told me, "You should meet General de La Laurencie. He shares your ideals and like yourself he craves action."

A lunch was organized at the general's home a few days later.

*A technical school that trains specialized social workers to mediate between labor and management in industrial plants—Translator.

Pétain Is France, France Is Pétain

Robert Guédon had not yet left for the occupied zone, so the two of us went together to the residence of the onetime delegate-general of the Paris government.

We were warmly and simply received. The meal was frugal but tasty, especially for those austere days. As the dinner conversation progressed it became clear that La Laurencie trusted us and vice versa. Though we had never seen one another before, we understood one another instinctively. Though our ages and ranks were different, we were all officers and graduates of Saint-Cyr. We spoke openly. Our host bore no grudge against Pétain, who had relieved him of his duties in Paris; on the contrary, he deferred to him frequently during our conversation. For the Vichy government, however, his contempt was absolute. When he spoke of Admiral Darlan, one sensed that this contempt was accompanied by a deep hatred.

Then Guédon and I spoke. We inflated the little that we had done, and at times we disguised our projects as accomplishments. Yes, our remarks contained a large element of bluff, but how could I ever have recruited the first resister if he had known that he was the first?

"I congratulate you on what you've already done," the general told us as he escorted us to the door. "Let's stay in touch. You know where I live and you've told me how to contact you. I want very much to help you, and I believe that I shall be able to. But above all, please be careful!"

"You know, Robert," I said as we went out, "he's a damn good contact! His connections are legion, even in foreign embassies. He's very close to Admiral Leahy. And he knows how poor we are. When he says that he'll help us, I think he's hinting at financial aid."

"I hope to God you're right. And if you do get any money, why, just think of me up in the occupied zone!"

Sometimes I arrived at the Hôtel du Parc just as Marshal Pétain was coming out to take his daily walk. The ritual was sober and unchanging: The company of guards would pay its respects, and the Marshal, hat in hand, would salute it and nod to the large

The Night Will End

crowd of curious onlookers who attended the little ceremony. In fact they were more than onlookers; they were pilgrims. Most of them were neither from Vichy nor from the surrounding region. They came from far away, with their children, solely to glimpse their venerated chief of state, their "Father," as Maman had called him back at Sainte-Maxime. Every social class was there. Gazing at these faces, I could sense their joy and ecstasy to the point where I myself felt acutely embarrassed. The men would uncover their heads while their eyes filled with tears; once, the members of a whole family even crossed themselves. Only rarely were there cries of "*Vive le Marcéchal!*" for usually utter silence reigned—a churchlike hush.

Again and again I tried, without success, to discern some sign of emotion in the Marshal's face. I never found any; no smile ever enlivened that marble impassivity. Perhaps he was simply indifferent. Off he would go with his confident stride, usually alone, sometimes accompanied by Dr. Ménétrel, his personal physician and confidant (and also, it was whispered, his illegitimate son).

I usually attended Sunday-morning Mass at a small chapel near my hotel. One Sunday—I can no longer remember exactly when or in what church—a religious ceremony was held in the presence of the chief of state. I didn't attend, but I did wait outside amidst a large crowd. As the service ended, the great double doors opened and the Marshal, in uniform, paused briefly in the courtyard. He was escorted by the apostolic nuncio, the bishop and numerous other priests. A great cry arose, echoing over and over, accented by the piercing voices of the women: "*Vive le Maréchal!*" School children, massed before the church, struck up a song I'd never heard, though in fact its singing was a required morning activity in every school in Vichy:

> *All the children who love you*
> *And hold your years dear*
> *To your supreme call*
> *Have answered smartly, "Here!"*
>
> *Marshal, here are we*
> *Before you, O savior of France,*

Pétain Is France, France Is Pétain

We your little buddies swear
To follow where you advance.

For Pétain is France,
And France is Pétain.

A little farther on I saw delegations from the French provinces, which had resumed their ancient names: Anjou, Berry, Rouergue, Quercy. They presented the old soldier with gifts symbolic of the characteristic occupations of their regions. One delegation had brought a tiny white lamb with a pale-blue ribbon in its fleece.

The crowds' outpourings caused me a certain anxiety. No, France was not Pétain! She existed before him and would exist after him. Although I did trust Pétain's integrity and disinterestedness, he was, after all, a fallible human being. No doubt he really had kicked out Pierre Laval several weeks earlier; yet this fact could not erase from my mind the memory of Montoire and Pétain's handshake with Hitler. What were the man's real inner thoughts? He was now eighty-four years old. His stability had inevitably weakened with old age. Did he still have enough strength to hold the line? Intrigues were multiplying daily in the corridors of all those Vichy hotels glorified into cabinet ministries. Would he be able to unmask and foil them?

On January 19 an important and, for me, decisive event took place. Opening my newspaper, I read a brief communiqué: "Marshall Pétain, Chief of State, has conferred with Pierre Laval. They had a lengthy discussion in which the misunderstandings of December 13 were dispelled."

I knew that the Marshal hated Laval. He had said so covertly before Laval's arrest and openly after it. Everybody knew it. Therefore, he himself had not initiated this interview. It had been imposed on him.

Yet Pétain had plenipotentiary power, more than any French king ever had. The pressure on him could not have been of domestic origin. It was the Germans who, directly or no, had forced him to make up with Laval. This reconciliation was to smooth the way for Laval's re-entry into the government. To the

The Night Will End

great discontent of my friends the diplomats, Pétain had bowed before a *fait accompli*.

So! Darlan was dancing to Hitler's tune, while Pétain met secretly with Laval. The cards were on the table.

I asked Baril for a short leave, for my morale had plummeted. On the way to Sainte-Maxime I stopped off in Marseilles at Recordier's. Maurice Chevance was buoyed by the contact he had recently made with the boss of an army special-service unit located in Marseilles. He wanted me to meet him too.

"What's his name?" I asked.

"Captain Paillole."

Recordier fairly leaped into the air. "Paillole? Did you say Paillole? But he was a childhood friend of my brother Maurice. He's like a member of the family!"

I hadn't been able to get a word in edgewise, but I too knew Paillole. Not only had he been one of my *bazars** in Saint-Cyr, but I myself had taught him on the Marschfeld** how to stand at attention and present arms. We had been good friends.

We met at a café. Paillole himself knew only that he was to see Chevance's unidentified "boss" in the clandestine movement. When he saw me come in he couldn't believe his eyes.

"Good heavens! It's you!"

"Yes, it's me, old boy. Does that surprise you?"

"No . . . but talk about the long arm of fate!"

In essence, Paillole was the head of the counterespionage unit attached to Rivet's special services and installed in his villa, Eole, on the Promenade de la Plage in Marseilles. His activities took place under the label "Rural Constructions," his role consisting primarily in identifying German agents and, if possible, in penetrating the enemy's espionage services. At this he was rather successful.

Of course I spoke quite openly to this old friend. I told him how my ambivalent feelings about the government and my hostility to

*Student officers of the following class.

**The exercise field inside Saint-Cyr.

Pétain Is France, France Is Pétain

the collaboration led me to clandestine activity. He found me a bit hard on our military chiefs. We agreed to stay in touch secretly. Chevance would be our liaison.

I had faith in the Deuxième Bureau and the S.R., but they were only a cog in the army machinery, which itself was answerable to the government. The government: What did it really want, what could it really do, and where was it really headed? Pétain had arrested Laval, but then he had patched things up with him several days ago in Hauterive. Why? In Paris, General de la Laurencie, recently relieved of his duties as the government's delegate-general, had been replaced by Fernand de Brinon, an avowed collaborationist. Marcel Déat, Jacques Doriot and Marcel Bucard were actively creating their own quasi-Nazi parties, a fact that didn't seem to bother my friends the diplomats at all. Admiral Darlan's influence was growing. Everyone knew how personally ambitious he was and how much he hated England. Yet England remained our one great hope. Several weeks later, Darlan was to be appointed vice-president of the Council of Ministers, Minister of Foreign Affairs and Minister of the Interior. Finally, it was he who was eventually designated the Marshal's heir apparent.

If Pétain was not free, what sense was there in blindly following his orders? "I address you as a leader," he had said. "Follow me!"

No doubt about it, the army *would* follow him. Of course it might itself have influenced him positively if its leaders had had any character. But character, it seemed, was inversely proportionate to the number of stars a general wore. Yes, the army would obey—above all because obedience was an ingrained military habit.

"Discipline being the principal strength of an army, it is essential that every commanding officer obtain total obedience and complete submission from his subordinates. . . ." So read Article 1 of our army's disciplinary regulations—the first lines of the first book placed in our hands at Saint-Cyr. Soldiering, like the novitiate, entails total submission.

Clearly the government, firmly under German control and ruling only half of France, was no longer its own master. In the shadow of the doddering Marshal various clans now jockeyed for

The Night Will End

power—the anti-German faction, the temporizing or opportunist faction and the full-fledged collaborationists.

The army, with its reduced man- and firepower, was predominantly anti-German, but it was commanded by unimaginative and irresponsible dolts. Above all, these men were duty-bound to obey orders, just as I myself was. It was the fundamental condition of our profession. My profession had thus come into direct conflict with my underground activity.

I began casting about for an honorable way to quit. I couldn't just disappear one fine day without telling anybody, including Baril. That would be the same as deserting. London was out of the question, for I wanted to stay in France and continue my resistance work. To resign was impossible for an officer in wartime, and France was legally still at war; an armistice is not peace.

The following Sunday I went to Clermont-Ferrand to see Lieutenant General Desbordes, the second-in-command of our regional general staff. I had met him in Toulouse in 1938–39, and I respected his judgment. I disclosed to him my clandestine activities and explained the troubled state of my conscience.

"Frenay," he said, "I thank you for confiding in me. I sympathize with your activities, and if I can help you out some day, without neglecting my own duties, I'll be only too glad to do so. If you're looking for an honorable way to leave the army, I happen to know of a ministerial form that enables you to apply to do so. I'll find out more about it and pass the information on to you."

Then we talked about my official work in Vichy, the public figures whom I had approached and the general mentality of that comic-opera capital. At the end he walked me to the door.

"If you leave the army I know you'll suffer. But you'll also be rewarded by the satisfaction of having acted according to your conscience. God be with you."

In Vichy I obtained a copy of the ministerial form in question. It had already expired. What to do? Berty and I wracked our brains and eventually came up with an answer: request a discharge without fully revealing my opinions and projects.

On January 24, 1941, I drafted my request in the form of a letter

Pétain Is France, France Is Pétain

to General Huntziger, the Minister of Armies. It was easy to compose, much easier than I had thought. A ministerial circular dated October 25, 1940, and addressed to the entire army specified the proper attitude of personnel desirous of staying in active service. All I had to do was contradict it.

In my letter I criticized the methods and spirit of the army, concluding: "My ardor I reserve for my country alone; I have none left for institutions. Thus the only honest course is for me to leave active service. For this reason, I request permission for an armistice leave."

I gave this letter to Colonel Baril, who forwarded it through the proper channel. He read it without surprise, for he knew my thoughts and had surely guessed my activities.

"Frenay, I know you've thought this over. Your father was an officer, your brothers are officers, and you're an officer yourself. If you resign from the army, you'll also be leaving a part of yourself behind."

"What you say is true—yet I cannot do otherwise. If I want to remain faithful to myself, I have no choice. I'm resigning so that I may act without constraints. Can I rely on your support, Colonel?"

"Well, as your boss I regret your departure. But I do understand your reasons for it, and consequently I shall speak in your favor."

Two weeks passed. One morning the telephone rang.

"This is General Staff Headquarters, General Picquendar's office. Captain Frenay? The general wishes to see you about your request for an armistice leave. He expects you in his office the day after tomorrow at eleven o'clock."

"Very well, sir, I'll be there."

On the appointed day I arrived and was immediately shown into Picquendar's office. He was the number-one brass in the entire military hierarchy. He motioned me to sit down opposite him. We were alone.

"Monsieur," he said, "I have before me a letter in which you have requested an armistice leave. It is couched in terms that led me to believe that I was dealing with a lunatic. Naturally I asked for your dossier. Here it is. I have studied it carefully, and I find myself obliged to admit that your performance has been excellent. Your superiors have spoken of you in unusually favorable terms.

The Night Will End

Your case interests me, because I cannot understand your attitude. Explain yourself."

Of course I had expected this—it was the only imaginable reason for my having been summoned—and I had my answer ready. I rather mildly criticized the acceptance of defeat, the policy of collaboration and especially the spirit of the army. I did not say all that I wanted to and revealed very little indeed of what I was actually up to. Yet, however honeyed my words, they took on, in this place and before this man, a scandalous ring.

Picquendar listened attentively, without once interrupting. His solemn eyes were riveted on mine. He wanted to understand, but he simply could not. How I longed to speak in total candor!

"Monsieur, the defeat has dealt a severe blow to your morale. Of course you are not alone in that. You find it difficult to recover from defeat, and now you want to throw in the towel. But you're wrong. If France is ever to rise again, it is the army that will lead her. And you want to quit! You can't actually believe that the General staff's sympathies lie with Germany. Come now! Allow me to tear up your letter. We have need of officers like you. Granted, the climate here does not agree with you. Good. You may go wherever you wish, in metropolitan France or abroad. Just tell me where, and I shall reassign you to the place of your choice."

His words touched me. They were sincere. Yet he had missed the point. I had lost confidence not only in the army but in the government it served. Yet I dared not confess the latter fact, for I dearly wanted my discharge.

"I am deeply touched by your words, General, and by your kind offer. But how can I accept it? I am in the position of a priest who has lost faith and to whom the diocese proposes a mere change of parish."

Irked, he threw up his arms in a gesture of disappointment. "Enough! You'll regret this decision. I shall pass your letter on to the minister and ask him to relieve you of your duties."

I left him with a heavy heart. Several days passed. Then one morning Colonel Baril called me. "Frenay, Marshal Pétain has requested your presence tomorrow at five o'clock. I don't need to tell you how important your words to him will be, not only for you but for all of us. You have a great opportunity. Make the best of it!"

Pétain Is France, France Is Pétain

But that opportunity never came, for the audience was countermanded. The chief of state, held up by other business, asked the grand chancellor of the Legion of Honor to receive me instead.

His name was General Bricard. Apparently he was an old aviation ace. This refined and courteous aristocrat was obviously quite loath to question me. Though the Marshal had asked him to receive me, he did so with little zeal or curiosity, which he clearly would have regarded as inappropriate. The interview lasted no more than twenty minutes. Soon I was back in my office—but for how long?

Meanwhile, events were confirming my pessimistic analysis of the political situation. P.-E. Flandin, Laval's successor in the Ministry of Foreign Affairs, was forced to resign. Darlan became the Marshal's heir apparent and took over three cabinet portfolios, including Flandin's. The opportunist clan had temporarily gained the upper hand.

Baril called me in again in late February and gave me my armistice leave papers. My request had been accepted! I was satisfied but joyless. I had the feeling of having accomplished a particularly somber duty.

An armistice leave is not a total discharge from the army. Pending a Franco-German peace treaty, a soldier on armistice leave was simply placed on the reserve list. Though he could begin a civilian career, he retained his military status and could ask to be reinducted into the service. But my letter must have displeased General Huntziger, because a memorandum attached to my papers stated: "In conformity with the instructions of the Minister's cabinet, Captain Frenay is advised by the Army High Command that his departure from the Army must hereby be considered in principle as definitive."

"In other words," I said to Baril, "they've kicked me out."

"Be a little more objective, Frenay. Try to put yourself in the minister's shoes. Your letter attacks everything that's been done in the army under his authority. How would you feel about it if you were he?"

"Sir, I'd never have put myself in a position to get such letters."

In honor of my departure, the chief of the Deuxième Bureau organized a reception for our officer corps. He did not criticize my

The Night Will End

conduct but publicly upheld it as a lesson worthy of serious consideration by all our officers.

He ended with these words: "I know, Henri, that you've no intention of remaining idle. I salute you and wish you the best of luck and much success in your new endeavor."

In the army it is not customary to answer a speech in one's honor, so I remained silent, profoundly touched by my fellow officers' friendship. But in the pit of my stomach it was fear that I felt, the fear of a young boxer the first time he enters the ring.

Pétain Is France, France Is Pétain

CLANDESTINE PRESS

In early March, 1941, I arrived in Lyons. My cousin, Marcel Deville, a lawyer, gave me the run of his place at 43, Rue de la Charité. It was in the old neighborhood where I had spent my entire Lyons life. I was entirely at ease in this familiar apartment, but I could not decently remain there and risk compromising my host, who knew nothing of my clandestine activity. I had to find a reasonably priced lodging for myself. It would not be easy.

As it happened, I simply lucked out. One day, standing on the Quai Gailleton beside the Rhône, I spotted a notice that had been posted on the wall that very morning. It said: "Two rooms, furnished, to let." I climbed the stairway, rang the doorbell and immediately put down my deposit—for, miracle of miracles, the price was within my range. The flat was bright and charming, with a view of the Rhône and its riverport where lawn-bowling fans used to gather in summertime. I was to live here for four months. It was the last dwelling I openly rented in my own name. Wary lest anyone in officialdom should know my new address, I gave out that I had gone to spend my leave in Sainte-Maxime.

To my dear mother, more than ever an admirer of Pétain, I was forced to explain

4

why I was no longer in uniform; otherwise she would have been severely pained, for she believed me destined for a distinguished military career. I led her to believe that the Deuxième Bureau had reappointed me to a position in mufti, a secret mission that I was not at liberty to reveal. It was a plausible explanation, and she accepted it.

Shortly after my arrival Berty joined me. She had succeeded in getting herself a job in Lyons as regional women's unemployment officer. She brought along our "archives" in two fat valises.

Berty wasted little time in finding herself an apartment, at 165, Avenue de Saxe. A convenient streetcar led directly to her professional office in the main square of Villeurbanne, a Lyons suburb. As soon as she arrived we held a meeting, for we were both itching to get started. But before drawing up a plan of action we had to take stock of our new situation.

In mid-March 1941 the movement was still very weak. Nonetheless, it had taken root in four departments of the Midi: the Bouches-du-Rhône, the Vaucluse, Var and the Basses-Alpes—at least, so Chevance had informed us. It was also represented in Toulouse by Jean-Paul Lien, an Alsatian railwayman, but we had no idea what he was up to, for he never wrote and didn't even acknowledge receiving our bulletins. We had also placed some of our people in Vichy and in the neighboring departments and also at the demarcation line. Finally, we possessed the addresses in several cities of unknown but apparently sympathetic persons to whom we regularly mailed our bulletins. So much for the free zone.

In the occupied zone we knew that Guédon and Froment had gotten in touch with Jeanne Sivadon and the people at Fulmen. But what they had actually achieved we didn't know. From them we received infrequent mail, illegally posted just on our side of the demarcation line. Though their letters contained much information, they were silent concerning the development of the movement. I decided to go to Paris myself, for I had a hunch that in the occupied zone underground activity did not obey the same rules and did not command the same resources that it did in the free

Clandestine Press

zone. For example, in the occupied zone military activity apparently took priority over intelligence-gathering and propaganda. However, I believed that before I made any excursion into the occupied zone I should see to it that the movement had taken firm root in Lyons, for here a large staff would very soon be required. I also planned a tour of our militants in the free zone.

I had one other worry. My contacts with the government ministries had now evaporated, and all the efforts of our Vichy informants could not fill this void. Our information and propaganda bulletins no longer had any real sources.

My plan was to reach a gentleman's agreement with the Quai Saint-Vincent in Lyons where, under the cover of a commercial business, the Deuxième Bureau had installed its "German section." In utter disregard for the armistice convention, it was gathering intelligence on Germany and her army. I knew some of the officers there, and I was very eager to contact them.

Such was our plan of action. But to accomplish it, as we knew only too well, we needed money. Of course we still practiced systematic "mooching," thanks to which we had been able to achieve the little we had. But the inherent limitations of this method we knew only too well, for we had already reached them.

We needed the cooperation of businessmen and entrepreneurs, financial angels who could enable us to set up a genuine budget instead of living from hand to mouth. But we did not know a single wealthy businessman. Our scant experience with them had proved quite disappointing. The head of one large business, an old schoolmate of mine at the Lycée Ampère, with whom I had remained on good terms, had given me 5,000 francs; I had been hoping for ten times more. The owner of a well-known shipyard had offered me another sum so tiny that we were obliged to refuse it. Dignity above all!

We might well have obtained money from the intelligence people who were perhaps working alongside us without even suspecting our activities. But who were they? As for De Gaulle, though he had not yet sent us a single emissary, we believed a liaison with him to be essential from every standpoint.

Seated before a blazing fire that evening, Berty and I drew up a program for our future activities: (1) a major recruiting effort in

The Night Will End

Lyons, (2) an inspection trip to the free zone, followed by one to the occupied zone, (3) intelligence-gathering, and (4) a renewed quest for financial support.

On the following day I presented myself at the Quai Saint-Vincent. There, in a modest six-room apartment, the Deuxième was organizing its illegal, and hence underground, activities. They were directed by an officer called Serre, a small chubby man who rarely spoke and was imperturbably calm. With him worked two old friends of mine. One of them, Captain Gaton, was an artillery officer. Guédon, he and I had been in the same class at the Ecole de Guerre. We had also been in the same work group, so we knew each other quite well. The other was Captain Cossé-Brissac, a cavalryman. He and I had taken courses together in the Centre d'Etudes Germaniques in Strasbourg. Several times I had been invited to his home and had met his wife (née Rohan), who was following a tardy medical vocation at Strasbourg University.

These men believed that the very existence of their service branch, which was directed solely against Germany and financed by Vichy, was ample proof of the government's good intentions. Hitler was still the enemy, collaboration only a decoy designed to distract him. They also knew, as I did, that still other military branches were involved in underground activity against the Third Reich. Among them were the Bureaux M.A. (Bureaux de Menées Antinationales*), which were none other than our disguised counter-espionage service. Serre and his men knew that the Bureaux M.A. had been set up with the aim of detecting German agents (we shall witness a remarkable example later in this narrative). But they were also ferreting out English agents, as well as those whom Vichy referred to as "Gaullists" or, when its propaganda deemed necessary, as "Communo-Gaullists" (labeled "antinational" purely because they were hostile to Pétain and his regime). None of this displeased my two ex-colleagues, however, for both were still traumatized by Mers el-Kébir.

They also knew that on orders from our general staff the camouflage of arms was being practiced on a vast scale. We were among the few who were aware that in each region, on orders from

*Menées Antinationales: Anti-National Conspiracies.

Clandestine Press

Colonel Vigier, soldiers officially on armistice leave were recruiting personnel, usually reserve officers, to conceal on their property or in the vicinity—in barns, granaries, cellars and caves—materiel of all kinds, including howitzers and tanks.

Regimental Benevolent Societies were also being set up to take a census of our reserves in view of an eventual remobilization.

We were also aware that the so-called *Chantiers de la Jeuneese* (Work Farms for Youth) were intended to play an important role in the eventual armed uprising envisaged by our general staff. Under a standing order from General la Porte du Theil, every young Frenchman of the free zone was required to spend eight months in one of these *Chantiers.* Officially they were aimed at reducing unemployment and at channeling the energies of these young men, most of whose fathers were prisoners of war, into public works. But in the mind of the general staff their real function was to provide military instruction—the rudiments of discipline, hygiene and endurance—and also to gather all the statistics normally required by a military recruiting office.

How clear it all seemed to my intelligence friends! Steeped in military history, they compared our current situation to that of Prussia after the debacle of Jena. France, according to this view, would one day join the Allies and participate in our national liberation.

Likewise all was clear to the many camouflage officers who, clad in work overalls, were toiling deep into the night. For these presidents of benevolent societies, for these gentlemen-farmers on whose estates the weapons of revenge were stockpiled, Pétain was not only France's shield but also her sword. Yes indeed, the old Marshal would show the Germans! De Gaulle they abhorred. To them he was a mere criminal, an overambitious general in the pay of the "foreigners" and the "Judeo-Masons."

Soon I put Serre the big question: "*Mon commandant,*" I said, "I know that you gather and file away all kinds of intelligence here. No doubt some of it is reserved exclusively for Colonel Baril. But the rest, the greater part, is useless both to official bodies, who already know it, and to the press and radio, who are forbidden to broadcast it. We, however, could publish it in our clandestine newsletters, which we hope to expand in the near future."

The Night Will End

Then I showed him several copies of our bulletin. He thumbed through them, stopping here and there to read more closely. He was obviously intrigued.

"Frenay," he said, "we know you and we trust you. That's the only reason I'm able to discuss this matter with you at all. What you are requesting is, as you undoubtedly know, unorthodox. But as we're certainly aiming at the same goal, I'll agree to grant your request. However, I do impose one proviso—that it be you, and you alone, who comes each week to pick up the information. Nobody but you must know our address."

"It's a deal. No one will ever know the source of this material. I'm truly grateful, *mon commandant*. This information is bound to open the eyes of some of our less enlightened readers."

For many long months I made my weekly pilgrimage to the Quai Saint-Vincent. Garon usually helped me check and sort out the intelligence reports. I would invariably leave with a large number of them after providing the intelligence people with the latest copy of our own bulletin (later, our newspaper). Garon's intelligence reports, along with those I received from the occupied zone, provided us with the bulk of our news copy.

Now that we had this steady source of copy, we decided that during my frequent absences Berty would take charge of the editing and mailing of the bulletins. She lost no time in finding a new helper and a new work place. Then I left her for the provinces.

In Marseilles I stayed with Recordier, who treated me like a brother. He was rather upset over my decision to leave the army. Maurice Chevance also spent an evening with us. He had done his best to expand both his agency and our movement. He'd created six-man cells in most districts of the city. There was a rising clamor for our information bulletins: a hundred were now required in Marseilles alone. We sent them to Chevance in packets, and he took charge of their distribution. This ploy avoided the dangerous alternative of having a central address file. I also learned that Gemahling's intelligence-gathering had begun to yield fruit.

But I was not content. It was clear that Maurice had in fact given priority to his agency. It had made great progress and was already

Clandestine Press

outdoing its competitors, as he told me with his incurable optimism. Meanwhile, our recruitment was faltering, and our growth outside Marseilles was just too slow. Maurice finally realized that he could not run both his agency and our movement. He proposed, and I accepted, that Bellet take charge of our activities in the region.

At the local officers' club I ran into an old friend from my class at Saint-Cyr, Jean Chapelle, a captain in the colonial infantry, currently at home on furlough. Naturally I spoke to him about my situation, my activities and, of course, my impecunity. I do not remember if I "mooched" any money off him, but it's quite likely I did, for mooching had become a reflex with me. His personal contribution must have been modest, for the following day he called me up to propose a meeting with two potential angels. They were wealthy men who had made their fortunes in commerce and banking. Both French Jews, they detested the Nazi regime. We arranged a rendezvous.

I met Jean Chapelle in a little café near the Vieux-Port. Beside him were three elegantly attired women. I was rather surprised and doubtless I showed it.

"May I introduce Henri Frenay, the man I mentioned to you," he said, and then, turning to me: "Madame Paulette S. . . . Her sister Odette L. . . . and Chilina Ciosi, a physician and friend of my family."

The latter was a young woman about thirty years of age, slender, olive-skinned and with jet-black hair. Her profile was that of a Roman medallion. She was discreet both in her speech and in her appearance. I gathered from the conversation that she was unattached.

"Monsieur," began Paulette S., "kindly forgive our husbands for being absent. They were planning on coming but were detained at the last moment. Jean Chapelle has told us a little about your activities, but we'd like to be able to tell our husbands a little more before you actually meet them."

"Madame, since I have met you through our common friend Jean Chapelle, I shall trust your discretion. However, allow me to caution you that our discussion here today must be kept secret by your husbands and yourselves. I think you can see why."

The Night Will End

Then I told them about our ideas, our rudimentary organization (which I inflated somewhat) and our objectives. I later discovered that my eloquence had been impressive, though not impressive enough to make the long-awaited funds tumble eagerly into our coffers. Pressed for time, I never did get around to presenting my case in person before S. and L.

As we parted at the door of the café, Chilina Ciosi offered me her address in Paris. Apparently I did not hear her, and later I discovered that this had rather piqued her. But destiny had decided that one day I would know that address very well indeed.

My visit to Toulouse was very disappointing. Lien, who had taken charge of our effort there, had done absolutely nothing—at least, he had had absolutely no results. He set up three successive appointments for me, one of which was with a certain M. Raymondis, a lawyer who apparently enjoyed a solid reputation in the city. Elsewhere I was received suspiciously and often had to submit to veritable cross-examinations. I was extremely irritated, and I gave Lien a piece of my mind. He didn't even try to excuse his idleness. And yet, with all the refugees from Alsace-Lorraine in his region, he disposed of a really exceptional recruitment pool!

No doubt about it: I was dealing with an incompetent, a shallow, characterless man who possibly—and here was the real danger—lacked the courage of his convictions. I had to replace him, but with whom? I tried for twenty-four hours to look up some of my old friends in these parts (for, two years earlier, I myself had been garrisoned in Toulouse). I did not find a single one. All officers, they had been transferred elsewhere. After vigorously reprimanding Lien, I headed back to Lyons—but without harboring any illusions.

Berty greeted me in the Lyons railway station. She was in good spirits. She had just made a fine new recruit called Jacqueline Bernard. A young Jewish refugee living in Lyons with her parents, she had immediately agreed to help us and had begun typing our bulletins. (We never suspected that Berty had just netted a tireless worker who, until her arrest by the Gestapo in the spring of 1944, was to be the linchpin of our entire underground press.)

Clandestine Press

Jacqueline Bernard arranged for me to meet her parents. They were obviously well-to-do, otherwise the entire family could not have lived in the Grand Hôtel. In the same hotel resided the delegation of the German Armistice Commission, no doubt heavily seasoned with Abwehr agents.

Colonel Bernard was a slight, trim man with bright eyes and a pencil mustache yellowed by tobacco. He was a brusque, voluble speaker who regarded his opinions as definitive. Having served for many years in the colonial army, he had finally settled in Indochina, where apparently he had made his fortune. His lively wife had a certain penchant for good-natured jibes, which were sometimes taken amiss. Her laughing eyes had not been dimmed by the defeat.

The friendship of the colonel and his wife was unfailing right to the end of the war, despite the terrible ordeals they suffered on account of their two children. For they also had a son, Jean-Guy, whom I was soon to meet. He had entered the Ecole Polytechnique in 1939, but after the occupation of Paris he had sought refuge in Lyons, where he was now finishing his second year of study.

We had known each other only a few days when Colonel Bernard offered me 50,000 francs, a gesture he renewed on several occasions. Thanks to his generosity, our movement began to make great strides forward.

Through my friends on the Quai Saint-Vincent I had, since my arrival in Lyons, made the acquaintance of a certain Captain Besson. His activity was shrouded in mystery. Though he seemed to have no official business there, he had some kind of arcane access to the general staff headquarters of the military region. He was definitely not a career officer and was never in uniform. He had an "office" on the ground floor of No. 10, Rue de Castries, where there was no furniture and whence unmarked parcels departed almost as soon as they had arrived. He wasn't nosey, and neither was I. Perhaps he was from intelligence, perhaps from the counter-espionage, perhaps from the camouflage service. I never found out. One thing, though: He was remarkably efficient, as I was soon to discover.

The Night Will End

As much for security as for increased efficiency, we needed an office. Besson agreed to help me locate one. One day he said:

"I've found just what you want. Everything is ready. All you have to do is move into the offices of the S.N.C.A.S.E. (Société Nationale de Construction Aérienne du Sud-Est). It's on the Avenue de Saxe. The company's director, Raymond Moine, is a friend of mine. You'll have free run of two furnished and virtually separate offices, and you can use the telephone. You'd best give the postman a fictitious commercial name, unless, of course you want to use your own name, which is highly unadvisable."

As it happened, I had just seen a movie starring Victor Francen.

"I'll be Henri 'Francen,'" I said. I preferred to keep my own Christian name. Berty would never get used to any other, and my hatband and much of my wardrobe bore the initials H.F.

And so, in early April 1941, M. "Francen" and his secretary moved their typewriter, their stock of paper and their heavy file cabinet with its security lock into the premises of a nationwide business firm.

As I opened the door to our new offices I felt a crazy desire to dance a jig.

"Berty," I said, "before I leave for Paris, I must get a mimeograph machine. No typist could do this job. From now on we must produce five hundred copies, soon a thousand. Many of our militants and correspondents would like to distribute copies to their friends."

Unable to afford a new machine, we found a very old model on sale. A helpful stationer provided us with a considerable stock of stencils and paper. To get that mimeo rolling required heroic efforts. It was a truly comical contraption. Sometimes it devoured four or five sheets at one time, then it would refuse to take any paper at all. Often—and always at the least expected moment—it would vomit Niagaras of ink. How delighted we were when, having finally mastered this infernal machine, we began to see our bulletins rise before us by the hundreds.

It must be hard for those who read this narrative thirty years after the events, and who did not themselves live through the occupation, to grasp the significance of our modest underground

Clandestine Press

bulletins. We ourselves were only dimly aware of their importance.

We originated them—at least, in our own movement—to fill a very specific need: to counterbalance Vichy's propaganda (which itself simply mirrored Goebbels'). We also wished to offer our readers information denied them by the official press, as well as editorials that might provide them with some reason to keep on hoping—and, in the early days, that was pretty hard to come by.

Soon the bulletin, and the newspaper that succeeded it, began to play yet another equally important though unforeseen role. A solidarity born of complicity was cemented among all those who received our sheets. Since wartime conditions precluded the calling of public meetings, the newspapers served to bind our followers together. People sometimes forgot the name of our movement but never that of our newspaper.

At long and irregular intervals I received news of our movement in the occupied zone—not enough, however, to fill me in on what had taken place since my meeting in Vichy with Guédon. Then one day Berty rang me from her office in Villeurbanne.

"I've a very good friend of Jeanne Sivadon's in the office here with me. She saw Jeanne a few days ago. She just got in from Paris and she wants to meet you."

That was how I met Anne-Marie Boumier. She was a tall woman with pepper-and-salt hair, somewhere between forty and forty-five years old. With her severe dress, her lightning-fast retorts and her manners of a person used to positions of authority, she had been one of France's first factory superintendents. She was an old colleague of Jeanne Sivadon's and had needed no great prompting from Jeanne to enroll in our movement. Her incisive mind, her high position and her tremendous energy convinced us that she was a truly choice recruit.

"Things are progressing splendidly in Paris," she told us. "Robert Guédon is working like crazy, but he travels a lot, so we don't see much of him. He asked me to tell you that he'd appreciate your presence in Paris as soon as possible. I think he wants to straighten out some propaganda and liaison problems."

"Well, I was already planning on leaving shortly for Paris. But I

The Night Will End

haven't yet decided on how or when I shall cross the demarcation line."

"I'm leaving myself on April 12. Why don't we go together? It shouldn't be too hard for you to get a pass. I got mine in forty-eight hours."

A pass? I hadn't considered this possibility, for I could not imagine a plausible reason for requesting one. It was likely that the Gestapo was already aware of my activities, and I had no intention whatever of throwing myself to the wolves. My original idea had been to cross the line in secret, as so many others had done.

Perhaps I was silly, but the sheer speed and comfort of the railway tempted me. I mentioned it to my friend Captain Besson.

"It's a snap," he replied. "I'll simply leave you in the hands of Captain René Israël."

The very next day—for Besson always worked fast—I met Captain Israël. He worked in the army cartography service, an activity which, as his conversation indicated, had led him into some shady practices. Nothing was easier for him, he assured me, than to fabricate a phony pass bearing the name of "Molin", with corresponding identity papers. Why "Molin"? The name had occurred to me several days earlier when I was dreaming up euphonious pseudonyms. It was composed of the first letters of the words, *Mouvement de Libération Nationale*. To do the job, Captain Israël required only forty-eight hours.

"But are you sure this pass looks authentic?" I asked him as I received my forged papers. "And what about the stamps and signatures?"

He gazed at me with mingled pity and severity. "Monsieur 'Francen,' if such things had not been taken care of, I wouldn't conceive of letting you have the papers. You see, I assume all responsibility for the risks my comrades run."

As I inspected the pass my eye was caught by a misspelled German word. I called it to his attention.

"That," he replied, "is the fly in the ointment. Such a spelling mistake exists in the original. If I correct it, you're lost!"*

*Later, returning from a trip to England, Captain René Israël was arrested by the Gestapo, wounded during an attempted escape and finally murdered in a Lyons hospital bed on June 15, 1944.

Clandestine Press

I was ready to leave and knew my fake identity and civil status by heart. I agreed to meet Anne-Marie Boumier on the station platform. Shortly afterward Chevance called me on the telephone. I joyfully announced my departure for Paris and, in an undertone, the route I was taking.

Three days later, on April 12, I went to the Gare Perrache accompanied by Berty. We were a little ahead of time but found Anne-Marie already waiting. We both judged it safest to travel separately, as if we did not know each other, and we put our baggage in different compartments of the same coach. Berty and I paced nervously to and fro on the departure platform. A few minutes before departure time, a breathless dispatch runner grabbed my sleeve.

"I've just come from Marseilles with a letter from Maurice," he panted. God only knows how this fellow had recognized me, for I had never seen him before. I opened the letter and read these rather unnerving words in Chevance's own handwriting: "Henri, don't go! For the last forty-eight hours a bilingual notice has been posted at Châlon-sur-Saône announcing that all individuals caught at the line of demarcation in possession of a false pass will be summarily executed."

If Maurice had taken the trouble to send this messenger, the news must be true. Should I postpone my trip? I could always wait a few days and slip across the line at Moulins. Berty urged me to do just that, but in my mind's eye I could still see Captain Israël's gaze and hear his voice saying, "I assume all responsibility for the risks my comrades run." He was a man who meant what he said. And so I departed, under Berty's nervously watchful eye.

In the train corridor Anne-Marie and I exchanged a few words, as if we were people who had just met. In an undertone I told her about Chevance's letter. A bit farther on, toward Mâcon, I suddenly noticed that my hatband bore the initials H.F. I tore it off in the toilet and flushed it, returning to my compartment with a ludicrously large hat.

As we approached Châlon-sur-Saône the train cut its speed. This was my first contact with the occupied zone.

The train stopped and several people got off, but we were still six in my compartment. The loudspeaker advised us, first in French,

The Night Will End

then in German, to remain in our seats and to have our papers ready for inspection. Before each compartment stood an armed sentry. Two Germans arrived, one in a noncom's uniform, the other in mufti—probably a plainclothesman.

"Papers, please."

Everybody's papers were inspected and duly returned—except mine, which seemed to interest them exceedingly. Had something gone wrong?

"Monsieur 'Molin', are these your papers?"

"Yes. Why?"

No answer. One of the two men called in a third. He re-examined my pass even more closely. Through the corridor window they summoned a guard and posted him before the door of my compartment. They then disappeared with my papers. The guard's eyes did not leave me once.

I began to suspect that the game was up. I was terrified. How could I escape? It was impossible—too many soldiers, too many tommy guns. I began to play the innocent gentleman who, though exasperated by bureaucratic formalities, is essentially indifferent. I feigned deep absorption in my newspaper, though actually I was incapable of reading a single line. Several endless minutes passed. Then the inspectors—now only two—returned. Holding my pass up against the corridor window, they examined it through the light in comparison with another, authentic one.

"Monsieur 'Molin'?"

"Yes?"

Wordlessly they returned me my papers, which I methodically replaced in my wallet. Then they departed with the sentry in tow. The train shuddered. I had been saved by Captain René Israël.

Anne-Marie and I had agreed that I would stay in her Paris apartment at 14, Rue Emile-Duclaux in the XVth arrondissement. She lived there with a friend, Dr. Anne Noury, who welcomed me warmly. Little did I suspect that these two women would be the first in our movement to experience the horrors of the Gestapo, prison and deportation.

Occupied Paris! How many times I had pictured German troops in our capital! But to see them with my own eyes—that was

Clandestine Press

another story. Each day I had a sensation of rape, and perhaps it was on the Place de la Concorde and the Champs Elysées that my sorrow was most acute. The Hôtel Crillon and the Ministry of the Navy were draped with immense, swastika-emblazoned banners. Before the doors, sentries stood in stony immobility, while twenty yards to the left and right of them others goose-stepped up and down the pavement. And oh, that horde of rowdy, wisecracking German soldiers who meandered up and down the promenade of the Champs Elysées! Often young French girls hung on their arms, utterly unembarrassed to be seen in the company of a *Schleuh.* In vain did I remind myself that I too, during my 1926–29 stint in the Army of the Rhine, had often had a German girl on my arm.

The Marignan had become a *Soldatenkino,** and certain restaurants were reserved exclusively for German troops. They also invaded the department stores, especially those on the Rue de Rivoli that specialized in souvenirs. At twenty francs to the mark, a German shopping expedition was legalized pillage. The Unknown Soldier, whose flame still flickered on at the Etoile, received daily visits from the sons of those he had vanquished. Clocks were set to German time, with the result that even in April Parisian school children went to school in utter darkness. In the evening a blackout was strictly observed, and the curfew made the capital a dead city.

The day after my arrival I met Guédon in the Ecole de Surintendantes d'Usine on the Rue Princesse. He introduced me to Jeanne Sivadon, whom I already seemed to know from Berty's reminiscences. She was a blond, fortyish woman who radiated extreme youthfulness. Tiny and round, she communicated an intense *joie de vivre* to those around her. Her voice and her way of speaking were almost childlike. On her generous bosom reposed the Huguenot cross. Born a pastor's daughter in Mas-d'Azil, in the Ariège, she was still a militant Protestant, but her natural gaiety seemed to win out over the austerity of her religion.

These offices in the Ecole became the center of all our activities

---

*Cinema for German soldiers.

The Night Will End

in the occupied zone. Jeanne, under Guédon's direction, became a kind of secretary-general to the movement.

As I had expected, Robert had been very active. "Henri," he said, "I have not followed all your organizational directives, for experience has led me to different conclusions. Here in the occupied zone, and even more so in the prohibited zone, many unconnected groups have sprouted up spontaneously. Each is in the image of its leader and oriented either toward intelligence and propaganda or toward sabotage. I didn't see the point of still more potentially rival groups. They would have cost us precious time and created unnecessary conflicts. So I asked them only to distribute our bulletins, which they do, and to pass on to us whatever information they get their hands on."

"I think you made the right decision, Robert . . . on one condition—that these groups accept our coordination and follow our general orientation."

"Well, frankly, that's our whole problem. But fortunately it's not yet a burning issue. For the moment I simply visit them once a month to collect their information, and they really do distribute our bulletins. What we should do first is get them the money and arms they're clamoring for."

I wasted no time in sending them some money; but as for arms, alas! I simply had none. The first parachute drops were still a long way off.

Already many groups were affiliating themselves with us, especially in Champagne, Tours and Caen. In Tours there were really two sub-groups. The first was directed by a gendarmerie captain who had enlisted all his subordinates. They specialized in intelligence and in crossing the demarcation line. The second group was directed by the prior of Saint-Martin. He reigned over a chapter house packed with ex-army chaplains, as well as a convent of nuns for whom the dangers of clandestine activity were like a hot pepper in the calm of their monastic life.

The team in Caen was even more autonomous. It specialized in the rescue of English airmen downed by flak or by German interceptors. It also gathered precious information, which it managed not only to smuggle to London but also to transmit to Robert. This information included the number of planes missing

Clandestine Press

in Luftwaffe squadrons returning from air raids over England, the number of men drowned and cremated after disembarkation and landing exercises, troop transport schedules, the fortifications of the Normandy coast and so forth.

"In fact," continued Guédon, "if most of these people do listen to me, it's neither for my lovely voice nor for my politics. It's simply because they know that I'm a general staff officer, hence in their eyes a competent leader in touch with the Deuxième Bureau of the Army General Staff. Their faith in Pétain is total. They can't stand the very name of De Gaulle, whom they won't forgive for having left our national territory."

In Paris, Jeanne Sivadon had expanded her recruitment of ex-factory superintendents. From them Robert Guédon had obtained a lot of help with his propaganda and intelligence-gathering activities. He multiplied his contacts everywhere—always in the most reckless way. Though we were unaware of it, the Gestapo was already hunting us.

Several days after my arrival I rang at a fifth-floor flat at 25, Avenue Victor-Hugo. The address had been given to me in Marseilles by one of our first recruits, Robert Dupleix, who vouched for the reliability of his friend Jacques Dhont, a northerner like himself.

The door was opened by a thin, icy-looking fellow with almost completely white hair and wearing a sumptuous dressing gown. When I mentioned the name Dupleix he showed me in. I found myself in an elegantly furnished bachelor apartment. On a card table before the window I noticed an enormous jigsaw puzzle, which my host had obviously been busy with when I arrived. What an unusual activity and attire for a bachelor at eleven in the morning in the middle of occupied Paris! Perhaps our interests did not coincide.

I described our doings at length. In turn Dhont asked me some very incisive questions about myself and our movement. The man appealed to me. His speech was elegant, his courtesy almost old-fashioned (fortunately I happen to prefer this excess to the opposite one). He seemed quite relaxed. He knew how to listen,

The Night Will End

and when he spoke he weighed his words. His opinion of Germany coincided with my own. We drank a glass of port and the atmosphere become more informal.

Then he asked me offhandedly, "Well, what's my first job?"

Events were to prove that I had just enlisted a first-class recruit.

I was eager to see Froment again. Robert and I visited him in his uncle's place at 7, Rue du Colonel-Moll. With a characteristic regard for absolute precision, he calmly related his achievements. Several groups were now operating under his direction. The most promising one was probably that of Vierzon, where the director of the Fulmen factory, along with a M. Dor, a Dr. Duval and the principal of the local school, had set up services for propaganda, communication with the free zone and intelligence. They also had antennas in several nearby arrondissements.

In Amiens, on the border of the prohibited zone, an insurance agent called Edmond Hadengue had created his own group. Under the direction of Jacques-Yves Mulliez, a reserve officer and the son of an important northern textile manufacturer, his organization had spread to Lille and Roubaix. Since early 1941 he had been writing and mimeographing a newspaper called *Les Petites Ailes du Nord et du Pas-de-Calais*. Its circulation amounted to six or eight hundred copies in both departments. Later Froment was to extend its distribution to Béthune, Arras, Boulogne and Calais.

Groups had also sprung up in the Aisne, at Hirson, Saint-Quentin and Laon. Some specialized in propaganda, others in intelligence. At the latter they were particularly successful, for they happened to be in an excellent position to observe all the German railway transportation in the northern and eastern parts of France. They provided Froment with regular communications concerning the content and tonnage of railway convoys bound for Germany and laden with strategic goods such as wheat, copper, wool, etc.

Froment devoted some serious thought to the possibility of direct action against the occupier's convoys and installations. In the end he rejected such actions as premature. For the moment he was content to gather and stockpile arms. In fact, he managed to

Clandestine Press

conceal at his home in the Indre 150 tons of weapons that had been entrusted to him by army camouflage personnel.

As I listened to Froment I didn't know which I admired more, his dogged hard work or his sheer guts in boldly pushing our movement right into the very zone the enemy had the nerve to call "forbidden."

"Froment, old man," I said, "you've done a very good job indeed and in record time, too. Two or three more like you, and we'll cover the entire occupied zone. But for the moment our biggest task is to make the best possible use of the information we've gathered. And that means getting it to London. As for propaganda, what we need is a newspaper—a real, honest-to-God newspaper."

"By the way," said Froment, "I brought along a few copies of the one I mentioned to you."

He took several mimeographed sheets out of his briefcase—*Les Petites Ailes du Nord et du Pas-de-Calais*. Beneath the title was a drawing representing two little wings similar to those usually sewn on aviators' flight jackets. The implication was that by means of this clandestine newsletter the truth might fly from door to door.

"Why don't we expand its circulation to cover the whole of France?" I asked. "Perhaps Mulliez would agree to change its name to *Les Petites Ailes de France*."

"Sure he would," agreed Froment. "He's utterly selfless."

So we were going to publish a newspaper! Right away we began discussing its production and format.

Yes, we would call it *Les Petites Ailes de France*. As a motto we would add a saying of Bonaparte's that Guédon had read somewhere and jotted down: "To live in defeat is to die every day." We would put out two editions, one for the free zone, under my direction, and one for the occupied zone, under Robert's. As far as possible the editorial would be identical in each edition, and the paper would appear twice a month. Each zone would take care of its own distribution. Each central editorial bureau would also create its own regional distribution centers that would receive each issue in packages and circulate the individual copies. We agreed to start with a mimeographed sheet but to graduate to a properly printed periodical as soon as possible.

The Night Will End

"Why don't we try to bring out the first issue for the fête of Saint Joan of Arc?" suggested Robert. "Goebbels is already planning a publicity campaign based on Saint Joan, emphasizing the duplicity and cruelty of the English. Saint Joan's death at the stake in Rouen is supposed to serve as German propaganda. Why don't we reply by exalting Joan as the liberator of our national territory?"

I agreed. But it was clear that we'd have to move devilishly fast. At least Robert was right where he needed to be, whereas I was far from my Lyons headquarters in the free zone.

As dusk stole over that comfortable apartment in the XVIIth arrondissement, all three of us had the deep conviction that we had made a great stride in a single day.

My old classmate Jean Chapelle had asked me to take advantage of my trip to Paris to obtain news of Chilina Ciosi, who was apparently recovering from a nasty bout of pleurisy. One morning I mentioned her over breakfast to my hostess, Anne Noury.

"Anne, a friend wanted me to look in on one of your colleagues, Dr. Chilina Ciosi."

Before I had finished she had already lifted the receiver and dialed Chilina's number, which she obviously knew by heart. I was astounded at this latest coincidence.

"Chilina, dear, how do you feel? Listen, I'm going to put somebody on who wants to talk to you."

We made a date and met at the Brasserie Kléber, on the Place du Trocadero.

Though quiet and reserved, as Corsican women of the more fortunate classes generally are, Chilina was strikingly pretty. The morning was superb, the sky cloudless. It was pleasant to sit beside her, yet we were soon plunged back into the rude reality of the spring of 1941, for I detected a distant sound that soon turned out to be a marching band's rhythmic thunder. Suddenly a whole Wehrmacht batallion rounded the corner, deafening me with its fifes and drums. As the well-drilled platoons goose-stepped impressively by, Marshal Foch, high on his stone pedestal, seemed to doff his képi in salutation.

I had to get back to Lyons. But how? With my phony pass? What

Clandestine Press

65

a taunt to the gods after the severe warning they had already given me! Yet, on second thought, if my papers had stood up once to such a rigorous examination, why couldn't they do it again?

Guédon saw me off. We agreed that I'd return sometime during the summer.

At Châlon-sur-Saône the same ceremony again took place: the passengers restricted to their compartments, the sentries, the painstaking examination of papers. Yes, mine were in perfect order.

The Night Will End

A WANTED MAN

All the way back from Paris I was bursting with enthusiasm. The occupied zone was by and large ahead of the free zone. I soon realized that our team needed two things to be able to match theirs: greater resolve and additional resources. Here, as was so often the case in the years to come, luck was on my side.

Jean-Charles Demachy, our chief fisher of souls in the Lyons region, had arranged for me to visit Emanuel Mounier in his little apartment in the Croix-Rousse. I knew Mounier by reputation only. The founder of the review *Esprit*, he was also the father of "personalism," a much-discussed Christian existentialist doctrine of the prewar years. I also made the acquaintance of Stanislas Fumet, a major contributor to another periodical, *Temps Présent*, which he also virtually directed. Both men belonged to a branch of avant-garde Catholicism which the Church hierarchy tolerated only with some apprehension.

I can still picture Fumet, with his graying bangs and his air of a defrocked monk, saying as we ended our discussion, "Considering your present activities and plans, I believe you'd do very well to meet Father Chaillet. Give me about four or five days to notify him that you're coming. I'd be

5

quite surprised if you and he don't quickly find common ground."

Less than one week after our interview, I found myself ringing the doorbell of the Jesuit residence at 2, Montée de Fourvière in Lyons. I waited in the impenetrable silence of a long vestibule. A few moments later a man appeared and greeted me: "Monsieur Frenay? Won't you please come in? My friend Stanislas Fumet told me to expect you."

As we entered the little study that was also his bedroom, I could make out the man a bit better. What struck me most about him was not his baldness, a little premature for a man of my age, nor even his clergyman's habit, so rarely seen in those days. It was his look, a look of extraordinary intensity that alighted only furtively on me and soon fled my returning gaze. I felt that the reverend father did not wish me to guess his unspoken thoughts.

In the course of this initially rather stiff meeting, which soon became more open and eventually quite relaxed, I discovered a man whose whole personality was inclined toward direct action. Even before my visit he'd been involved in some resistance activity, a fact I divined but chose not to mention openly. The important thing was to convince him to work with me. He accepted.

In the first of my frequent return visits to his cell, I asked him to write a religious column for our paper. In each issue up to the end of 1941, under the pseudonym of *Testis*,* he addressed himself to the Christian conscience of our readers, in the language not of politics but of faith. His principal aim was the revelation of the true face of National Socialism, a task that seemed as important to him as it did to me, for a very large portion of Catholics, reflecting the position of almost all French bishops, supported Marshal Pétain and his regime of "National Revolution" and were thus dangerously exposed to the temptation to collaborate.

Happily for us, a small but very active number of Christians were on our side. Demachy wasted no time in introducing me to them: Marcel Poimboeuf, the Christian trade-unionist; Joseph Voyant; Michel Crozier; Jean Lacroix, a philosophy professor and later a brilliant sociologist; and Professor Hours, a historian whose

*Testis——Latin, "witness."

The Night Will End

courageous lectures had become the talk of Lyons. There was also the Reverend Roland de Pury, a Protestant pastor with whom Berty had already spoken. Through him she managed to achieve direct access to Karl Barth, the great Protestant theologian in Switzerland. The latter's firm and oft-reiterated rejection of Nazism was of capital importance to our propaganda. Often Berty and I went to the Huguenot chapel on the Rue Lanterne to listen to Roland de Pury's sermons. What a joy it was to hear this man preach before a full house almost exactly what we were saying in our clandestine newsletters!

I always had the impression—God forgive me if I slander the innocent—that plots were under way on every floor and in every cell of this Jesuit residence. For example, I later discovered that Fathers Faissard and Lubac were working all the while along the same lines as we were. Even today I would not swear that other cabals of a very different tendency were not being hatched in the same honorable quarters. No doubt only the Almighty Himself knew about all of them.

Our newspaper, *Les Petites Ailes de France*, had just come out. What joy and—why deny it?—what pride to know that at the same moment, and under the same title, the edition for the occupied zone was also appearing!

Yet we felt that our little effort in journalism really needed to be printed before it could be called a genuine newspaper.

"Berty," I said, "in a few weeks the number of copies we require will already exceed the strength of our poor old machine. Its health already worries me. What we need is a printer. Let's start casting about for some small artisan, preferably one who works alone and doesn't object to getting involved in underground activity. He should also be aware that our operation will expand as the months go by."

One evening in mid-June I arrived at Berty's for dinner. She wasn't home yet, so I chatted with her daughter Mireille. Time passed, but Berty did not come. We were beginning to worry when suddenly the door opened. Berty burst in, hollering like a madwoman: "I've got one, I've got one!"

We gazed at her dumfounded. She sat down, looked at us for a

A Wanted Man

moment and burst out laughing. Slowly she enunciated the following syllables: "A printer! His name is Martinet and he lives at 5, Rue Mozart in Villeurbanne. He works together with his wife and can provide us with enough paper for ten thousand copies. That's all he has in stock, but he thinks he can get hold of more."

Martinet—what an utterly appealing figure he was! A simple artisan in the old Lyons tradition, generous, obliging, hating injustice and loving liberty more than life itself, he was fast as quicksilver, too. The first printed number came out only a week later. It gave us real joy. Up to that day we had never laid eyes on a printed clandestine newspaper.

The discussions about Europe that I had with my friends in those days illustrate the variety of motives which spurred men to join the Resistance. Of course I'm speaking only of the early period, not of the final year when many who had contributed nothing to our struggle jumped on the bandwagon of certain victory. Like myself, some resistants made a clear distinction between Hitler and Germany, but they were very few. For the vast majority, Nazism was only the most recent manifestation of an eternal Teutonism. As I was later to learn, this was also De Gaulle's opinion.

Out of opposition to this Teutonism came certain men of the old French right, though most rightists, along with the greater part of the country as a whole, applauded the vanishing of the Third Republic and blindly followed Marshal Pétain. Some even actively collaborated with counter-Resistance execution squads. But inside the occupied zone, the very presence of German troops, resented as a form of rape, provoked many Frenchmen to strike back.

To all these motives were often added more private, even personal, considerations. Among these was the anxiety of Jews about the vicious anti-Semitism of the Nazis and certain measures enacted by Vichy, such as the exclusion of French Jews from so many public and private jobs that they felt increasingly pent up in a sort of ghetto. There were also disbanded Freemasons who had fallen under the prohibition against secret societies, and there

The Night Will End

were Communists hunted by the government just as their German comrades had been hunted by Hitler.

I knew and was proud that in our ranks we had all these types. For I believed that energy of any and every instigation should be welcome in the struggle against Nazism. Nobody was turned down. Unlike certain other groups, ours was unaffected by sectarianism.

I hummed contentedly to myself on the way home. Not only was it a lovely evening, but the day had been good. It was about eleven o'clock. Despite the late hour, the concierge was on the lookout for me.

"Monsieur Frenay . . ."

"Good evening, Madame. I see you're turning in late tonight."

"I was waiting up for you. I wanted to tell you that you had visitors today."

"Ah? And who were they?"

"Two men. They asked what floor you lived on. Lots of other questions, too—if you receive company, if you travel a lot, what hours you keep. I had a hunch they were from the police, but no, they said they were friends of yours. They said they'd be back."

I had always known this day would come, and, in a way, I was prepared for it. Though upset by this strange visit, I answered the good concierge calmly.

"Thank you, Madame. I know who those visitors were. I'm sorry to have missed them, and I hope to be home when they return. I'll be in tomorrow evening from six on. Oh, I forgot to buy a paper. Well, it's a nice evening. I'll go pick one up in the Perrache district."

I never again set foot in that apartment on the Quai Gailleton. First I rented a hotel room for the night, then I telephoned Berty. Already in bed, she was alarmed by my news. I asked her to send a messenger to my place early the next morning to pack my suitcases and to remove them from the apartment.

To tell the truth, I was almost pleased that the police had finally paid me a visit. It eased my mind. I had been anxious for some time. It seemed unthinkable that the Sûreté did not yet know

A Wanted Man

about me, and I was afraid that the police might swoop down and carry me off whenever they wanted. Better still, they could put me under surveillance, observe my activities and associates and haul in a huge catch whenever the net was full.

This day, then marked the beginning of my clandestine life, in the full sense of the word. There was no longer any point in concealing my "subversive" activities, since the police were already well aware of them. Moreover, from month to month, in the course of arrests and confiscations of archives and documents, they would find out much more about our organization and my role in it. Now that I was a wanted man my aim was simply not to get caught, first by the Vichy police, later by the Gestapo and the Abwehr.

Very early—in the spring of 1941—I began to take precautions that were still relatively rare in our movement. I forced myself to implement them despite the trouble and the delays they might entail. I also required my friends to follow the same security procedures. Unfortunately not all of them did so. Often they sacrificed security to comfort or to short-term expediency; often they were just careless. The typical Frenchman does not have a conspiratorial temperament, and only with considerable difficulty does he acquire a conspirator's reflexes.

What were these precautions?

First, the frequent change of pseudonyms, which often foiled our pursuers or completely threw them off track. Thus I was successively "Francen," "Molin," "Maurin," "Tavernier," "Gervais," "Lefèbvre," "Xaintrailles," etc.

Next, the obligatory use of false but inspection-proof identity papers. Naturally, we also had to have ready answers for all questions relating to these papers. After the Allied landing in North Africa, in November of 1942, many of us "decided to have been born" in Constantine, Algiers or Sétif. Sometimes, to ensure the authenticity of these new identities, we would resort to the following procedure. Suppose one of us wanted a new set of false papers. Two of our men, supplied with police identity cards, would walk up and down the street until they saw someone resembling the comrade in question.

"Police. Identity papers, please," one of them would say, flash-

The Night Will End

ing his card. Then every scrap of information on the pedestrian's papers would be scrupulously recorded. Our comrade would eventually receive a complete set of new papers bearing this stranger's identity.

Every appointment and every parley entailed serious risks. We shifted our meeting places constantly. In our correspondence and our messages they were designated by code letters or numbers meaningful only to a handful of us.

My own private retreats—with the Roussillon family in Villeu or with the Roujoux family in Charnay-lès-Mâcon—were known only to two or three persons, such as Jean-Guy Bernard and Dominique, who collected and delivered my mail. I never received direct mail at any of my hideouts.

At Mâcon or at Villefranche, my assignations were set for ever-changing places. Sometimes I arrived by train, sometimes by bicycle, and I would always survey each spot from afar before venturing any closer.

On trips to Lyons I got off not at the Gare Perrache or even at the Gare de Vaise but two or three stops before the terminal. From there I would resume my journey into town via streetcar.

I never went anywhere without checking to see if I was being shadowed. After a little practice I could easily spot a tail. I often changed my hat or overcoat—always the best way to transform one's silhouette. I also varied my hair style; wore and did not wear spectacles, with several types of rims; sported mustaches; and even grew a beard, which, however, I quickly shaved off, for beards were rare then. Eventually I decided to carry a gun—when and why we shall soon see.

No doubt fortune favored me—but it also seems clear that without these precautions I could never have escaped arrest and its inevitable aftermath.

My lawyer-cousin Marcel Deville occasionally loaned me his apartment on the Rue de la Charité. There I held a few infrequent meetings. On the 17th or 18th of June 1941 four of us were sitting around the table in the dining room: Berty, Jean-Guy Bernard, André Bollier and myself. At that time I did not yet really know the two boys who were sitting opposite me. They were classmates, just

A Wanted Man

finishing their second year at the Ecole Polytechnique. They were barely over twenty but had expressed a desire to join us.

Jean-Guy was a young man of medium height with slightly wavy reddish-blond hair. His look was direct, fixed, penetrating. He was sober in dress, precise in speech. He laughed only rarely, as if wanting to conceal his youth and the *joie de vivre* that one could sense welling up within him. A pilot and an air force second lieutenant (which was rather unusual for a resister), he was to become my personal delegate for every delicate mission. It was he who received my directives, sounded out those of our people who were directly involved in implementing them and relayed me their messages and final reports.

André Bollier, Jean-Guy's friend, had served in an armored outfit. When his tank was knocked out, he had refused to surrender and had shot down several of his assailants before being grievously wounded himself. Hospitalized, he had escaped as soon as he could regain his feet. Tall, thin and no more talkative than Jean-Guy, his look betrayed an ardent temperament and an ever-vigilant intelligence. In early autumn I entrusted him with the task of supervising the printing and distribution of our newspaper. It was he—along with the magnificent team he gathered about him and which he infused with his own dynamism—who changed our modest newsletter with its circulation of four or five thousand copies into the most extraordinary organ of the Resistance, with printings of over a million per month.

We were terribly depressed by the reports in the collaborationist press. The battle of the Atlantic was raging, with staggering losses to British convoys. The BBC tried to minimize these losses, but it did not conceal them. Britain's food supply, and hence the outcome of the war, was at stake. The battleship *Hood* had been battered and sent to the bottom by the *Bismarck*. Fortunately the German vessel was pursued by Admiral Torrey's fleet, which sank if off Brest. All England acclaimed the victor.

In the Mediterranean, the Luftwaffe had delivered a terrible blow to the Royal Navy, which lost, in a single engagement, four cruisers and six destroyers. A carrier, the HMS *Formidable*, had been severely damaged.

The Night Will End

The war had spread beyond Europe. Our comprehensive monitoring of all BBC broadcasts provided us with the knowledge the Vichy press denied us. The Germans had dispatched warplanes to Syria, directly threatening Suez. Pressure from both east and west could clamp the canal in a stranglehold. Since Syria was still under French mandate, we expected a strong reaction from Vichy. The secret truth we discovered only later: Admiral Darlan had already visited Berchtesgaden and ceded to Hitler the use of our air bases in Syria.

At the Quai Saint-Vincent, where I still went each week for my harvest of intelligence reports, an officer accosted me. "Have you read this? The English have invaded Syria with those Gaullist bastards in tow. The Gaullists have attacked our troops. Mercenaries, attacking French soldiers! What a nerve! I hope our boys push them right into the sea. One day this will be a matter for the high courts."

I didn't answer. I was too anguished by this eruption of fratricide. No doubt every soldier in the Levant was convinced that he was doing his duty according to his own lights; but for me our first imperative was not military obedience but the struggle against Germany. And yet, facing the English and General Catroux was the 16th Regiment of Tunisian Fusileers, a company of which I myself had recently commanded in the Djebel Druze and in Damascus. Men whom I knew still served in it. I wondered if it was really necessary for De Gaulle to commit his troops against them. Perhaps this battle was but the latest phase of the old Franco-British rivalry in the Levant. The traditional French "presence" in the Near East would surely vanish if the British were to enter Beirut and expel the Germans from French air bases unaided by French troops. But I felt utterly unable to rebut the anti-Gaullist argument. Anyway, the very look of that outraged officer at the Quai Saint-Vincent told me that such a rebuttal would be in vain. I sought refuge in vague generalities.

"Don't forget, the Germans are in Syria too. Doesn't that make the whole issue awfully difficult to judge?"

On my return to Lyons I learned that Colonel Rivet, the head of French intelligence, had asked to see me as soon as possible. Once

A Wanted Man

in Vichy I immediately presented myself at his office. He was expecting me under the name of Jean "Molin." As soon as I had been announced he received me.

The memory of *père* Rivet still fills me with tenderness. He was a man who knew his job and loved it passionately. It is all too true, however, that he failed to comprehend the new kind of war that Hitler had unleashed on the world. Only fifteen years later did the military become truly conscious of "revolutionary warfare," only belatedly did it recognize this phenomenon and begin to study its mechanisms. While it is true that Rivet had not adapted his methods to this new reality, he was nonetheless a staunch patriot, a faithful servant of the state and a profoundly decent man.

We were alone in his office, so he addressed me by my true name. "Frenay, I know what you're up to. There's evidence of it everywhere. Allow me to offer you my heartfelt congratulations. In both zones my people hear constantly about you and your movement. You seem to do awfully good work . . . and you're pretty damn fast, too!"

"Colonel, I thank you for your appreciation, but I myself am still unsatisfied. Of course we make progress every month, but our progress is nothing, absolutely nothing, compared to our goals. With more money and men we could really get to work. By the way, please believe me when I say that I've come here because you asked me to, not just to put the bite on you."

"Hmmm. You know I've wanted to speak with you for some time now. The reason is simple. I think it's a real pity that you and I work side by side without any coordination. It's obvious that your means are complementary to ours and that a truly concerted effort would be far more efficient. Some of the things you do could be done more easily by us and vice versa. Funds we can easily supply you with—men, too. Moreover, you are one of us yourself. Why, only a few months ago you were working in the Deuxième Bureau. My suggestion is that your group become a highly advanced, specialized and secret antenna of our service."

If I had not already experienced the army's ambivalence, if I had not spent two revealing months in Pétain's capital, if I had not sensed the depths of the government's submissiveness, the offer would have been tempting. It was terribly sincere, and I was

The Night Will End

mortified that I absolutely could not accept it. I knew how much pain my answer would cause this old soldier whom I esteemed so highly. But I also believed that no ambiguities should cloud his understanding of my position.

"Sir, I am familiar with the excellent work performed by certain of your services, and, as you know, my relations with the German section of the Deuxième Bureau are close and cordial. I am also aware of certain efforts on the part of our general staff to issue a fresh challenge to the enemy. However, I cannot accept your proposal. It would be equivalent to my reinstatement, morally speaking, in the army. Yet the very reason I left it was to avoid an eventual conflict between the duty to obey my superior officers and the duty to pursue my underground activity. I am ready if necessary to revolt against the present government, and if the need arises I shall feel morally free to do so. Anyway, as you know, I'm already a rebel, since my country's police is hard on my heels and I live in the shadows.

"You, Colonel, must obey orders. Like all officers in uniform, you may not and cannot do otherwise. But by obeying orders you may one day forfeit all that the army has accomplished, attempted or even hoped for. Please understand me, sir, and do not resent my words."

I could see in his eyes that he did not resent me. But he also did not understand me.

"Oh, come now, Frenay. How can you really believe that the Marshal and General Huntziger could tolerate, or actually bring about, a conflict between our soldiers' military duty and their patriotic duty?"

Alas, that was exactly what I did believe! For the war was leading inexorably to this very drama of conscience, dragging Colonel Rivet and the army along with it. (On his return from Berchtesgaden, where Hitler had pressured him furiously, Darlan had addressed the nation in a radio broadcast whose undertones had not escaped me. "For France," he had said, "it is a question of life or death. I chose life." Yes, there would be still more pressure, still more capitulation).

I bade farewell to Colonel Rivet. He clasped my hand in his two hands, looked at me fixedly and—perhaps a little moved—he said,

A Wanted Man

"I think, and above all I hope, that you are wrong. The future will cast the decisive vote. I am still very fond of you, Frenay. Good luck!"

I returned to Lyons by train. Had I really done well to refuse Rivet's offer? Had I accepted it everything would have been easier, and my morale certainly would have jumped. No, I could not accept! I decided to forget about the whole matter, and I swept all doubt from my soul.

On the morning of June 23, 1941, I had an appointment with Colonel Bernard not far from his hotel. He was to deliver a certain sum of money. The Rue de la République and the Rue du Président-Carnot seemed oddly changed. On the faces of passers-by, in the very air, one could feel a distinct nervousness. People clustered about the news kiosks. I bought a copy of *Le Progrès* and unfolded it. I couldn't believe my eyes: German troops had entered Soviet territory the day before, driving back the Red Army, which appeared to be in full retreat.

Once my surprise had passed, confused and contradictory thoughts assailed me. Among them hope and joy were dominant. Of course the real value of the Red Army was open to doubt. Not so long ago it had hardly shone against the people of little Finland. But its troops were numberless, and it was heavily armed. The country was immense, as Napoleon and the Grand Army had learned—yet the Emperor's Old Guard did not advance at the same lightning speed as Hitler's armored divisions. If the Soviet armed forces were defeated, it would not take the Wehrmacht long to arrive before the walls of the Kremlin. And perhaps the population itself, groaning under the yoke of Red dictatorship, would not resist the German troops but actually welcome them as liberators.

In any case, the threat to England had already receded, for Hitler could not attack on two fronts. In this sense, we had gained weeks, perhaps months. Churchill would be sure to take advantage of the breathing space afforded by the Russian war.

In effect, the war had just taken a decisive turn. We already sensed this, confused as we were. What we never guessed was the prodigious resources the Communist state, appealing to the spirit

The Night Will End

of Old Russia, would draw from its admirable people. It was long before we grasped this fact, so striking were the initial successes of the Wehrmacht, especially when broadcast by Dr. Goebbels.

I rang Berty. She had already heard the news and I could sense that she felt buoyed by it. However, the official telephone of the Unemployment Bureau was hardly advisable for a lengthy exchange of confidences. That evening we met in a little restaurant not far from the Place des Terreaux.

"Hitler will never defeat the Red Army," said Berty. "He has just signed his own death warrant. His end will come, in one, two, three or ten years—when exactly I don't know, but he will be beaten. I know the U.S.S.R. I've spent time there. Those admirable people cannot be conquered."

After a long, reflective silence she continued. "But you know, Henri, I'm very happy for all my Communist friends, some of whom you met at my place."

"Why for them, especially?"

"Well, it was easy for me to reject the Hitler-Stalin pact, since I'm not a member of the Communist Party. But they—they are sincere militants, entirely devoted to the party. They accepted that pact with despair in their hearts; it was moral torture for them to applaud the handshake of Molotov and Ribbentrop, for most of them were appalled by it. Today, for them and for the entire party, all is clear. They have returned to us!"

The vagaries in the prewar Communist attitude toward Hitler's Germany had often led to disagreements between myself and these Communist friends, who in the last analysis, always bowed to party discipline.

Already in 1935, two years after Hitler's seizure of power, when I was still at the Ecole de Guerre, I found it difficult to stomach Maurice Thorez's cry in the Chamber of Deputies: "Not one sou for military service!" Three years later, after the *Anschluss* and the invasion of Czechoslovakia, the very same Thorez declared, "The defense of France against Hitler has a very clear meaning for the working class: the defense of liberty, the defense of peace."

The Nazi–Soviet pact was signed in 1939, dispelling Hitler's nightmare of a two-front war and condemning Poland to death.

A Wanted Man

France mobilized her troops on the German border—but the same Maurice Thorez was strangely absent.

Today the French Communists had finally entered the war—at the required signal from the Soviet Union. Never again would my eyes fall on anything like those two curious clandestine issues of *L'Humanité* that my friends had shown me during my recent visit to Paris. The paper had editorialized that the Cross of Lorraine and the Nazi swastika were in the same bag and that De Gaulle was the lackey of the English. Now, at last, it was clear that we and the Communists were waging the same struggle—though no doubt for very different reasons.

All during 1941, about once a month, I would make the rounds of our groups in the provinces. This constant shuttling exhausted me. To save time and money I usually traveled at night and in third class. The gaps the Nazi war effort had left in our rolling stock and locomotive depots were more and more in evidence. As our railway schedules became skimpier our coaches became more crammed. How many times I sat propped up against my suitcase on the floor of a corridor or baggage compartment! At my destination some sorry restaurant inevitably awaited me, its menu unfailingly dominated by the rutabaga, a to me obscure vegetable that had suddenly conquered the French market.

Sometimes I stayed with friends in Cannes who must surely have equaled if not beaten the national record for austerity. They lived in a noble villa surrounded by extensive grounds. The Côte d'Azur, still devoted exclusively to the growing of carnations, offered absolutely no produce for direct local consumption, although such produce was slowly but surely appearing on the black market. Yet for the Pracontals, a family raised in the loftiest traditions and reared on patriotic sentiment, it was unthinkable to buy anything but the official rations allotted to each citizen. They would have considered it a disgrace to avail themselves of black-market produce. But oh, how miserable those rations were: 250 grams of bread and 15 grams of oil or fat per day; 180 grams of meat and 40 grams of cheese per week; 500 grams of sugar per month. Potatoes were irregularly distributed even in the best of circumstances at the rate of one kilo per month.

The Night Will End

For some time I had been wondering if General de La Laurencie had forgotten all about the visit Guédon and I had paid him in February at Vichy. Fortunately, I was mistaken. In June 1941, I believe, Laurencie's friend Jean Batault—also my friend—arranged to meet me in a little bistro not far from the Lyons produce market.

"The general is in good health," he said. "His activity fills me with admiration and his optimism is contagious. He has made so many friends that people now offer him their services spontaneously."

Surveying the surroundings, Batault leaned toward me. "This place is too crowded. Let's continue our talk outside."

On the landing, before my old school, the Lycée Ampère, he slipped me a long envelope and whispered in my ear, "Here's a hundred thousand francs from the general. He'll get you two hundred and fifty thousand more shortly, and he hopes from now on to provide you with the same sum each month."

Unbelievable! No doubt about it, I had lucked out! Now we could expand both the circulation of *Les Petites Ailes de France* and the membership of our permanent team—and even pass something on to help nourish the occupied zone.

I immediately wrote Guédon the good news, incontrovertibly proven by my enclosure of 80,000 francs.

On the Côte d'Azur, in Marseilles, in Montpellier and in Lyons, my friends had often mentioned a newspaper called *Liberté*, which had attracted my attention as early as the previous December. It seemed to have a very wide circulation. Some of our militants received it, and some were even approached and asked to serve as distributors, which in effect would have entailed their adherence to another movement. My comrades in Marseilles were troubled and sought my advice as to how they should respond. To accept would be to multiply the risks they already ran, and to refuse would be downright unfriendly. The best policy would be to conclude an accord at the highest level so that the two groups might intelligently counterpoint each other.

An investigation conducted by Chevance soon supplied the necessary information. The movement was directed, and the

A Wanted Man

paper published, in Lyons, by a small team probably headed by François de Menthon, a professor in the law faculty. Stanislas Fumet and Emmanuel Mounier considered him their friend. It seemed that he staunchly supported the same views as we did. I had little trouble in finding his address and obtaining an appointment. With Maurice Chevance, who was passing through Lyons, I presented myself at Menthon's home at 39, Rue Vaubecour, in my old neighborhood, the Perrache district.

The man who received me was tall and slender. He wore glasses. His handshake was irresolute; he seemed to offer it grudgingly. Naturally we discussed myself and our movement, for he was curious to learn more. Our conversation lasted a long time, over two hours. First I explained to him who Chevance and I were, and, as our military background seemed to intrigue him, I related how and why I had left the army. Our organizational concept, with its different services and its division into six- and thirty-men cells, rather perplexed him.

The principal if not unique activity of his movement was propaganda—that is, its newspaper, with the exception of a single action group in Montpellier. Menthon believed that the citizen's first duty was to fight back against cowardice, defeatism, official masochism and, of course, collaboration. The rest would come naturally.

Unlike our members, those of *Liberté* had a definite political direction. Virtually all their leaders had belonged before the war to the Parti Démocrate Populaire (P.D.P.), itself an outgrowth of Marc Sangnier's *Sillon*—that is, of left-wing Catholic circles—a fact I found encouraging.

Among them were many other law professors. Though *Liberté* had militants in all the principal cities of the free zone, it had no ties with Paris and the northern zone. Our rapid growth in this area, as well as our proliferating distribution centers in both zones for *Les Petites Ailes*, astounded my interlocutor, though he contrived not to show it.

I was for unified action, and I underlined the grave consequences that might result, especially in our common social base, from factionalization. We agreed to see each other frequently, at least once a month, and to inform each other of our achievements as

The Night Will End

well as our projects. And so our consultations became a regular event, either at Menthon's or at the home of some common friends or at the law school. Trust and solid friendship grew between us, despite the striking difference in our natures.

It was toward the middle of July, I think, that Menthon announced to me the birth of a new movement.

"Have you heard of *Libération?*"

"No, I don't recognize the name."

"Well, it's a brand-new initiative on the part of a former naval officer called Emmanuel d'Astier de la Vigerie. He resigned from the service not long after leaving naval college. He has just brought out a clandestine newsletter called *Libération.* I'll soon have a copy of the first issue. I don't know D'Astier, but I think he lives on the Côte d'Azur."

"Well, this is the first I've heard of him. My people haven't mentioned anything about such a movement. If it really exists, it must still be in the cradle. But we'd better try and contact it. Since you obviously are in touch with it, why don't you try?"

Shortly afterward an issue of *Libération* arrived from Clermont-Ferrand. It was subtitled *Organe du Directoire des Forces de Libération Francaises,* which naturally gave the reader the impression that it spoke in the name of the entire Resistance. I definitely did not appreciate this wording; in fact, I found it deliberately deceptive. I intercepted Menthon at the law school one day—he was still in his professorial gown—to confer with him about this. He seemed less shocked than I. But who was this d'Astier, and what was this *Directoire?* The question would be fully answered in a few weeks.

During this same period Demachy introduced me to René Cerf, whom we dubbed "Ferrière". As we strolled across the Place Bellecour I noted the similarity of our ideas. He struck me as a Jacobin radical-Socialist, a type of man that we did not yet have in our ranks. His self-assurance was marked, but I had the impression that it was more apparent than real. He had the delivery of an orator, but he also craved action. He already knew that I intended to put him to the test in connection with our newspaper or our problems with printing.

"You've joined us in the nick of time," I told him. "You can help

A Wanted Man

83

me out of a serious bind. You see, we have only one printer. If he's arrested, there goes our paper and with it the only concrete thing that unites our movement. We must find at least one more printer and not necessarily in Lyons, for the day will come when we must have simultaneous printings in several places, if only to multiply our chances for survival. The most important thing you could do for us is to scare up another printer. I'm also going to put you in touch with the person who manages the paper—" I was thinking of Jacqueline Bernard "—and gradually you'll take on a large share of responsibility for it. After all, you're a professional editor."

Cerf-"Ferriere" accepted.

I needed serious secretarial help. Simone Gouyou provided it. Our mail had become quite substantial in both zones. We corresponded with Paris in invisible ink (first the usual lemon juice, then a special product developed for us by a pharmacist). Our intelligence reports needed to be classified, typed and sent to the newspaper offices. My articles also needed typing. Occasionally urgent meetings were required, and sometimes a highly critical liaison would necessitate a traintrip. So Simone was pretty busy. To facilitate her job she came to work at our premises in the Avenue de Saxe, although Mlle. Péron, an old friend of hers who worked in the silk business, had offered her the use of her office in the Rue de Griffon.

"Simone," I told her, "I'll take you where Berty and I work. We never receive anyone there, except for extremely rare exceptions. We make as few calls as possible and never give anyone our telephone number. In other words, I'm ushering you into our inner sanctum. If one day the situation becomes desperate, if everything blows up in our faces, that's where we'll still be safe."

We were hardly in the room when the telephone rang.

"Monsieur 'Francen,' please," said an unknown voice.

"Speaking. Who's this?"

"A friend. I'm calling to tell you that M. will visit you tomorrow morning. He didn't say what time, but he's a morning person. Do you get my message? I repeat: M., tomorrow morning."

I no longer remember M.'s real name, but at the time I knew it very well indeed. He was the chief of police in Lyons. Some

The Night Will End

anonymous friend was obviously trying to warn us that he would raid our office tomorrow morning. Every imaginable proof of our activity was sitting right there, including complex time-lapse detonators.

"My dear Simone," I said, replacing the receiver, "the inner sanctum, the ultimate refuge, exists no longer. The gentlemen of the constabulary will be here tomorrow morning. Before becoming my secretary, you're going to be a professional mover."

Jouffray was summoned to reinforce us. In our ever-ready luggage we piled up every scrap of compromising material. To the police we abandoned our reams of paper, our stacks of envelopes and the old mimeo, which I glanced at tenderly in farewell. I watched at the window as Simone disappeared, followed by Maurice ten minutes later. Before leaving I telephoned Berty, though without announcing myself, for she knew my voice.

"Don't come this evening. I'll call you back tomorrow morning."

Right on cue, the police raided our abandoned offices the following morning.

Who was the mysterious person who had saved us from arrest and imprisonment or, at the very least, from the kind of internment which had already been inflicted on General Cochet, Loustaunau Lacau and others? I never found out. If by any chance he is reading this now, I offer him my tardy but heartfelt thanks.

Summers in Lyons are hot, and this one was premature as well. The Place Bellecour was an oven. As I crossed it I was trying to decide where to lunch. For safety's sake I changed restaurants often. Passing the Charité, I turned into the Rue des Marronniers and—God knows what inspiration seized me—entered the Trois Tonneaux restaurant.

The dining room was breezy, the marble tables refreshingly cool. I sat down and opened my newspaper. A man entered several seconds later. I raised my eyes momentarily. But—I knew that fellow! Our eyes made contact. No, there was no mistaking him.

"Soulage! Robert! It's you!"

"Frenay! What incredible luck to run into you!"

We embraced each other. Soulage was a friend whom I hadn't seen in years. In 1932 I'd known him when he was a reserve officer

A Wanted Man

85

in Hyères in the Third Alpine Infantry Regiment in which I myself commanded a company. We had become fast friends in the course of many philosophical discussions and—these were rarer, thank God—a few memorable drinking bouts. He had decided to stay in the army, thanks partly to my own advice; for his ardent and generous nature, as active as it was reflective, seemed to me to dispose him more toward soldiering than toward teaching, the career he'd originally chosen. The war had separated us; he was in the Far East, I was on the frontiers of Germany. I hadn't even known if he was dead or alive. What pleasure it was to be seated beside him on the good old imitation leather of a Lyons restaurant seat!

He told me how he had spent his last few dangerous years and how they had enriched him; for if he had fought a lot, he had thought even more. His conversations with Father Teilhard de Chardin had greatly impressed him. The mysticism he'd always borne within him had blossomed; his expression and his words bore witness to it. He had just arrived in France proper and still knew nothing about her current situation. He found himself in an occupied land, and he wanted to know all.

I talked with him for almost two hours, acquainting him with my own activities, which had already made me a pariah in the eyes of officialdom.

"Robert," I concluded, "I know you too well to think that you'll stay in the army as it is today. Work with me. We sadly lack men, above all men like you. Fortune decreed that we should meet here today. Do you think it was just for nothing?"

How could he understand or believe me—he who was just back from the antipodes? He was troubled by my words, but he quite naturally wanted to experience it all for himself. But his personal experience of France's disastrous state did not last long—only a few months, in fact—before he too resigned his commission. Under the name of "Sarrazac" he was to play an essential role in the *maquis*, especially after 1943. His weapons—as he put it himself, though not without scandalizing his comrades—were prayers and bombs. He'll soon reappear in our narrative.

The police raid on our old premises had given me food for

The Night Will End

thought. Though it seemed to have transpired without any harm to our host, Raymond Moine, it was proof that the police found us highly interesting, especially me. Somehow we had to cover our scent. We decided to alter our identities entirely. We had already changed location; we might as well now change our aliases, our paper stock and maybe even our newspaper's title. The latter idea did not appeal to Berty, but in the end we decided to go through with it anyway. For several days we toyed with new titles. It was Jouffray who hit on the word *vérité*, truth. There was something appealing about it, but it was somehow too philosophical, verging on pretentiousness. Who really knows the ultimate truth? Who can claim to have grasped it? Then it occurred to me that we might use the plural of the same word. That changed everything! In the reign of the Big Lie truths must be told—such, in fact, was our role. And so *Vérités* became our title, and at once a statement of Pétain's from 1940 popped into my head: "I hate the lies that have done us so much harm." We were to use this sentence as a motto on the front page, and I must admit that this reference to the Marshal amused me no end. Why, in a sense, he seemed to be vouching for us!

A "publishing conference" was called to discuss the contents of the new paper. Except for its format, we agreed that it should be much closer to an ordinary, above-ground newspaper. We wanted it to be more varied, more entertaining, more complete than *Les Petites Ailes de France*. Headings were to be gaily complemented by little tailpieces. The editorial would be signed *Veritas*, and in principle it would be drawn up by me. Under the title "Your Opinion and Ours" we would discuss and analyze crucial topics. The heading "Events of the World at Large" would precede a column on foreign politics usually written by Georges Oudard, a journalist with *Illustration*. And of course Father Chaillet would continue his religious commentary. Finally, a column on "The Truth About . . ." would list brief news items, almost in the raw state, on Nazi acts in various European countries, including France. The newspaper would have six pages. Since we had no folding machine, they would simply be clipped together. It would come out every ten days, and the first issue would consist of five thousand copies.

A Wanted Man

In Marseilles, in June, during one of my many tours of the free zone, I received a message from Reverend Howard, one of the bosses, I believe, of the Joint Committee, an American relief organization. I had already met him the previous year when I was still serving in the garrison bureau. This time he urged me to accept the visit of a certain high French official who was about to leave for England and whose reliability he vouched for. Perhaps we had at last found a way to set up a liaison with London. I say London because I made no distinction between De Gaulle and the British government. I simply couldn't let the opportunity slip by, and I agreed to meet this mysterious person in Recordier's apartment.

At three o'clock, in the good doctor's living room, I awaited his arrival with extreme curiosity. Presently Marcel showed him in. He was a man of middle height, his hair slightly graying, his face heavy, his look direct. He introduced himself.

"Jean Moulin. Captain Frenay?"

His handshake was frank. Recordier retired discreetly.

"Before we discuss the precise reason for my visit, I'm sure you'd like to know who I am."

In fact, Moulin was still a total stranger to me. During the invasion he had been the prefect in Chartres, where he had had the sorry duty of receiving the conquering Germans. Refusing to yield to their demands, he was thrown into prison, where he tried to commit suicide by slashing his throat with a piece of broken glass. Hospitalized, he was able to resume his duties shortly thereafter. In late 1940 he was dismissed for his overattachment to the Republic.

Though his opposition to the Vichy regime was total, he spoke of it not with hate but with contempt. Nazism horrified him. He planned to leave France with the sole aim of joining General de Gaulle, who, he claimed, sorely needed men.

"However," he continued, "I'd like to be able to supply him with as much information as possible about France. So far I've met many opponents of the regime, but no one who was actually in the Resistance. That's why I was so eager to see you, because I've been told that if anyone is in a position to help me out, you are."

The Night Will End

We talked together for several hours without a single interruption. I began with the M.L.N., whose history I sketched beginning with its birth in this same city of Marseilles just one year earlier.

On his knees, armed with a little notebook and a pencil, Jean Moulin took notes. Sometimes he would ask me a brief question. He was very attentive to details.

Next I told him what I knew of the other movements, including my initial contacts with François de Menthon, the existence of *Libération*, whose leader I did not yet know, and the groups in the occupied zone which I would soon visit again in Paris.

"My description is surely incomplete," I confessed, "for there may be clandestine activities of which I'm unaware, especially in the occupied zone. I can also confidently predict that even more will soon spring up. It's a sign of improving health in this country that has until now been consumed by such sloth and cowardice. But we must guard lest such a proliferation lead straight to anarchy. Efficiency, logic and even security all require some minimal coordination of our efforts and, if possible, a division of labor among our various teams and individuals."

"But just how do you intend to focus all these disparate forces?"

I explained to him that to require the allegiance of every resister to a single movement, formed around the nucleus of one of the current underground groups, would doom all our efforts to failure. Such an artificial reorganization would light and fan the fire of unquenchable personal rivalry. Our ultimate success required a symbol outside the Resistance, a symbol whose very remoteness would endow it with a federal authority acceptable to all.

"Only the Cross of Lorraine and De Gaulle can play such a role," I told him. "That's exactly what I intend to explain to my friends in the occupied zone, and that's what you should tell the general. Tell him also that we desperately need direct access to him—for a thousand reasons. From the standpoint of intelligence alone it's pathetic that we have no means of transmitting our information directly to London. And then we have financial problems."

I explained to him how we obtained our slender resources. He smiled and continued his note-taking. He questioned me about the

A Wanted Man

role of the army during the armistice, about its attitude toward the Marshal and toward collaboration. He seemed astounded by my excellent relations with the Quai Saint-Vincent.

"I intend to depart as soon as I can. If all goes well, I shall arrive in England toward the end of the summer. I shall faithfully deliver your proposals—that I promise you. I believe that you are right in your wish to consolidate your scarce manpower, so I shall have no trouble in being your advocate."

I was satisfied with our interview but skeptical of the returns it might bring. At times I had the feeling of having set adrift a message in a bottle. Yet, in a deeper way, I believed that I had found a faithful messenger. My impression of Moulin was really excellent. He was calm but reacted passionately to certain topics. He was his own master. I liked the expression in his eyes, and my experience told me that a man's look hardly ever plays false.

I called Recordier back into the room. He served us some refreshing *pastis* with ice water. At last we could relax informally, for the essentials had been said and understood.

It was almost seven o'clock when Jean Moulin left. I opened the blinds and watched him disappear in the direction of the prefect's office. I sighed. It was one more contact among many, and so many had already proved fruitless!

I had no intimation that this day had been of capital importance to the French Resistance and its relationship with London. No, I had no such feeling as I drew my chair toward the Recordier dinner table, where I had lingered at their friendly insistence—and at the insistence of an aromatic Provençal dish.

During my visit to Marseilles I stayed with Chevance on the Place d'Aix. I hardly saw him, as he was very busy with his company. His employees had more than tripled, and he now exported more parcels than all his competitors put together. He had grandiose projects for further expansion. On the other hand, he was disturbed by the slow progress of the M.L.N. in the Marseilles region. Luckily Chevance had just recruited a young officer on armistice leave, Henri Aubry. Aubry had recently arrived from Brittany, where he had barely escaped from the

Gestapo's clutches. Chevance had delegated to him the task of planting the seeds of our movement in Provence and on the Côte d'Azur. This new activity was financed out of the local treasury, thank God, without recourse to me.

"Maurice," I told him, "you need someone like Aubry for your own region. And I need someone like him here, too. How can I possibly be at the helm in Lyons at the same time as I'm making the perpetual round of the provincial departments? So listen here: You and I are already old friends, and you were the earliest resistant. I want you in Lyons with me. You'll be a sort of itinerant inspector for this movement which you know so well. Yes, I know you have your agency. But give my proposal some serious thought. There's no rush, since I must first get hold of the necessary funds, which I do not expect to find tomorrow morning."

"But, Henri, I can't leave everything here in mid-air!"

"Think about it, my friend. You've found a reliable assistant for the M.L.N. in Aubry, and you can find one for your agency too—unless, that is, you decide to turn it over to a managing director. You must ask yourself this question: What takes priority in your life, the Resistance or your parcels?"

My words upset him no end, for he had already turned his company into a flourishing business. Besides, it was his only means of support. And yet, a month later, when I again put the question to him, he agreed wholeheartedly. And so he left Marseilles and his agency to become my lieutenant in Lyons.

Once again I was required in the occupied zone. Correspondence between the two zones remained fitful; nothing seemed to replace personal contact. Before leaving I devoted some hard thinking to the role that Chevance had assigned to Aubry. Granted, Aubry was a kind of "regional inspector." But what was the region? What were its exact limits? This sort of imprecision would inevitably lead to overlapping activity, to crossed wires, perhaps even to disputes over authority. We had an urgent need to draw fixed boundaries and to appoint "capital cities" for each of our departments. A certain amount of reflection convinced me that the administrative map of the M.L.N. should coincide with

A Wanted Man

that of the Vichy government, an arrangement that would later afford us great advantages. The southern zone would comprise six regions, which I baptized as follows:

R.1—chief municipality, Lyons	10 departments
R.2—chief municipality, Marseilles	7 departments
R.3—chief municipality, Montpellier	6 departments
R.4—chief municipality, Toulouse	9 departments
R.5—chief municipality, Limoges	9 departments
R.6—chief municipality, Clermont-Ferrand	5 departments

This administrative map was adopted and used until the end of the war, first by us, then by all the other resistance movements and finally by the English and French services in London.

My second trip into the occupied zone was less harrowing than the first. Not far from Moulins one of our men slipped me a border pass and an identity card. I affixed my photos, he stamped them, and we drove up to the German inspection station. The controller glanced distractedly at our papers, opened the barrier and we were through. Nothing could have been simpler.

As everything was running smoothly, I spent only a week in Paris. Robert Guédon was an enthusiastic as ever. Of all his activities he preferred propaganda, with the result that his newspaper, now called *Résistance*, had made spectacular progress.

Information was plentiful. Robert had even succeeded in placing an informant close to the writer Jean Luchaire. Luchaire, who socialized a lot, was probably the best-known collaborationist in the summer of 1941.

Another source of intelligence was Father Riquet, whom I met twice in his office on the Rue d'Assas. A Jesuit, like Father Chaillet, he was as cool as the latter was flamboyant. His expression was glacial, his smile constrained, but his jaw and his lips bespoke a resolute and steadfast character. Once accepted within our confidential circle, he urged others to come to see us. It was he who introduced me to André Noël, who undertook an intensive recruitment campaign that lasted until the black days that befell us several months later. Upon his return from deportation after the

The Night Will End

Liberation, Father Riquet became the predicant of Notre-Dame in Paris.

For the editorial management of the paper, Jacques Dhont netted a truly capital recruit, Maurice Bourdet, who before the war had been the managing director of Poste Parisien, an important broadcasting station. For the preparation of each issue Bourdet would hold a veritable editorial conference in his home in Versailles. There his editorial board would settle matters of news coverage, editorial focus, design and layout.

Guédon arranged a meeting between myself and Captain Touny, one of the chiefs of the O.C.M.,* with whom I developed excellent relations.

My conception of our struggle was similar if not identical to that of the O.C.M., perhaps because Touny and I both had received a military education. However, one thing is certain: My interlocutors in the O.C.M. and elsewhere felt absolutely no need to rally to De Gaulle. In fact, the idea hadn't even occurred to them. Thus I was utterly dumfounded to read the following passage in Jacques Soustelle's *Envers et Contre Tout,* which appeared well after the war: ". . . There was only one principle of unification: the name and the appeal of General de Gaulle. The spontaneous Resistance was spontaneously Gaullist." It was a strange claim to be put forward by a man who, by his own admission, was outside France in 1941! Had he been there, he would have discovered that De Gaulle's June 18 Appeal was unknown to nine out of ten Frenchmen and that the Resistance, a full year after its birth, was unaware of De Gaulle's supposed leadership—even his moral leadership. The Resistance was, if not reluctant, at least very hesitant to place itself under his banner. Yet Soustelle, though badly informed, was sincere. He was not the only one in London to entertain such ideas, but they betokened a serious lack of understanding that was to have fatal consequences.

Before my return to the free zone I conferred in Jeanne Sivadon's office with Odile Kleinlen, the secretary of the Ecole de Surintendantes d'Usine, and Robert Guédon. Jeanne herself was

*Organization Civile et Militaire.

A Wanted Man

also present. Despite a generally satisfactory balance sheet, Robert was troubled by the position on De Gaulle that I had defended before various interlocutors in Paris. Not only did he regard my position as blatantly political, and hence controversial, but he also believed that it might provoke the ire of several of his groups who had retained their faith in Marshal Pétain. Guédon himself was a strong believer in the so-called double game of Vichy—and, in fact, with some reason: Captain Dupré, a member of the chief of state's cabinet, had delivered him 30,000 francs straight from the Marshal's own privy purse.

What Robert wanted was a totally political action, aimed solely against the occupying army and the Nazis. Here a certain disparity in the mentalities of the two zones had already become clear. In the occupied zone, opposition to the overbearing and sometimes cruel German presence overrode all other complications. In the free zone, however, opposition to Vichy and its laws had become, in the mind of the resistants, more and more inseparable from opposition to Nazism itself.

The Night Will End

COMBAT

Back in Lyons, I dis-
covered that nothing of great importance had happened during my absence, However, a large stack of mail awaited
me. It was the usual stuff—except for a letter from
my mother. She wrote me often, more often than I
wrote her, under a borrowed name I had suggested. She
addressed her letters to a post-office box. This time she had
included in her letter a circular from the Army General Headquarters that invited me to join my fellow officers in taking a loyalty oath to Pétain.

Of course I still distinguished between the Marshal and his
ministers, such as Pierre Laval. But nobody who attaches any
value to his signature can sign a blank moral check. After all the
trouble I'd taken to get out of the army I wasn't about to pledge
myself unconditionally to anyone. I never returned that circular.

In her letter, which reflected deep anxiety, my mother begged to
see me. Since the appearance in my life of the Vichy police I
had avoided visiting Sainte-Maxime. Unaware of my reasons, my mother was both surprised and hurt. She offered
to come to see me in Lyons.

A friend escorted her from the station to the
house where I awaited her. My poor, dear
Maman! She was still dressed in her

6

usual way, wearing a severe black dress and a wide-brimmed hat. She carried a sort of woven-straw basket that served her as a combination handbag and valise, and she wore a white ribbon around her neck, for she was ill-resigned to the ravages of age. This is the Maman I seem always to remember; the other, the young and beautiful Maman, is lost in the deepest recesses of my memory.

As we embraced I could already sense that something was amiss. She was tense, nervous. The idea of my having arranged a rendezvous in an unknown apartment really bothered her, and it was clear from her most recent letters that she had begun asking herself some hard questions about my real activities.

"Henri, about that General Staff circular with the loyalty oath to Pétain, you filled it out, right?"

I didn't have the courage to lie. "No, Maman, I didn't. I'm not signing that oath."

I tried to put the conversation on a different, more abstract plane. I attacked the idea of a citizen of the Republic, a Christian, pledging allegiance to a mere individual. Unconvinced, and barely able to control herself, she turned pale, then interrupted me curtly in a quiet but terrifying tone.

"*Mon petit*, at last I've admitted to myself what I've long suspected. You've been lying to me. You're plotting against the Marshal and his government. Before the war you were sympathetic to the Communists. Now maybe you're one yourself."

"But, Maman . . ."

"No, shush, listen to me! You're trying to hurt our country, and I'm sure you're doing your utmost, just as you always do. And if you think I'm just going to keep quiet about it . . . well, you're wrong! I love you dearly, as you know—my children are my whole life—but I believe that patriotic duty comes before maternal love. I'm going to denounce you to the police! I must stop you from doing evil and, yes, from doing yourself harm as well!"

I was more stunned than indignant. My poor dear mother! She was returning my gaze unwaveringly. She obviously expected something—but what? That I renounce my underground work? Suddenly I heard myself saying, "Maman, I know how much it pains you to say what you've just said. I admire you more than

The Night Will End

ever, for I know that you believe that you're simply serving your country, perhaps even serving me. But your denunciation wouldn't tell the police anything they don't already know. Frankly, they're already after me. I beg of you, try and understand one thing: Such an act on your part would cause an irreparable breach between us. I respect your conscience; please try to respect mine. But if you insist on doing what you've just threatened to do, don't bother to call for me on your deathbed, for I shall not come."

I kissed her goodbye and left. We didn't meet again until after the Liberation. I was by then a member of the government. She had not denounced me.

Public opinion was divided over Marshal Pétain. In fact, it continued to be so well after the end of the war. I remember Chevance telling me about the Sicé family in Marseilles. Surgeon General Sicé was in De Gaulle's service in London. His wife, who had stayed in France with the rest of the family, suffered desperately and unavailingly through the daily arguments and occasional violent fistfights between her two sons, one of whom shared her father's views, and the other of whom was still loyal to Pétain.

The Marshal both claimed and in fact possessed supreme responsibility for the nation. "I alone am responsible," he had said. "It is I alone whom history will judge." In my eyes, according to all available international and domestic evidence, history's verdict seemed more and more likely to be negative. Since Montoire and my visit to Vichy, my initial trust had grown steadily weaker. The hopes which the Marshal had once aroused in me had now all but vanished. And yet, oddly enough, I failed to draw the obvious conclusion from my otherwise correct assessment of the Vichy government.

My father and brothers were Saint-Cyriens, and so was I. Despite growing and indisputable proofs, I felt a sort of repugnance to admit to myself that the old Marshal, whatever his intentions, was actually serving the enemy. My judgment was muddied, my initiative constrained, by the powerful influence of my own social background.

It was Claude Bourdet who, as we were strolling one day on the

Combat

Boulevard Dugommier in Marseilles, forced me in my heart of hearts to abandon the *Pétainiste* myth. The facts now spoke for themselves. Moreover, my rejection of Pétain was really already implicit in my acceptance of the symbolic leadership of De Gaulle, whose cause I had so strongly defended in Paris. In the depths of my soul I now radically rejected my earlier hope that De Gaulle could be France's sword while Pétain remained her shield.

About this time I met Emmanuel d'Astier de la Vigerie. He was tall, thin and slightly hunched. His wavy hair was graying at the temples. He told me that his movement, Libération, had a positive leftward lean. Socialists and trade-unionists made up 90 percent of its membership. He was clearly buoyed by a recent agreement with Léon Jouhaux, the veteran trade-union leader, who had begun urging C.G.T. militants to join Libération to the exclusion of all other groups. D'Astier expected to include qualified representatives of various unions and the Socialist Party in his governing board. He had already approached André Philip, a socialist deputy from the Rhône, who had agreed to join the committee. D'Astier didn't even bother to mention Nazism, for his opposition to it was self-evident. But the liberation of national territory and the overthrow of the Vichy regime were, in his mind, only two sides of the same coin. I had to admit that his political consciousness was much more advanced than my own.

The man not only had talent; he had class as well. What's more, he knew it and used it. His frank and boyish smile was probably his secret weapon. But that smile, as I later realized, did not reflect his true inner personality.

I was impressed by his account of Libération. It was clear that the massive enlistment of Socialists and trade-unionists would greatly enhance the experience, maturity and sheer size of the movement.

In comparison, what I told him about the M.L.N. seemed pretty skimpy. Our organizational structure seemed to have little interest for D'Astier, to judge by the polite smile with which he greeted my description. Though he recognized the need to coordinate the efforts of Libération, Liberté and the M.L.N., he shrank from any idea of a merger. It was out of the question, he believed, for the political tendencies of the various groups were simply too divergent. However, he did agree that we should contact De Gaulle as soon as possible.

One early morning in late August—I had been back from Paris for two weeks now—Jouffray and I were chatting at Berty's place. Offhandedly he asked me if I had seen the daily paper yet. No, I hadn't even listened to the radio.

"Well, you've missed the big news. There's been an assassination attempt against Laval in Paris."

It was thus that I learned of the young Colette's courageous act. He had opened fire just as Laval was arriving to preside over the ceremonial constitution of the Legion of French Volunteers Against Bolshevism, a group of young men who, several weeks later, openly donned the uniform of the Wehrmacht and solemnly pledged allegiance to Hitler.

Two letters from Guédon that followed closely upon the news of the assassination attempt spoke of a radical change in the political atmosphere in Paris. Several additional attempts had been made on the lives of German soldiers, and the German reaction had been brutal. Guédon transmitted to us the text of a handbill that had been posted on the walls of the capital. It announced that the German command had executed French hostages in reprisal. All the cinemas and theaters in Paris were closed. The evening curfew now started two hours earlier than it had before. People were afraid, and this fear had taken its toll on the morale of the underground. If only Robert would try to be a little more cautious!

Georges Batault, General de la Laurencie's right-hand man, arrived from the Midi with an important communication from the general.

"The general has organized an important secret meeting here in Lyons," said Batault. "Two important Americans will be present. Your task will be to acquaint them with the present state of the French resistance and to inform them of its most pressing requirements. Colonel Thierry and I shall also be present. Please understand that the future of your entire movement depends on this interview."

"Who are these two Americans?"

Combat

"Well, I know who they are, but I'm afraid that I can't disclose their names. Please forgive me. I can only tell you that they are very important and that they have considerable influence on the highest levels in Washington."

"All right, then. When do we meet?"

We met in mid-October 1941. The time: early afternoon. The place: the home of a Lyons businessman, not far from the Place Bellecour.

I arrived right on time, for clandestine living had reinforced my native punctuality. A maid ushered me into a large, ill-lighted room. To my surprise, I was obviously the last to show up. I noticed some empty coffee cups on a tray. They had already lunched, and perhaps even conferred, before my arrival.

They rose as I entered, and General de la Laurencie shook my hand firmly.

"My dear Frenay—I'm calling you by your real name, for everybody here knows you, even if they have never met you—I'd like you to meet Mr. 'Smith' and Mr. 'Scott,' two very good friends of mine who're now friends of yours, too. You already know Thierry and Batault, so I won't bother to introduce you."

It was really impossible to see anything in this sitting room, with its high ceilings and heavy wall tapestries. I was straining to get a good look at the faces and expressions of those two Americans. It was particularly difficult because they had placed themselves directly in front of the window, intentionally, no doubt. From where I sat they looked almost like Balinese shadow puppets.

"Gentlemen," said La Laurencie, "now that Monsieur Frenay is here, we may begin our discussion. Shall I begin?"

The general was no orator—he just didn't have the gift of gab—but he started rather auspiciously, with a searing critique of the Vichy government, which he pictured as having become willy-nilly an accomplice in the collaboration. By degrees this collaboration had become so intense that Marshal Pétain was by now powerless to curb it. Such a policy was in the interest neither of France nor of the Allies. Turning toward the two shadows, La Laurencie added, "I hope you'll permit me to anticipate a bit by including you among the Allies, although I know of course that you're not at war—yet. For us Frenchmen there is only one way to

The Night Will End

reverse this policy of collaboration, and that is to get rid of the present government. Believe me, all France will rejoice at the replacement of the Vichy regime by a provisional resistance government. It is just such a government that I desire to form."

Had I heard wrong? Looking around me, I realized that nobody else had even batted an eyelash. Obviously there had been quite a little parley before my arrival!

Continuing, La Laurencie drew a piece of paper from his pocket; it was none other than the composition of his future cabinet!

"But just how do you intend to oust the present government?" asked the American called "Smith." "After all, German troops are only a few days' march from Vichy."

"I cannot foresee the exact date or the circumstances of this change of government," said the general. "But we've got to be ready to exploit any opportunity that may occur during the course of the war. With the support of public opinion and the organized Resistance, such a seizure of power is not impossible or even improbable. As far as this organized Resistance is concerned, my principal agent here, Henri Frenay, will tell you something about it."

I was dumfounded. What sort of trap was this? Suddenly I had become the general's "agent"! I noticed that Batault, who *was* his agent, had averted his eyes. I felt a strong desire to walk out and slam the door behind me. I was incensed that I had been tricked into this comic-opera conference. And yet—we were in the presence of important emissaries. It seemed foolish to have an argument right here in front of them. Wouldn't it be wiser to make out as strong a case as possible for the M.L.N. while pointedly mentioning our problems and needs? Later, when the Americans were gone, I could put an end to La Laurencie's daydreams.

Aware of my own grim and resentful expression, I began. Since people often asked me to talk about the Resistance, I carried a ready-made speech about in my head. I spoke at some length, without the help of notes, but my *précis* was well organized and to the point. I didn't try to bluff and quoted hard figures whenever I could. When at last I reached the military aspect of the Resistance, the so-called "Secret Army" that we were beginning to mobilize, I said, "Tomorrow our men will be like a detachment of commandos

Combat

who have been parachuted behind enemy lines. They'll be poised for attack wherever the Allied command wants them. Of course we are aware that the liberation of our country will be accomplished mostly by the Allied armies. But if we ourselves did not participate in it we'd never be able to forgive ourselves. And our contribution to the struggle will save you valuable lives and equipment."

Despite the feebleness of the light, "Smith" was taking notes. The Americans wanted an exact idea of what our optimal budget might be. I told them we needed at least a million francs for immediate use, as well as twelve two-way radio sets capable of eluding radiolocators of the sort the Germans had inside the occupied zone. As for arms, I promised them that I could easily draw up a list of much-needed light weapons and explosives.

When I had finished, Batault and the general accompanied me to the door. With a sour look I said, "I've got some pretty serious reservations about the way this meeting's been handled. We'd better get together soon and talk it over."

I later learned just who those two American gentlemen were. "Smith" was Colonel Legge, the American military attaché in Berne. "Scott" was none other than Allen Dulles, the head of the American secret service in Europe and the future head of the CIA. They had come all the way from Switzerland expressly to confer with us. Here was at least one point about which Batault had not deceived me: The conference really was of the utmost importance.

I was mad as hell, but I had to admit that La Laurencie's financial aid was indispensable to the rapid growth of our movement.

Soon Chevance moved from Marseilles to Lyons. By now we had the means to finance his inspection tours throughout the entire free zone. As our inspector general, he was responsible for setting up cadres, firing their zeal and supervising their activity. For several weeks he was joined by Marcel Peck, a man whom Claude Bernheim, one of our first militants, had recruited.

Peck had come from Tunisia expressly to work for the M.L.N. He was an entirely new type to us. He was of medium height and dark complexion, slim, elegantly but soberly dressed, with a small

The Night Will End

mustache and a fondness for dark suits and Homburgs. A graduate of the Ecole de Sciences Politiques, he was exceptionally polite and had a somewhat British sense of humor. His trips with Chevance acquainted him with our movement and its men. Later, under the name of "Battesti", he took charge of region R.1 in Lyons. His efficiency, methodical hard work and unwavering courage (he escaped from jail no less than three times) made him one of the truly first-rate regional chiefs of the entire Resistance.

In Marseilles, Jean Gemahling was devoting himself increasingly to intelligence-gathering. He became in effect the head of our own private intelligence arm. Not only did he put to work all the intelligence people whom our militants could scare up, but he also recruited his own men. His military and non-military information was a big boost to our newspaper, and we hoped one day to transmit to London the vast quantity of intelligence his service had garnered for us.

In Toulouse, Jean-Paul Lien was still sitting on his hands. I dispatched Jean-Guy Bernard to replace him. Before long Jean-Guy had laid a solid organizational foundation in region R.4, especially in the Gers, the Ariège and the Lot-et-Garonne. He also helped to raise considerably the local circulation of *Vérités*.

He told me about a new group operating in Tarbes in the Hautes-Pyrénées. This group, which he hadn't yet been able to contact, was already pretty well known. It printed and distributed leaflets and had also burned down the depot of the Légion des Combattants as well as various newsstands that featured collaborationist periodicals. The team was apparently directed by an engineer in the Hispano-Suiza company.

We followed up his report, and, sure enough, we soon identified the leader of the group. His name was Henri Garnier, and we easily prevailed on him to affiliate his team with the M.L.N.

In October we finally succeeded in regularizing our Paris–Lyons postal communications. Here is how we solved this delicate problem: At Saint-Pourçain, in the Allier, we had a very active militant, a retired noncom named Jacquinot. As well as working for us, he stockpiled arms for the General Staff. He had also happened upon a real windfall in the person of Henri Devillers, a professional messenger for the Messageries Hachette. Devillers

Combat

seemed like a reliable fellow, and he had a valid pass that was routinely renewed. In his van, which was always loaded with books and periodicals, he crossed the line of demarcation at least once a week, a veritable one-man "M.L.N. express." This rescued us from the infantile business of having to conceal our mail in the pages of publications which themselves had to be enclosed in cumbersome packages. Berty and I checked out our new dispatch rider over coffee in a Lyons café. Although he made a good impression on us, we decided to continue our practice of always using invisible ink. We just couldn't be too careful. We decided that Jeanne in Paris and Berty in Lyons would serve as the two post-orderlies at either end of the chain. What tremendous progress we had achieved—at least, so we thought.

In early September André Bollier showed me a pamphlet against Vichy and the occupying Germans. It was signed *Le Front National pour la Libération, la Renaissance, et l'Indépendance de la France.* Still another movement! It was the third we had come to know of since Libération (the one D'Astier had initially claimed to speak in the name of the entire Resistance). We wondered what this one stood for and who its members were. Not one of our regions had ever encountered it. We knew that to mimeo a bunch of tracts is one thing, to create a real movement quite another. But the style, which smacked of Red Army communiqués, left little doubt that the group was Communist-inspired.

Thinking it over, I began to form my own hunch. Why, of course! This new organization conformed perfectly to the "transmission belt" concept of activism taught at the Communist Party school for party cadres in Bobigny. The "transmission belt" was conceived as a small group which, while concealing its actual obedience to the Party, would rally the French masses with a theme of universal appeal. By means of this front the Party could disseminate its propaganda among social strata that were usually unreachable. This same concept explains how the Front National, which was always directed by Communists, had accepted men like François Mauriac in its directing committee.

It was a dangerous new challenge. Should we try to impose a "publicity quarantine" on this CP front, or should we simply

The Night Will End

unmask it? We opted for the latter solution. In our September 25 issue of *Vérités* we published an article on the Front National:

"The anti-German front which Moscow wishes to set up is already in existence here. Our ranks are composed of men who, as a consequence of the defeat, have sincerely examined their own consciences. Among them are members of all the prewar political parties. We have members of Action Française* as well as of the Communist Party.

"But when France was trying to defend her national soil against the German attack, Thorez** deserted her. At that time his propaganda was practically indistinguishable from that of Dr. Goebbels'. It was aimed at demoralizing France. This we have not forgotten. Today the same Thorez is trying to exploit the purely patriotic devotion of our citizens for the greater good of the Soviet Union."

By the next post I asked the regional chiefs to inform me immediately of any signs of activity on the part of the Front National. The first timid signs of such activity did not appear until late 1942.

As the leaves started to fall in the autumn of 1941, the morale of the French people had dropped to an all-time low. Even to provide an adequate food supply had become an apparently insoluble problem. It was also estimated that there was insufficient fuel for domestic heating in the event of a harsh winter. Moreover, most people were still wearing clothes of prewar manufacture, and there was no way of replacing them. It was increasingly difficult for us to get the BBC on the radio; German jamming techniques seemed to have made great progress. There were evenings when we couldn't pick up the BBC at all. And what news we got from England was quite distressing anyway. Yet the RAF had been able to bombard Berlin despite the distance of the German capital and the strength of the Luftwaffe. British aircraft were still regularly pounding the cities of northern Germany.

In the east the German armies were driving deeper and deeper

*The prewar ultra-conservative movement.—Translator.
**Secretary-general of the French Communist Party, 1930–1964.—Translator.

Combat

into Russia. They had arrived at the gates of Stalingrad, which was, at least so we believed, about to fall. In a recent address to the German people, a self-confident Hitler had proclaimed, "The enemy on the eastern front will be crushed before the onset of winter." I had great difficulty in preserving my optimism, especially because, as I listened to conversations here and there, in shops or in streetcars, for example, I had the impression that for 90 percent of the French people this was somebody else's war and that they believed Russia had already been beaten. Soon it would be England's turn. The important thing was to have enough to eat, something to wear and a roof over one's head.

Such was the sad state of affairs when Robert Guédon reached Lyons at the end of October. Devillers was also in town, so I lunched with them and Berty. Devillers informed us that the Gestapo had arrested Anne-Marie Boumier and Anne Noury in their apartment on the Rue Emile-Duclaux, where I myself had stayed. There had been no warning, and there was no explanation. What could we do? What would become of them?

"Two loyal friends have fallen," said Robert, "and their arrest deeply affects us all. But things would have been a lot worse for the movement if they'd hit Jeanne's place on the Rue Princesse. They would have picked up all our files and documents."

Anne Noury was to die in Ravensbrück in 1945, the very day the camp was liberated. Anne-Marie survived, after hiding out for a year and spending two more in prison and in a concentration camp.

After considerable trouble I managed to obtain an interview with La Laurencie. I was supposed to meet him in Valence—why there I have no idea. I asked D'Astier and Menthon to come along, for the meeting was sure to have important political implications. I figured that the solid front of our three organizations would be sure to impress him. However, only D'Astier could make it. As we headed toward Valence we agreed to dispel the general's hopes for our support in his ridiculous project. We found him fatigued and dejected. Apparently he traveled a lot, and he was no longer a young man.

I didn't beat about the bush. *"Mon général,* I'm afraid that I

The Night Will End

must tell you how dismayed I was that you did not inform me in advance of the true nature of that conference with 'Scott' and 'Smith.' You put me in a terribly embarrassing position. Because I was loath to start a quarrel in front of them, you probably got the impression that I was in agreement with you. Well, I must disabuse you of that notion."

"But, my dear Frenay, what can you possibly have against the overthrow of the Vichy government?"

It was a long and trying discussion. Essentially, we told him that we thought his action premature. The war would go on for a long time, and Vichy could not be ousted until the Allies had liberated the bulk of the free zone. Moreover, the British had already recognized De Gaulle as the leader of the French freedom fighters. This made De Gaulle the prime candidate to become the chief of state of a liberated France. We ourselves were seriously considering throwing our movements behind the Gaullist banner.

It soon became clear that La Laurencie was basically not amenable to political reasoning. For example, when D'Astier asked him if he thought he could count on the support of the French left, the question simply struck him as irrelevant.

"But you can't just ignore General De Gaulle," I insisted. "He really does exist, you know, and when the Liberation takes place, believe me, he'll be there. Have you considered that possibility?"

"Of course. I'll grant him amnesty."

We were astounded. I could see that D'Astier was as hard put as I to keep a straight face.

"*Mon général*, you may recall that you presented me to the Americans as your agent. Such an introduction was unexpected, to put it mildly. The fact of the matter is that you and I are not in any kind of hierarchical relationship. Even if we were, this relationship would not be founded on your stars and my stripes. I'm no longer in the service. I'm an independent agent, and my organization too is independent. We are ready to talk with anyone, including yourself, to try and find a way to realize our common goal. But your project, sir, is totally unrealistic. D'Astier and I reject it categorically. Consciously or unconsciously, you threaten to divide the entire Resistance at the moment when it is seeking unity around De Gaulle."

Combat

D'Astier obviously concurred. The general's disappointment and annoyance were clearly visible. Incapable of understanding us, he obviously preferred to go on beating his head against the wall. We parted very coolly. As far as D'Astier and I were concerned, the case was closed.

Shortly thereafter I learned that La Laurence had hit the road again. He had stopped off in several large cities in the free zone, even meeting with several of our people to solicit their aid. Naturally they told us about it. In order that our militants not be seduced by his overtures, I published a small paragraph in our paper to warn them. Just to keep the general well informed, I sent him a copy too.

This was the end of our contacts with La Laurencie. We had squelched a revolt within the revolt, but at the same time I had, with my own hands, poisoned our financial well. What I did not know at that time was that the Americans themselves were backing General Fornel de la Laurencie! They wanted an alternative to De Gaulle, a more docile figure whom they could unreservedly support. I was still unaware of Roosevelt's hostility to De Gaulle, a hostility that was to provoke the latter's lifelong resentment against the United States.

And so, unwittingly, I myself had nipped this American initiative in the bud. Yet it was not to be the last such initiative. For La Laurencie was soon succeeded by a new American favorite— General Henri Giraud.

How were we going to survive without La Laurencie's money? I was pretty worried, for our expenses had skyrocketed. But this was only the beginning of our troubles. As everyone knows, troubles tend to gang up.

Toward the end of October I paid a routine weekly visit to French intelligence on the Quai Saint-Vincent. The atmosphere had changed drastically. When I requested my usual bundle of intelligence reports—the same I had been receiving every week for the past six months—Garon told me he hadn't had time to compile it yet.

"When should I come back?"

The Night Will End

"I don't know," he answered. "Let's talk about it outside."

We walked over to the Place des Terreaux. Garon, though at first outwardly calm, became more and more obviously nervous. It seemed that his service had noticed a growing Gaullist tendency in *Vérités*. Just what, he asked, was my position on De Gaulle?

I sensed the danger that lurked in this subject, but I could not simply brush off an honest question. Yes, I admitted, we intended to join up with De Gaulle's services as soon as possible.

Garon's whole demeanor instantly changed. "In that case, we have nothing more to say to each other. You are a Gaullist—we are not! We are loyal to the Marshal. Frenay, we're simply not in the same camp. I hope you'll understand that you'll no longer be welcome at the Quai Saint-Vincent. Today you've closed the door on yourself—forever."

I've forgotten whether we shook hands, but I remember how sad I was as I watched Garon walk back in the direction of the intelligence office. I had lost not only some good friends but also the invaluable intelligence reports they had provided me.

Disaster followed disaster. Several days later a communication informed me of two more arrests. In one fell swoop the police had picked up Jean Gemahling, the head of our own intelligence, and young Bourlier, who worked in our radio and telegraph monitoring center in Vichy. In the other arrest they'd netted Robert Mouzillat and Raisin. It was an absolute catastrophe for the M.L.N. in the Allier. Then Berty herself was apprehended. She was taken to the Lyons police headquarters, interrogated for several hours—mostly about me—and finally released. We felt the net tightening around us. With the loss of Bourlier and Gemahling our major source of intelligence had simply vanished. Now our only source of copy for *Vérités* was the information Robert sent us via Devillers. If that final communication line was cut, what would become of our movement?

The three-man meetings with D'Astier, Menthon and myself became increasingly rare. Menthon was very busy with his teaching and, besides, he had to commute back and forth between Lyons and Annecy, where his wife lived in their old family chateau. I was obliged to meet with each of them separately, which

Combat

was a pity. However, I finally managed to convince my two colleagues of the necessity of a long working conference devoted to the detailed examination of the principles of our organizations in view of a possible merger. Menthon proposed that we meet in Grenoble, midway between Annecy and Lyons, where the risks would be minimal. Each one of us would proceed there separately.

We stayed in a comrade's apartment. It was early November and the weather was cold and gray. Menthon and I waited in vain for D'Astier, though not for very long, for I was sure he wouldn't show up anyway. The idea of putting our cards on the table, of disclosing details about our various movements, their cadres and the means at their disposal, didn't seem likely to arouse his enthusiasm. Thus the head of Liberté and I began our work without him.

We began with an inventory of our still modest forces and the men who commanded them. Menthon admitted that the M.L.N. was larger than Liberté both in numbers and in geographical extension. While our cadres were highly developed all over the nation, Liberté's were practically nonexistent. On the other hand, we agreed that the direction of four of the six regions should be assumed by Menthon's people. Those were Montpellier, Limoges, Toulouse and Clermont-Ferrand. Demachy and the Chevance–Aubry duumvirate would continue to head the Lyons and Marseilles organizations respectively. The administrative breakdown into six regions would remain unchanged. The organization and cellular structure of the M.L.N. would be extended to the entire unified movement.

Our fusion would be total; the current names of the two movements would be dropped. From now on we agreed to call ourselves the Mouvement pour la Libération Française. It would be directed by a governing committee of six members, three from Liberté and three from the M.L.N. I had initially intended to hold out for an M.L.N. majority, but on second thought I put aside this idea. For our triumvirate I designated Bourdet, Chevance and myself; Liberté would be represented by Pierre-Henri Teitgen, Alfred Coste-Floret and Menthon. (Later Georges Bidault joined the committee.) Since I had no other job, it was understood that I would be in charge of the daily administration of the movement,

The Night Will End

while Menthon would replace me during my frequent out-of-town trips. The directing committee was in principle to meet every six weeks.

Next there was the newspaper. Menthon told me some bad news from Marseilles. The editorial staff of *Liberté* had been arrested, including Menthon's brother-in-law Guy de Combault, and Roger Nathan. That was all he knew, but naturally he was pretty upset. We agreed to scuttle both *Liberté* and *Vérités*. They would be replaced by a single newspaper. But what should we call it? Casting about for a title, I hit on *Combat*. With the subtitle *Organe du Mouvement de la Libération Française*, it was virtually self-descriptive. The simplicity of this formula appealed to Menthon, and we adopted it. A little later I added the following epigraph from Clemenceau: "In war, as in peace, the last word belongs to those who never give up."

In conjunction with the title and subtitle, this epigram perfectly expressed the nature of our struggle. The editorial direction of the new paper we entrusted to the tandem team of "Ferrière" and Jacqueline Bernard. André Bollier was to remain in charge of production and distribution. I would draft the first editorial and submit it to Menthon for his approval. To throw the police off our track—if that was still possible—we would present ourselves as an entirely new movement, with no mention of the merger that had taken place.

It was comforting to realize that we were in full political agreement. Both movements had stood for the struggle against Nazism and collaboration in all its forms and for the unification of the Resistance around De Gaulle (though we had no wish to alienate Pétain, whose prestige was still great with many of the people whom we hoped to attract). Menthon seemed content with this arrangement; as for me, I was overjoyed. We had shown the nation the way toward unity. Soon others would follow us. I wasted no time in visiting the six regions to meet with the local representatives of Menthon's groups, as well as to inform my own resisters of the merger and to insure a reliable communications network. Menthon and I drew up and signed a short statement announcing our accord. It was to serve me as a credential with those of his people who didn't already know me.

Combat

No sooner had our meeting broken up than Menthon was arrested on the road to Annecy. Only later did I find out about his incredible adventure. He was transferred to Marseilles and incarcerated for several days in the Prison des Baumettes. He was then taken to Vichy, where, after a long conversation with Rollin, the boss of the D.S.T. (Direction de la Surveillance du Territoire),* he was released. Soon he was back at the university, giving his courses as usual. To his great surprise, he had discovered that Rollin was openly anti-Nazi. Though obligated to blow the whistle on Menthon's activities, which were considered "anti-national," Rollin seemed more interested in convincing Menthon of Pétain's rectitude than in punishing him.

As soon as I got back from Grenoble I notified Bourdet and Chevance of the results of my meeting with Menthon. Then I packed my bags.

My first stop was Clermont-Ferrand in R.6. Alfred Coste-Floret was its new boss. A law professor, he had recruited his following exclusively in legal and academic circles. He introduced me to Walter, a professor in the medical school who, in his spare time, concocted explosives in his laboratory. I also met Sadron, who taught in the science faculty. The entire town was in ferment, for it was here that the faculty of the University of Strasbourg had sought refuge. It was rich humus for the Resistance.

For his part, Colonel Borgnis-Desbordes had virtually no experience of civilian life. It seemed to me that he really hadn't done much to attract his potential clientele of Auvergnats.

Coste-Floret and his friends apparently had little feeling for organization. The new organizational form that I proposed was greeted by them with ill-concealed sarcasm. I could easily sense what they thought: It was the typical brainchild of a befuddled general staff officer. However, they were delighted with the merger.

The seat of R.5 had been shifted from Limoges to Brive-la-Gaillarde, where Edmond Michelet lived. I was very taken with him even at our first meeting. The father of an enormous family,

*Vichy's political police.

The Night Will End

he seemed never to flinch at the incredible risks to which it was subjected. He was a devout Catholic, and his language was vigorous and frank, though under the stress of his intense and fast-moving mind his words often came out oddly jumbled. He was to become a very dear friend of mine. He had a practically evangelical effect on the region, for he was a Christian who knew how to communicate his faith to others. We got along well right from the start.

In Toulouse I was received by a Dr. Parent. From our conversation I got the impression that he was very busy and probably unsuited both by temperament and age for an important role in the movement. Decidedly this region was under a bad spell.

In Montpellier it was the reverse. Here we had two captains, Pierre-Henri Teitgen and René Courtin. One was Catholic, the other Protestant, a not insignificant fact considering the proximity of the Cévennes. Their courses in the university consisted primarily of anti-Nazi and anti-collaborationist speeches. Larger and larger audiences attended their "classes" in Montpellier University, and the students listened openmouthed.

And then there was Jacques Renouvin. An ex-*camelot du roi,* or member of the most extreme royalist faction within Action Française, he was an experienced brawler who always hankered after a good fight. Though he stressed propaganda—the holy war between the Cross and the swastika—his aggressive nature and political background predisposed him more to direct action. Violently anti-German, he had gained a certain notoriety with a gesture that had delighted many of his compatriots. Following the shameful appeasement in Munich, P.-F. Flandin had sent a telegram to congratulate Hitler. Jacques Renouvin was incensed. A tall man with a long reach, he had calmly slapped Flandin in the face while the ex-president of the Council of Ministers was about to place his ceremonial wreath on the Tomb of the Unknown Soldier.

Rather at loose ends in Montpellier, Renouvin had decided to devote his energies to recruiting a band of men ready to engage in punitive expeditions against the collaborators in the region. This band eventually matured into a whole network of Groupes Francs that extended into several departments, including Hérault, Gard and Lozère.

Combat

A towering, big-boned, partially gray-haired man with a mild strabismus clearly visible through his thick glasses, Jacques Renouvin was a *bon vivant* out of *The Three Musketeers*. He was a marvelous leader, and men of all ages followed him with passionate devotion. We soon became fast friends, and he accepted my authority without qualms.

He also agreed to become the national chief of the G.F. (Groupes Francs). It was his job to recruit and to train one or more direct-action groups in each region. All France was soon to know of them.

From this first contact with Jacques Renouvin I got the germ of an idea for a new organizational principle. Gradually it ripened in my mind. Already in 1940, under the name of Choc, I had encouraged the founding of paramilitary units trained to launch armed attacks on the occupying troops. By this time we had put together, with uneven success, several six- and thirty-men cells of these commandos.

Our problem was this: If these cells were to open hostilities immediately, they would not only run the risk of their own annihilation but also endanger the whole paramilitary wing of our movement, which might be decimated before it ever had the chance to act. Did we really want the same type of individual for these daring, immediate operations and for the long-range liberation struggle? I thought not.

We needed two entirely discrete paramilitary organizations. Their sole liaison would be through the local regional chief. The direct-action commandos would keep the name that Renouvin had already given them: Groupes Francs, or G.F. But what should we call the other, larger paramilitary body? Its title would have to emphasize both its flatly military aspect and its clandestine character.

I decided to call it our "Secret Army."

The weather became raw; we could feel the winter coming on. And winter was our great hope. The situation on the Russian front had become so critical that Stalin had taken personal command of the Red Army. We prayed that the snow might halt the powerful

The Night Will End

offensive the Wehrmacht had recently launched against Moscow. Hitler had promised absolute victory to his troops in the east; several weeks later, he himself took over command of the front.

In the Far East, the Royal Navy had sustained a grave defeat. Two of its finest vessels, the battleships *Prince of Wales* and *Repulse,* had been sunk by the Japanese. By word and picture the collaborationist press acclaimed the successes of the Axis. There wasn't a single ray of hope anywhere on the dark horizon of war. And yet . . .

On December 7 I stayed in my room all day to revise the contents of the forthcoming issue of *Combat* and to write an article. That evening I tried as usual to get the BBC, an increasingly difficult task because of German jamming. Over the radio I learned of the one thing that I never had suspected would happen: The Japanese air force had attacked the American Pacific Fleet at Pearl Harbor, sinking or severely damaging most of its ships. The United States was at war with Japan!

It was wonderful news. It didn't even occur to me to think about the terrible American losses, about those burned-out hulls in Hawaii. Only one thing mattered: America, the great and powerful America, was now on our side!

About December 15 I received a visit from Jacques Dhont. He'd crossed the line of demarcation to come to see me in Lyons.

He told me that our movement in the northern zone had entered a period of severe crisis. Robert Guédon's wife had recently died. Overwhelmed with grief, Robert came less and less often to Paris. The German military police was hunting all over Normandy for him, so he moved incessantly from one place to another. He surfaced only rarely, and since it was he who ran the whole show, the resistance groups were receiving fewer and fewer concrete orders. They now had the perhaps exaggerated but highly depressing sensation of noisily racing their engines, of attracting the attention of the occupation authorities while accomplishing substantially nothing. They accused Guédon of being a blunderer, of starting all kinds of projects he couldn't finish. According to Jacques Dhont he no longer commanded his comrades' loyalty or trust.

Combat

"The movement's melting away like snow in a spring thaw. You'd better come up to Paris right away to help us find a way out of this debacle. All our friends begged me to ask you to come as soon as possible."

Guédon was a dear old friend of mine. I was deeply pained by what Dhont had said but only half surprised. I knew that Guédon had very little ability to delegate authority and that his tumultuous thoughts were often difficult to follow. In any case, my friends wanted me in Paris, and I had no choice but to go.

Within a forty-eight-hour period I conferred with Berty, Menthon, Jean-Guy Bernard and his sister Jacqueline. Leaving the direction of *Combat* in their hands, I left with Dhont for Paris.

I had no time to fuss over a well-prepared crossing of the demarcation line. I simply trusted in my good angel. Oddly enough, it was this imprudence that actually saved our skins. If I had arranged the day of my crossing in advance, the Gestapo would have been awaiting me in the Gare de Lyons along with my Parisian friends. Although we didn't know it at that time, our courier Devillers was actually a Gestapo agent.

We took a bus from Mâcon to where the demarcation line ran just south of Montceau-les-Mines. On the bus a pretty young blonde, not more than twenty years old, was sitting next to us. As usual I started a conversation with her. During a short rest stop I bought her a cup of coffee. She was heading for Montceau, just inside the occupied zone.

"How do you intend to get through?" asked Dhont. "Do you have a pass?"

"Oh, I don't need one—not me," she answered. "I know the area like the palm of my hand and the schedule of the German patrols, too. I just slip across whenever the coast is clear."

"Suppose we come with you," I said.

"Sure. Just follow me and do exactly as I do."

We followed her for an hour and a half through a marvelous snowscape, and, behold, we were in the occupied zone. It was as easy as pie.

The girl's parents, who were simple working people, received us as if we were old friends. We didn't say a thing about ourselves, and

The Night Will End

they didn't ask any questions. After a good night's sleep in their home, we boarded the train for Paris.

My friends in Paris were expecting me and had found me a place to stay. It happened that Chilina Ciosi was one of those who had offered her apartment, at 131, Rue de Vaugirard, to the movement, for the lodging of underground transients. By pure chance she was designated to put me up. In any case, I spent my brief stay at her place, including Christmas Eve, which was to be an important date in both our lives.

First I talked to Guédon. I didn't try to dissimulate the fact that I'd heard a lot of harsh criticism of him. Our friendship was strong enough to withstand total frankness. He didn't seem surprised, but I could sense that he was pained. Deeply affected by his wife's death, tracked by the Gestapo, feeling the dragnet tighten around him, he had lost his earlier morale—and who could blame him?

First I embarked on a long investigation of my own. Separately or in groups, I met with everyone who belonged to what was in effect the movement's general staff (and Robert was very wrong not to have conferred recognized official status on it). It included Jeanne Sivadon, Odile Kienlen, Elisabeth Dussauze and her brother Paul, Tony Ricou, André Noël (a friend of the Reverend Father Riquet and a militant in the Pax Romana group), Father Riquet himself and the Abbé Vallée. Each of them, with his own emphasis and nuances, told me the same story: We needed a better-knit organization with more decentralization and delegation of authority—in a word, we needed a hierarchy.

Yet, however sloppy and disorganized, we were still making progress. *Résistance* continued to appear and to be distributed, and our sources of military and political intelligence had not dried up and were in assiduous contact with our headquarters at the Ecole des Surintendantes d'Usines on the Rue Princesse.

It was New Year's Day, 1942. I counted on returning to the southern zone within a week. I had already met individually with most of the important people in our movement in Paris. But to rescue it from the throes of its present crisis and give it new

Combat

self-confidence, I had to get the whole team together. We had to talk as a group and perhaps to redistribute some of our tasks.

At my behest Elisabeth Dussauze organized such a meeting for January 3. It was attended by André Noël, Paul Dussauze, Jacques Dhont, Tony Ricou, Jeanne Sivadon, Odile Kienlen and Henri Ingrand. There were also three men whom I hadn't yet met: Jacques Lecompte-Boinet, Charles Le Goalez and François Morin. Robert Guédon was absent, as he had not yet returned from Normandy.

I began by retelling the story of the movement and explaining the organizational structure toward which it was groping. They rather pointedly asked me where our funds were coming from, and I was obliged to answer that, though we had very little money at all, it was entirely of French provenance. My comrades seemed to suspect that it really came from the United Kingdom.

Then I explained why I believed that we should throw our weight behind De Gaulle. Principally, it would help us to steer clear of feudal struggles between the various clandestine movements and their leaders. I concluded by saying, "Nobody has to join us, nobody has to request or to accept positions of responsibility. But from the moment that you do decide to assume them, you take on certain obligations and duties which may—and in some cases already do—weigh quite heavily on your shoulders.

"We are fighters, not boy scouts. We are involved in a war, not a war game. Our discipline should be all the tougher precisely because it is voluntary, and weakness in leaders is even more intolerable than weakness in rank-and-file members."

They listened in silence. Nobody asked any questions. Immediately after the conference the steering committee of the northern zone was set up. It was to be headed by André Noël and Elisabeth Dussauze. It would be their responsibility to designate further chiefs for propaganda, intelligence and commando operations and to reorganize our entire movement under these three categories, including the straggling groups in the provinces.

After this decisive meeting I was not to see my friends again. I did not know it, but a terrible threat was hanging over them.

I don't remember how I first met Michel Brault, the man who

was soon to be known as "Jérôme." A specialist in international law before the war, he had important business contacts in England and the United States. Through them the British intelligence service had requested him to form an intelligence and action network, in which he was already energetically involved. He continued his legal work all the while.

We made an appointment and met in an enormous loft. He came with two other men. One of them, Pierrat, had a big scar on his face and had been awarded the Croix-de-Feu. He was an editor of *Le Petit Journal*. The other, who was introduced to me simply as "Lucas," was really Pierre de Vomécourt, as I learned after the war.

They were well informed as to my activities. They were particularly intrigued by what seemed to be Combat's unique ability to take firm root in both zones. The real purpose of our meeting was for a reciprocal exchange of information.

For them the problem of communication with London had been solved long ago. They also possessed many two-way radios and got answers to their messages to London within forty-eight hours of the original transmission. They received foreign agents continually and had a regular line of communications open with the Allied embassies in Switzerland.

"You're very lucky," I told them. "We haven't got anything near your communications network. For eighteen months we've been making do with whatever information we could get our hands on. We send messages to London erratically and by very circuitous routes, and we never know if they arrive."

"Well, now you're in a position to improve that situation," said Lucas. "But, frankly, I'm not surprised by what you've told me. The British services are very efficient, much more so than the French—as you've probably noticed. And then, as we all know, the two of them share no mutual trust whatsoever. Anyway, if it's efficiency you're after, the English are the ones who can help you."

"Jérôme" and his people offered to assist me. What a temptation! All I had to do was say yes, and our whole position would improve enormously. Our isolation would be over. It would be the end of our nightmarish difficulties in providing for our full-time militants and in arming our six-man cells. But what would then become of

Combat

the unity of the Resistance, which I myself was championing with such zeal both here and in Lyons?

"I can see that you're right," I replied, "but, however great my admiration for the English, I'm still a Frenchman living in France. Just imagine for a moment what would happen if the entire Resistance, out of a desire for money and material, put itself at the disposal of Great Britain. Why, we'd be mercenaries at the beck and call of a friendly though still foreign power! If De Gaulle were not in London I'd accept your offer immediately. I assume that you are indeed making me a proposition . . ."

"Well, a suggestion . . ."

"But, you see, De Gaulle *is* in London, and one day before long we'll be sure to get in touch with him. De Gaulle can legitimately speak in our name and represent us. In a word, he can and must be the incarnation of that part of the French people that fights back against oppression. That's why I and certain of my friends have been doing our best to encourage the entire Resistance to rally around him. If we succeed, the real France will stand up to the traitors and make them pay for the collaboration."

"Jérôme" remained silent, but I could see that he was not unaffected by my words. A month later he admitted as much himself when he arrived to join me in the free zone (after barely escaping from the clutches of Mathilde Carré, a member of his ring known as "La Chatte" and who had become a double agent for the Abwehr).

"Lucas" disagreed. "This is total war," he said, "and I'm willing to serve with any group that gives me the opportunity to fight, especially if it represents a friendly power."

For the time being at least our viewpoints were irreconcilable. We went our separate ways. But I notified "Jérôme" of a channel whereby he could get in touch with us. It was to come in handy for him.

Once out in the street, as I passed a few German soldiers, I couldn't stop myself from feeling a certain regret over my intransigence.

Berty Albrecht came up to visit me in Paris. She was overjoyed to be with her old pals from the Ecole de Surintendantes again.

The Night Will End

She shared with them all the tricks and subterfuges she'd picked up in the course of her underground experience. It was with Berty that I returned to the free zone early in 1942. We simply walked across the line, as I had done on the way up. We did it near Montceau-les-Mines, with the guidance of the same pretty young blonde who had helped us last time. I happened to know that she was longing for ice skates, so I brought a pair along and gave them to her as a token of thanks.

Combat

THE SPIRIT OF REVOLT

Shortly after my return from Lyons, I received the following brief note from Recordier: "URGENT: Come to Marseilles immediately. The high official whom you met in my house last July has returned. He has been staying with 'Georges' and he wants to see you."

In our lingo, "Georges" meant London. Apparently Jean Moulin had made it to England as he had promised, and now he was back. How? Why did he want me? Well, the answer was right there in Marseilles. The following evening I boarded a train for the Midi.

A meeting had been organized at the home of Agnes Bidault, Georges Bidault's sister. She lived in a little two-story house at 103, Rue Kléber. Burning with curiosity, I immediately headed there at a brisk pace with Chevance by my side.

It was indeed Jean Moulin. He was overjoyed to see us. He told us of his journey through Spain to Portugal and how his departure for England had been subjected to endless delays. He described his first conversation with General de Gaulle, noting the vivid impression the man had made on him, as well as his stay in London. The resolute courage of the people of that city had deeply affected him.

7

Sitting in Recordier's little kitchen, we were in a flash transported into another world. We were devouring the words of this man who, only a few days ago, had actually been in London. For us, the voice of the BBC seemed always so near and yet so far away.

Then he told us about his unfortunate parachute landing in the swamps of Fontvieille and about how he had lost track of his radio operator, which worried him no end. Having been dropped at night, they had landed at some distance from each other. Unwilling either to call out or to exchange signaling flares, they had searched for each other in vain.

"I now believe," he said, "that your desire to unify the Resistance will soon be realized. I myself will be able to offer you concrete help. That's the real import of the mission that De Gaulle has assigned me."

Then, drawing a matchbox from his pocket, he opened it and took out a handful of tiny slips which fit the box's contours exactly. He handed us the first slip—it was a microfilm—along with a magnifying glass. By the light of the small lamp over the gas stove I read, "I hereby appoint Jean Moulin as my personal representative and as the delegate of the French National Committee to the zone of metropolitan France not under direct occupation.

"M. Moulin's mission is to bring about the concerted action of all elements which resist the enemy and the collaboration. M. Moulin is to report to me directly upon the accomplishment of his mission."

And, beneath these lines, was that simple, laterally extended scrawl that I'd never before seen: C. DE GAULLE.

Here at last was what we had so long awaited: contact with Free France, miraculous contact on the highest level! What a powerful spur this would be to our unity drive! We read pure joy in one another's faces.

It was our turn to speak. We had made much progress in our efforts at unification since Moulin's departure. I informed him excitedly of the birth of *Combat*, of D'Astier's failure to appear in Grenoble, of my two trips into the occupied zone and of the recalcitrance of the organizations there to rally to De Gaulle.

"By the way," said Moulin, "I have not forgotten that you're itching for a communication line to the general and his services.

The Spirit of Revolt

When I've relocated my radio operator, which I'm sure I'll do before long, you'll be able, through me, to send London whatever messages or information you want. I have an airtight code. Later we'll work out the exact details of our liaison, as well as a mechanism for supplying you with aid of various kinds. From now on, if you don't mind, you'll be calling me 'Max.'"

"And I shall be 'Charvet,'" I said. "As for Maurice, we'll call him 'Bertin.'"

"I've also brought you some money. I know that you were desperately hard up when I left, and you're probably even worse off now."

Removing a wad of banknotes from his hip pocket, he chucked me 250,000 francs.

"However, I want you to know that Colonel Passy's people are very upset by the fact that the various resistance operations—the political, the intelligence, the propaganda services—are so terribly intermingled, even to the point of often being run by the same men. In his opinion this could be disastrous for security. It increases the vulnerability of both units and individuals. They could be knocked out even before they get started. The British Secret Service shares this view, and, after all, they're the ones who have all the resources, especially arms and ammo. All this is by way of explanation for the dispatch that I've brought you."

He then showed us several more pages of microfilm that contained extremely precise instructions covering everything down to the tiniest details of our operation. In fact, they were *orders*.

Chevance and I exchanged a sidelong glance under Max's watchful eye.

"You know, it just isn't as simple as that," said 'Bertin.' "Sure, in theory all this is perfect. But in practice it's utterly unfeasible. For example, we have, as you know, a certain number of commando squads at our disposal. How can we possibly forbid them—as this dispatch demands—to receive and distribute *Combat*? How can we possibly order them not to transmit some important intelligence report they've received?"

"I'd like to add," I said, "that these activities are really the only

The Night Will End

124

plausible role for a resistance movement in the free zone. Our men have got to have something to do while they're waiting for D-Day. We'll want them in place when we need them, and while they're waiting it's not a bad idea at all to have them get used to taking risks. Also to receive our newspaper is an important symbol of adherence to our movement. Granted, London's orders are theoretically valid, and in fact they correspond with our own initial ideas. But if, in practice, they're going to hurt our cause, then what real good are they?"

We hashed out these problems for three hours. It was already light outside when we finished. "Max" had a train to catch that evening. We agreed that I should arrange a meeting between him, Menthon and D'Astier. A few days later I did in fact introduce him, in the chateau of Menthon-Saint-Bernard, to the founder of *Liberté*. D'Astier he met separately when I was elsewhere.

Before breaking up the meeting we agreed that Aubry would help supply "Max" with men if he needed any. "Max" asked us to get started right away checking out what he thought was a good site for parachute drops. From now on we were to see him very often, usually several times a month.

Back in the nearly deserted streets, Chevance and I headed toward the Place de Castellane, off which Recordier had found me a small, furnished two-room apartment on the ground floor. It was very badly heated but conveniently equipped with two exits. A sense of foreboding clouded our happiness. Of course we were aware that we had just made a great stride forward. Our twin problems of obtaining funds and communicating with London had probably been resolved, which was no small matter. Furthermore, with "Max's" help the unification of the movement would surely be accelerated.

"You know, these guys are really too much," said Maurice. "They sit around in London absolutely convinced that they know what should be done in France."

I fully agreed with him. It was natural that our purely military targets should be predetermined, but how exactly to attack them should be left up to us who knew the ropes. After all, they weren't

The Spirit of Revolt

our superior officers. Moreover, London's organizational proposals made absolutely no sense; they hadn't consulted us on anything.

We discussed this problem late into the night. It was a serious snag, and we planned to raise the issue before *Combat*'s steering committee.

We wouldn't have been nearly so taken aback by those microfilmed instructions if we'd had the slightest inkling of London's real opinion of us. Only three years after the war, when his impressions were still fresh, Colonel Passy wrote*:

When "Rex"** arrived in France nothing had yet been accomplished. . . . He had to start virtually from scratch. . . . His task was to impart some order to a heterogeneous mob in which everybody tried to manage everything at once. . . .

In the unoccupied zone he found an abundance of well-meaning desires, courageous ideas, and exalted theories, which inevitably translated themselves into chaotic and ineffective actions. . . . Here people were no more than well-intentioned. . . .

Apparently the most pressing matter for Passy and his services was that our groups "outgrow the inorganic chaos in which they had been vegetating. . . ."

To be sure, our organization was far from perfect, but it did exist and existed at the cost of enormous effort, especially considering the absence of resources and the indifference of the population. Our six- and thirty-men cells had become a living reality, and it was a fact that since 1940 I had set up three distinct, functioning bodies: Choc, our intelligence arm, and our propaganda service. Thirty years later I'm still amazed that Passy could ever have written, "'Max's' primary task was to replace their purely political concept of resistance with an understanding of the military aspect of revolutionary action."†

*Colonel Passy, *10 Duke Street*, Editions Raoul Solar, 1948, page 96.
**"Rex" was Jean Moulin's alias in radio communications. Inside France it remained "Max."
†Colonel Passy, *op. cit.*

The Night Will End

At the time I never suspected that we commanded so little sympathy, so little recognition. On the basis of what information, I wonder, had such a misconception of us been formed? For, with the exception of my meeting with Moulin in July 1941, no contact between London and ourselves had ever before taken place.

Whatever Moulin had said in London, it is quite clear to me today that the very notion of an underground resistance movement was totally foreign to the French Special Services. For example, in June 1941 Colonel Georges Groussard arrived in London from France. In the occupied zone, as in the free zone, he had already managed to organize both commando units and an important intelligence network. In his memoirs he writes*: "I was prepared, as I told Passy, to make these two important weapons available to de Gaulle."

Passy's reply**: "We discussed his intelligence network until midnight. *It was the only thing that really interested me.*"

This is so terribly true that it was not until January 1942, a year and a half after De Gaulle's June 18 appeal, that his special services changed their name from S.R. (Service de Renseignements, or intelligence service) to B.C.R.A. (Bureau Central de Renseignements et d'Action, or Central Bureau of Intelligence and Action).

This failure to recognize the kind of warfare we were waging was exacerbated by the greatest imaginable indifference until the moment when London suddenly took notice of the advantages of having a Resistance in the free zone.

When Christian Pineau, the first of us to reach London, finally managed, in March 1942, to talk to De Gaulle several times, he described the Resistance in great detail. Pineau writes†: ". . . He [De Gaulle] mentioned the Free French, the troops in Africa, as if they were the sole representatives of the French Resistance. . . ." And again: "He put me not a single question about the Resistance, not a single question about my own activities. Perhaps it seemed too humdrum to him to ask if I'd had a good journey to London,

*Georges A. Groussard, *Service Secret, 1940–1945*, Editions de la Table Ronde, 1964.

**Colonel Passy, 2e *Bureau, Londres*, Editions Raoul Solar, 1947, page 197.

†Christian Pineau, *La Simple Vérité, 1940–1945*, Editions Julliard, 1960, page 158.

The Spirit of Revolt

but in my eyes it had been no ordinary journey, and it merited some small word of acknowledgment."

This indifference was a serious matter indeed. Though we hoped that the presence of "Max" among us might help to dispel this attitude, in fact it only made matters worse.

It wasn't easy to organize at short notice a meeting between our extended steering committee and a representative group of regional chiefs. But we had to break the ice concerning the serious problem posed by the orders "Max" had brought us from London.

The meeting was eventually held in Nîmes. There were many familiar faces around the conference table that day: Menthon, Alfred Coste-Floret, Claude Bourdet, Chevance, Berty, Demachy, Aubry, Jacques Renouvin, Courtin, Teitgen and myself. Chevance and I reported our long conversation with "Max," emphasizing that he was De Gaulle's sole emissary in the free zone. We also mentioned the money he had given us as well as the promise that it would now be provided on a regular basis. Finally, we told them about that curious microfilmed list of instructions.

Of these we furnished an explicit account. Aubry and Demachy fully concurred with our own initial opinion. Here was our dilemma: To accept them would indeed be to place us under the command of the Special Services in London, but to repudiate them, inappropriate though they were, would cause incalculable damage to our new relations with our allies. After a long discussion we decided to make a loyal attempt to carry out London's directive to segregate the Secret Army from the rest of our activities.

All during the year 1942 we tried our utmost to accomplish this, but to no avail. It was so much wasted effort. Though it was possible to separate our political arm from our military arm on the national, regional and departmental levels, as we approached the rank-and-file membership the resultant dislocation seemed appalling. In the last analysis, it was simply impossible to bring about the required political/military articulation.

This was a consequence of the nature of our guerrilla struggle, a fact that London had totally overlooked. Across the Channel they were still thinking in terms of classical warfare. Their services were

The Night Will End

still totally oriented toward intelligence; the very notion of a clandestine movement was utterly foreign to them.

As soon as she had arrived at Nîmes to attend our meeting Berty drew me aside. "Henri," she burst out, "if what I've heard is true, our dispatch runner Devillers is a German spy. . . . Yes, I know. I'm still stupefied myself. I just can't believe it, and yet . . ."

"A German spy? Are you out of your mind, Berty? Who in God's name has been handing you such nonsense?"

"Jean-Paul Lien. He came from Paris especially to tell me."

"From *Paris*? But he's been living in Lyons for several weeks now."

"Please, listen to me! I'm only trying to tell you what Lien told me. You see, in Paris he frequents a restaurant on the Left Bank where he often runs into the Germans. Well, one day at lunch he heard two civilians speaking German at the next table. He knows German quite well, since he's Alsatian. Well, he started eavesdropping. He quickly gathered that his neighbors were plainclothesmen. Twice he heard the name 'Molin,' then 'National Liberation Movement' and finally 'Combat.' There could be no doubt: It was you they were talking about.

"Naturally he started to pay very close attention, but there were still parts he couldn't make out. Then he contrived to address a few words to them in German. Little by little he joined their conversation. He revealed his Alsatian origin and conveyed his satisfaction that his native land had been returned to the Reich. By the end of the meal they had joined tables. In order to coax more out of them, Lien ordered them a few bottles of champagne topped off by cognac, which loosened their tongues until they were speaking quite confidentially.

"It seems that they were Abwehr men assigned to maintain surveillance over us. Henri, they know all about you! They even know that you visited Paris in December! They were planning to arrest you then, but, according to Lien, they decided to hold off until they knew more about our movement. Lien played along with them and asked if they weren't afraid that you might slip through their fingers. One of them, already half drunk, answered,

The Spirit of Revolt

'No way. We know every move he and the other big shots make, because the guy who works as their messenger between Paris and Lyons is one of our boys.'

"Well, that's it, Henri, just as I heard it."

How much could I credit this report? Lien couldn't have invented it. But, then again, if true it meant that Devillers was a German agent! Chills ran down my spine. For three months he'd been our liaison between Paris, Vichy and Lyons. He knew many important addresses. As for the contents of his messages, though our letters were almost always written in invisible ink, they could surely be detected and read by any decent counterespionage service.

"Berty," I said, "if this is true, it's pretty damn serious. Did you warn Paris?"

"Immediately. I put Lien on the train for Paris right away. He'll be alerting Jeanne Sivadon on the Rue Princesse, and she'll relay the warning to all our endangered comrades."

Perhaps Jeanne's own security precautions were too rigid; perhaps she didn't recognize our messenger; perhaps the password we'd given Lien was for some reason unacceptable. In any case, she never got that message. And we never knew that she hadn't got it, because Jean-Paul Lien never came back to tell us.

I was terribly worried by the accusation that was hanging over Devillers, not on my own account—he didn't know my address— but on account of our comrades in Paris. Devillers should have been back in Lyons several days earlier; he had vanished. The atmosphere became tense.

Night was descending stealthily as I accompanied Berty home along the Rue Victor-Hugo. We were walking toward the Hôtel Dubost on the Place Carnot where she had been staying. We were both very uneasy. As a precautionary measure we split up. While she crossed the street in front of General Staff headquarters and the Hôtel d'Angleterre, I remained in the shadows of the trees on the square, following furtively to make sure she got home safely.

Suddenly, forty yards ahead of me, facing the hotel lobby, I detected three motionless silhouettes. In a flash I understood: the police! What should I do? Turn and run? No, they must have

The Night Will End

noticed me already. I raised my collar, pulled my hat brim down over my eyes and continued to walk toward them, neither slackening nor quickening my pace. When I reached where they stood I simply walked right past them, raising my hands to my mouth and coughing noisily. Given the cold, it was a natural thing to do. They had not seen my face. But as soon as I'd passed them I heard one of them whisper, "That him?"

I continued on at the same pace, straining my ears but never turning, ready to take off. Silence. Perhaps they weren't following me after all. Arriving at the Cours de Verdun, I slipped behind a streetcar stationed at the terminal, then raced as fast as my legs would carry me to the Gare Perrache, occasionally consulting my watch as if I were late for a train. I'd escaped by the skin of my teeth!

The next day and for several days thereafter, my comrades informed me of the avalanche of arrests that had befallen us. One of our liaison agents, André Koehl, had been stopped in Clermont-Ferrand carrying a suitcase bursting with issues of *Combat*. On his person, alas, he was also carrying a long list of names and addresses written "in clear." Dismayed, I listened hour by hour as the reports of the arrests came in: Demachy, Peck, Simone Gouyou, Colin, Crozier, Mme. Fradin de Clermont, Emmaneul Mounier, Langlade, Michel Renouvin in Montpellier; Colette Braun in Toulouse; and, finally, Chevance and Berty herself. There were many others whose names I didn't recognize. All in all, forty militants had been arrested. They were interrogated by the police, then imprisoned in the Prison de Saint-Paul and the Prison de Saint-Joseph in Lyons. Finally, they were transferred to Clermont-Ferrand.

That night I sat dreadfully alone before my untouched dinner in a little workingman's restaurant a few paces from where I was lodging. I felt overcome with fatigue. Crushed, oh, I was utterly crushed! For the first time in my life I understood the full meaning of this word. It was all over. I couldn't eat. One by one the faces of all those dear comrades rose up to haunt me. They seemed to be smiling. What could I do for them, my God, what could I do! I felt ashamed to be free, spared in the battle into which I had led them and in which they had fallen. Should not I too have been among

The Spirit of Revolt

them? It would have been so simple for me to surrender to the police, and I would have found such peace.

"You just happened to miss me," I would have confessed, "but you got all my friends. Well, I am their leader. Take me where you have taken them!"

Brokenhearted, I trudged back to my room. The next morning I would see things more clearly.

The following day Jean-Guy Bernard came to see me. His youth, his ardor and the effect of a good night's sleep afforded me a measure of solace. The blow had been hard indeed. But Jean-Guy was still there, as was his sister Jacqueline and André Bollier. Our steering committee, with the exception of Chevance, had been spared, and our regional groups were still functioning. Jacques Renouvin's nephew had been captured, but he himself and his Groupes Francs were still intack. Our printing presses were still operating.

The casualties had been severe, but the battle must go on; our friends in prison surely wanted it that way.

Jean-Guy headed off to alert Menthon, in case he still didn't know of the arrests, and to dispatch a warning to all regions to change their letter boxes and meeting places. We reminded them of the regulation against keeping lists of names and of the need to conceal all secret papers in socks or in coat linings.

Still no sign of Devillers! What was going on in Paris? A disturbing and inexplicable answer soon arrived. In the mail I received a brief note from Robert Guédon, postmarked in the free zone near the demarcation line. With Reine, who had become his wife, he had left the occupied zone for good. He wanted to cross over to North Africa and was making his way toward the Spanish border. No explanation. Only a list of names of the various regional chiefs in the north, along with directions on how to locate them and announce oneself to them. Why had he left so precipitately, without even stopping to see me? Had he had a premonition? A conflict over our newly adopted course? I didn't know, but I was troubled and uneasy.

Chilina Ciosi arrived from Paris, right in the midst of sheer chaos. A pulmonary attack had forced her to leave for a sanitari-

The Night Will End

um. The message she brought us from Jeanne Sivadon, written, as always, in invisible ink, made no allusion to the grave suspicions hanging over Devillers. She told us only that no one had seen him for two weeks.

I was at a loss. I decided to go to see Menthon in his chateau. Together we would decide on a course of action. Chilina came with me. From Annecy she could easily proceed directly to Sancellemoz, where she was to be hospitalized.

We arrived at Annecy in the middle of the afternoon and decided not to go on to Menthon-Saint-Bernard until the next morning. We wanted to spend a quiet evening together. We were just getting up from the dinner table when—I couldn't believe my eyes—there was Berty, entering the hotel lobby!

"Berty! Berty! You're free!"

"Oh, Henri, I was so afraid that I might not find you! Chilina!" The two women embraced.

"Let's go into this alcove. . . . There. . . . Now I'm going to tell you what happened to me. It's scarcely believable . . . but, oh, it's good to be free again!"

I made her eat a little something. It was really she, more self-possessed than ever, and dressed as always with elegance and sobriety.

Directly following the arrest, she had been brought to the Prison de Saint-Joseph, where she found the other women from the movement. A few days later she was taken to the offices of the D.S.T.* in Lyons. There the police commissioner, Triffe, had informed her that Devillers had been apprehended at the demarcation line on a tip from Paillole's services (the Bureaux de Menées Antinationales—Bureau of Anti-National Conspiracies). Although the latter were responsible to the Vichy government, they took every opportunity to strike a blow at the Abwehr. Devillers, after long interrogation, had been recognized as one of its agents.

"For three months," she continued, "there hasn't been a single communication from Lyons or Paris that has not been turned over to the Germans, opened and read without a trace by their

---

*D.S.T.: Direction de la Surveillance du Territoire—Directorate of Territorial Surveillance, Vichy's political police.

The Spirit of Revolt

specialized services and then sent on to its destination. Paillole's Bureau de Menées Antinationales has investigated the matter and it won't be long before Devillers is prosecuted before a military tribunal."

So Lien's information had been correct! Yet Jeanne hadn't said anything about him or the message he was to have given her. This was unthinkable! Had not Lien delivered our message? There was no way of knowing, for we hadn't seen him again since his departure. In the midst of this dramatic uncertainty we still had to warn our comrades in Paris. They were in mortal danger.

"That's not all," Berty continued. "Triffe told me that he had received orders to take me to Vichy, because his boss, Rollin, wanted to talk to me."

This colloquy had indeed taken place and, oddly enough, under the most courteous conditions. Rollin was aware of the important role Berty occupied at my side. He seemed very well informed about our organization and had still not gotten over the fact that it was led by a former officer. Berty had been released solely on condition that she inform me that he, Rollin, the director of the D.S.T., wanted to talk to me. He had actually requested that I come to Vichy to meet him.

"Of course I let him know that you were wanted by the police and were not inclined to give yourself up to them," Berty told us as she finished her dinner. "He gave me his word of honor that if you accepted his offer he'd guarantee you safe passage there and back."

I was in a quandary. What should I do now? What did this bizarre invitation signify?

Berty counseled me to go. In Lyons, as in Vichy, she had been shown so much consideration that she was convinced that the offer was not a trap. Since we were to see Menthon tomorrow, we could arrive at a definitive conclusion then.

Once again, that night, I hardly slept. I kept thinking about all our comrades, those imprisoned here and those under Gestapo surveillance in Paris. How weak I felt in this ordeal! How, how could I help them?

I wondered if I should follow Berty's advice and go to Vichy? It seemed unlikely that Rollin's proposal was a trap, but then there was no ironclad guarantee. If I were to get arrested on the way

The Night Will End

back from this interview, I would truly deserve the accusation of having been insanely careless. Moreover, the kind of truce that Rollin was proposing had something unhealthy about it.

I ended up solving the matter with a sleeping pill.

The next day Menthon had us to lunch. Once again Berty told the story of her own astounding adventure and Rollin's offer. Menthon was not surprised. Hadn't he himself been led before Rollin last autumn? Hadn't he too been released after their conversation? Nevertheless, to comply with his request posed a basically *political* problem that could be settled only by our steering committee. We agreed to call a meeting as soon as possible, but Menthon, like Berty, recommended that I accept the offer. Still, "Max" had to be notified.

To help ward off the danger which threatened our comrades in Paris, Berty, as soon as she was back in Lyons, dispatched a liaison agent with a memorized message. He was given one address only, that of Jeanne Sivadon. The message was not delivered. Why, we would never know.

On January 27 I held a meeting of the steering committee. We were all present, with the exception of Alfred Coste-Floret. After a lengthy discussion we concluded that the invitation for me to visit Vichy was not in fact personal but addressed to me only as the acting representative of the movement. Hence the movement as a whole was involved and might in some way be compromised. On the other hand, we could not remain indifferent to the fate of our imprisoned comrades, and the proposed interview might have a beneficial outcome for them. Finally, it would be highly interesting to know more about the mentality of a man who, while hunting us, also wanted to talk to us and had also recently arrested an Abwehr agent.

In the end we decided that I should accept the invitation. We agreed that I should listen more than speak and make use of even the slightest opportunity to intercede on behalf of our arrested comrades.

Only twenty-four hours after this last session of our steering committee I presented myself under my true name at the D.S.T. in Lyons. A few moments later I found myself sitting face to face

The Spirit of Revolt

with Rollin. We were alone in his office. On his desk I noticed two stacks of papers. One contained our underground newspapers, the other was labeled "M.L.N." It was the evidence for the prosecution!

Our interview lasted two hours. The man opposite me was an ex-naval officer who, like D'Astier, had gradually gotten involved in journalism. I knew that before the war he had written a book called *L'Apocalypse de Notre Temps*, a fiery indictment of Nazism. It was a fact that he hastened to remind me of himself.

What a strange conversation! Here was the spectacle of the head of the D.S.T. trying to explain to an outlaw hunted by his own detectives that his government's motives were in no wise pro-German! The government's subtle policy, he claimed, was being thwarted by a bunch of troublemakers who thought of themselves as a resistance movement. Our demonstrations and newspapers only hobbled the government and at times seriously undermined the arduous negotiations it was holding with the occupation authorities to obtain better conditions for France and her people. An ex-officer like myself should be able to understand that our efforts were divisive and counterproductive. Just what was it, after all, that we wanted?

What we wanted, I replied, was the solidarity of the French people behind the only political themes capable of unifying it: to join the Allies in the struggle for the liberation of our national territory and to recover the full measure of our sovereignty in both domestic and foreign affairs. Our own movements were in the vanguard of the struggle; I painted a highly flattering portrait of their strength and cohesiveness. Total unity was on the verge of being achieved, and our strength waxed daily.

"What I should like," said Rollin, "is for you to try to re-examine your conscience, to ask yourself if your behavior is really likely to serve our deepest interests. It's too bad that you cannot meet Admiral Darlan, but unfortunately he's out of town. However, perhaps you would be interested in talking to the Minister of the Interior, M. Pucheu."

I had to think fast. To agree to an audience with Pierre Pucheu, an egregious collaborator, might be to exceed the mandate I had

The Night Will End

been given by our steering committee. Considering my opinion of the Interior Minister, and considering the way we'd vilified him in *Combat*, was it wise to talk to him at all? I was walking a tightrope, for my refusal might offend Rollin and eventually result in harm to our comrades. Moreover, I felt a certain curiosity to meet this man Pucheu, who, for us, was one of the principal villains of the piece.

"Our newspapers, which are sitting right in front of you, have no doubt given you an inkling of our feelings about Pucheu. But I'd be no more compromised in his office than I already am in yours. I do not object to meeting him."

The plot was thickening. I knew Pucheu was no pushover, and if he had read our newspaper, he certainly bore us no love. A few moments later I entered his office. He rose and examined me skeptically.

"So you're Captain Frenay. You're young indeed for the task you have undertaken."

"No less than you to be a minister."

He must have been four or five years older than I. He sat down, a surprised smile on his face. I had no doubt that he was a good poker player. We were not alone. Rollin was with us, of course, as well as two gentlemen in civilian dress. Later I was to learn their identities. One was M. Rivalland, the secretary-general of the Ministry of the Interior; the other, M. Johanna, a naval officer and the head of Pucheu's staff.

"Well, then, it seems that you take me for a traitor."

Indeed, that is exactly what we had called him. The attack was direct, embarrassing, but I couldn't suddenly change my opinion.

"*Monsieur le ministre,* if you are not a traitor you have every appearance of being one."

"Ah, yes, I know, I have the reputation of being the puppet of the Germans. But don't you find it curious that with this brilliant reputation in the free zone I am attacked for the opposite reason by the Parisian press?"

"You're also accused of being a sellout to the pro-Nazi Parti Populaire Français, whose commander strolls openly about the Paris streets in a German uniform."

The Spirit of Revolt

"Yes, in fact I founded the P.P.F.—with Doriot, of course. But I haven't belonged to this party for a long time. Tell me, what is the gist of your position? I don't understand it."

"The movement in which I and others are working is, first and foremost, straightforwardly anti-German."

"But why have you taken this *a priori* attitude? It is mere sentimentality. France has been defeated, and it is altogether natural that a certain number of new factors must now influence her policies. The German factor is one, but there are also others—the American, the English, the Russian and so on. We in politics must keep our eye on the facts, not only on the vagaries of public opinion."

"It would appear difficult to govern without consulting public opinion, much less against the public's deepest wishes."

"One molds public opinion; one leads it. Believe me, one does not allow oneself to be led by it."

"I beg to disagree. Though it may be true that in a parliamentary situation one tries to lead public opinion, reverse conditions obtain in the present circumstances. Your policies are directly contrary to the people's will. The best proof is the failure of your official propaganda despite the considerable means at its disposal."

In fact, I knew that the drift of public opinion was far from being as I had described it. The vast majority of the French people was utterly apathetic and still believed that Germany would win the war. But there was no harm in drawing for Pucheu the picture of a less resigned, more virile, public.

"Captain, you are one of those who are preventing us, or at least hindering us, from achieving unity. The government wages a perpetual holding action against German demands. To be successful, it requires that the public remain calm, that no hotheaded demonstrations impede it from reaching its intended goal. Moreover, allow me to point out that you reveal appalling presumption in your opinions. Do you claim, for example, to possess solid information on which to base your newspaper articles?"

"No, certainly not. Our sources of information are imperfect and, in any case, quite unequal to your own."

"You are often guilty of grave errors. For example, your pamphlet on the Weygand affair."

The Night Will End

The previous December, General Weygand, the government's delegate-general and supreme commander in North Africa, had been recalled to metropolitan France. His authority had covered the entire Maghreb: Morocco, Tunisia, Algeria. I was not unaware of his opinion of the Vichy government, in which Pétain alone commanded his respect. He was an avowed enemy of Germany and the collaboration. The fact that he had been kicked upstairs was an unnecessary anticipation of German demands, an unasked-for sign of submission. In consequence, we had vitriolically blasted Vichy (not in a pamphlet, actually, but in *Combat*) for its servility toward the occupier.

"You tried to inflame public opinion over an issue you didn't understand. I shall now explain to you the Weygand affair. Listen carefully. From the very moment he set foot in North Africa as the government's delegate-general, Weygand never passed up a single occasion to demonstrate—often in public—his anti-German opinions. Naturally, the Armistice Commission in Algiers was aware of this and had formed its own opinions of Weygand.

"Now, as it happens, we desired to rearm our troops in North Africa. I'm sure you can guess why. Ergo, we were convinced that as long as Weygand was in charge, the Commission would discountenance any such rearmament. And I must add that Weygand's relentless and quite venomous attacks on Admiral Darlan had become utterly insufferable. Therefore, we recalled him. We were right to do so."

"I'm entirely convinced, sir, that the government must indeed yield frequently to German demands. Such a state of affairs was the obvious consequence of the Armistice. If France were still fighting beside her Allies, things would be quite different, and our country would be paying no more dearly than she is today."

"You know very well that it was impossible for us to continue the war. You should also realize that our behavior since the Armistice has placed the French state in a far superior position to those of the other occupied states, whose governments are in London. I recently received a visit from the secretaries-general of the Interior Ministries of Belgium and Holland. We compared the situation in our three countries. France is in a better state than they in all respects, especially in the economic sector.

The Spirit of Revolt

"Your position is really rather simple-minded. You exploit the emotions of the people; this is demagoguery pure and simple. If I wished to be the most popular man in France tomorrow, I would give an incendiary radio address this evening against the Germans. How easy!"

"Yes, indeed, it's ever so easy, but you're not about to do it, and that's exactly what the nation holds against you. For my part, I'm profoundly convinced that nothing can be done in a country without the support of the people. And the people are against you. It's not only the government's foreign policy they detest but its domestic policy as well. Pétain's so-called 'national revolution' is a sham. Everyone knows very well that it doesn't exist, precisely because its mainstays are the same privileged classes who ran the old regimes—that is, the middle classes, who have shown themselves to be utterly selfish and incompetent."

"On that point I agree with you. I don't believe in this 'national revolution' business either—especially not now. The idea should never have seen the light of day. But tell me about your movement."

It was a good occasion to stress the power of our organization. Naturally I didn't hesitate to exaggerate its strength. I carefully stayed in the realm of generalities, emphasizing our ability to act in both zones, the wide circulation and impact of our newspapers, the nearly achieved unity of the various groups, the many different social strata that had rallied to us and our alliance with the labor unions (of course this in fact applied only to D'Astier's movement). At this point Pucheu interrupted me.

"Perhaps you've had discussions with certain labor-union leaders, but you do not have the unions behind you. Believe me, I know them better than you. I'm a worker's son, and I know the workers. You don't get the support of the labor unions that easily.

"Understand this, Captain: If I agreed to see you, it was because I thought I was dealing with a reasonable man whom I believed might benefit from some clarifications concerning a government's true policy, a policy that cannot be expounded in the streets or in public squares. I hope that I have given you something to think about."

"*Monsieur le ministre*, I am both a private individual and the

The Night Will End

representative of the Resistance. What I may think or decide as an individual is of no immediate concern to the various resistance groups. I share with a certain number of comrades the responsibility for directing these groups; hence I must first report to them the results of these negotiations."

"I beg your pardon, Monsieur. These are not negotiations. I am simply giving you a warning before proceeding to repress your organizations with extreme severity."

"Quite so," I continued. "If you prefer, I shall call them not negotiations but discussions. In any case, it was not I who requested them. I repeat that I must first report your position to my comrades. I cannot prejudge the decision they will make. In any case, I should like to inform you of it, and for this I need ten days without being hounded by the police."

"Rollin here will see to that. In any case, Captain, you may come back to see me if you so desire."

I left his office with mixed feelings. I knew that I had very little room in which to maneouver. Pucheu was a strong man, there was no doubt about it. But since he had expected me to return, it seemed unlikely that he would try to arrest me in the meantime. His language was tough, his statements utterly frank. He was not one to shilly-shally around. He said what he thought and he said it forcefully. His policy seemed clear enough, and I had no doubt that it was also the government's. It was simple: One must be in the victor's camp; for the moment, the victor was Germany; if victory changed camps, so would the government. In the meantime, the French population should be as carefully protected as possible.

In any case, I had won precious time by insisting that only our steering committee could arrive at a final conclusion concerning Pucheu's statement. Together we would examine the possibility of deriving from our relations with Pucheu some benefit for our imprisoned comrades.

As we entered his office Rollin said, "Monsieur Frenay, I'm going to write you a note that will keep you clear of cop trouble in the event that you're arrested before having seen Monsieur Pucheu again. Hold on a moment."

He went into the next room. After a brief spell he returned

The Spirit of Revolt

carrying a slip of paper which he signed and handed to me: "In the event that the bearer of this letter is apprehended for whatever reason before February 10, 1942, kindly advise me immediately by telephone. By order of the Minister of the Interior. *Rollin.*"

That was that! So armed, I could venture back out into the world.

I was just about to leave Rollin's office when he said, "Are you free for dinner this evening? My wife would be delighted to meet you."

Well! So we were already old chums. I accepted his invitation, and at eight o'clock Rollin, his wife and I were seated at a table in the Hôtel Albert.

What a bizarre situation! What luxury! And what fine fare in this elegant restaurant! Mme. Rollin was a very refined woman and not indifferent to political questions; in fact, she was bursting with political observations. She was a Russian, one of those whose accent never lets you forget it. Perhaps because of her origin she was sympathetic to the Allies. She tended to minimize all German victories, always implying that they were transitory, insubstantial. As I listened to her I began to wonder whether it was I or she who was representing the Resistance.

Back in Lyons I immediately called the steering committee into session. They were very eager to hear my report. We agreed that we might derive certain advantages from the situation as it now stood. What we had to do was to exploit the government's inborn opportunism. It was obvious that as soon as a clear-cut victory was achieved by either side the government would swing over to the victor. Since the Allies were bound to win, it would be illogical, if not dangerous, for the government to persecute those whom, one day, it would find by its side. The government was going to be obliged to slacken its persecution of us and to liberate our prisoners.

Our own position must not change. We would continue to mobilize public opinion, to recruit and organize our militants. However, as collateral for the release of our people, we would have to make some kind of conciliatory gesture. We decided to renounce all attacks on the Marshal and, in the event that his

The Night Will End

government were to lean in our direction, gradually to drop all attacks on his cabinet ministers.

This position seemed felicitous to all of us. In effect, while yielding on no important points, we were declaring our neutrality toward the Marshal, who still commanded considerable prestige anyway. Now we could look forward—at least in the unoccupied zone—to the progressive diminution of the risks we had previously run and to the imminent liberation of our comrades.

This was the basic theme of a memorandum we drafted and which I was to read before Pucheu. It was introduced by a trenchant preamble, founded on hard facts, which unequivocally criticized the policy of collaboration. My friends recommended that, once in Pucheu's office, I refrain from adding any mollifying asides.

Before returning to Vichy I wrote a new article for *Combat* called "The State Police Against the Patriots." It was sure to be read in Vichy, for Rollin would soon have it on his desk. It would also be read by those who had arrested our comrades:

All over the free zone, resisters have been thrown into prison and treated like common criminals. Shame, shame on you, foreign-appointed myrmidons of the law! Oh yes, you may continue the sorry work you have begun. . . . But you shall not silence the voice of France. For it is through its martyrs that a cause achieves nobility. . . . The day is coming when, thanks to these martyrs, thanks to us, France shall once again be free.

At the hour of the Liberation every citizen shall be obliged to account for his acts. But it is we who shall judge them.

(*Combat*, February 1942)

I returned to Vichy in the same way that I had the first time. It was February 6, 1942. After a brief talk with Rollin, I once again entered Pierre Pucheu's office.

"Well, Captain, have you come around to our point of view?"

"*Monsieur le ministre,* as I told you during our last meeting, I was obliged to discuss the matter with my friends. I disclosed our conversations to them, and it is their opinion which I offer you today."

The Spirit of Revolt

"I am listening."

"This opinion has been set forth in the form of a memorandum which I have in my hands at this moment. I request permission to read it to you while retaining the document on my person."

To draft that memorandum was one thing; to read it to the Minister of the Interior in his own office was quite another. Here, in this place, our condemnation of the government's behavior took on a more disturbing ring, and our request for the liberation of our comrades surely smacked of wild temerity. The Minister sat there, silent, nervous, drumming his fingers softly on his desk.

"Your note contains a certain number of errors. You speak of anti-Semitic legislation, but you know very well that I have always been an anti-Semite. We have proceeded with the Aryanization of all French firms, and I believe that we have done well. What can you possibly have against such measures? Do you dispute the rightness of our measures against such Jewish banks as Lazard Frères and the Banque Rothschild?"

"I hold against you all measures inspired by anti-Semitism. I have noticed, however, that even this anti-Semitism has certain limits in your mind. For example, the Banque Worms has been spared."

It was a direct frontal assault, for I knew that Pucheu held power of attorney for the Banque Worms. I felt a heavy pall of silence fall across the room.

"Well, everything you have told me requires further reflection. But kindly tell me, what the hell are you doing with a man like Emmanuel Mounier* in your ranks. I've been watching this Mounier for years; he's a real gutter democrat!"

"In our movement there is a place for men of all persuasions. Mounier is a man of uncommon spiritual value."

As it happened, Mounier had been imprisoned along with our other comrades. In a flash I saw that I now had occasion to downplay his role, so I added, "Besides, Mounier doesn't work with us—not in the exact sense of the word."

*Emmanuel Mounier: founder of the leftist Catholic review *Esprit*. An outstanding representative of Catholic humanism in the interwar period.—Translator.

The Night Will End

Another silence. Pucheu stood up, consulted his watch and stationed himself directly before me.

"You must understand that I'm not going to let myself be hoodwinked by anybody. I'll think over what you've told me. Rollin! Make sure that I can get in touch with Monsieur Frenay in case I have something to tell him."

He went out, and Rollin and I moved into the adjoining office.

"Do not forget," I said, "that a number of my friends are in jail and that it will be highly difficult for me to continue these meetings as long as they're in prison. I request your sincere consideration of this fact."

"Well, something should be done on their account," Rollin admitted. "We'll think about it. In any case, we'll call off our surveillance of you during your discussions with the Minister. Kindly hand me the note I gave you last time you were here."

Over his signature he scribbled, "This order is valid until February 28 inclusive."

My visit had not been without positive results. Soon several of our comrades were provisionally released from prison. Among them were Chevance and Peck. They had been detained for one month. Why they and not the others? I would never know.

Once again I informed our steering committee of my latest conversation. In turn they told me that my contacts with Pucheu had been divulged in Lyons. The news had spread like wildfire in Resistance circles. In these rumors the facts were often twisted or presented in a positively defamatory manner: I was supposed to have concluded a pact with Pucheu whereby I received personal police protection. I had a meeting called so that I might supply the explanation that numerous resisters were now demanding.

After setting my friends straight, I once again departed for Vichy, with the steering committee's blessing, to try to detect some sign of a forthcoming liberation of our friends. I also took advantage of my visit to denounce the government's policy, as well as to try and shame the conscience of those who claimed to be playing a double game when in fact they were only playing the enemy's game.

The Spirit of Revolt

The attitude of some of my supposed comrades gave me an indication of just how deep the malaise ran. D'Astier, I was informed, was now waging a campaign against me and against the entire movement. At first I refused to believe that he could be so perfidious. I lunched with him and "Max" in the Hôtel Terminus in Lyons. "Max" understood my position (at least, that's what he told me), but D'Astier, though he dared not pronounce the word "treason," spoke of "serious errors" and "grave compromises." In his eyes I never should have agreed to any compromise whatsoever with the chief of the D.S.T. and the Minister of the Interior, even though it might benefit our prisoners. I deserved better from D'Astier, and I was on the verge of extreme anger. I knew that he was using this rather poor pretext to deliver a low blow to Combat, (which he could not forgive for being more important than Libération). I also had to protect myself, for D'Astier's venom was sure to be cunningly distilled. I decided to make a tour of the regions.

In less than a week I visited all six. I was stupefied. Everywhere it was already known that I had visited Pucheu. In Toulouse and in Montpellier the information had been leaked to my friends by the prefecture, which, by all evidence, was acting under received orders. The only possible explanation was that somebody wanted to spread dissension in our ranks. Yet I had little trouble in re-establishing a climate of trust, for, after all, my comrades knew me well and had been informed that the steering committee had unanimously approved my talks with Pucheu.

The last few days had been terribly taxing. In the circle of those whom I regarded as my friends I still commanded trust and was able to act with candor. I expected some reciprocity. For the first time, and in the midst of a grave situation, I was encountering slander, prevarication and defamation. It was not to be the last. It was in vain that a jesting Bourdet had warned me that slander was the lot of a public figure and that I had best get used to it. I was not only revolted but also morally offended, especially in view of the ordeal of our Paris comrades who had now fallen into the hands of the Gestapo. I thought, too, of those in the free zone, incarcerated in the prison at Clermont-Ferrand.

In any case, I could not simply let Pucheu's calculated leakage of

The Night Will End

confidential matters go unanswered. As I was getting ready to leave for Vichy and demand an explanation, I heard that Rollin had again asked to see me. After getting Menthon's okay, I presented myself at Rollin's office on February 25.

Rollin motioned to me to sit down.

"I have asked you here that I may put you abreast of the situation of your jailed friends. At present some of them have been provisionally released from detention. Monsieur Pucheu mentioned the matter to the cabinet, and the Marshal has decided to take charge of the affair personally. Consequently the case will be transferred to Lyons, where a judge will examine the prosecutor's brief and report his conclusion to the Marshal. There will be no trial. What I expect is an all-around dismissal of charges."

"What advantage does this formula have for my friends?"

"It's very important—even if the charges are not dropped. In the latter case, the Marshal himself would condemn them to simple administrative internment. You see, unlike a sentence passed in a criminal proceeding, administrative internment can be commuted at any time by a simple executive order.

"Now, sir," he said, changing the subject, "I'd also like to know if you are responsible for this outbreak of window-smashing in Montpellier and the surrounding area."

In fact, Renouvin and his irregulars had, in less than a week, partially blown up several collaborationist lairs.

"Yes, indeed," I replied, "and we intend to generalize these operations."

"They gravely compromise the maintenance of public order. It would be advisable for you to restrain your impetuous colleagues."

"That is absolutely impossible. I'm sure that you yourself have noticed the kind of people we chose to chasten. They're the presidents of Collaboration, the enrollment bureau of the Anti-Bolshevik Legion. They're notorious scoundrels, dyed-in-the-wool traitors. We cannot promise to refrain from attacking such people or their property."

"All right, all right, but don't you see, the whole thing could easily degenerate into street warfare. The P.P.F. is just itching for an opportunity to get out into the streets."

"I understand your concern, but I'm afraid we simply cannot

The Spirit of Revolt

modify our position in this matter. If the P.P.F. wants street warfare, they'll have it. Your job is simply to arrest the troublemakers. You'll be doing your job, and we'll be doing ours. Business as usual!"

In the midst of all this, Rollin received a telephone call from the Keeper of the Seals* to request that he meet the Lyons public prosecutor concerning our imprisoned comrades. The following day, February 26, we met in the office of the secretary-general of the Ministry of the Interior, M. Rivalland, who, in the absence of Pucheu, had requested to see me.

I launched an immediate attack.

"I have noticed with some consternation that the results of our latest talks have been leaked right down to the smallest detail. Yet they were supposed to have been secret. The immediate broadcasting of these facts cannot be imputed to the very few friends with whom I discussed the matter and whose discretion I can vouch for. I am obliged to conclude that the Minister of the Interior himself is responsible."

"You are wrong. We have no interest in such disclosures. As I have assumed responsibility for the continuance of our discussions, all such publicity is highly dangerous for me as well. No, I rather suspect that the culprit is the Army General Staff. They're incensed at your contacts with us because you won't meet with them. They'll do anything they can to torpedo our arrangement."

"Whatever the case, I find myself caught in a vise. These rumors, as you might well imagine, have seriously upset my colleagues. Some of them are ready to cry treason. This I can't tolerate, any more than I can stand idly by and watch the destruction of all that we've built. Our struggle shall go on."

"Think about it. There's still time."

I left Vichy, never to return. The balance sheet of these three conversations was, at least to my eyes, largely positive: No new arrests had been made, the provisional release of certain comrades had been announced, the courts were not going to proceed with

*Title of the Minister of Justice in the French cabinet—Translator.

The Night Will End

the case, and I had been informed of the likelihood that no judicial inquiry would ever be opened. The professional slanderers could go about their business, but the fact of the matter was that I had done my duty. Upon their release from jail, Chevance and Peck also approved my action.

Shortly after my second dialogue with Pucheu, Jacques Dhont, having miraculously escaped the clutches of the Gestapo and fled Paris, informed me of the terrible wave of arrests that had overwhelmed our movement in the northern zone.

On February 4 Jeanne Sivadon and her secretary had been apprehended, and they were followed in the next forty-eight hours by all our people Jacques knew in Paris: Elisabeth and Paul Dussauze, Andre Noël, Tony Ricou and others. In reality, the raids had been much more comprehensive than even Jacques knew. By my later reckoning fully forty-seven of our comrades had been arrested, including members of our groups in the provinces.

It was mid-February. I did not yet know that several of our militants who had been arrested in the free zone were shortly to be released, and now here was Jacques announcing to me the complete destruction of our movement in the northern zone. I wondered where they were now, these comrades whom I could still picture sitting about me during our last meeting less than two months ago. How were they being treated? What fate awaited them?

Crushed and disheartened, on the verge of tears, I saw the entire edifice that we had so painfully constructed over the months lying in ruins and rubble.

These Parisian comrades arrested in February 1942 were only just beginning a long and dolorous Calvary. It was only after the war that I was to learn their tragic story.

All of them, both men and women, were first incarcerated in the Prison de la Santé and in Fresnes, where they were forced to submit to lengthy interrogation. They could hardly deny their activity, for Devillers had furnished proof of everything. Three months later they were transferred to the prison of Saarbrücken

The Spirit of Revolt

and designated N. N. (*Nacht und Nebel**). Only one, René Parodi, remained behind in France. He had hanged himself in his cell on April 17.

In Saarbrücken they were all put in solitary. Certain of the prison guards, as well as the Protestant chaplain, Wolf, helped ease the harshness of their detention. Disregarding their official orders, they sometimes authorized the prisoners to receive books and to visit with one another.

Seventeen months later, on October 12, 1943, a large trial was held before the Volksgerichthof,* the court responsible in peacetime for the trial of defendants indicted for high treason.

The tribunal, presided over by a very high-ranking judge, was composed of officers from the Wehrmacht, the Luftwaffe and the Hitlerjugend.† Though each defendant was offered legal counsel by the state, all the defending attorneys were Nazis. Moreover, the evidence for the prosecution, seized during the house searches in Paris, was both voluminous and damning.

The prosecutor read the indictment with pitiless zeal. He concluded that the activities of the defendants, as well as the consequences of these activities since the actual date of arrest, had "seriously endangered the German Army." It was only then that our comrades, so long cut off from the outside world, learned that the cause for which they had sacrificed their liberty had grown considerably in the free zone, that it possessed large quantities of arms and that it was in close communication with the United Kingdom and General de Gaulle. To their utter stupefaction, the Nazi judges witnessed these accused men and women—many of whom were clearly about to lose their lives—turn to one another with radiant joy on their faces. They now knew that their sacrifice had not been in vain.

The dignified and courageous bearing of the defendants impressed the tribunal and lent the trial an exemplary quality. The judges recognized the patriotism that had inspired these French-

---

*"Night and Fog." This appellation, invented by Hitler himself, designated prisoners judged so dangerous that they were to cut off from all contact with the outside world.

**People's Tribunal.

†Nazi youth organization.

The Night Will End

men. The public prosecutor, while conceding the virtue of their motive, was extremely severe. Against twenty-three of them he demanded the death penalty.

After he had presented his indictment and the lawyers had pleaded their cases, the defendants were granted the right to speak. Their declarations gave proof of their lofty spirit. First Tony Ricou rose and said, "Even now, at the very moment when you are demanding my head, I still have no hatred against Germany. Before the war I backed the idea of an entente, at least an economic entente, between France and Germany. But now my country is at war, and my attitude has changed accordingly. Was it not the great Schiller who said, 'Before even life itself comes honor'?"

Then André Noël spoke:

"I too harbor no hatred toward your country. It was again one of your own writers, Fichte, who told the youth of Germany during the Napoleonic occupation: 'Always preserve your dignity before the occupier and do not slacken your resistance.' We have simply followed his counsel."

Embarrassed, the judges gaped at one another.

The tribunal sentenced twenty-three of the prisoners to death—seventeen men and six women. The others received stiff prison terms.

Shut up again in their cells, shackled day and night, they now expected nothing but death. For three long months, hearing each morning the footfalls of the prison guards, they would think that at last the fatal hour had arrived.

On January 7, 1944, almost two years after their arrests, the male prisoners (with one exception) were taken to Cologne and decapitated with an ax. The sentence against the six women was commuted to life imprisonment. Four of them died during the deportation: Odile Kienlen, Hélène Vautrin, Gilberte de Marthay and Mariette Martin-le-Dieu. Only Elisabeth Dussauze and Jeanne Sivadon survived.

And so ended the great and tragic trial that came to be recognized as one of the noblest moments of the Resistance.

As for the traitor Devillers, he had already been tried by a Vichy military tribunal, condemned to death and shot at Fort

The Spirit of Revolt

Montluc only one day before Laval, newly promoted to power, was to demand his release from prison.*

As soon as I got back from my second meeting with Pucheu I decided to change my residence. I needed a new hideaway.

Before her arrest, Simone Gouyou had introduced me to a certain M. Roussillon, a Lyonnais businessman who had become one of our most active militants in the propaganda field. He now proposed that I stay in his country home, which he himself visited only when the weather was exceptionally fine. And so, one chilly February day, I found myself standing with two suitcases and my typewriter on the station platform at Villieu, a town in the Ain only a few miles from Lyons.

Roussillon's place was a big mansion set in a large garden. Its upkeep had been left to a caretaker who lived with his family in a little annex on the property. They had been told I was a professor on prolonged sick leave who had come to find some health-giving peace and quiet far from the hurly-burly of the city. As I'd become quite thin, the story was plausible. Naturally, the caretaker and his wife had been instructed to look after my diet, and they managed to feed me very well considering the austerity of those days.

As the caretaker's family was sure to notice the frequent visits of Jean-Guy Bernard and my secretary, as well as my habit of spending the entire day at the typewriter, I explained to them that I was writing a paper that required the help of several research assistants.

I felt much more comfortable in this house, where I was absolutely alone, than I had in Lyons. The city had become a very risky place, for there everything of importance took place in a small area between the Place Carnot and the Place de la Comédie, a district the police could easily put under close surveillance. Furthermore, the Service d'Ordre Légionnaire (S.O.L.),** now

*After the war we learned that Devillers was an ex-POW who had been freed by the Germans on the condition that he engage in espionage for them.

**Service d'Ordre Légionnaire: Legionary Service of Public Order, a right-wing veterans' organization created in 1942 by Joseph Darnand. It was dedicated to stamping out "democracy, the Jewish leprosy, and the Gaullist dissidents."

The Night Will End

in active collaboration with the police, was using its thugs as volunteer informers who would point out to the authorities any suspect goings-on.

Twice a week I would go into town for assignations or the regular sessions of our steering committee. The location of these meetings was routinely shifted about. I would never get off the train in Lyons itself but always in some small suburban station whence I would enter the city proper by streetcar.

I was to stay in this country hiding place for three months, sallying forth only for a brief trip to Lyons or to the provinces. I had no contact with the outside world besides that which my two friends brought me in the form of mail. Often they merely delivered oral requests, then left with the instructions, notes and articles that I had typed since their last visit. These security precautions contributed to my feeling of safety, but I was also glad that the house had so many exits.

Berty had also moved. Taking Mireille with her, she had rented a new apartment at 87, Quai Pierre-Scize, right on the Saône. Her time was now entirely her own, for her superiors in the Unemployment Office had told her in no uncertain terms that the fact that she held so much attraction for the police had made her continued performance of her duties dispensable. She had resigned without regrets.

"Henri, several of our comrades are still in prison, ill fed and ill clothed. Often their families too are subject to grave financial and mental strain. We can't simply abandon our fallen comrades on the field. We must do something to help them."

"Berty, you have a point. Every army has a medical corps that rescues the wounded and attends to them. We ought to have something analogous—but what?"

"Well, if we have enough money, we should create a specialized corps. Why don't we found a Social Service?"

A few days later I mentioned this project to "Max," for the two of us had been meeting regularly to hash out some budgetary problems. He agreed to ask London for the necessary funds. They arrived by the next parachute drop.

The Spirit of Revolt

Expanding in response to the persecution of our militants, the Social Service soon became the ministering angel of many of our imprisoned comrades and their families.

It was no mean task in 1942 and the years that followed to collect the foodstuffs our imprisoned comrades so sorely needed. We had to go prospecting in the countryside, usually by bicycle, to find peasants who would sell us eggs, butter, meat and other foodstuffs. Their prices were frequently quite steep. We also had to outwit the government inspectors appointed to crack down on blackmarketeers. As if the inherent danger of underground activity were not enough, we now ran the risk of being taken for speculators and starvers of the people.

The produce often had to be stocked in places ill suited for such a function. In Lyons, for example, two spinster antique dealers on the Rue Vaubecour turned the back of their shop into a transit warehouse whose odor often pricked the appetite of some browsing fancier of a Louis XIV chest or a Directoire chair! We were to visit the *demoiselles* Buisson very often in the coming months, for they performed many other services for us as well.

First we had to find out where a given comrade was interned, then visit his family to give them his food parcel. Sometimes we also had to provide social welfare to a household whose sole breadwinner had been captured. Yet the very knowledge that they had not been abandoned was a great solace to the prisoners and their families.

Thus, even inside the prison walls, a kind of purely humanitarian solidarity was cemented. Occasionally it blossomed into full-scale collusion with the prison authorities, enabling the Groupes Francs to organize jail breaks. Certain chaplains and prison guards quietly but efficiently aided us.

One of my major concerns was the belief held by the police that our ranks had been decimated and our leaders demoralized. It was up to us to prove them wrong with some kind of spectacular action. Yet the southern zone offered our Groupes Francs no properly military objectives (that is, until the German invasion in 1943). It was primarily against the collaboration, and its conscious or unconscious representatives, that we were struggling. Hence, in Montpellier, Jacques Renouvin began, with my blessing, to attack

The Night Will End

some of the more obviously pro-German newspapers and periodicals.

It was a simple operation. First the owner of a newsstand would receive a letter signed "Combat." It would explain that nothing forced him to display magazines like *Signal* (the wartime equivalent, as far as format is concerned, of the *Paris-Match* of today but whose staff was at Goebbels' beck and call). An appeal would be made to his patriotic sentiments. If this "friendly persuasion" went unheeded, a second letter would arrive, warning him that he was going to be "leaned on." If he remained equally deaf to this warning, his stand would be blown up. At this point a circular explaining his misfortune would be mailed to all the merchants in town. This procedure soon produced excellent results.

We also wished to prove our breadth to those who minimized it. In such cases we used the time-honored technique of the graffiti campaign. I distributed to our various regions a booklet of brief and incisive slogans whose quasiuniversal reproduction in chalk or paint proved our pervasiveness to the police. Our people in Montpellier outdid themselves by writing in immense black characters on the town aqueduct (which was seven or eight yards above the ground), "COMBAT PUNISHES TRAITORS."

An anti-Semitic film called *Le Juif Süss* also provoked frequent outbursts. These gave prudent cinema owners something to think about.

All records for mischief were broken on March 28, 1942. On that day the celebrated Berlin Philharmonic Society was scheduled to play in Lyons. Planque, Harmel and Fontoynont, Combat's principal operatives in the city, felt that such a concert was an intolerable provocation. Without any assistance from our national leadership they organized their own welcome party. They distributed throwaways calling for demonstrations on the Place des Terreaux and in front of the Salle Rameau. The text ended with the words, "The Berlin Bosch shall not play!" They were glued to the walls, deposited in letterboxes, even boldly showered into the streets. Naturally the police was alerted and began to guard the concert hall (thereby impeding us from setting explosive charges, as we had originally intended). On the appointed evening an ever denser crowd of Lyonnais congregated in the Place des Terreaux.

The Spirit of Revolt

The streetcar lines were halted, the police intervened, fights broke out, and many people were arrested. The following day this imposing demonstration was the talk of the town.

True, such activity can hardly be considered warfare, yet there were no military targets in the preoccupation days in the southern zone. Our demonstrations, with their invaluable proof of our existence, not only awakened the desire of many to follow our lead in opposing the collaboration but also satisfied our militants' craving for direct action.

About this time a newcomer appeared in the clandestine world. From Lyons and Saint-Etienne I received issues of a newspaper called *Franc-Tireur*. It didn't take me long to meet its boss. Jean-Guy Bernard, who had ferreted him out, introduced us one day in the Brasserie Thomassin in Lyons. His name was Jean-Pierre Lévy.

A tall, swarthy young man, he must have been between twenty-five and thirty years old. He greeted me warmly. His expression was frank, but his speech was impeded by a slight stutter. He had already brought out three issues of his newspaper, and he was beginning to organize—as we had already done—a resistance movement. So far, it had made its greatest impact in the Lyons area.

Combat was of course the elder of the two movements, a fact he recognized with remarkable candor. He was very surprised by what I told him about our organization. He had never suspected that our movement was already articulated into specialized services each with its own regional and departmental subsidiaries. We decided to keep in touch through Jean-Guy Bernard.

Since the big February raids I had been out of touch with the occupied zone. Were all the risks our northern comrades had taken, all their work, all the ordeals they had withstood to have ultimately been in vain? I wondered if we should try to repair the damages to the movement or just resign ourselves to the difficulty of simultaneously forging movements in both zones.

I discussed this quandary with Michel Brault ("Jérôme"), who had just arrived from Paris. Though I'd seen him quite recently I

The Night Will End

barely recognized him. His hair was cropped and dyed, and he was wearing glasses. His own network, he said, had been picked clean; the whole operation was a mere carcass now. It was a miracle that he himself had escaped the clutches of Mathilde Carré ("La Chatte"), a resister who had gone over to the Abwehr and informed on every single one of her ex-comrades.

Brault had decided to put himself at our disposal. Following the latest wave of arrests, he no longer had any contact with the British intelligence services, yet he wanted to continue the struggle. He urged me to abandon the idea of reconstructing our movement in the occupied zone. The distance, the communication problems and the difference in outlook between north and south all suggested that we should simply concentrate our efforts on the southern zone.

I too had come around to this viewpoint.

"Let's work together," I suggested. "Maybe we should devote some thought to the role you could play here."

"Yes, but I'm not much good for anything now. Don't forget, I'm quite a bit older than you . . . and by now I'm a nervous wreck as well. So many of my old friends have disappeared. I'm going to head down to the Midi for a few weeks' rest. I'll get in touch with you in a month or so."

It was true: Brault seemed greatly changed, and, considering our own afflictions, I had no difficulty in sympathizing with him. He left shortly to recuperate on the Côte d'Azur. When he returned, fully self-possessed, he replaced Jean Gemahling (who had been arrested the previous December) at the head of our intelligence arm. In 1943 Brault was to become the national leader of a new service called Maquis.

In the silence and isolation of Villieu I had plenty of time for reflection. After finishing my daily work, which consisted largely of typing instructions on that yellow notepaper which my correspondents had come to know so well, I would listen to my short-wave radio. I had some difficulty in getting the BBC, but how delighted I was each evening when, after long minutes of fiddling with the dial, I would finally hear the voice of the BBC spokesman for Free France, Maurice Schumann, saying, *"Ici Londres."* Then

The Spirit of Revolt

would come the call signal, struck upon a gong: *ta-ta-ta-tah!* Three shorts and a long: V for Victory.

Victory: Yes, I still believed in it. Yet we in France still seemed lost in a pitch-black night that would never end. The news was undeniably bad. In the Far East the Japanese were scoring victory after victory. In February the supposedly impregnable fortifications of Singapore had fallen along with their garrison of 80,000 troops. The Mikado's soldiers had occupied Java and landed in the Solomon Islands. In the Indian Ocean the Royal Navy had lost three major warships, one of them a carrier. The BBC stressed the American war effort, that enormous giant who was slowly girding himself for battle. The question was, would the giant arrive in time?

In Russia, Hitler's troops had indeed been halted by winter, but now it was spring again. As soon as the ground was dry they would resume their eastward march. How much longer could the Red Army hold out? It was a race against time. If the U.S.S.R. were to collapse, all the firepower of the Wehrmacht and the Luftwaffe would be brought to bear against the Channel coast and the Straits of Dover.

In the midst of this global warfare, what was the point of my antlike struggle here with my typewriter and my ream of paper? All our contacts, all our recruits—of whom so many had been mowed down like grass—all our voyages, all the earnest sessions of our steering committee, what real value did they have? And yet, however insignificant my work, what else could I do—give up? All during the bitter year of 1942 I was to ask myself these same disheartening questions. On more than one evening despair looked over my shoulder.

A messenger came to announce the arrival of Robert Soulage in Lyons. We arranged a rendezvous. I hadn't seen him since last June when I had invited him to join our ranks. As the reader may recall, he had wanted to experience our defeated France for himself. He had ended, as I had, by leaving the army. This act, along with his political opinions and his friendship with me, had caught the attention of the police, who had already interrogated him. Though drawn to resistance action, he wanted first to think

The Night Will End

over the deeper causes of the present conflict, the deeper objectives of the struggle he was soon to join. Soulage always thought long and hard before acting; now he wanted to go off by himself and come to some personal conclusions. He needed a precise conception of where he was going. He promised that as soon as he had found his bearings he would join me.

April 18: The news came like a thunderbolt. Laval, the biggest collaborator of them all, had been called back into power. The following day Marshal Pétain addressed the nation. His voice seemed even wearier than usual; one could sense his terrible fatigue. The speech was brief. It ended with the words: ". . . People of France, the new government will provide fresh reasons for faith and hope."
And then the "Marseillaise."

The Spirit of Revolt

THE SECRET ARMY

It so happened that the steering committee of Combat had arranged two weeks earlier for a meeting to be held in Clermont-Ferrand on the same April 19 on which Pétain delivered his speech.

We were all there. As usual, I summarized the movement's activities since our last meeting, but I was brief, for we were very apprehensive over Laval's return to power.

Though so far we had tried to get along with the Marshal, we now found ourselves in unanimous agreement that after today's speech such an accommodation was no longer admissable. From Vichy we had got wind of the withering pressure to which the German authorities had been subjecting the chief of state. Once again he had capitulated. No, he had done worse—he had delegated his powers to Laval! I proposed to devote *Combat*'s next editorial to this subject, for I was even more revolted by this turn of events than the rest of my colleagues, perhaps because I had always harbored a remote hope that one day the old man would repossess himself.

We also discussed the kind of May Day demonstrations we wanted. "Max" had planned to ask De Gaulle to deliver a May Day broadcast over the BBC, and of course we all col-

8

laborated on the new initiative. As soon as I returned to Lyons I instructed our regional chiefs to mobilize their men for the May Day demonstrations. May 1, 1942, was to be a landmark in the history of the Resistance.

I was alone again in Villieu, in the house of my friends the Roussillons. I could smell the first shy flowers of spring. Before the garden window, in a great flood of spring sunlight, I wrote an "open letter to Marshal Pétain," to appear in the forthcoming number of *Combat.* I think it was the only article I ever wrote in one sustained burst:

April 18, 1942: Having exploited to the full the cowardice and amorality of your servile cabinet ministers, Hitler ordered you to fire them. He wanted a new cabinet, one more firmly committed to the path of treason. You obeyed. To lead this band of traitors you chose the biggest traitor of them all, the very man you yourself had once kicked out of the government. He now avenged himself by taking your place. At this we rejoiced, for at last you had dispelled the ambiguity which you had earlier so willingly created. And yet there were still men and women who believed in you. Your white hair and your star-studded sleeves inspired their trust. Your propaganda led them to believe that you were cunningly deceiving Hitler.

Yet the traitor of Bordeaux, whom you yourself have appointed, not only appeases Hitler in every possible way but also banishes every possible doubt as to the government's intentions.

The policy of détente with Germany, he says, must be loyally and unambiguously supported. A lasting agreement can only be based on sincere words and actions.

In a word, you have made France Germany's ally. Yet you had a real choice: either to knuckle under or to resign. It was your duty to step down, to leave to others the business of betraying our homeland. But you preferred to stay on, no longer even half free but now in total bondage to your role as protector and abettor of treason.

At last, all is clear. The myth of Pétain is dead. Your stars have burned themselves out. . . .

It was you who once told us: "Follow me; have faith in eternal France."

Yes, we have kept our faith in our homeland. For her we are willing to

The Secret Army

sacrifice our freedom and, if need be, to lay down our lives. But we shall not follow you.

The entire French people, always implacably opposed to Laval, is now implacably opposed to you. It is you yourself who have wished it so!

Two days later, when Jean-Guy came to pick up my communications, I showed him my declaration. After reading it he said simply, "Now *that* gives me real pleasure."

His expression was worth a thousand words.

Our steering committee's rejection of Pétain entailed grave problems. Despite everything, the old Marshal still had considerable prestige.

Even at this late date we were running a serious risk of alienating many of our colleagues. Moreover, we were now obliged to sever all contact with the special services of the Armistice Army. Yet these were minor matters. Pétain had been right about one thing: "Life is never neutral," he had said. "One must boldly pick sides."

My mail did not consist exclusively of Combat-related letters. Chilina wrote me often and sometimes even sent me some parcels from Corsica. They pleased me enormously, although I was hardly ill nourished. They often contained dried figs stuffed with nuts, sometimes jars of preserves and always two or three packs of cigarettes.

What luck she'd had to fall ill and leave Paris! It was only later that she realized just how lucky she'd really been. The Gestapo was now relentlessly telephoning her apartment at 131, Rue de Vaugirard. Obviously she too had been on Devillers' list. In effect, her tuberculosis had saved her.

She wrote me that she'd left Sancellemoz for a chalet in Aillères. She'd fled not only the atmosphere of the sanitarium but also a frightening operation proposed by one of its resident surgeons. She was thrilled by her new surroundings. Her window gave on a great fir tree that stood out against the towering range of Mont-Blanc. From her letters I could sense her anxiety, her worry that she might never recover. In early May she wrote me how she dreaded the thought that her life might slowly be snuffed out far from those

The Night Will End

she loved. She felt that she must serve some purpose, and, since she was physically incapable of leading our kind of existence, she requested that we designate, in Vichy or elsewhere, an important enemy whom she would undertake to assassinate. She was at our orders, she said. Touched by her sad words, I replied, "Take care of yourself, get well; then we'll talk about it."

Night fell. How long had I been here in this house? I added up the days. Why, almost three months! I had enjoyed perfect working conditions, and there wasn't the slightest hint of danger. Nonetheless, I had to leave. It was a basic security precaution.

My contacts with D'Astier had not improved our relationship. First, as the reader may recall, I'd been shocked by the subtitle of his newspaper (*Organe du Directoire des Forces de Libération Françaises*), for it implied that somehow it represented the entire Resistance. Next he'd ducked out on Menthon and myself at that Grenoble meeting where we'd created Combat. Now, in a new move, he was pretending to represent the trade-unions, a claim that several of their leaders had hotly contested. His movement, he insisted, also represented the Socialists, but by now the party organ, *Le Populaire,* had reappeared in an underground version and the Socialists seemed ready to reunite. Moreover, none of our comrades had ever found a trace of Libération outside Lyons and the Côte d'Azur. Above all, D'Astier and I had absolutely antipodal temperaments.

I never fully believed a word he said. Perhaps he was one of those men who unconsciously mingle fact and fiction. His disarming smile—which he so patently exploited—I now found phony and embarrassing. Moreover, I knew from several sources that he was continuing to spread unpleasant rumors about my talks with Pucheu. What finally broke my patience was a scribbled note from Bourdet in Cannes telling me that D'Astier, from whom I had never concealed anything and whom I had included in so many of my projects, had left for England in a submarine under the sponsorship of "Olive," an agent for the S.O.E. (Special Operations Executive*). D'Astier had never breathed a word to me about

*The British espionage service operating on the Continent.

The Secret Army

it! But the worst was yet to come. Here's what "Olive" had told Bourdet:

"D'Astier introduced himself to me as the representative of all the resistance movements in the unoccupied zone. For this reason I thought that he should go to England, and I arranged for his departure. After he had already left, a number of incidents, including my conversation with you, led me to realize that his declaration had been false. I immediately telephoned the S.O.E., telling them—and these were my very words—that 'D'Astier represents only the group called Libération, which, from the military standpoint, is of minimal importance. The only militarily important movement in the unoccupied zone is Combat, whose chief is Frenay.' It is my deepest wish to make up for the harm I've done your movement in having sent D'Astier to London."

I was terribly irked to realize that my already diminished trust in D'Astier was still unwarrantably large. Well, now I knew all I needed to know—at least, so I thought. I later discovered that Jean Moulin himself had been aware of D'Astier's departure and that he had even entrusted him with a message to London.* Moulin too had told me nothing.

As planned, we directed all our regional groups to throw their weight behind the May Day demonstrations in the free zone. Libération and Franc-Tireur did the same. Thousands of announcements and inserts were run off on *Combat's* presses. They called on the citizens of every municipality to assemble at an appointed place and demonstrate against the occupation, against Vichy and for the restoration of public liberties.

It wasn't so easy to get the French people to come out into the streets. Though De Gaulle had spoken, urging his countrymen to demonstrate, I wondered how many people had actually heard him. If we were to fail, our failure would both weaken our militants' morale and be trumpeted as a great victory by Vichy. And so, as I headed toward Lyons that first day of May 1942, my curiosity was not unmixed with deep misgivings.

The demonstration was to be held on the Place Carnot, the

*Colonel Passy, *10 Duke Street* , page 107.

The Night Will End

location of the statue of the Republic. I walked there along the Rue Duhamel where I had spent so many of my childhood years. I was not alone; the street, usually so placid, was now crowded with people. Many men and women, mostly in groups, were heading in the same direction as I, despite the fact that I was early. I walked around the Place Carnot. From every access—the Rue Auguste-Comte, the Rue de la Charité, the Cours de Verdun—numerous other "strollers" were converging.

By the appointed time the plaza was crammed with people. The crowd spilled over onto the Cours de Verdun, invaded the lawns, mounted the benches and even clambered onto the fountains surrounding the statue and onto its pedestal. The police were out in force, and though they didn't try to prevent anyone from joining the demonstration, they did oblige the crowd to keep circulating. Then the cry "Death to Laval!" rang out, accompanied by a rhythmical stamping of feet. Two women beside me began to shout "*Vive de Gaulle!*" but their cry found no echo. Then, from beside the statue, arose a timid "Marseillaise" which, gaining force, soon billowed forth until, at the line "*Aux armes, citoyens,*" the whole crowd was singing in unison. A great war song had arisen from the multitude! Our wager was won!

It was impossible to estimate the size of the crowd, but it must have been between 50,000 and 100,000 strong.

In the following days reports from our regional chiefs came in saying that the demonstrations had been a huge success everywhere. "Max" had been right to suggest them. It was a bitter day for Vichy.

Attempts on the lives of Wehrmacht officers were multiplying, not only in Paris but in several cities in the occupied zone as well. Sinister black-and-red posters covered the walls. "*Bekanntmachung,*" they said ("Notice"), followed by an announcement of the assassination committed and the names of the hostages shot in reprisal.

We were familiar with the Communist belief that, since war inevitably involves the death of innocent persons, the execution of hostages had an essentially positive effect in that it aroused the hatred of the people against the occupier. They insisted that ten

The Secret Army

volunteers would rise up to replace every hostage who was shot.

Though I understood this viewpoint, I could not share it. That war kills innocent people is of course only too true. But that I, of my own free will, should sign what would in effect be somebody else's death warrant, for the sole reason that it might instill a greater combative ardor in the people (and this without any serious damage to the enemy)—no, I could never have consented to such a policy!

Between the Communists who held this "utilitarian" point of view and those who thought as I did, the quarrel was of a philosophical or religious nature and hence without any practical solution. And yet their cold determination compelled my respect, for it never flinched, even when the hostages themselves were party members. A good example was the case, announced over the official radio and in the press, of the execution of twenty-seven hostages in the prison of Châteaubriant. Confronted with the courageous death of these men, philosophical niceties hardly seemed important. In the May issue of *Combat* we wrote:

. . . twenty-seven hostages were chosen by the subprefect from among the Communists interned in Châteaubriant . . . among them was one child of seventeen, Guy Moquet . . .

As they left the prison camp, their interned comrades sang the "Marseillaise" and the "Internationale." . . . They died as Frenchmen struggling for the liberation of their homeland, struggling for their ideals. . . .

Vichy is selling our French brothers to the enemy. These shameful crimes shall one day be avenged! . . .

A few days after that unforgettable May 1, I left Villieu. Somebody had found me a lodging among friends who lived not far from Mâcon, M. and Mme. André de Roujoux.

A tall, blond fellow of the rotund Celtic type, he had joined us about a year earlier. He spoke volubly, stressing his words with gestures. He was a man of action, a prompt decision-maker, a true force of nature. His wife was a quiet and cultivated a musician who effaced herself behind her often tempestuous husband.

André, like many others in the Mâcon region, was an amateur

The Night Will End

winemaker. Every once in a while, plunger in hand, he would take me down into his wine cellar to see how his *petit Mâcon blanc* was doing.

They lived in the old gatekeeper's cottage on the large family estate, which had been inherited by André's brother, Guillaume. The cottage was surrounded by a kitchen-garden devoted primarily to strawberries. When the season came, my color-blindness did not prevent me from doing a bit of picking. They ate well, the Roujoux. I still remember their fresh garden salads, dressed in the local Mâcon style with white wine and cream.

I had a large, bright room on the first floor, with ample space for my files, my faithful typewriter and my habit of pacing up and down while thinking.

As in Villieu, only Jean-Guy and my secretary had direct access to me. To avoid having to go too often to Lyons, I had the address of four persons, two in Mâcon, one in Saint-Laurent (a town on the far side of the Saône) and another in Villefranche. I was thus able to farm my appointments out among these four locations. To this list I later added a fifth address, that of Cerf-"Ferrière," in Beaujeu, where two or three meetings were later held.

The biggest attraction of my new lair was not so much its greater safety as the opportunity it afforded me to think things over in peace, far from the apprehension in which I had hitherto been living. Here, in this peaceful family atmosphere, I was at last able to find my bearings, to look back over two years of progress.

Since July 1940 my thinking had undergone an almost imperceptible evolution. In this spring of 1942 I recalled with astonishment the final sentence of my first manifesto: "May Marshal Pétain live long enough to see the day when success crowns our efforts."

At that time there had been no inherent contradiction between joining the struggle against Nazism and retaining one's faith in Pétain. De Gaulle was a still little-known officer in London whose true character had been disfigured beyond recognition by Vichy's propaganda.

So much had happened since then! On leaving the army I'd had a desire to put a distance myself and Vichy, for my doubts were growing stronger by the hour. Where was France headed? Both in

The Secret Army

London and on the esplanade before the Hotel du Parc in Vichy, French troops dressed in identical uniforms saluted the same flag and sang the same "Marseillaise." Which group truly represented my country? No Frenchman since the Revolution had been forced to ask himself such a question. Aside from the obvious symbols— the tricolor, the national anthem—it was necessary to search carefully and often painfully for our abandoned national ideals. I found my conscience confronted by a profound political question, a question that I could answer only by consulting those eternal values which our country should exemplify on pain of spiritual self-negation.

As the Marshal's government gradually yielded to Germany's demands, as it began to enforce various Nazi-inspired measures, the gulf between it and us slowly but steadily widened.

Before the hearth in the Roujoux' sitting room—for the evenings were still rather raw—I outlined to André and his brother Guillaume the successive phases of my own growing disillusionment: the collaboration that Hitler and Pétain had initiated in Montoire, the Reich's annexation of Alsace-Lorraine and its subsequent massive and brutal expulsion of much of the local population, the transformation of the north and the Pas-de-Calais into a prohibited zone—obviously a prelude to more annexations—the agreement ceding several of our Indochinese air bases to the Japanese, the anti-Jewish edicts, the handing over of our Syrian airbases to the Luftwaffe and, finally, to top off the whole infamous business, the return to power of Pierre Laval, the pawn of the Germans and the man whom Otto Abetz had rescued from jail with armored cars in 1940. It was this man who today had received plenipotentiary power from the Marshal!

"Our struggle against this regime," I told my two friends, "is now as intimately connected with domestic affairs as it is with foreign policy. This is an inescapable consequence of what's happening in Vichy territory. Henceforth the anti-Vichy struggle will be inseparable from the struggle against Hitler's Germany. Moreover, opposition to a regime necessarily implies the desire to oust it and replace it with another. Our action, whether we like it or not, is political as well as patriotic."

The Night Will End

"There's one hitch, though," said André. "If our action is political we may well end right back where we started—with the Third Republic. If that's our ultimate goal, I'd prefer to sit the whole battle out. I've got a wife and kids, and I'd rather remain a good daddy who looks after his family and his little wines than go running off to reinstall the same old buzzards who got us into this pile of shit in the first place."

He was saying in his salty language what each of us felt in his heart. In July 1940 the Third Republic had simply disappeared in a morass of public indifference, and it must be frankly admitted that the trial of the prewar politicians in Riom had awakened little sympathy in the public, which was only too happy to find a scapegoat on which to vent its frustration.

In the autumn of 1940 Paul Reynaud, Edouard Daladier and Léon Blum, all ex-presidents of the council of ministers, as well as Vincent Auriole and Georges Mandel, former ministers, and Léon Jouhaux, the ex-secretary-general of the C.G.T., had been put under house arrest and then transported to a fortified place of detention. The indictment against them had been drafted in such a way that one could not tell whether the kangaroo court was trying them solely for criminal negligence in France's defeat or for other alleged acts as well.

What infuriated me at the time was that the prosecution was preparing its brief under German pressure. The occupation authorities were obviously trying not so much to victimize certain individuals as to exculpate Hitler and to blame France for the war itself.

As for the political parties that supposedly represented the various blocs within the nation, they seemed to have evaporated after the defeat. Yet it was they, not unknown people like us, who should have initiated the Resistance. Unable to foresee the war, they had been willing to accept the defeat. They had disqualified themselves. Only the Communist Party was still alive, though it was more felt than seen and, of course, still unconditionally loyal to the U.S.S.R. Yesterday the Communists had been against the Resistance; today they were part of it; tomorrow where would they stand?

The Secret Army

"You see, André, our days of innocence are over. It's our duty to decide the kind of France we want and to fight for it."

By "we" I meant all our comrades, whether or not they'd been involved in politics before the war. Our defeat had been an occasion for them to re-examine their hearts. With their willingness to risk their freedom and possibly their lives, they had gained a chance to translate their new beliefs into action. Such a willingness to take risks is a true test of fire—perhaps the only one.

Some of my comrades had already formed more mature political ideas than I, perhaps because their political consciousness was more advanced than my own. For example, Pierre-Henri Teitgen and René Courtin, the leaders of Combat in the Montpellier region, had already set up a study group on postwar problems that corresponded with Emmanuel Mounier and his Christian Socialist circle.

Parallel to this growth in political consciousness, which was soon reflected in our press, was a gradual tilt toward De Gaulle and the Free French. Early in the spring of 1941 I had begun to feel the need of formal ties with them. My reasons had not been political. I wanted simply to avoid the squandering of our energies, the splintering of the Resistance into rival groups and subgroups. I felt that De Gaulle carried a standard around which we could all rally. Remote from our quarrels, located in the capital of the fighting free world, struggling like ourselves for victory and liberation and willing to speak in our name and in the name of those who had no voice, only De Gaulle could be the symbol and the spokesman for the Resistance.

Yet, if events had indeed politicized us, then part of the coordination of London and the Resistance would be a frank exchange of views. Since cooperation with London was vital, "Max's" role became ever more precious. Only through his coordinating effort could we forge the unity required by the struggle for victory and a new national life.

As I climbed the stairs to my room, suddenly D'Astier popped into my mind. He must be in London now—lucky fellow! Why had he concealed his departure from me? Perhaps he'd been afraid that I might want to accompany him. In that case, *he had wanted to be in London alone.* But why?

The Night Will End

Since Simone Gouyou's arrest, Jean-Guy Bernard had been in charge of all the communication lines between the movement's domestic groups and myself. This job was soon taken over by Dominique Pagel, a young student at the University of Lyons who turned out to be a precious co-worker.

One day in late May 1942 Jean-Guy arrived at my door drawn-faced and minus his usual bright-eyed expression.

"What's the matter, Jean-Guy? Some new disaster?"

"Yes." He was staring at the floor. "'Victoire's' been arrested."

"Victoire" was the pseudonym Berty had assumed on moving into her new apartment on the Quai Pierre-Scize.

"Berty arrested! How? When?"

He told me the story. Later, Mireille, who'd been with her mother when it happened, filled me in on the details.

Early in the afternoon there was a knock on their door. "Police! Open up!" Berty glanced out the window: Three black Citroëns were parked in the street, and several men were stationed on the sidewalk before the entrance to the building. Calmly Berty walked to the door, on which the police were now knocking impatiently, and drew the latch. Turning the key in the lock, she whispered to Mireille, "Quick—my papers!"

Rapidly they lighted a fire in the fireplace, then chucked the crumpled papers into the flames.

From behind the door the blows and cries redoubled. Then there was a long silence. They had gone to fetch their locksmith. Soon there was a sound of groping in the keyhole. After some time the door flew open and five men rushed into the room, blind with rage when they saw the embers smoldering in the fireplace.

"Madame, what have you been up to there?"

"Look for yourself. I was burning some papers that were none of your business."

They set about systematically and exhaustively searching the entire apartment, including the mattress stuffing and the down of the bed bolsters. The search lasted three hours, but, despite the fact that there were ten policemen, including those downstairs, they found not a shred of evidence. They questioned Berty harshly, but she haughtily replied that she had nothing to say.

"Just do your job. I certainly prefer mine to yours."

The Secret Army

Berty and her daughter were confined to separate rooms, where they spent a sleepless night under a police guard. The following day they were conducted to the central police station on the Place Bellecour. Though Mireille was released, Berty was immediately committed to detention in Vals-les-Bains in the Ardèche. Her internment was to be long and hard.

Our organization was expanding methodically, with results that varied according to the region. I was furiously at work on our nationwide services. For the most part this work consisted in finding the most qualified man for the job of national director of the service in question, in providing him with the wherewithal to carry out his job and in making sure that he organized each region and each department with painstaking care right down to the basic six-man cells.

It was unnecessary for me to improvise new structures. We had already taken on the characteristic structural articulation of any sizable administration with a large-scale interpenetration of vertical and horizontal channels. For example, though a regional Secret Army or Social Service chief was answerable to his national superior, his actions also had to be coordinated with those of the other services in the region.

The Secret Army of the Lyons region (R.1) was directed by Captain Billon. A fighter pilot, he was tiny as a jockey. His fiery look hinted at his passionate temperament. Under the direction of Marcel Peck, his regional chief, he was in several months to become the chief of the Secret Army, which now regrouped the united paramilitary units of all the original resistance movements of which Combat was composed. (He was arrested before the end of 1942 but managed to escape. Recaptured after the German invasion of the free zone, he was incarcerated by the Gestapo in Vichy and fiendishly tortured. Feeling his physical resistance give way and unwilling to betray our secrets, he hanged himself in his cell.)

In the Toulouse region the Secret Army was developing along two parallel lines. One of these two groups was directed by a young man of twenty-two named Francis Crémieux. The son of Benjamin Crémieux, the writer who had introduced Pirandello to the

The Night Will End

French reading public, he was bursting with hope and ardor, though in constant danger on account of his marked Semitic features. The other group was directed by Colonel Ganeval, whom I had already known in 1928 in the Army of the Rhine, where we served in the same regiment. After the war he was to become head of the French military mission to Berlin, later chief of the Maison Militaire of President René Coty. He agreed to help us out in Toulouse, where he provided the Secret Army with several crack units, though at the same time adopting an attitude of reserved caution toward Francis Crémieux, whose youthful zeal rather worried him.

Our intelligence was also making great strides forward. Jean Gemahling, who had been arrested in November of the previous year, had recently been released on parole. Reinstalled in Marseilles, where he now disposed of considerable resources, he was greatly assisted by Maurice Chevance. Thanks to Maurice, his service gradually expanded in the political as well as in the military field. London was highly to appreciate this fact later on.

I myself was deeply involved in propaganda. Though a clandestine sheet cannot be compared with a proper newspaper, *Combat* had achieved a certain structural unity. Its editor-in-chief was Cerf-"Ferrière," its editorial secretary Jacqueline Bernard. Georges Bidault, Pierre Scize and Georges Oudard were regular contributors. I usually wrote the editorials, though Bidault also wrote a few. Later Claude Bourdet took over. Thanks to the funds that "Max" procured for us, the May 1942 issue reached 40,000 copies. I wanted to push this figure up to 60,000.

I asked Jacques Renouvin to visit me in Lyons, for I wanted to know exactly how his Groupes Francs were coming along. I awaited him in the apartment of the Buisson sisters, the two old spinsters whose antique shop was used as a food warehouse by our Social Service.

What delightful old ladies they were! These tiny, delicate-limbed women, who had never parted from each other since birth, attended to each other with the utmost consideration. In their nineteenth-century dress, they had the kind of profile one finds on old cameo brooches. Their voices were as diminutive as their

The Secret Army

173

Roi, too! We've been in some pretty wild brawls together, but we've had some pretty good times too. His name is Pierre de Bénouville. He tried to make it to England but got caught. As soon as he was out of the clink he joined up with the English secret service. He didn't even know about Combat. One day I'll bring him around. You'll see he's a real sonofabitch. I know you two will really hit it off."

"Joseph" was smiling and his eyes were twinkling as he departed. No doubt he was dreaming of his "carnival," that mysterious event I'd soon be hearing about.

In June 1942 a fellow called Jacques Lecompte-Boinet turned up, one of the survivors of the Paris raids. He'd been trying to pick up the pieces of our movement in the northern zone and had come to Lyons to get further instructions. We agreed that it was now very difficult to maintain a unified command for both zones. I helped him out with a little money so that he could continue to take inventory of the groups that had escaped the Gestapo's clutches. We agreed that once he had finished this task we would reconsider the future of our movement in the northern zone. He returned in September, right before my departure for London. We agreed that henceforth he would enjoy total autonomy. The upshot was a new movement called C.D.L.R. (Ceux de la Résistance*).

In the half year since January, Combat had made enormous progress, largely as a result of the financial resources "Max" placed at our disposal each month. Jean-Guy Bernard picked up the money right in the street (though never twice in the same place). There would be a brief conversation, then an envelope would change hands. The money was farmed out according to my instructions. I kept only 5,000 francs for myself. Though the needs of our various services were strictly calculated, I often found myself involved in highly trying "budgetary arbitrations."

In January 1942 Moulin had given me 250,000 francs (the equivalent of about 72,000 of our francs today). In February 1943

*Ceux de la Résistance: "Those of the Resistance."

The Night Will End

176

Combat was to receive no less than 5 million francs (or about 1,500,000 of today's francs). Between these two dates our resources, and our expenditures, had irregularly but steadily mounted.

Our strength had of course also grown. By now experience had taught me that working responsibility for a regional command post could be effectively assumed only by a man or woman who was entirely devoted to it—that is, who had left his or her job and/or family to become a regular operative. Those who, having been arrested and released, wished to continue the struggle were obligated to become full-time cadres. Hence the membership of Combat continued to snowball.

Our liaison with England was an outstanding problem. One parachute drop had taken place, in the Midi, not far from Avignon. Here an Alsatian refugee, the Abbé Krebs, had found "Max" a suitable site and reliable men. But one parachute drop was hardly enough.

"Max" came by to see me and we discussed these problems at some length in a little Mâcon bistro. We agreed that there were two possible solutions: either to let each individual movement find its own sites for its own parachute drops or to create an autonomous air-lift service for the entire Resistance under "Max's" own direction. In either case, officers trained in England would have to serve as advisers, for the sites would have to conform with the strict R.A.F. norms.

We preferred the second solution. It seemed more rational and economical. I proposed a name for the new service: the S.O.A.M. (Service des Opérations Aériennes et Maritimes). It was to be responsible for all parachute drops of men and material, as well as for the departure of personnel by air or sea.

Of course we still had to insure that the S.O.A.M. and the various movements would function smoothly together. I asked "Max" to give me a memorandum establishing the precise functions of the new service and its exact relationship to us. It was to be passed out to "Max's" officers and to our own regional chiefs.

In the absence of D'Astier, the three movements' negotiations for fusion, or at least better coordination, were dragging badly.

The Secret Army

However, regular meetings were held between the representatives of the three movements and "Max." We limited ourselves to trying to arrive at a better understanding of our major problems. It was during one of these meetings that "Max" announced his intention of founding a new body, which, he believed, would be of great service not only to De Gaulle's but also to our own newspapers. It would serve as a clearinghouse for all information of a political, economic and social bearing, to the exclusion of military intelligence. It would not only classify this information but also work it up to coherent articles. It would be a press agency serving London and the resistance movements.

At that time I had not yet realized that the creation of such a service was a prearranged part of "Max's" mission, nor that our own intelligence and propaganda services were in fact already fulfilling this role. I saw it only as further progress toward unity and rationalization. For that reason I approved the creation of the new service, which we dubbed the B.I.P. (Bureau d'Information et de Presse). Georges Bidault, soon assisted by a large team of journalists, directed it. He had his own budget and was directly answerable to "Max."

In much the same way, Jean Moulin created the C.G.E. (Comité Général d'Etudes), whose members had the task of trying to find a solution for the principal problems of the liberated France of the future. This committee was composed of six men: François de Menthon, Pierre-Henri Teitgen and René Courtin, all from Combat; Paul Bastid, an ex-Radical Socialist deputy; Alexandre Parodi, an ex-member of the Council of State; and Robert Lacoste, an ex-official in the Ministry of Finance. The B.I.P., largely by relying on outside help, was able to continue its important work in the political and juridical fields right up to the Liberation.

In June 1942 the news was particularly depressing. Marshal Rommel's Africa Corps had taken several key positions from Britain's Eighth Army. The BBC praised the valor of the Free French troops under General Koenig* at Bir Hakeim, but the sad

*General Koenig: commander of the 1st Free French Brigade Group attached to the British Eighth Army in North Africa.

The Night Will End

truth was that the Allies were in full retreat. Twenty-five thousand British troops had been forced to capitulate at Mersa-Matrouh, and the way to Suez was now open to the enemy. In Russia, German troops had invaded the Crimea and occupied Sebastopol. In the Far East, the Japanese had managed a successful landing in the Aleutian Islands, thereby threatening American territory from the north. It had taken them only a few weeks to conquer Burma.

In France, too, German pressure had become more intense. The Jews in the occupied zone were now forced to wear yellow stars. Obviously this was only a prelude to more vicious persecutions.

Then Laval addressed the nation. That evening I listed to his radio speech in the Roujoux' sitting room. Wishing to sound especially persuasive, the chief of state had adopted a solemn tone:

. . . A new Europe will inevitably arise from this war. . . . To build this Europe, Germany must make enormous sacrifices.

She cannot be thrifty with the blood of her youth. . . . I welcome Germany's victory, because only such a victory can save the world from being conquered by Bolshevism. . . . Germany has an urgent need for labor. . . . A new hope has arisen for our prisoners. . . . Their relief [relève] has begun. . . . Workers of France! In exchange for the liberation of our prisoners, you must go and work in Germany. . . . You must heed my appeal, so that France may take her rightful place in the new Europe. . . .

My countrymen! A great soldier whose life is an example of sacrifice and discipline presides over the destiny of our homeland. I address you tonight in his name. . . .

I had great difficulty in listening to this speech right to the end. I was not only angry; I was also afraid. Laval's appeal to the nation was diabolically clever. One million, eight hundred thousand Frenchmen were prisoners in Germany. Their families probably hoped that Laval's speech would indeed be heeded, that our workers would flood across the Rhine to share the burden of war and defeat with their brothers in the POW camps. The "relief" labor service in Germany could even be construed as a national duty. The fear of Bolshevism was also very real, as Laval knew only

The Secret Army

too well, and his call for European unity against Communism had doubtless found an echo.

What could we in Combat do to stop French workers, already threatened by serious unemployment, from going to Germany to serve in her war machine? Our only weapon was our press and the slogans our militants were spreading in town and country. I worked late into the night on two directives, one for our regional chiefs, the other for *Combat*'s editorial board.

The very next issue of *Combat* vitriolically attacked the slave merchant who had "welcomed" Hitler's victory. The article appeared under the title "Not One Man for Germany!"

Put the unemployed to work in your fields, your gardens, your houses.

Every worker who remains in France is one less prisoner in German hands.

Every patriot must strive to create work.

A country that wants to live in freedom and greatness must be prepared to fight for its liberation.

Frenchmen! Frenchwomen!

With us, against misery and slavery—	fight!
for your daily bread—	fight!
against pillage and oppression—	fight!
for your freedom and your children's freedom—	fight!
for Liberation, for Victory—	fight!
for France—	fight!

This issue came out in 80,000 copies.

The Night Will End

In Marseilles, August 1940. (Author's Collection)
Berty Albrecht, head of Combat's Social Service. (Author's Collection)

JOURNAL HEBDOMADAIRE   **7 AOUT 1941**   Tirage de zone libre

LES PETITES AILES

À lire attentivement.
A faire circuler prudemment.

«Vivre dans la défaite c'est mourir tous les jours»
Napoléon 1er

Malgré les nombreux appels que nous avons faits à notre public, malgré les appuis que nous avons déjà reçus, la situation financière des Petites Ailes l'empêche de continuer à paraître. — Nous nous efforcerons de maintenir le contact avec nos lecteurs par des feuilles dactylographiées. Nous supplions ceux qui ne nous lirons plus de poursuivre notre combat, la Libération du Pays.

COMMENTAIRES & CITATIONS

Pourquoi la France, seule parmi les pays vaincus a-t'elle été sollicitée de collaborer avec l'Allemagne

On a beaucoup parlé de la "collaboration", on en parle toujours, on en parlera encore. C'est elle qui divise la France en deux clans: celui des "collaborationnistes" et celui des "non collaborationnistes".

Cette politique amorcée par Mr. Pierre Laval, subit une éclipse entre le 13 Décembre et le mois de Février, date à laquelle l'Amiral de la Flotte Darlan se vit confier, outre le Portefeuille de la Marine, ceux de l'Intérieur et des Affaires Étrangères.

En ce qui concerne la France, Hitler s'est donc trouvé non pas face à un pays livré sans contrôle à sa domination, mais face à un pays qui s'était donné un Chef vénéré à qui le peuple français vouait une profonde et respectueuse affection. Seule sa haute personnalité était garante dans ces heures troubles du maintien des liens entre la France et son Empire.

Le Führer eut-il voulu obtenir de la France ce qu'il obtenait par la contrainte des autres pays sans avoir au

---

Maurice Chevance, coordinator of Combat's military arm. (Photo Christian Boyer, Jours de France)

Dr. Marcel Recordier, Combat's first militant. (Author's Collection)

Our first underground newspaper. (Author's Collection)

The Chamber of Deputies: "Germany victorious on all fronts." (ERL Archives)
Jacques Dhont, one of the top Resistance men in Toulouse. (Photo Harcourt)

Jean-Guy Bernard, Combat's staff secretary. (Author's Collection)
Jean Gemahling, head of Combat's intelligence service. (Author's Collection)

Claude Bourdet, director of the N.A.P. (Infiltration of Public Administrations). (Author's Collection)

Jacqueline Bernard, one of Combat's top propaganda specialists, with Marcel Peck, Combat's chief in Lyons. (Author's Collection)

JOURNAL INDÉPENDANT   Nº 11   le 15 Septembre 1941

VÉRITÉS

« Je hais les mensonges qui vous ont tant fait de mal. »   Philippe PÉTAIN

VOTRE OPINION ET LA NOTRE

COMMENT "ILS" FONT L'HISTOIRE

"L'histoire se chargera de refaire ce livre".
(Hitler parlant de Mein Kampf)

Il faut que chaque Français sache ce que pense de la continuité française tout jeune allemand éduqué par les nazis. Car l'éducation hitlérienne ne prêche pas seulement l'orgueil de la race germanique et le mépris d'une France "abâtardie et négrifiée". Elle fausse systématiquement le passé pour justifier des revendications territoriales, dont la plupart des Français n'ont aucune idée.

Aussitôt au pouvoir, les chefs hitlériens travaillèrent fiévreusement au "redressement" des perspectives historiques. Dans ce domaine, comme dans beaucoup d'autres, ils dépassèrent de loin, en rigueur, en cynisme et en habileté, les chefs bolchevistes. On n'exécuta pas les historiens bourgeois, m............... On ne chassa pas tous les n............................", mais on leur impo........................storique.

Ma............................ leurs
élève..............................
tr....................

de sa fraîche puissance de nouveau-riche, se cherchait une glorieuse galerie d'ancêtres. Mais le Troisième Reich, en violentant l'histoire, a donné le jour à des monstres bien plus redoutables. Des monstres déguisés en agneaux, en chevaliers du droit, en envoyés de Dieu!

Sachez donc ce qu'on lit dans les récents manuels des écoles allemandes. Voici quelques extraits cueillis au hasard : "La civilisation germanique est la plus ancienne du monde.. La culture grecque elle-même doit sa naissance aux races venues du Nord.. Ceux que le monde romain et chrétien a appelés les Barbares furent en réalité les rénovateurs et les libérateurs... Malheureusement ces barbares se laissèrent abâtardir par la doctrine chrétienne... Les grandes invasions ne sont pas venues à bout de cette horde d'esclaves... Enfin Hitler est venu, qui nous enseigna la pureté et la dureté. Grâce à lui, le peuple allemand, conscient de ses origines, ignorera désormais les hésitations et les demi-mesures... Il ne se laissera plus berner par un Luther ou un Richelieu. Il ne tolérera plus que les Welches lui impose un autre Diktat comme celui de Westphalie ou celui de Versailles!.. La France, notre éternelle ennemie, n'a eu jusqu'ici raison du grand Reich que par la ruse et la fourberie, en s'alliant successivement à tous ceux qui haïssent la lumière et la vertu.. Mais nos justes aspirations renverseront irrésistiblement ces misérables digues..."

Simples phrases creuses, direz-vous, sans vous rendre compte peut-être que ce lyrisme vague, qui plaît à la jeunesse allemande, cache des appétits féroces et précis. Prenons quelques exemples qui nous intéressent. Que dites-

---

"In the reign of the Big Lie truths must be told." (Author's Collection)
The author wearing a beard and glasses to evade detection. (Author's Collection)

Georges Bidault, noted resister and later General de Gaulle's Foreign Minister. (ERL Archives)

Pierre-Henri Teitgen, Combat's chief in Montpellier. (Photo Star)

Alfred Coste-Floret, Combat's chief in Clermont-Ferrand. (Photo J. Stara)

Francois de Menthon, founder of Liberté. (Photo OFIC)

AOUT 1942

combat

Dans la guerre comme dans la paix le dernier mot est à ceux qui ne se rendent jamais - Clemenceau.

Je détruirai la France.

(Hitler)

Je tiens les promesses, même celles des autres. (Pétain)

ORGANE DU MOUVEMENT DE LIBÉRATION FRANÇAISE

PAS UN HOMME POUR l'ALLEMAGNE

Tous les journaux, tous les jours, et des milliers d'affiches, dans les villages comme dans les villes, appellent inlassablement les Français à aller travailler en Allemagne. La propagande manie simultanément tous les thèmes : hauts salaires à relève des prisonniers, construction de l'Europe nouvelle, lutte contre le bolchevisme, etc.

Après plus de quarante jours de cette campagne, on peut juger du résultat : ce résultat est misérable. L'Allemagne réclamait 350.000 ouvriers. Il a du en partir une vingtaine de milliers, y compris une forte proportion d'étrangers et de nord-africains.

Encore pour aboutir à ce chiffre a-t-il fallu ramasser tout ce qu'on a pu trouver de clochards, de propres à rien et d'indésirables (hommes ou femmes). Je n'en veux pour preuve que les déclarations faites récemment à Vichy aux journalistes de la zone non occupée par M. FLEJO, chef du service social du bureau de recrutement des travailleurs français en Allemagne. M. FLEJO qui était prisonnier de guerre a été rapatrié pour faire ce joli métier. Cela suffit à dépeindre le personnage dont il s'agit.

Et bien, tout marchand d'esclaves qu'il est devenu, M. FLEJO n'en a pas moins du reconnaitre que, contrairement aux accords internationaux, il était impossible de connaitre les conditions exactes du travail en Allemagne, pas plus que d'obtenir des précisions sur la proportion dans laquelle s'opèrerait la fameuse "relève". En outre, le même FLEJO a du signaler que le recrutement portait surtout sur de pauvres diables qui n'ont rien à se mettre sur le dos et, en ce qui concerne les femmes, sur des "ouvrières" préoccupées de savoir si elles pourront faire commerce de leurs charmes.

Enregistrons avec satisfaction l'aveu tombé d'une bouche aussi autorisée. Cet aveu a donc du paraitre trop convaincant à l'un des journalistes présents, car il n'a pas hésité à protester au nom de la Kollaboration contre ces propos décourageants. Epinglons, en attendant le règlement des comptes, le nom de ce salaud. Il s'appelle Léopold BLOND, rédacteur au "Petit Dauphinois", et père du fameux Georges BLOND de "Je suis Partout" et des fossés de Vincennes.

Enregistrons cet aveu, mais pas d'excès de satisfaction ni d'optimisme. D'abord, si peu qu'il en parte, il y en a trop. Ensuite, il faut s'attendre à ce que la main allemande s'appesantisse de plus en plus lourdement sur la France livrée par Vichy à mesure que la situation économique et militaire de l'Allemagne s'aggravera.

(suite pag. 2)

DERNIÈRE NOUVELLE

ALERTE DANGER

La police fait imprimer « COMBAT » sur les presses de « L'EFFORT ». Ses moutons se présenteront à vos amis comme distributeurs de nos journaux, afin de pénétrer dans le mouvement.

Contre cette odieuse manœuvre, une seule parade :

« N'ACCEPTER LE JOURNAL QUE PAR LES VOIES HABITUELLES »

Le sort du mouvement peut en dépendre.

"In war as in peace, the last word goes to those who never give up." —Georges Clemenceau.

Jacques Renouvin, head of the Groupes Francs. (Author's Collection)

Jean Moulin, De Gaulle's envoy to the metropolitan Resistance. (Photo Harcourt)

General Delestraint, titular head of the Secret Army. (Photo Comité d'Histoire de la Seconde Guerre Mondiale)

Pierre de Bénouville, director of Combat's foreign relations. (Author's Collection)
General and Mme. de Gaulle in their wartime residence outside London. (Photo Keystone)

Emmanuel d'Astier de la Vigerie, founder of Libération. (Photo OFIC)

NEW RECRUITS

One day my secretary, Dominique Pagel, brought me a note from "Max." He was eager to give our steering committee an important communication. A few days later we all assembled in Rémy Roure's place on the Rue Cuvier.

"Max" said, "I've just received a message addressed to the French Resistance from General de Gaulle in London." It was the first time the leader of the Free French addressed us (not us alone, of course, but the entire Resistance). He spoke of "the battle objectives of the French people": the restoration of our territorial integrity and our domestic freedom, the punishment of traitors, a secure national and social life, equality of opportunity for all. He promised that the Liberation would be followed by the election by universal suffrage of a National Assembly and by the constitution of a world council dedicated to the maintenance of peace in a context of respect for the rights of peoples.

"My request," said "Max," "is that you publish this text as soon as possible in your newspaper. The other movements will do the same. The result will be a spectacular proof of the unity of all those who are fighting for freedom and victory."

De Gaulle's message was soon published simultaneously, as Max had requested, in

9

Combat, Libération and *Franc-Tireur.* It was the first visible sign—and it was a spectacular one—that the French Resistance was rallying to De Gaulle and that he had established close ties with us. It left no room for any pretense of doubt by the Americans or the other Allies. To stress our unity we introduced a new symbol consisting of the *C* of *Combat* inserted within the transverse bars of the Cross of Lorraine.

This message marked a decisive turning point in the Free French leader's conception of his own role. Until now—that is, for two years—De Gaulle had been a leader in battle whose only objective—and it was a pretty grandiose one, at that—had been to keep France on the Allied side that she might share in the final victory. But on June 24, 1942, he ceased to be a mere standard bearer in the battle and became a political leader whose ambitions reached well beyond the end of the war.

Of course we were totally unaware that this text had in fact been "wrenched out of him" by Christian Pineau, the first Resistance leader to reach London. Later Pineau was to note in his memoirs*: "I realized that, like Passy, he knew nothing about the Resistance. . . . When I mentioned that the Resistance wanted a sign from him, a message, he was obviously quite surprised and had no conception of what I expected on his part."

Hence we may infer that the day of his meeting with Pineau was the very day on which he first saw the enormous role he was to play in the destiny of France.

Mireille Albrecht, terribly alone for a girl of sixteen, was still living in Berty's new apartment on the Quai Pierre-Scize, where she was frequently harassed by police interrogators. The school she attended had felt obliged to drop her on account of the haze of doubt that hung over her person and her name. Our Social Service had allotted her a modest monthly allowance, enough for subsistence only, and to save money she ate at the Salvation Army. Her only solace was her weekly visit to her mother in Vals-les-Bains, through which we also maintained our correspondence with Berty.

*Christian Pineau, *op. cit.*, pages 157, 158.

The Night Will End

In Vals-les-Bains the "administrative internees" were confined in the Hôtel du Vivarais. Berty discovered that several other friends were also there: Emmanuel Mounier, Crozier, Langlade and Demachy.

The regulations were strict but not inhumane. Each "internee" had his own room and was forbidden to communicate with his fellows. However, the latter regulation was often waived by the friendly gendarmes who served as prison guards.

Yet Berty was bristling with indignation. The arbitrariness of her "administrative internment," whose length was entirely at the discretion of Vichy's executive, absolutely revolted her. "There are courts of law in the land! Let them try me!"

This outrage against internment without trial became an obsession with her, as it also did with Mounier and Perrin. Eventually the three of them agreed to hold a hunger strike and, if they did not receive satisfaction, to pursue it to the bitter end. Mireille brought me a letter dated Friday, June 19, in which her mother declared to me her absolute determination: "I have decided to go right to the end. In losing my life I shall win an ineffable peace. . . ."

On the twelfth day of the hunger strike, Vichy yielded. They had won. An arrest warrant was filled out and a judicial inquiry opened. The case was laid before a court of France. After three weeks of convalescence, a radiant Berty was transferred to the prison of Saint-Joseph, the Lyons women's house of detention.

In early May of 1942 our movement faced an important new issue: Should we merge with Libération and Franc-Tireur? The answer to this question would clearly determine our new orientation.

It was difficult to decide on a safe meeting place. In the end we opted for the home of Charles d'Aragon, the director of Combat in the Tarn. He lived in Saliès, not far from Albi, on his family estate, which consisted of a run-down chateau surrounded by a vast park. Since all the caretakers were themselves in the movement, absolute discretion was guaranteed.

We gathered in early July. Our steering committee was present in its entirety, along with Marcel Peck, Henri Aubry, René

New Recruits

Courtin, André Hauriou, Jacques Dhont and Edmond Michelet.

I was the only person who knew everyone there, for most of my colleagues were absolute strangers to one another. Yet so powerful was the bond that our common struggle forged among us that no more than a day was required for the birth of strong friendships. For three days we worked together each morning and afternoon in an atmosphere of warm camaraderie.

We adopted all our decisions in total unanimity. Although in four out of the six regions there were either very few or no members of Franc-Tireur and Libération, all our regional chiefs were in favor of the proposed merger. Naturally we also agreed on the idea of a unified Secret Army. In this case, however, we of Combat would retain command, for nowhere had any of our people detected any paramilitary units belonging to the other two groups.

At the end of the meeting Claude Bourdet, André Hauriou and I agreed to present our conclusions in a manifesto, a sort of charter of the Resistance, to appear in *Combat*. Several of my most cherished ideas were to appear in this manifesto, in particular the goal of a United States of Europe.

Since July 14, 1939, we had not celebrated a true Bastille Day. In 1940 and 1941 we had, instead, commemorated it in sorrow and in self-communion. Now, in early July of 1942, "Max" informed us that General de Gaulle wanted to turn this July 14 into a great patriotic demonstration of national unity. He was planning to urge the French people over the radio to deck the streets with flags and to gather in every city to sing the "Marseillaise."

We made ready accordingly. As we had for May Day, we printed leaflets and distributed them widely. Wherever there existed a Place de la République our countrymen would assemble, for the Quatorze Juillet is indeed the fête of the Republic.

On the eve of the Quatorze, every member of Combat sat with his or her ears glued to the radio. Suddenly we heard the words ". . . And now, General de Gaulle":

Tomorrow, in that part of France they call "unoccupied," the tricolor shall hang from every house. In every town and village Frenchmen and

The Night Will End

Frenchwomen shall march to the appointed place, and with a strong voice and tears in their eyes they shall sing the "Marseillaise." . . . These flags shall be our pride! These marches shall be our hope! This "Marseillaise" shall be our rage! For we have need of our pride, our hope and our rage, and we have preserved them. Tomorrow we shall prove it!

De Gaulle's appeal was heard and widely answered. There were few flags hung from windows, but a massive, gay and noisy crowd gathered in the Place de la République. Whole families came, from every social class, with children in tow. It was impossible to guess their number. The police tried to disperse the demonstrators, who immediately regrouped. Mounted troops intervened, people were trampled, yet whenever the "Marseillaise" was silenced in one place it billowed forth in another. The cry of "Death to Laval!" was heard over and over again. At least a hundred persons were arrested.

France, returning at last to the eternal source of her revolution, celebrated a real Quatorze Juillet.

After three months' absence, Emmanuel d'Astier returned from England. "Max" and I met him in Lyons.

He'd left so precipitately, he said, that he hadn't had the chance to inform me. I told him how shocked I'd been that he'd claimed to represent all the movements in the southern zone. He reacted with apparent surprise. Since he'd been the only one with an opportunity to make the trip, it was natural for him to inform London of the desires and needs of the rest of us. I feigned to accept this explanation, but I was not duped. Still, there was no point in poisoning our relationship.

Beginning in late July 1942 "Max" began to meet more and more frequently with the chiefs of the three movements. With the greater bargaining power that Saliès had given me, I held out for a complete fusion of the movements and the creation of a unified Secret Army. Jean-Pierre Lévy shared my opinion. D'Astier, however, stuck to his guns. He was satisfied with the simple coordination of our efforts. However, he did agree to a merger of our paramilitary outfits, with the proviso that the head of the Secret Army not be a member of any of the three movements.

New Recruits

I objected: "As you know," I said, "for two years we in Combat have developed our Secret Army in a way that simply has no parallel in Libération and Franc-Tireur. If you consider my own military background and my experience in underground operations, I believe I am better qualified than some neophyte to assume this responsibility."

I was very well aware even as I was talking that I did not have the concurrence of my two colleagues. Even Moulin was opposed to my proposal. He reminded me of the order he had received from London: The paramilitary outfits of the resistance organizations were to be kept rigorously discrete. Yet, clearly, if the leaderships merged, so, in the end, would the rank-and-file. D'Astier and Jean-Pierre Lévy fully agreed with this line of thought.

Now, I knew that Combat would account for over 80 percent of the personnel and trained cadres of a unified Secret Army. I wondered if I could ever accept the idea of placing them in the hands of an unknown. Did I have the right to put some stranger over thousands of men who'd given me their implicit trust? It would be appalling if, through pure rivalry, I should be dismissed from the leadership of this Secret Army that I was already successfully commanding within Combat.

I decided to submit the matter to a review by our steering committee. As it turned out, the steering committee counseled me to accept D'Astier's and Lévy's offer; I was being asked to make a painful sacrifice on the altar of unity. To my eyes, the decision was unfair, and it evidenced rank suspicion born of the purest jealousy, jealousy that I had in no way incited. Lastly, and most significantly, I was afraid of the decision's consequences.

Later, Henri Noguères, one of the best historians of the Resistance, was to write*:

Objectively one must recognize that Frenay was by no means without reason in presenting his candidacy [for the command of the Secret Army]. The official constitution of a Secret Army was the final consummation of an idea that Frenay had been the first to formulate, and it was

*Histoire de la Résistance en France, Vol. II, Robert Laffont, 1969, page 613.

The Night Will End

to rely upon positions that he had secured and to operate under the very name he had chosen. Moreover, considering that the Secret Army was to be composed of already existing irregular outfits, it is incontestable that Combat alone contained more men than its two partners combined.

This latest decision afforded no pleasure to my comrades in Combat. They reproached me heatedly for having yielded. Irony of ironies, it was now my turn to think up arguments for what I myself had decried.

In any case, we now had to find a man to lead the Secret Army. What sort of "profile" should he have? He should not have been a member of any of the three movements, nor of the collaboration, nor of the Vichy government, nor of any of its dependent authorities; yet he should have earned enough prestige to be able to throw his weight around with the Allied general staffs. In other words, he had to be top military brass.

One day Marcel Peck, the regional chief of R.1, came to see me in my favorite little café in Mâcon.

"Henri," he said, "I've a candidate for you. He's an anti-Vichy reserve lieutenant general called Delestraint."

In early August 1942 I went to Bourg-en-Brest, where General Delestraint was then living. The general showed me into his modest apartment. He was a man of average height and quite young for his high rank. He couldn't have been more than sixty. He was in his undershirt. There were none of those panoplies or lance pennants one so often sees in the homes of career officers.

I introduced myself with a brief description of the various stages of my military career. I sensed that our shared background inspired confidence in him. I explained why I had left the army and how our refusal to accept defeat and collaboration had led us to an intransigent opposition to Vichy. Finally, I explained how, progressively, we had rallied to General de Gaulle.

"Did you know," he said, "that De Gaulle was my subordinate when I commanded an armored division? I've great admiration for him, as much for his quick mind as for his tactical skill. He was a brilliant regimental commanding officer."

So far, so good, I thought; but would Delestraint, after having been De Gaulle's superior, now agree to serve as his subordinate?

New Recruits

Anyway, I gave my little lecture on the Resistance, noting that he followed me attentively as I spoke. Yet the questions he asked me only proved how difficult it was to assimilate in a few hours what we had learned in two years. At last I came around to the object of my visit.

"General, the Secret Army must become a well-armed, perfectly trained instrument of war. It must play a large role in the battle for our liberation, and so its actions must be integrated with the Allied battle plan. At its head should be a soldier with top-flight command experience who can deal confidently with De Gaulle and the Allies. General, I've come to ask if you could accept such a responsibility."

Delestraint let a long silence elapse, then rose and paced thoughtfully across the room. Then, turning to me: "I'm sure you realize that your proposal requires serious reflection. . . . Of course I cannot answer you today. . . . But in any case I can tell you two things: I shall consider your offer, and the fact that I would be placed under the command of an ex-subordinate will have no bearing on my answer. However, if I say yes, I shall also require a written order signed by De Gaulle himself."

I liked this man. His last words had given proof of real character, for the army pecking order is rigidly determined by the number of stars on a general's sleeve. But was he fully aware of the risk of the adventure I was proposing?

"General," I said, "I must warn you that an acceptance on your part would entail your exposure to mortal danger, a far greater danger than you've ever met on the battlefield. The Gestapo does not spare—"

"Monsieur," he cut in, "mortal danger is the career officer's lot."

All during the early summer of 1942 our organizational work in Combat was progressing at a furious pace. I've been accused of taking a freakish delight in organizational charts, and I suppose there's some truth in that charge. Each week new needs arose, and to fill them I decided to create a number of autonomous nation-wide services, each with its own director. Gone were the lean days of the "one-man band," when we had lacked the money to fund such services.

The Night Will End

Thus was created our False Papers Service (F.P.), which operated in conjunction with André Bollier's printing works. Its job was to provide phony identity cards, driver's licenses, rationing cards and passes, and sometimes it even counterfeited police papers with glorious embossed stamps. Of course all this required the complicity of many specialized artisans.

Our Liaison Service provided the messengers we so urgently needed to maintain daily communication between the national center and the provincial regions and departments. In late 1942 and in 1943 a system of underground telegraph communications was perfected with the complicity of the major post offices in the southern zone.

The Housing Service was responsible for finding safe dwellings for full-time militants hunted by the police.

It was this organizational effort that led Henri Noguères to write: "Of the three largest movements [in the summer of 1942], Combat was by far the most solidly constructed."

The movement also spread to Algeria. Through the intermediary of Chevance in Marseilles, we organized a communication line with the Algiers resistance under René Capitant. We spirited him our newspapers and our mail a couple of times a month. Aside from that, he was free to organize his group as he saw fit. Our experience in the occupied zone had led us to conclude that different situations always require different methods.

Whenever Capitant came to metropolitan France he had the right to sit in our steering committee. The Resistance was to hear more of him.

Jacques Renouvin was still combing the free zone for recruits. Isolated paramilitary operations were beginning to take place all over France and not only in the large municipal centers. Every operation was signed "Combat."

The Groupes Francs had by now managed to blow up many collaborationist lairs, as well as the enrollment bureaus for the labor draft for Germany and the Anti-Bolshevik Legion (which Laval was soon to dub the "Légion Tricolore") and the offices of the J.F.O.M. (Jeunesse de France et d'Outre-Mer), a neo-Nazi organization designed to regiment young Frenchmen. Already we

New Recruits

were a big topic in the police stations and among the population in general. Our punitive operations were also good public relations. They attracted young men who yearned for action.

In late July 1942 I finally learned about that famous "carnival" Renouvin had been planning for me. He'd devoted much time and care to organizing it. Inside one hour on July 29 in fully ten cities of the southern zone all the offices of the labor draft were blown to smithereens! In August still more targets were simultaneously destroyed. One day it would be the Service d'Ordre Légionnaire, that sorry auxiliary of the Vichy police; another day it would be the headquarters of the Fascist Parti Populaire Français (P.P.F.), under Jacques Doriot.

The indefatigable Renouvin rushed from town to town, recruiting, organizing and sometimes personally directing an operation. What a natural leader he was!

Yet he still needed explosives and even revolvers. Why didn't we get weapons from London? I was to wonder about this for a long time to come, and all the Resistance would be wondering with me.

In this same summer of 1942 several comrades who'd been "burned" in their usual place of work came to request new reassignments in the Lyons area.

One of them, Marcel Degliame, Bourdet's labor-organizer friend, had just fled the Côte d'Azur. For several months he'd served as André Bollier's assistant; now the steering committee requested him to create a new service called "Workers' Action." His new role was to organize resistance against the labor draft for German industry, later against the S.T.O.* promulgated in early September. Within an ever-growing number of industries, first in the area around Lyons and then in other regions, Degliame organized a network of three-man cells composed of determined propagandists who soon moved on to industrial sabotage. And so began a far-flung operation whose consequences we shall witness later on.

Henri Ingrand, whom the Abwehr had arrested in Paris, had

*S.T.O., Service de Travail Obligatoire: compulsory deportation to forced labor in Germany instituted after the failure of the volunteer labor draft (known as *la relève*).— Translator.

The Night Will End

190

been released in circumstances that seemed highly suspect. Before we could make further use of this marvelous organizer and idea man we were obliged to put him under surveillance. In late 1942, reassured by his obviously innocent behavior, we put him in charge (under the name of "Mazière") of R.6 in Clermont-Ferrand.

But the most valuable new arrival in Lyons was Claude Bourdet. I had known him for a year, and we'd had countless conversations; he'd also participated in every single meeting of our steering committee. I deeply appreciated his swift and penetrating mind, his understanding of political problems and his unclouded serenity, which some mistook for nonchalance.

Sought by the police in the Alpes-Maritimes, he'd left Philippe Monod in charge of that department. From now on Bourdet spelled me during my own trips out of the Lyons area, and it was with him that I first talked in confidentiality about all the key problems that arose. In effect, Bourdet now became the number-two man in Combat.

Early in August 1942 he came to visit me in Mâcon.

"Henri," he said, "we're now convinced that the insurrection against Vichy will be part and parcel of the Liberation. We have to prepare for a power-seizure right down to the departmental level. The most efficient way would be to infiltrate every ministry and prefecture with agents who could get to know the political views of the principal officials. Then, at the Liberation, we could immediately replace the rotten part of the old administration with our own 'shadow' teams."

"Claude," I said, "you've had a real brainstorm. And there's nobody better suited than you to implement this new Resistance branch. But what should we call it?"

After a few moments of reflection he replied, "Let's call it the N.A.P. for 'Noyautage des Administrations Publiques' ["infiltration of public administrations"]. That's a pretty straightforward title. May I add that while awaiting the insurrection we'll already have intelligence agents in all the right places. They can double as spies."

At first limited to the infiltration of administrative organs in the narrowest sense, the N.A.P. was by degrees extended to the

New Recruits

public-utility companies. Later we were to form an N.A.P.-Rail, an N.A.P.-Energy and an N.A.P.-Public Communications.

Since May we had been anxiously following the actions of General Giraud. He had pledged allegiance to Marshal Pétain, and he seemed to be holding consultations with the commanding officers of the Armistice Army. Little by little we realized that he was hatching some sort of plot. We had to get to the bottom of it.

In July, Menthon, with the blessing of the steering committee and "Max," had succeeded in meeting the general in the Lyons suburb where he now lived. He'd been very unfavorably impressed. To be sure, the man was deeply anti-German and hostile to Vichy, but he was also unduly respectful of the Marshal. Moreover, he acted idiotically self-important. What was his game?

It didn't take us long to find out, thanks to Claude Bourdet, who visited the general in Cannes.

"If I had to sum up my conversation with him," said Claude, "I'd say that on all available evidence he's setting up a broad military action against Germany. He's got some important backing, probably American, which has bolstered his confidence. He has great moral authority within the Armistice Army, and he intends to wield it. But he knows almost nothing about the Resistance, and he wants nothing to do with De Gaulle, who, he claims, has no pull with the Allies. In effect, the general seems utterly impervious to political reasoning."

It was indeed a discouraging picture. What would become of us if Giraud, backed by the United States, were to initiate his own independent action? There would then be three Frances: Vichy France, De Gaulle's Free France and Giraud's France. We who had already rallied to De Gaulle could never accept this.

Before my open window in Charnay I carefully drafted a letter to Giraud. First I reminded him who I was. Then I explained my evolution toward De Gaulle, concluding with an explanation of our organization and its goals. About Vichy I wrote:

The noblest words and symbols have been . . . prostituted. Honor, dignity, work, fatherland, the flag itself, all have become mere . . . tokens that veil the hidden designs of those who govern us. The time has

The Night Will End

come when a Frenchman can no longer proclaim his ideals by his attachment to the flag but rather by his attachment to the one who bears it. The French people has two such standard bearers: Pétain and De Gaulle. It has chosen De Gaulle. . . .

The workers and peasants, the middle classes, the vast majority of Christians are united in their recognition of General de Gaulle as the representative of their deepest hopes. I adjure you, General, to take cognizance of this fact. If you wish to put your prestige at the service of France, listen to what I now tell you . . . if you follow the Marshal, and . . . disregard . . . De Gaulle . . . you will surely fail. . . .

The National Committee in London, over which the general presides, has been recognized *de jure* or *de facto* by all. . . . our Allies. Moreover, these Allies have recently recognized De Gaulle as chief not only of the Free French but also of all the French troops in metropolitan France and abroad who are fighting for our national liberation. In brief, our Allies have recognized the unity of the French Resistance. We must offer them a single representative who can rally the entire Resistance to him. . . .

General, it is in France's vital interest that you try to reach an accord with De Gaulle.

With the best will in the world, I ask you to consider my words. If I seem insistent it is only because I know that if you come to agree with [me] you will be able to perform a great service for our homeland.

In early December I received the following brief note: "I am grateful for your letter and the information it contains. The hour of decision is not yet upon us. When it is, I shall act in complete independence."

In complete independence? Just what did that mean? Independence from us? From De Gaulle? From the Americans? I had no idea. But Giraud's laconic reply seemed like a bad omen. And so it was.

On September 14 I left for Marseilles. I had just received a message from Jean Moulin informing me that D'Astier and I were to embark for London from the Riviera.

New Recruits

LONDON MISSION

In Marseilles I stayed again off the Place de Castellane in the little apartment reserved for me. It seemed that I was to embark with D'Astier from the cove of Port-Miou. My two friends undertook to provide protection for the embarkation.

We picked up the BBC signal for my departure on the evening of September 16. I was to meet D'Astier the following day in one of the restaurants of Port-Miou. A guide would take us to the cove.

On September 14 I arrived early at the appointed place. Port-Miou was a tranquil little town, and its café was almost deserted. The season was over; the summer folk gone. I was just ordering my dinner when D'Astier arrived, along with our guide.

After an hour's walk we arrived at the little pebbly beach at the bottom of the cove. Each one of us was equipped with a pocket flashlight. We were to point our flashlights seaward and flash a Morse "A": a short and a long. We were to receive the same signal in return.

It was I who began. Every five minutes I flashed an "A." In this way an hour passed. Then D'Astier spelled me. I stretched out on my back with my head on my portfolio—it was all

10

I had for baggage—and gradually drifted into a light slumber.

Suddenly D'Astier roused me with a tap on my shoulder.

"They're here!"

Twice more, from the now dark sea, came the long-awaited flashes. We heard the plashing of invisible oars. Gradually two bright forms grew out of the darkness and glided toward us. Now they were beside us in their yellow oilskins, maneuvering their pneumatic dinghy.

We waded into the water and climbed aboard. As we waved farewell to our guide, the night enveloped us. We inched our way out of the cove and into the open sea, our two companions paddling in silence. We wondered what sort of vessel we were about to board. A submarine? A cutter? Suddenly we were astounded to be drawing alongside one of those fishing boats known in Marseilles as *pointus*. This was a very large one, about fifteen yards long.

Several pairs of arms reached out to help us aboard, then hoisted up the dinghy as well.

"How are you, gentlemen?" said a voice in English.

In fact, they were not Englishmen but Poles. Almost noiselessly, at a snail's pace, we put out to sea.

Ah, how delicious that first cup of coffee was, set off by the simmering milk we passed around in an enamel mess tin! It was genuine coffee, a taste we had almost forgotten, and the milk was the same creamy milk that we had so casually drunk before the war.

The commanding officer, a tall, blond fellow of about my age, looked on, smiling.

"Smoke?" he asked.

He held out a package of Cravens. I can honestly say that in my whole life no gift ever seemed more exotic. Oh, that first puff! Thirty years later I still seem to feel it on my tongue.

"Well now, Skipper," said D'Astier, "you're not going to tell us that this vessel of yours can take us all the way to England."

"Oh, no. I'll just take you out to the open sea, beyond the French territorial limit. We'll stop there."

"Stop?"

"Yes, that's right. You see, I'm under orders to carry out six

London Mission

missions of this type. We won't be leaving for Gibraltar for another week."

"You've got to be kidding."

"Nope. I've got six more embarkations to take care of. It's an order. And orders are orders."

All night long we stood out toward the open sea. During the day the vessel cut her motors, and we passengers would swim or sunbathe. Then, in the early evening, we would start back toward the coast, each time standing off a new point and picking up new passengers. On the last evening we had ninety on board!

We had been warned, in case of an air-raid alert, to cover ourselves with an immense net. Once a plane was spotted, and we quickly hid ourselves. Peeking up, I saw a pair of tricolored cockades streak by. The plane buzzed us twice at an altitude of two or three hundred yards. Then, satisfied that all was as it should be, it flew off. What a feeling, to have to hide from a French airplane!

It was impossible for me to put any questions to the commanding officer, for I would have to walk right across the top of that mass of huddled bodies. But I was itching with curiosity to know what he intended to do with us. One morning just after dawn we sighted two imposing and apparently motionless vessels. Before we could make out whether they were Allied or enemy ships, our *pointu* headed straight for them. Soon we could see the British sailors making ready to help us aboard.

I ended up on the larger of the two ships, which D'Astier, an ex-naval officer, identified as a cruiser. From the height of a companionway we watched the minuscule fishing boat and its Polish crew sail into the distance.

"Messrs. 'Bernard' and 'Charvet,' please."*

A midshipman courteously led us to our private staterooms. What luxury! We had hot and cold water and little reading lamps over our beds. Showered, washed and shaved, we were cordially received in the officers' mess room, despite our ragged clothes.

That evening, for the first time in my life, I saw the Rock of

*During the war I had many pseudonyms, among them "Molin," "Maurin," "Tavernier," "Xaintrailles," and "Custines," but London always knew me as "Charvet."

The Night Will End

Gibraltar—that great bastion of the British Empire and portcullis of the Mediterranean. We disembarked onto a launch that zig-zagged to the jetty among vessels of all descriptions. A waiting limousine took us to a villa where a double bedroom had been prepared for us. We were also informed that Her Majesty's Governor, Lord Gort, was expecting us for lunch.

Lord Gort, in shorts and a linen summer shirt, welcomed us into his garden. He had a dark, florid complexion in which whiskey, as well as service in the Raj, had played its part.

D'Astier and I spoke in general terms of our clandestine press, our Secret Army, our Groupes Francs. It was an unknown world to him, but he politely refrained from any show of unseemly curiosity. Like all well-bred English gentlemen, he was sparing of word and gesture, and he learned little enough from us. For him the victory of the Allies was a foregone conclusion. It would take time of course, but then, eternity itself stretched out before the British Empire.

When we arrived in Bristol by seaplane on September 26, no one was expecting us and no one even knew who we were. However, as it happened, a British officer and another from the French services were awaiting us in the London railway station. We were taken directly to 10 Duke Street, the seat of the B.C.R.A.*

I was living in a dream. The last ten days had seemed like an eternity to me. Never again could any voyage give me the feeling of sheer wonder and exoticism that I then felt. At last I was in London, only two paces from the BBC, whose gong we had awaited in France every evening with our ears glued to the radio. In this ordinary Duke Street building, which seemed no different from so many others, worked my still-unknown comrades. I was flying with joy!

We were received straightaway by Lieutenant Colonel Passy, the head of the B.C.R.A. He was a man with thinning blond hair, a direct look and a frank handshake. He must have been four or five years younger than myself, hence about thirty. We already knew

*Bureau Central de Renseignements et d'Action: Central Bureau of Intelligence and Action. The Free French secret service.

London Mission

each other in a sense, through Jean Moulin. We set an appointment for the following day. In the meantime we had to find a place to stay and to buy some new clothes. We were given a few dozen pounds sterling, and I was driven to the Mount Royal Hotel near the Marble Arch.

During this sojourn, which began in late September of 1942 and was to last rather longer than I expected, I found the spectacle of the British capital at war utterly fascinating. I saw, heard and registered as much as I possibly could.

But where were the ruins of those devastating Luftwaffe raids? It took me a while to realize that the wooden palisades along which I seemed to be walking so much of the time actually concealed destroyed houses and ruined buildings. To ward off the morale-weakening effect of these shattered hulks, the day after each blitz an army of workmen and soldiers would arrive to clear away the wreckage and throw up a concealing screen. Thus the capital seemed utterly intact, and the war took its course without any glaring evidence.

It was considered bad form to discuss a recent bombardment. Such bombardments were quirks of fate, unworthy of mention, much less complaint. It often happened that a Londoner, arriving late for work, would quietly apologize, and later, during lunch, or on the following day, his colleagues would learn that his house had been totally destroyed the previous night.

Though rationing was in effect, the department stores seemed well stocked. To one arriving from France they were overflowing with luxuries. And the restaurants and dance-halls were packed.

Quietly an RAF pilot would tuck his kids into bed, kiss his wife goodbye, drive to the airfield, then let out the throttle of his fighter-bomber to wing his way over Cologne and Hamburg, sowing the seeds of death and destruction. The flak was murderous, the losses severe. Upon his return, if there was a return, he would tiptoe back into his home so as not to awaken his family.

The blackout was all-embracing and very strictly observed. Batallions of women served in the anti-aircraft squads or regulated the kite balloons, for right in the center of London the sky was bristling with "sausages" to ward off low-altitude bombing raids.

The Night Will End

During my stay we were bombed several times. Calmly the hotel guests would descend into the street and walk to the nearest bomb shelter, where they would inevitably encounter various acquaintances. Our shelter was an Underground station, and once inside I was surprised to observe these Londoners chatting amiably with one another as if in a parlor, while the earth shook with nearby explosions.

De Gaulle had just returned to London after several days' absence. He had visited first the Levant, then French Equatorial Africa. Grave misunderstandings had arisen in Lebanon and Syria between De Gaulle and the English, who were trying to oust the French from the area to enlarge their own sphere of influence. In mid-August the English had also landed in Madagascar and commenced operations against Vichy's troops there, but Churchill had refused to grant the French National Committee* the right to represent French interests on that island.

This situation had become the principal subject of conversation in the offices of the Free French, both in the B.C.R.A. and in André Philip's interior *commissariat.***

On his return from his earlier trip to London and Washington, D'Astier had told us about Roosevelt's hostility toward De Gaulle, but even then we never imagined that the conflict with the English had gone so deep.

We had been confident that in the midst of this global struggle the English and French would unite in a common front. Yet here in London I saw nothing but anxious expressions and heard nothing but disquieting suppositions. It was in this utterly unexpected atmosphere that I found myself invited to lunch with General de Gaulle himself in his country house fifty miles north of London.

I was ushered into a large room that gave directly onto a garden. The furniture was comfortable but simple. On one table was a

*A number of resisters had gathered around De Gaulle in a body called the French National Committee, which was in fact the authoritative command of the Fighting French.

**Commissariat: the functional equivalent of a ministry within the French National Committee. Each was headed by a commissaire.—Translator.

London Mission

knitted sweater and some English magazines, on the other a tray with two bottles, one of whiskey, the other of sherry.

Before I had had much time to examine my surroundings, a door opened and the general was walking across the room, his hand extended, his face impassive and unsmiling.

"*Bonjour, 'Charvet.'*"

I had not seen De Gaulle for fifteen years. He was as thin as ever, very erect, and without one gray hair on his head. He wore no decorations on his khaki uniform, but there was a Cross of Lorraine on the right side of his tunic. He approached me slowly, with a grave expression, as if he'd seen me only yesterday and known me since time immemorial.

"Have a seat. Fix you a drink?"

I accepted a glass of sherry. De Gaulle himself drank nothing.

"Smoke?" He offered me a cigarette.

I gave De Gaulle a cursory picture of the state of mind of the population in the free zone, noting the progressive enlightenment of the public since Laval's return to power, the growing curtailment of personal freedom, the persecution of the Jews and the repression of the Resistance. Lastly, I mentioned that Marshal Pétain's prestige, though waning, was still considerable. This surprised him.

"You mean the French people still don't understand?" he asked me.

"General, many of them still believe in the so-called 'double game.' Some even think that there is a secret agreement between you and Pétain: You are the sword, he the shield."

"Yes, I can see how comfortable such an attitude must be. It allows them to avoid choosing sides."

Then I spoke to him about Combat and the development of our movement. I also defended the idea of a merger between Combat and Libération and Franc-Tireur.

"I've been told," he said, "that your relations with D'Astier could be better."

"Our temperaments are different—very different. Furthermore, our personal conceptions of the unity of the Resistance are widely divergent. I stand for the merger of all movements; he prefers

The Night Will End

simple coordination. Our arguments over these subjects have often been rather vehement."

"What about your relationship with 'Max'?"

"On the personal level, it's very good indeed. Yet I find that he has become something of an unnecessary barrier between Free France and ourselves. Of course, he has the money and the means to forward messages and supplies; he is also the one who provides us with the hardware we so desperately need. His role is valuable as long as our movements remain separated. If they fuse, it should be altered."

"As far as I can tell, 'Max' is a man of great qualities. He's a true *homme d'état*, and you should trust him implicitly, as I do."

Then I mentioned the Secret Army and the decision we had made to organize all our paramilitary outfits into one corps. "I believe that I have found the right man for the command of the Secret Army: General Delestraint."

"Delestraint? I know him well and have great respect for him. Will he accept?"

"If you endorse his new role."

"I shall write him—in fact, you yourself may bring him my letter. Delestraint seems a good choice to me."

We were joined by Mme. De Gaulle. She was quiet, very simply dressed, almost self-effacing. She hardly joined at all in the conversation. I believe she was raised by nuns; she certainly bore all the outward marks of such an upbringing. We sat down at table, where we talked of daily life in France. By the time coffee was served I was again alone with General de Gaulle.

Then De Gaulle mentioned the Free French. "The English think that they can do as they like in Syria and Lebanon," he said. "Our nineteen forty-one accord is no longer respected. Neither is that which I concluded with Churchill in nineteen forty.* The English want to evict us from the Levant by taking advantage of

*In 1940 the British government and De Gaulle had signed an agreement recognizing the latter as the leader of the Free French and specifying the relations to obtain between the two parties. In July 1941, after the tragic events in Syria, the "Littleton–De Gaulle" agreement was concluded in recognition of De Gaulle's right to represent French interests in the Levant.

London Mission

our temporary weakness. They wish to organize elections to give their policy of despoilment a democratic façade. As these elections are to be held under their supervision and in the presence of their troops, the results can easily be guessed in advance.

"This I shall not tolerate," he continued, stressing each word. "I shall not trade the interests of France for a mess of pottage. You can guess what they'd say about such a sellout in Vichy. If necessary I shall leave England and pitch camp in Brazzaville, and I shall let the whole world know why. It was to France and not to England that the League of Nations granted the mandate over the Levantine states. I am not going to be the one to strike our flag."

I didn't want to leave before mentioning the contacts between Combat and General Giraud. De Gaulle listened to my account with the appearance of sovereign indifference.

"I know all about this business. It's an American machination. We can expect it to hang fire indefinitely."

It was almost four o'clock now. I got ready to leave.

"Of course we shall meet again before your departure, but until then you've got plenty of work cut out for you."

"Yes—you know, we in France are expecting a lot, especially in the way of arms. We must have arms!"

"I know. Try and explain that to the English. *A bientôt.*"

As I returned to London I thought long and hard about this meeting. It had neither disappointed nor comforted me. I had felt no exchange of human warmth, but De Gaulle had at least listened carefully to everything I said. The general's impassivity disconcerted me somewhat, but, in the depths of my soul, I still admired him deeply.

During the first two weeks of October meeting followed meeting at an ever faster pace. They were held either in the B.C.R.A's Duke Street headquarters or in the Hill Street location of André Philip's *commissariat* of the Interior and always with the full participation of the Free French general staff. André Philip himself was still passionate, muddled and overflowing with enthusiastic ideas.

My meetings with Pucheu last February obviously intrigued my interlocutors, who asked me if I had not by chance maintained

The Night Will End

some obscure contact with Vichy. Since almost everyone seemed curious about this, I drew up a report for Passy on my meetings with Pétain's Interior Minister. In mimeographed form this report was passed around to the principal official representatives of Free France. My statement was clear; no one ever mentioned the matter to me again.

Day after day I met men who for varied reasons were focussing their attention on metropolitan France. One of them was Jacques Soustelle, our new information *commissaire*, a brilliant young ethnologist who had worked for the Musée de l'Homme before the war and had returned from Mexico the previous year to work for General de Gaulle.

It was with Pierre Brossolette that I had the most in common. He was Passy's assistant and had become his close friend. He had a degree from the Ecole Normale Supérieure and had been a militant Socialist before the war. His political experience was so rich that he became a kind of adviser on political affairs to Passy. Brossolette and I had already met in France. He was one of the few people in London who had solid experience of clandestine life and the resistance movements. Unlike so many others, he knew what he was talking about and was familiar with our potential and our limitations. I was delighted to reach agreement with him on several burning issues.

Like myself, he'd realized that the strict sealing-off of our paramilitary cadres was impossible. The rank-and-file militant, whether we liked it or not, was at once a propagandist, a recruiter and, perhaps, an intelligence-gatherer. How in good faith could we forbid him to join the Secret Army?

Brossolette also thought that the powers conferred on Jean Moulin were excessive and possibly dangerous, for there was no way to tell how he was using them. Unfortunately his opinion, so close to mine on these issues, was shared by virtually no one else in the B.C.R.A.

During my London stay several sessions were held on the issue of fusion versus coordination. Once again I bowed to D'Astier's stubborn opposition to fusion; after all, coordination was better than chaos. On the conclusion of the two sessions in early

London Mission

203

October, the B.C.R.A. formalized our accord in a memorandum to be distributed throughout France. The following were its essential provisions:

A Coordinating Committee was to be set up, composed of four members: Jean Moulin (chairman), plus the chiefs of the three movements, each of which was to preserve its autonomy.

In the political domain, the French National Committee in London would be required to consult with the Coordinating Committee prior to all decisions. London would remain free, however, to determine the ways and means by which any decisions would be carried out.

The head of the Secret Army would be allowed to attend the sessions of the Coordinating Committee.

Depending on the situation, the orders of the committee would be carried out either by the movements themselves or by the Secret Army.

The committee would provide "shadow" administrative cadres to take over on the liberation of our territory.

The existing study groups were to be merged and placed directly under the control of the committee.

In reality, these directives were never followed. Jean Moulin soon managed to capture all the real power in the Coordinating Committee. As we shall soon see, with the exception of Moulin the committee played only an episodic and consultative role.

The functions of the Secret Army, as well as the hardware it required, were carefully studied. The army was to accomplish three different types of missions: (1) to knock out certain industrial targets; (2) to wipe out the enemy's rear communication lines on D-Day; (3) after D-Day to harry the enemy's columns relentlessly.

These plans were well conceived and quite realizable—on the condition that we received the necessary weapons. After having checked on the most useful type of weapons and the minimum quantity to be parachuted each month (at least 1,000 tons), we had to wheedle these arms out of the English, along with the planes necessary for parachute drops.

Accompanied by Passy, we brought this request before the

bosses of the S.O.E.*: General Gubbins, Colonel Hutchinson and Robin Brook. Our proposals were received with that indifferent courtesy that so often characterizes relations between Britons and Continentals. The final decision, it appeared, lay not with the S.O.E. but with Lord Selborne, the Minister of Economic Warfare.

D'Astier and I met him in the presence of his principal private secretary, and by the time we left we were very discouraged. Yes, they understood our needs, but other countries also required aerial assistance of the type we had requested. Moreover, it was simply impossible to divert too many aircraft from the bombing raids over Germany. However, we could rest assured that the question would be submitted to the most sympathetic study.

What the upshot of these conversations was I never knew. Neither London nor Jean Moulin ever revealed the number of tons parachuted into France. In any case, for many months the Secret Army and the Groupes Francs received nothing but a dribble in the way of arms.

Our stay in London was drawing to a close. We'd done what we could to carry out our mission. De Gaulle received D'Astier and me in his office in Carlton Gardens.

"Well, now, 'Bernard' and 'Charvet,' I see you're about ready to go. Passy has told me that you've accomplished some important work. The fusion of the Resistance is now complete, and the Coordinating Committee will direct its operations. I'm writing to 'Max' to ask him that all organizations other than Combat, Libération and Franc-Tireur contribute their supporters to one of these three movements."

"But we're still worried about hardware," I said. "The English showered us with kind words, but we were unable to extract a commitment from them."

"Well, now you've seen for yourself that with the English nothing is easy. They're playing their hand; we must play ours. Here and in France, the struggle is the same. Tell your people back home that against Hitler, against Vichy and in our dealings with

*Secret Operations Executive.

London Mission

the English, we must present a united front. That is the essential. We have many hurdles ahead of us, as I hope you've realized during your stay here."

De Gaulle was staring at the ceiling now, his long legs stretched out under his desk, his fingers interlaced, that ever-present cigarette protruding from his mouth.

"The Vichy clique is groveling at the feet of the Germans. The Americans are up to some form of mischief with Giraud. The English are supplanting us in our overseas territories. If France wishes to remain France, she must rally to De Gaulle."

D'Astier once again raised the issue of our relationship to "Max," who was too avid of authority and too personal in his wielding of it for both D'Astier's taste and my own. However, we were assured that from now on the Coordinating Committee, and not "Max" alone, would have the last word. This was to be the guarantee of our *bonne entente* and hence the condition of success.

My final night at the Mount Royal had come. Tomorrow we were to set forth on our return journey. I tried to draw up a sort of balance sheet of what we'd accomplished. First, there was De Gaulle. The truth was that there had been not the faintest spark of human contact between us. He was a cold and calculating strategist. The Resistance, for him, was one pawn among others. The devotion and courage of its members, the dangers, the arrests, the executions were for him only an inevitable tithe paid to the god of war.

Despite his 1940 accord with Churchill, De Gaulle's status as France's legitimate representative was still questionable. The Americans flatly refused to recognize the accord, and the English, by no means blind to the lingering prestige of Marshal Pétain, were still wondering just how popular De Gaulle really was. Even much of the French community in London had refused his authority.

In the B.C.R.A. itself I'd found an ambience reminiscent of the youth, fervor and gaiety of Combat. There I'd had the impression that we of the Resistance had been heard and understood. True, I hadn't insisted on all the positions that I believed correct. Indeed, I'd accepted, both for the Secret Army's high command and for

The Night Will End

the coordination of our movements, decisions that I found less than optimal. As Henri Noguères wrote long after the war: "It was at the price of great concessions, especially by Frenay, that the London talks were at last adjourned with an accord . . . resolving every question on the agenda."*

I spent the morning of the following day, October 20, on a round of farewell visits. At nightfall a car driven by a British soldier and containing a B.C.R.A. officer came to pick up D'Astier and myself.

We sped off southward. Not a breath of wind was stirring, and the moon rose clear and bright and unshrouded. After passing several inspections, we stopped before a small barracks. Then we were ushered into a vast, bare but well-heated room. In a corner, two civilians and a British officer were conversing in hushed tones. Perhaps they too were clandestine travelers. We sat down in the opposite corner.

On our departure from London we had each been given a viaticum preparing us for every conceivable eventuality. It contained powerful sleeping pills, "ups" to keep us awake and, last but not least, a giant "horse pill" of cyanide, in whose use we were carefully instructed. Since the poison was sealed inside a rubber membrane, its user could safely keep the capsule in his mouth until he chose to die, at which point all he had to do was to bite. The cyanide required only a few seconds to do its job.

We were called up for departure at about ten o'clock. An R.A.F. man escorted us on foot to the end of the airstrip, where at last we got a good look at one of those famous Lysanders. It was a solid little monoplane. I drew lots with D'Astier as to who would sit behind the pilot. He won. We clambered into the cockpit and squeezed ourselves into place along with our luggage—first the pilot, then D'Astier, then I. The propeller spun into motion; the engine was revved all the way up. Menthon turned around and raised his eyebrows for my okay signal. I held up my thumb. The plane edged forward, gathering speed, and we were off.

Hardly had we taken off than we saw the coast of England glide

*Histoire de la Résistance, Vol. II, page 618.

London Mission

past beneath our wings. Its dark receding mass stood out sharply against the scintillating silver of the Channel. Our plane was still climbing when France appeared below.

As we approached the coastal promontories I saw luminous balls of light begin to glide slowly toward us. It took me a few seconds to realize that this was the famous flak, or German antiaircraft fire. The spectacle had an unearthly, fairy-tale beauty about it.

Because of the weak momentum of these projectiles, they left the earth with astonishing slowness, but as they arrived at our altitude they would rush by at several hundred feet per second. They came in different sizes and colors—yellow, red and blue. And so, half quailing, half applauding, we watched this extraordinary fireworks display. Happily for us, it was soon over. We had overflown the German coastal defenses and were humming along over the French countryside.

The blackout was so strictly observed that we couldn't make out a single point of light, but the rivers, meadows and copses were perfectly visible. We crossed the Loire, then the Saône. Less than ten minutes later we saw the pilot scrutinizing the terrain. The plane swung sharply to the right and described a wide circle, then repeated this procedure on the left. We soared and circled in this fashion for several minutes, searching for the agreed-upon signal and the welcoming triangle of beacons.

But our search was in vain. There was nobody there. They had missed the rendezvous! We were obliged to return to England.

Though I had not taken a sedative, I fell into a deep sleep. Then suddenly I was roused by a brilliant light. Our plane's wings seemed to have been lit by a powerful spotlight. I looked downward and froze with horror. Six or eight searchlights, their beams converging, were trained on us. I had the eerie impression that we were naked and totally vulnerable.

But our pilot knew his business. As my stomach rose into my mouth, the plane plunged vertically downward. Then, at only two or three hundred yards from the earth, it suddenly shot up, riveting me to my seat. Behind us the searchlights groped vainly about the sky.

When we landed I discovered that by some navigational error we

The Night Will End

had overflown Dijon, where a whole squadron of Luftwaffe interceptors was based.

By the light of the October moon we made two more vain attempts to return to France, each in that same fairyland setting—the sea, the flak, the fields and woods of France—but neither time did we venture beyond the Loire, where shrouds of fog and clouds turned us sternly back.

And so we remained in London. It was now November 1942. The war was approaching a decisive turning point.

Our London mission had already been accomplished, so I decided to get in touch with those Frenchmen who had either refused to rally to De Gaulle or had quit his service.

I asked the B.C.R.A. officers how I could get in touch with the notorious Admiral Émile Muselier. Though my curiosity awakened their anxiety, I found Muselier's case especially intriguing.

A vice-admiral—and thus of higher rank than De Gaulle—he had nonetheless agreed in June 1940 to serve under De Gaulle's command. He had become the number-two man in the London hierarchy. As it happened, the Free French disposed of numerous warships of low and medium tonnage; in fact, they were the principal military resource of the French freedom fighters. Naturally Muselier became their commanding officer. Moreover, it was actually Muselier, not De Gaulle, who had "invented" the Cross of Lorraine as a counter-symbol to Hitler's swastika. Finally, on orders from De Gaulle, Muselier had landed an expeditionary force in the islands of Saint-Pierre and Miquelon to bring them under Free French suzerainty.

A number of serious incidents had occurred between Muselier and De Gaulle in 1941 and early in 1942. Apparently he had tried first to oust the general, then to entice the Free French navy into seceding from the French National Committee and putting itself directly under English supervision. Following this attempted coup, he had been relieved of all his duties, including the command of the navy, and he had even been subjected to disciplinary sanctions.

Muselier was a man of average height, with intelligent eyes,

London Mission

lightly graying hair and a hawk's profile. He must have been terribly nervous, because he could barely control his trembling hands. He warmly expressed his pleasure in meeting me. Like all the French in London, he was eager for news from France.

"Is the Resistance really behind De Gaulle?" he asked.

"It's entirely behind him, and I myself have been one of the prime movers in this direction."

"One day you'll regret it. You don't know what De Gaulle is really like yet, but you'll learn."

From the fiery tirade that followed I gathered that in his eyes De Gaulle was a reactionary dictator. De Gaulle's men were mere marionettes. He pulled their strings, then threw them out when they had served his purposes. The members of the French National Committee were pure papier-mâché. As for the Special Services, they were packed with *cagoulards*.* They were no more than a secret police made up of right-wing hooligans.

I said goodbye to Muselier and walked out into the crowded London streets. The sheer vituperativeness of his words had caused me not to take them too seriously. Yet perhaps all that he said was not false. I began to wonder if I'd not best be more vigilant toward De Gaulle.

Early in my stay I'd met Mr. Albrecht, Berty's husband. Cut off from all news of his wife and children since the defeat of France, he was gnawed by terrible anxieties. He had been absolutely thunderstruck to learn of our activities, of his wife's part in the Resistance, her imprisonment and her subsequent victorious hunger strike.

A Dutch citizen of pacific temperament, he was an excellent musician and a discerning gourmet. Now in his fifties, he did not in any way participate in the war effort. He was a financial expert who practically lived in the City, where his talents were renowned.

"Berty in prison!" he exclaimed. "Impossible!" I could tell that for him the word *prison*—even in this case—had a scandalous ring. I felt sorry for this man, whose fear for his family could hardly be allayed by his admiration for his wife's courage.

*Members of the extreme royalist faction of Action Française.

The Night Will End

I saw him again early in November. The evening before, a telegram had arrived for me from France via the B.C.R.A. Fifty members of Combat had been sentenced by a Lyons court. This trial—in which the defendants had been charged with endangering the domestic and foreign security of the state—had created an uproar. Chevance, Peck and I had each been sentenced *in absentia* to an incommutable ten-year prison term, a fine of 120,000 francs and the confiscation of our possessions. Only three of the defendants had been released, one of them Mounier; the others had received prison terms ranging from one month to five years in jail. Berty had been condemned to two years in prison.

When I informed Mr. Albrecht of this, he exploded at Vichy in a torrent of abuse. Alas, it was well justified, for Berty was soon to be "administratively interned" once again.

After the war I was to learn the reasons adduced for the negative verdict against the entire group:

. . . the distribution of leaflets of foreign inspiration . . . the formation of a subversive organization, financed by England, whose ringleader is the former* General de Gaulle

. . . the fomenting of a revolution aimed at the denunciation of the Armistice and the taking up of arms.

Since my arrival the tone of the press had grown steadily livelier. The war news was heartening. In London itself American uniforms were more and more common. Wave after wave of American bombers crossed the Atlantic to be based in Great Britain. Their participation in the attacks against German cities was ever greater, despite Goering's promise to his countrymen that never would the aircraft of the Allies penetrate the air space of the Third Reich.

In Russia, the German army was wearing itself out in the siege of Stalingrad (whose fall, however, still seemed imminent). Despite the ice and serious losses of men and materiel, convoys of Allied cargo ships, plying through the waters of the frigid zone, were

*The general had been condemned to death *in absentia* and stripped of his rank by a Vichy military tribunal.

London Mission

bringing the Soviets the cannons, tanks and ammunition they so sorely needed.

However, what really swelled the pride of the British was the news from Libya and Egypt. In early November, after a fierce battle, General Montgomery, the victor of El-Alamein, had forced Rommel and his Africa Corps into full retreat. After so many setbacks, so many humiliating surrenders in North Africa and the Far East, here at last was a clear-cut victory.

In London there existed a top-secret S.O.E. center whose sole function was to conceive and fabricate materiel specifically designed for underground warfare. To this center D'Astier and I were invited. Its staff consisted of doctors, chemists, ballistics experts and physicists. They were hard at work inventing the most extraordinary gadgets, not only for France and Europe but for all the other theaters as well, including Egypt, Libya and the Far East. We ourselves had only a very partial view of these inventions, but we did get to see a suitcase that, when unlocked, automatically destroyed its contents. We also saw different types of guns with silencers, pens that were actually pistols, anti-vehicle mines with the most startling shapes—including those of stones and camel turds—pills that put to sleep or killed the swallower, puncturing devices shaped like jacks and many others that I've now forgotten. In the cellar of this quiet house was a shooting range. It was here that we first saw a demonstration of the Sten guns that were later to arm the Resistance so abundantly.

About eight o'clock on the morning of November 8 I was in the midst of shaving when my phone rang.

"Hello? Frenay? This is Mamy speaking." Mamy was a captain who worked in the B.C.R.A. headquarters. "Heard the news? This morning the Americans landed in Morocco and Algeria. Our info's pretty skimpy but it seems that Vichy's offering some resistance. Anyway, all night long our monitoring service has been picking up the same message: 'Franklin's here . . . Franklin's here.'"

I wondered whether General Noguès, Vichy's resident general in Morocco, had really given the order to open fire on the

The Night Will End

Americans. What would Vichy's reaction be? Surely the Germans would pressure Laval to declare war on the United States. And what about Hitler? He could hardly sit by and idly watch while Rommel's rear was threatened by Allied troops. But did he have any extra divisions of his own to land in Algeria and Tunisia? Above all I wondered what Capitant and our people in the Algiers Combat were up to, now that they suddenly found themselves on the front lines.

I was just going out when the telephone rang again. It turned out to be a colleague of Sir Charles Hambro, the head of the British Special Services. Apparently Hambro, whom I'd never met, wanted me to lunch with him at his club near Pall Mall. He had an important communication for me.

I informed Passy of this invitation, then met Hambro at his club.

"Thank you for accepting my invitation," he said. "I thought a meeting between us might be useful. Of course, you know the news."

"All I know is that the Americans are landing in North Africa."

"Well, the situation is confused. Beachheads have been secured, though I'm not entirely sure that the Americans have firm control of the situation. The attitude of the French army seems ambivalent. However, General Giraud has spoken over the radio in Algiers to ask the troops and civilians to welcome the American and British troops as friends, and I believe that he will be heeded. You see, our government is concerned about the problem of future relations between a North Africa under Giraud and a Free France under De Gaulle. Don't you believe that it's in France's interest that some sort of bridge be built between them? Now, Giraud knows that you have an important role at the head of the French Resistance. Don't you think that now he'd consider a mediation offer from you more seriously than he has in the past?"

"It's hard for me to say. Our relations with Giraud have shown just how stubborn the man is. Furthermore, where could I possibly see him to talk the matter over?"

"Well, if you think an overture by you might meet with success, we'll fly you to North Africa. But we're pressed for time. You'd have to leave tonight."

London Mission

That was the last thing I'd expected!

"Frankly, I think that little is likely to come of a meeting between Giraud and myself," I said. "But it's worth a try. Of course I'm ready to go any time, but General de Gaulle must be informed first. I can't leave without his okay."

Sir Charles frowned. "Well, then, will you kindly ring me and tell me the outcome of your consultation with De Gaulle?"

We parted. I'd obviously disappointed my host. It was clear enough that he expected no good to come of my forthcoming consultation with the general.

Soon I stood before a frowning, tense-jawed De Gaulle.

"Well then, 'Charvet,' it seems you have something to tell me?"

I told him of Hambro's proposal, concluding, "Of course I can't leave without your okay."

He lit a cigarette, "There can be no question of your leaving for Algiers alone. We must show Giraud that the French freedom fighters have formed a united front, that the Resistance and the Free French are marching in step under De Gaulle's leadership. Tell Hambro that you'll leave this evening, accompanied by Lieutenant Colonel Billotte and Gaston Palewski."

"General, don't you think that it might be very dangerous to send Giraud an official delegation? Suppose he rebuffs it or fails to prove amenable to an agreement. Any failure sustained by a delegation from you would be a blow to your own prestige. If I went to Algiers alone, your prestige wouldn't be at stake."

After a moment's thought he replied, "I prefer my own idea. When you've got your Englishman's reaction to it, ring my staff."

He walked me to the door. "Listen, 'Charvet.' Only one thing matters—that the maximum number of French citizens, and the maximum amount of French territory, enter the war. Everything else is secondary."

Back in my hotel, I rang Sir Charles Hambro and told him about De Gaulle's counter-proposal.

"Ahhh," he said icily. "That's not exactly what I had in mind."

Why had De Gaulle opposed the idea of my flying alone to

The Night Will End

Algeria? I was reduced to guesswork. The most plausible explanation was that he was apprehensive lest the Resistance assume the role of mediator between Giraud and himself.

That same evening I listened to De Gaulle on the radio:

" . . . French leaders, soldiers, sailors, airmen, civil servants, colonists: arise! Help our Allies! The France that is struggling for her freedom adjures you to rally to her without reservation! Pay no mind to names or formulas. Only one thing counts: the welfare of our homeland! All those who have the courage to stand up and fight, despite the presence of the enemy and the traitors whom he has enticed into his service, are hailed and acclaimed by all of Fighting France. Have nothing but contempt for the traitors who try to persuade you that our Allies wish to claim our empire for themselves.

"Arise! The great moment is upon us! The hour of reason and courage has arrived!"

On November 11 several cablegrams informed us that the Wehrmacht had crossed the demarcation line and was pushing furiously into the southern zone. This was Hitler's rejoinder to the American landing. That day also marked the end of the myth of Vichy sovereignty. Henceforth the swastika was to float over the entirety of metropolitan France. For Combat, for my comrades and for myself, the battle was to change radically. We were now confronted by the Gestapo itself.

On the afternoon of the same day, all the French in London, both military men and civilians, were invited to a mass meeting in the Albert Hall. Fog has settled on the British capital. As I entered the enormous auditorium I found that a noisy, festive crowd of thousands had already gathered there. Flags decked the area around the dais, over which hung an immense Cross of Lorraine. Glancing about the hall, I realized that every face was young; the average age of the audience was surely under thirty. One by one the national *commissaires* filed into the front row, directly before the podium.

Though I was lost in the crowd and infected by its joyous fervor,

London Mission

215

my thoughts did not once leave my comrades in France. As the German troops advanced toward the Mediterranean they were sure to launch major raids. We already knew that one month ago almost three hundred Gestapo and Abwehr agents had entered the former free zone and had been provided by Vichy with French police papers.

Several speakers addressed the crowd. They were men who had just arrived from France in unusual and dangerous ways. Among them were workers, office clerks, fishermen. In their humble language, all the more touching for its occasional clumsiness, they recounted their adventures, the vicissitudes of life in France, their joy to be here under the Cross of Lorraine and their desire to participate in the liberation of their homeland.

Then De Gaulle appeared. The entire audience rose to its feet and applauded wildly. Yet the leader of the Free French wore a worried look. Even before this vast and enthusiastic crowd, not the faintest smile brightened his face.

He reviewed the recent successes of the Allies, our growing hopes, the new position of France in the conflict. It was with especial emotion that I, who had never stopped campaigning for total unity in our struggle, heard the words "It remains our duty to see that this war is won with the help of France. When I say France I mean one nation, one territory, one empire [a discreet allusion to Giraud], one law. . . . All France must now flock to join the ranks of that France that is already at war. . . . The aura of French unity is the blood of the French people. . . ."

Then he invoked the sacrifice of the sailors, airmen and soldiers of Free France and of the men of the Resistance who had been tortured or executed by firing squad: ". . . with your dying breath you said: '*Vive la France!*' Oh, sleep in peace! France shall live because you gave your lives for her. . . . We shall not allow anyone to divide the war effort of our Fatherland by any . . . separate undertakings. . . ."

Each of these rhetorical periods was greeted by frantic applause from the audience. Then, all at once, we were engulfed by the total silence that reigns in church at the moment of the elevation of the Host. Then I heard the words "France judges men and their deeds in accordance with what they do to save her life. The

The Night Will End

hierarchies established in the past, the consecrated figures of public life, the old rules of the game, have lost the faith once accorded them. The nation no longer recognizes any cadres other than those of the Liberation. Just as she did in her great Revolution, she will accept only those leaders who lead for the people's welfare. . . ."

And, in the midst of a tremendous ovation, he concluded: "Today France looks to her heart with one hope and one will. . . . One struggle, for one Fatherland!"

I was happy and filled with hope. What De Gaulle had said corresponded exactly with our own thoughts and wishes. I could tell my colleagues in France that we and De Gaulle were marching in step, that our hearts beat in unison.

Two days before my departure General de Gaulle invited D'Astier and me to dinner for the following evening, November 16, at the Savoy Hotel. Also invited were Colonel Passy, Colonel Billotte and Pierre Brossolette.

During the dinner the conversation revolved around the difficulties resulting from the now total occupation of France. Over dessert we discussed a new project that might give the Resistance a more representative character and so impress our Allies with its legitimacy. After all, up to now we had had a serious handicap: The Resistance was by nature secret, and the names of its leaders—our names—were new and virtually unknown.

Wouldn't it make sense to create a counterpart to the French National Committee in metropolitan France itself, an organism in which both the resistance movements and the old political parties would be represented? Opinions diverged, but in essence De Gaulle, Passy, Billotte and D'Astier favored the idea, whereas Brossolette remained circumspect. This idea prefigured what was to become, three months later, the National Council of the Resistance (C.N.R.).

"General," I said, "I'm opposed to this idea for several reasons. First, with the exception of the Communists, all the pre-war political parties—the Socialists, the Radical Socialists, the Democratic Alliance and the Republican Federation—have disappeared. To give official representation to these defunct parties would be an

London Mission

invitation for them to reconstitute themselves and thus to create the Third Republic all over again. That's exactly what we don't want. The body we are discussing would, as a representative council, feel called on to pronounce on all the nation's problems. Yet inside France men's perspectives are very different from what they are here. Doesn't it seem likely that such differences will lead to hostility?"

"In that case," said De Gaulle, "we'd just have to try to find a way to work things out."

"And if we failed, we'd be up a one-way alley," I insisted.

"No. In that case, I'd just issue orders."

Now we had arrived at the heart of the matter: the nature of the relationship between De Gaulle and the Resistance. A pall of silence fell over the table.

I said, "We are resisters, free to think and do as we choose. Our freedom of choice is an inalienable right. It is up to us to decide whether, in the political domain, we shall carry out your orders or not."

The general remained silent for a few moments. Evidently he found my words unseemly.

"Well then, 'Charvet,' it seems that France must choose between you and me."

The Night Will End

THE MAQUIS

Back in France, I re-
alized that I'd just turned thirty-
seven. What joy I felt to see my friends
again, to read the warmth and trust in their
eyes! Nothing serious had yet resulted from the new
German invasion. The Gestapo needed a certain amount
of time to cast its net over the whole southern zone. My
first concern was to form a good understanding of the
changed situation, in the company of the steering committee
of Combat and the principal chiefs of our movement. I asked
Jean-Guy to organize for me a series of rendezvous in Mâcon,
Villefranche and Lyons.

In Saint-Clair, a Lyons suburb, D'Astier and I met Moulin and
gave him the instructions and twenty million francs from London. It was a cordial meeting. Moulin and I left on foot, chatting
amicably. He asked me a great many questions about my meetings
with De Gaulle and the B.C.R.A. officers in London. A feeling of
trust and relaxation was beginning to characterize our relationship.

"Why don't you, like myself, become an official emissary of the C.N.F. [French National Committee]
or the B.C.R.A.?" he asked me. "Given your role
at the head of Combat, you'd get the highest
rank, that of P.1 agent. You'd also re-

ceive a considerable monthly soldier's pay that would be deposited in London in your name."

"My dear 'Max,' I appreciate your offer. However, I cannot accept it. Your apparently simple question in fact poses a problem of vast importance—that of the rapport between London and the Resistance.

"In the beginning we forged an organization without any help from London. None of us were 'agents,' for to be an 'agent' means to be at somebody's orders. We followed no orders but those of our own conscience.

"No less freely, we rallied to De Gaulle. You know that I championed De Gaulle's cause even before your return to France. But this cause had a value only because it was freely accepted by the groups involved. Our loyalty will remain valuable only if that implicit freedom is retained.

"I'm not at all sure that London yet appreciates the difference between the various existing 'rings' and our full-fledged movement. The former are, and must be, at London's orders. Otherwise they could not fulfill their intelligence-gathering role. The movements, on the other hand, in the fulness of their organization and their propaganda, are the expression of free men struggling at once against the occupier and against the Vichy regime. These men want to be soldiers *while remaining citizens,* and citizens cannot become 'agents' without renouncing their right to free expression.

"If, tomorrow, we all became 'agents,' each with his London bank account getting fatter by the month, do you think that we'd still command respect? No, to command respect, political expression must be free. I cannot accept your offer."

"My dear 'Charvet,' we are at war. In war it is necessary to have one supreme commander, and our commander is General de Gaulle."

"Militarily, yes; politically, no. To put the Resistance at De Gaulle's political disposal would be to go out of our way to confirm the charges of the anti-Gaullists that De Gaulle is an apprentice dictator. In the interest of our cause, I must decline."

I sensed that Moulin was angry now. But why? Was he afraid that I might prove disloyal to De Gaulle? Did he really imagine that

The Night Will End

my fidelity could be won with a lump of sugar—that is, with a salary and a pension?

We parted. Our rapport had distinctly suffered from this talk. I could see that I was now suspect in his eyes.

After the war I was to learn that during his first trip to London in April 1942, D'Astier had requested and received a position as "P.1 agent."

By now I felt that my comrades were my family. It felt good to be with them again. Though many called me "boss," I was really their friend. We were almost all between twenty-five and thirty-five, young enough to preserve our *joie de vivre* in the midst of danger. Our youth gave us strength.

The Marseilles region (R.2) was still organizationally superior to the others. Shortly after my departure for London, Chevance had even succeeded in implanting Combat in Corsica under the direction of Charles Giudicelli and Canavelli. However, since the occupation of the free zone our communication with them had been severed. According to the last word the movement was developing rapidly and had secured the precious collaboration of Senator Paul Giacobbi.

During my absence Henri Ingrand had been appointed by Bourdet to take over the direction of R.6 (Clermont-Ferrand), where he had replaced Alfred Coste-Floret, who, because of his record, seemed a likely target for Gestapo arrest.

In the R.3 region (Montpellier), Pierre-Henri Teitgen and René Courtin, both threatened by the Gestapo, had sought refuge in Lozère after appointing suitable replacements.

I at once dispatched Jean-Guy Bernard to Montpellier to study the situation and to appoint a new regional chief. The man whom he selected was Cauvet ("Cals"), a militant Socialist who was chief of R.3 until the spring of 1943, when he was arrested and deported. He never came back.

The printing of propaganda material had made great leaps forward. André Bollier had surrounded himself with a very able team, including Lucienne Guézennec, Fernand Beucler, Lucien Gros ("Lulu") and Désirée Chatain ("Dédé"). Our first printer, Martinet, was still serving us faithfully.

The Maquis

Bollier had bought a press and installed it in the cellar of an isolated house in Crémieux (Ain). In Nice, Villefranche and Toulouse he had also enlisted many printers, for the size of our newspaper's printing runs had shot up sharply, and we were also publishing numerous pamphlets against the labor draft. Thanks to the cooperation of a photography studio, we now used photographic plates instead of letterpress foundry type, which was much more dangerous to move about.

Bourdet was highly satisfied with the development of the N. A.P., in particular, the N.A.P.-Rail and the N.A.P.-Police. The direction of Sabotage-Rail was entrusted to René Hardy ("Didot"), who'd made an excellent impression on both Bourdet and myself. A thin, blond fellow with a determined mouth, he exuded energy and determination. A professional schoolteacher, he'd later become involved in railway management. Before the war he'd been the stationmaster of the Gare Montparnasse. The N.A.P.-Police was also beginning to render great services. Often it would warn a comrade of his imminent arrest, thus allowing him to vanish in time. Then, too—and for this we were also indebted to our accomplices in the city halls—it provided us with administrative stationery, blank identity cards and stamps, thus enabling André Bollier to organize an important reserve of false papers with all the hallmarks of authenticity.

General Delestraint's staff was also beefed up. Morin, Aubry and Castaldo were now joined by some newcomers from Libération: Raymond Aubrac*; his wife, Lucie, a certain "Valrimont," whose real name was Kriegel**; and Pascal Copeau,† who'd stood in for D'Astier during his trip to London.

Quite a few new faces had appeared in Libération: Pierre Hervé‡; his wife, Annie, who had been placed in the B.I.P. (Bureau d'Information et de Presse) beside Georges Bidault; and a fellow called Malleret ("Joinville"). Although we didn't know it at the time, all were Communists. Only later were we to realize that

*Aubrac: government civil engineer and future *commissaire* of the Republic.
**Kriegel: A future deputy.
†Copeau: son of Jacques Copeau, actor, author and theater director.
‡Hervé: schoolteacher and future deputy.

The Night Will End

they were the harbingers of the infiltration of the Resistance via Libération.

On November 27 the first meeting of the Coordinating Committee was held in a Lyons suburb. There were five of us sitting around the table that day: Jean Moulin, who chaired the meeting, Emmanuel D'Astier, Jean-Pierre Lévy, General Delestraint and myself.

First, D'Astier and I gave a résumé of our trip to London, mentioning the role and powers of this new committee, the confirmation of Delestraint as the supreme commander of the Secret Army and the promise of more parachute drops containing arms.

I called to mind that I had argued for the fusion of all our movements rather than the simple coordination I'd been obliged to accept. I said that I would loyally uphold the decision we had adopted, for it did signal some progress, but that I remained convinced that even this experience would eventually lead us to weld our three organizations together into one powerful movement.

We decided to meet at least twice a month.

While our Coordinating Committee was in session serious hostilities broke out all over the former free zone. Toward late afternoon rumors were circulating in Lyons that German troops had clashed with various units of the Armistice Army.

The following day, November 28, the press (and the BBC, which obviously had been swiftly apprised of the stiuation) informed us that the Wehrmacht had invested the fortified harbor of Toulon and that the entire French fleet had been scuttled to prevent it from falling into enemy hands.

Thus disappeared a powerful naval force that might have proved of vital importance in the war had it passed into Allied hands. I pictured the captured crews and the smoking wreckage in the great Mediterranean roadsteads. These sailors had been forced to destroy with their own hands the instrument the nation had entrust-

The Maquis

ed to them and which they themselves had so painstakingly perfected.

On that same November 27 the Wehrmacht had invaded the barracks and offices of the Armistice Army. The latter had been disarmed without putting up the slightest resistance.

When, almost two years earlier, I had quit that same army, I had known that all its hopes for revenge were mere vanity, that eventually it would have to bow before the government's submissive policy. Indeed, this had been my reason for quitting. Yet I had loved that army too much not to understand the heart-rending suffering that it was experiencing today and the distress of those officers, my old comrades, whom Vichy had led into this tragic impasse.

It was De Gaulle himself who, that sorrowful evening, best expressed our shared feelings: "The fleet of Toulon, the fleet of France, has just disappeared. In one brief moment our sailors have seen the veil of untruth that has blinded them since June 1940 torn from their eyes. . . . Added to all her earlier sorrows, this sorrow unites all France. . . . [We must have] victory. There is no other way, there has never been any other way."

The occupation of the free zone, the dissolution of the Armistice Army and the disaster of Toulon finally opened many eyes which, through loyalty to Marshal Pétain or through simple ignorance and egoism, had refused to see the cruel truth.

The demarcation line had divided France into two parts and two different regimes, one of which had preserved an illusive sovereignty. Paradoxically, the presence of German troops on the entirety of our national territory served partially to reunite the nation. Yet many Frenchmen, both soldiers and civilians, had been hoodwinked by official propaganda into seeing De Gaulle as a poltroon general who had deserted our soil in the hour of need. By backing not De Gaulle but General Giraud they were able to break with Vichy without having to condemn their own past conduct. And so, in opposition to us "Gaullists," the "Giraldists" came into being.

From now on all Frenchmen were to recognize one common

The Night Will End

enemy, Nazi Germany, and one common objective, the liberation of national territory. Yet profound differences were to persist between the Gaullists and the Giraldists.

The vast majority of the Giraldists remained attached, in one way or another, to the phony "national revolution." Their veneration for Marshal Pétain had been changed into mere pity.

Our movements, on the contrary, were republican. Contemptuous of the "national revolution," they were struggling to reconquer our freedoms. For them Pétain was only a tool in the hands of the enemy.

The conscience of many Frenchmen was sorely troubled. In Lyons, *Le Temps* and *Le Figaro* were scuttled along with the fleet. Their editorial staffs preferred this expedient to obedience to Goebbels. Other papers chose servitude over death.

Immediately after the meeting of our steering committee I summoned François Morin, the Secret Army's chief of staff. I disclosed to him our decision to commit all our resources to seizing the Armistice Army's arms depots, and I told him to contact General Revers.

"We've got a good chance of success," said Morin. "I've heard that Revers is already trying to reorganize his officer corps as an underground operation."

Yet once again I was to experience the sad results of blind military discipline.

Ten days later Morin reported back. He had indeed met General Revers and had been courteously received. However, Revers had referred him to General Picquendar, who, in his turn, had referred him to a regional commander called Mollard, who resided in the southwest of France and who, within the army general staff, had been the organizer of the arms-concealment program. It was Mollard who personally knew each and every camouflage officer, and he agreed to put us in contact with them on condition that he receive an order to that effect from General Frère (who, as I recall, had himself retired to the Limoges area).

Morin had driven to Frère's residence. He found the general in the midst of pinning toy flags on a map of the Russian front. No,

The Maquis

225

Frère did not feel competent to give such an order. He considered himself to be Giraud's subordinate. Unfortunately, Giraud was in Algeria.

As I listened to Morin's report I was seized by a fit of rage. I grabbed my pen and at one blow dashed off a note to Picquendar (who of course knew me already from the time in January 1941 when he'd tried to persuade me to stay in the army). This letter, signed in my own name, ended with these words:

The army's weapons belong to the nation and not to you alone. It is your duty to give them to those who will use them for the liberation of our homeland.

If through your stubbornness they fall into the enemy's hands, you shall answer before the courts of our liberated land, and I myself shall be your accuser.

The letter was never answered. Soon afterward, Laval ordered that all existing arms caches be turned over to the Germans, which, with a few exceptions, they were.

Jacques Renouvin came to see me in Mâcon.

"Chief," he said, "I talked about you to my friend Pierre de Bénouville. He wants to meet you."

My memory of my first meeting with Bénouville is still crystal-clear. The first thing that struck me was the light blue of his eyes and the intensity and liveliness of his expression. Although at first glance I thought that he was under twenty, I soon noticed that his only remaining hair was on his temples. His voice was cracked. Apparently he'd used it a lot before the war in the public meetings of Action Française.

Like many French resisters, Bénouville had not even bothered to distinguish between the English and the Free French, both of whom seemed to be waging an identical struggle. Now that he knew of their divergences, he had also discovered that our movements had rallied to De Gaulle as part and parcel of their unification. He was eager for his current chief, "Carte"—a British agent of French nationality—to join up with us. He had decided

The Night Will End

that if "Carte" were to refuse he would leave him and work instead for Combat. We concluded that it would be best to hold another meeting that this "Carte" himself would be invited to.

About a week later the three of us met again. This meeting Bénouville had organized in the Château de Bavière, the estate of his friends the Valette-Vialards. It was a luxurious home in the midst of a vast park and surrounded by a detachment of guards.

I hoped that we might succeed in merging "Carte's" undercover ring and our own organization. An agreement with "Carte" would enable us to procure the arms we were so desperately lacking.

Alas! There was to be no such fusion, for my essential condition was "Carte's" allegiance to De Gaulle. Perhaps on orders from the S.O.E., perhaps from personal repugnance, he refused. Sitting before a fire in the hearth of that elegant parlor, we were obliged to admit that we had reached an impasse.

"Carte" was forever lost to us. His organization gradually withered away. On the other hand, with the arrival of Bénouville, whom I rebaptized "Lahire," the movement gained life-giving force and I a dear friend. He was soon to provide stunning proof of his talents. His first exploit was his immediate removal, at my request, to Switzerland, where he established a communication line between us and the Swiss and English secret services. While we provided them with intelligence about the German troops in France, they closed their eyes to our activities and even helped us. And precious help it was, too.

Lyons, my dear birthplace, had become the number-one hotbed of the Resistance. Later we were to call it "the capital."

Yet danger stalked us everywhere. The Gestapo had just enlisted several hundred stoolies. Their role was simply to watch in the streets and cafés for secret meetings and to take note of the participants. By cross-checking the cards in its index the Gestapo could identiy suspect persons and meeting places. The Hôtel Terminus in the Gare Perrache and the military public-health school on the left bank had both been requisitioned by the Gestapo. We soon learned of the tortures the Gestapo was using on resisters and mere suspects to make them talk.

The Maquis

Soon I was packing a loaded pistol whenever I went out. That way, if the enemy were to appear, he and I would be a little more evenly matched.

Winter was upon us. Coal was still scarce, and French homes were cold. Clothes were worn out and hard to replace. Wood now often took the place of leather for shoe soles. Food was scarce for all but country dwellers and the lucky clients of the black market. An overwhelming majority of Frenchmen had only one preoccupation: to stay alive.

We resisters were feeling an upsurge of hope. The German army was wintering in Russia for the second year, and the Soviet counter-offensive had been successful. The army of Marshal Paulus had been surrounded before the walls of Stalingrad.

In Tunisia, the Afrika Korps had briefly resisted the Allies, then fallen back on Bizerte, where Hitler had beefed it up with new reinforcements. Under the orders of Admiral Derrien, Vichy's troops had surrendered to the Germans after a brief skirmish, but the British First Army and several American divisions were rapidly converging on Tunis, and their victory was certain. Shortly all of North Africa would be liberated—from the Germans, that is. But not from Vichy. During the almost four weeks since I had returned from London, Vichy had steadily deteriorated. Darlan, backed by the Americans, was now the kingpin. In the name of the Marshal (who, however, had disavowed him under pressure) he already reigned over Morocco and Algeria. The supreme command of our troops was entrusted to General Giraud. Through its viceroys, Vichy and the spirit of Vichy still reigned in Algiers and the North African littoral.

In the silence of my little room in Charnay I wrote an article for *Combat* entitled "In North Africa, As in France, One Leader Only: De Gaulle":

. . . though the total liberation of our African possessions is now only a matter of weeks, the political situation created by the American government poses grave questions and arouses deep apprehensions. . . .

Admiral Darlan, the servant of the capitulation, the avowed enemy of

The Night Will End

the Anglo-Saxon countries . . . and the man who shook Hitler's hand and applauded the departure of French workers to Germany, this despised and detested personage has been set up by the Americans as the supreme civil and military commander in Algiers. . . .

General Giraud, ignorant no doubt of the realities of the French situation, has unhesitatingly backed this cowardly and traitorous armchair admiral. . . .

The American people and their leader, President Roosevelt, are democrats; as such they have borne the hopes of France. Now they must hear her voice. Our nation, struggling for her freedom under the heel of Germany, cannot admit that any form of dictatorship be safeguarded by those who are struggling against the idea of dictatorship itself. America has broken with Vichy. Yet Darlan is Vichy.

Ever since the sinister day of the Armistice, there has been one man who never doubted, never weakened . . . one man who kept France from losing her soul. . . . In him, France recognized herself. . . .

It is behind him that all Frenchmen must march, to him that all French territories must fall, in a single combat for a single homeland. There is only one Resistance, just as there is only one France. The unity of our struggle is our law. This unity shall be formed behind De Gaulle, because the French people have willed it so.

Libération and *Franc-Tireur* published similar articles. The groaning voice of our clandestine fighters would surely be heard by the Americans. It was heard, all right—but not heeded.

Several days later, Justice pronounced her verdict. On December 24 Admiral Darlan fell beneath the fire of Bonnier de la Chapelle, a young student and member of the Resistance in Algeria. He was sentenced by a kangaroo court and shot by a firing squad. It was now Giraud's turn to rule.

Meanwhile, about December 10, Mireille Albrecht informed me that Berty had just pulled off a risky gamble. She had simulated insanity to such perfection that the doctors had ordered her transferred to the psychiatric hospital of Lyon-Bron. Here she could continue to receive visits from her daughter, for during the day she was free to use a common room. Only at night was she

The Maquis

229

confined to a private chamber. Mireille gave us an exact description of these places, including the position of the annex in which she was confined and that of her room on the second floor.

Next Sunday I mingled in a throng of Lyonnais who had come to Lyon-Bron to visit their relatives. I strolled about freely and at length in the great hospital complex, carefully noting the disposition of the buildings. The retaining wall was only about ten feet tall. Her escape was possible. All we needed was the keys to the annex where she spent the night. The doors were carefully bolted after the evening meal.

From a friendly nurse Mireille obtained a positive wax "dupe" of the keyholes. Within a few days we had a set of keys. During her next visit Mireille advised her mother to be ready to fly the coop on Christmas Eve. There was a good chance that surveillance would be lax during the holiday.

André Bollier assured us that he could arrange the escape himself. At midnight on Christmas Eve, with the aid of two other comrades, he climbed the asylum wall with a ladder. He easily opened the annex door. One comrade, revolver in hand, stationed himself before the door of the night watchman's room. Without a single hitch Bollier and the other fellow opened the door to the second floor, then Berty's itself. They had brought a set of her clothes. Silently, bursting with joy, she dressed. Then the three of them descended the stairs and carefully locked the doors behind them. The night watchman never heard a thing. They helped Berty over the wall and sped away in a car.

Berty was driven to Vernaison, a village beside the Rhône thirteen kilometers south of Lyons. The following morning I saw her. It had been seven months since the beginning of her imprisonment. We fell into each other's arms.

Her long detention had tried Berty sorely, but her light-blue eyes were still as bright as ever. She was very thin and still haunted by the horrible memory of the two weeks she had spent among the authentic madwomen on whom she had modeled her own behavior.

She wished to take her proper place in our ranks as soon as possible. I had to tell her that she'd best spend some time regaining her health and putting on a bit of weight.

The Night Will End

A snowy New Year's Eve. Six of us had gathered near Lyons: François Morin, Henri Aubry, Michel Brault, Pierre de Bénouville, Claude Bourdet and myself.

Our meeting was interrupted by the arrival of a messenger from Marcel Peck. He informed me that some young people, most of them from the Paris area, had evaded the S.T.O. labor draft and hidden in the mountains, where they now lived clandestinely. Refusing to be sent to Germany, they had procured side arms and were ready to defend themselves against arrest.

"In other words," said Michel Brault, "They've taken to the *maquis.*"*

It was the first time, to my knowledge, that this word had been so employed; it was a fitting expression, and it soon became current usage. There were to be many more of these maquis; indeed, a new form of resistance had spontaneously arisen. Neither Degliame, the head of our Workers' Action, nor Soulage, who was soon to create a school for maquis cadres, nor any of the rest of us had ever dreamed of this new kind of warfare. But we were all conscious of the need to help these young men to survive and fight on.

By now the Groupes Francs had swung into action all over the place. In the Hautes-Pyrénées, Henri Garnier, ("Ledoux") had put together several bands of irregulars. Despite the presence of many German sentries, he had succeeded in blowing up the transformer of the Hispano-Suiza factory, as well as the fuel reservoirs of several railway stations. One perfectly realized operation had given him especial satisfaction: the destruction of the regional jamming station that blocked all BBC broadcasts.

Soon directions were sent to the provincial regions enjoining them to organize operations against troop trains, trains for soldiers on short leave and freight trains bound for Germany, factories producing war materiel and French and German Gestapo agents.

Arms were still rare, but they were at least beginning to arrive. Three regions had received parachute drops and had armed their G.F.s. The parachute containers provided them with Sten guns,

*Scrub-wooded upland—Translator.

The Maquis

pistols and the appropriate ammo, as well as radio tubes, grenades and explosives with detonators.

In February I was informed by the N.A.P.-Rail that they would shortly furnish us with the exact schedules of all trains transporting German troops and war materiel.

On February 29 I addressed an instruction to Jacques Renouvin, René Hardy and to R.1 and R.2.:

. . . The Groupes Francs will train in the shortest possible time a six-man cell specializing in the sabotage of German trains. . . . This cell will receive from the Secret Army railway specialist technical indications concerning its future mode of operations.

These actions shall be considered full war operations. Prepare for action at top speed.

The day of depot sabotage and derailment had come.

By early 1943 D'Astier, Jean-Pierre Lévy and I all had the impression that the Communist-inspired National Front had made definite progress in the ex-free zone, especially in the Lyons region.

Still, the National Front seemed almost purely phantasmal to me, and I saw no point in granting it formal recognition, especially in view of London's directive that all new organizations should be placed under Combat's umbrella.

My position on the Communist Party was clear. The thorough reforms for which we yearned, the radical transformation of society, would be inconceivable without the support of popular elements trained or influenced by the Communist Party. To work with the C.P., not only in our daily struggle but also tomorrow, in a campaign for a socialist government, struck me as an indubitable necessity.

Yet the risks inherent in such an alliance did not escape me. The Party had always followed the Kremlin line, and there was no evidence that it had ceased to do so. However, the fact that since June 22, 1941, it had been, as we put it, "sleeping with France,"

The Night Will End

232

that it was fighting by our side, seemed likely to have a positive effect on its militants. Such was my hope.

Yet constant vigilance was necessary. In the clandestine world one can, with a small committee and a mimeo, put across as reality that which in fact is no more than a dream or a confidence swindle.

To recognize the existence of the National Front, whose strings were obviously being pulled by the Communist Party, would eventually entail its representation among us. This would be the first step in a chain of events that would inevitably lead to the C.P.'s preponderance in the French Resistance.

Hence, in Combat at least—and these were the instructions I gave out—we would maintain periodic contact with the C.P. but not with its fronts. The C.P. would thus be forced to assume responsibility for the decisions it took "in cooperation with" what were merely its own satellite organizations, or, to use the Marxist–Leninist jargon, its "transmission belts."

At this time our agreement with the C.P. on forthcoming operations was total, except on one point: while we were opposed to assassinations of individual German soldiers, the Communists continued to order such attacks both in the southern zone and in Paris.

Early in 1943 a clear distinction began to appear between those whom we called the "temporizers" and the "activists." In general, the former wanted to put the Resistance "on ice" until D-Day. They reproached the "activists" with prematurely exposing our cadres, the majority of whom might well be knocked out before the decisive moment came. The "activists" replied that such immobility would be very poor preparation for combat and that it would squander men's energies and hinder them from adjusting to the conditions of war.

Though I deplored attempts on the lives of individual Germans, I inclined more toward the camp of the "activists." Perhaps it was a matter of temperament. Perhaps it simply reflected my memories of the "phony war" and the sinister effect worked on the morale of the French army by nine months of inaction.

There were about 1,800,000 French prisoners of war still in

The Maquis

Germany, but some POWs had already been liberated. Among them were aged men, men of indispensable value to French factories working for the German war effort and sick men released for public-health reasons.

On my return from London I had learned that some of these ex-POWs were trying to carry the spirit of resistance into the world of the returned prisoners and their families. Thus it was that I first made the acquaintance of Michel Cailliau and François Mitterrand.

Both were about twenty-two; both had escaped from POW camps. The former, as it turned out, was De Gaulle's nephew. The latter, who of course was later to pursue a meteoric political career, struck me as a brilliant and cultivated fellow. Thin, elegantly dressed, and with a spirited look in his eye, he nonetheless awakened misgivings in me, for his smile reminded me of D'Astier's. He had worked in the Prisoner-of-War Commission, where, he said, he had earned the Francisque* on account of his devotion to the cause of our captive soldiers.

The two of them roundly detested each other. Since each wanted to create his own movement, their rivalry was intense. Yet their objectives warranted attention. They wanted to combat the official propaganda in POW circles, to base a new movement upon the "prisoner infrastructure" that Vichy had created. They believed it possible to recruit from among these POWs action groups that could establish clandestine communication with the camps inside Germany. Such were the actions they proposed and which, they believed, should be supported by us.

I mentioned them to the Coordinating Committee, which upheld my opinion that they ought to be aided. Beginning early in 1943 we were to have frequent contact with them and to furnish them with financial aid, which, of course, was too slender to suit them. And so began the M.N.P.G.D. (Mouvement National des Prisonniers de Guerre et des Déportés),* of which I shall have occasion to speak again.

*A rare Vichy decoration whose buttonhole pin bore the enameled image of a *francisca*, or Frankish battle-ax.

**National Movement of Prisoners of War and Deportees.

The Night Will End

234

In order to resolidify all my old contacts, I had remained in the Lyons region since my return. Now I decided that I had best visit the provincial regions again. I inspected all of them with the exception of Clermont-Ferrand.

Marseilles (R.2) was doing fine. Chevance had built up a solid general staff that now included a refugee from what had been the northern zone, a man by the name of Lunel ("Multon"). Here each national service had a correspondent, and the Secret Army outfits now comprised over 15,000 men. In every department of the region but two we had at least one Groupe Franc.

In Montpellier (R. 3) the situation was murkier. "Cals," who had replaced Courtin and Teitgen, still didn't have the situation fully in hand. The only people here who seemed to be doing much were the Groupes Francs. They had already punished, both corporally and through the destruction of their property, ten collaborators.

Gilbert de Chambrun was efficiently directing the Secret Army while at the same time running his home department of the Lozère. A diplomat of patrician origin, he nonetheless was to represent his department after the Liberation as a progressive member of the Chamber of Deputies.

André Hauriou was our regional chief in Toulouse, but Jacques Dhont, a full-time underground militant from way back (whom we consequently allowed to move about as he wished), was its real animating force. He organized his regional and departmental services with a northerner's cool deliberation.

I also met Colette Braun, the head of the Social Service, which, alas, already had plenty of work cut out for it, and Léo Hamon,* an ex-Communist who had developed the Workers' Action in the region. I also made the acquaintance of a refugee Parisian industrialist called Barlangue, who devoted more of his time to the department than he did to his own inner-tube factory.

Here the N.A.P.-Police was particularly efficient, thanks to the help of the local police chief, Philippe, and that of Firman Gamel, the ex-police chief of Toulouse (fired because he was a Freemason). They were in a sense the guardian angels of the movement in that city and in the surrounding department. The former provided

*Later to become secretary of state from 1969 to 1972.

The Maquis

us with bogus identity papers based on his police station's own files. The latter, thanks to the good relations he had retained with the police, made a point of warning Dhont in advance about all planned arrests or searches. For almost a year hardly a single one of our comrades had been apprehended in Toulouse. Philippe himself was later arrested by the Gestapo and tortured horribly. He died of his wounds.

On my first day back I sent a note to Chilina Ciosi, who, in November of the previous year, had left the sanitarium of Sancellemoz for a spot in the French Cerdagne not far from the Spanish border.

Though we had not seen each other for a year, we had corresponded regularly. She had managed to do without a surgical operation and already felt much better. However, it was necessary for her to remain under observation. She'd been appointed resident physician in the bone-tuberculosis department of the Sanatorium des Escalades. Since the high altitude of this institution was suitable for her own convalescence, she was able to resume her own profession while at the same time continuing her cure. (Along with the sanitarium chaplain, the Abbé Ginoux, who was to bless our union after the war, she also helped to smuggle many resisters through the Pyrénées into Spain.)

In my note I told her I was in Toulouse and that I very much wanted to see her.

In the little apartment where I was staying we talked halfway through the night. It was then that I asked her, "Chilina, if God wished us to have a child, how would you feel?"

She replied, "I'd be the happiest woman in the world."

Little Henri was born October 6, 1943, while I was still in Algiers. For the safety of both mother and child, he was declared to be of unknown parentage and placed in a foundling home until the end of the hostilities. After the Liberation we had no trouble recognizing him.

On the way back I stopped in Brive, where I saw our regional chief, Edmond Michelet. He was the same old Edmond: enthusiastic, generous, bursting with activity. He received several resisters

The Night Will End

each day, right in his home. This made my hair stand on end, and I told him so.

"Edmond, your carelessness really worries me. For two years now you've been the Resistance boss in this neck of the woods. You've received hundreds of our comrades in your house. It's absolutely impossible for such activity to escape detection. You've got to find some pretext to disappear, to go underground. It's not only a matter of your own safety; it's in Combat's interests as well that you stay alive!"

"But I just can't leave my family. They need me. My star has protected me so far. Why shouldn't it go on protecting me?"

Alas, Edmond's star soon failed him. Several weeks later he was arrested by the Gestapo and deported.

A few days after my return to Lyons, the Coordinating Committee began meeting under the chairmanship of Jean Moulin. General Delestraint was usually there too. There were several such meetings before Delestraint and Moulin left for London.

It was clear that Delestraint had not grasped the nature of the organization that had been entrusted to him. He now planned to "address my troops" with an epistle, written, by the way, in the most outdated military style. Our boys were partisans, sans-culottes; I could already picture them snickering as they read this piece of eloquence. Much against his wishes, Delestraint was eventually convinced to abandon this project, sour over our having "trespassed upon my prerogatives." It was now clear—to me at least—that if we did not carefully guide him, we would soon run into serious trouble.

The first maquis had been followed by many others. Virtually every new courier brought news of more of them. Lately, S.T.O. evaders had been gathering in the Hautes-Alpes, in the Cévennes and in the Montagne Noire. Each maquis usually comprised no more than a dozen men. Still more such groups, this time in Le Puy-de-Dôme and in Corrèze, had been reported to D'Astier and to the Franc-Tireur people.

We established contact with them through our departmental and regional chiefs. Usually these little maquis voluntarily fol-

The Maquis

lowed our instructions, in return for which they expected food, arms and ammunition. Of course, with our puny resources we could not satisfy these demands. Only London—De Gaulle or the English—had such means, but first we had to make them understand our situation.

It seemed to me that these groups, which were now hiding out all over the French mountain country, might well be transformed into an awesome combat weapon. The *maquisards* were all young, all volunteers, all itching for action. The question was, what action? It was up to us to organize them and to give them a sense of their role in the struggle.

This problem was to preoccupy me all during January 1943. If we couldn't put forward a coherent strategy, we'd have no chance of getting from London the money and arms the maquis so sorely needed. By the middle of the month my plan was ready. I recommended the creation of a certain number of "redoubts" in the Alps, the Juras, the Massif Central and the Pyrénées. These redoubts could be supplied by parachute with arms, equipment and food. Thus they could support highly mobile units of about thirty men each. Their role in the period before the Allied landing would be limited to hit-and-run operations. They would avoid participating in anything resembling a drawn battle.

Obviously it would be impossible for us to create such redoubts without the necessary supplies. This condition was never met, and even my conception of the maquis and their action was to encounter strong opposition from Moulin and General Delestraint.

In the committee's meetings of late January and early February 1943 we examined the progress of our coordination at the regional and departmental levels. Just when we needed a flexible, and hence highly hierarchized, organization, which would be able to carry out its decisions with maximum speed, this pyramid of committees was weighing us down badly, multiplying our dangers and sparking potentially nasty conflicts.

By degrees my friends in Libération and Franc-Tireur had become aware of this and, however joylessly, had come around to the position I'd adopted so long ago: the necessity of total fusion.

The Night Will End

I couldn't help thinking that we'd taken a good many months to arrive at this obvious conclusion, but I was still delighted that they'd finally seen things my way. One last meeting was planned to arrange the mechanics of this fusion.

De Gaulle's suggestion to D'Astier and me in the Hotel Savoy just before our departure had not been abandoned. This idea was to create in France an organism that would, in his eyes at least, represent French public opinion and admit delegates of the Resistance, the old political parties and the labor unions. Now it was Moulin's turn to put forth this proposal. Claudius-Petit, the then delegate of Franc-Tireur, was rather opposed to it, D'Astier more hesitant, and I was totally against it.

After the meeting Moulin asked me to return to Lyons with him. Once again I tried to explain how this project would hobble us. To gussy up the Resistance in the costumes of the now defunct political parties was to me unacceptable. Soon the tone of our discussion became strident. I reiterated the arguments I had voiced to General de Gaulle:

"If, refusing our advice, you aid and abet the reconstitution of the political formations of the Third Republic, you will snuff out the revolutionary spirit of our movements. You will be the undertaker of the Resistance."

"I hope that your words do not reflect your true thoughts," he replied, "for I believe that this project has merit, and it seems that General de Gaulle shares my opinion. In any case, in a few hours I'll be with him, and I shall ask him to settle the matter out of hand."

Once in London Moulin easily won out and received a mandate to create a "National Council of the Resistance" (C.N.R.). On that day, by the combined will of General Charles de Gaulle and Jean Moulin, the Resistance took a new and fatal direction. Politics, in the ugliest sense of the word, were to regain their old privileges. Already the Fourth Republic, with all its weaknesses, had appeared on the horizon.

Leaving Moulin, I felt overwhelmed with sorrow and disgust. It seemed that France's morally defunct politicos were indeed

The Maquis

to be resurrected. At this point I wrote an article for *Combat* called "The Hour of Trial":

For over two years . . . France has been subjected to martyrdom. . . . Yet it is in the hour of trial that character and fidelity to one's words are judged. . . . Where are those elites who only yesterday were representing France? . . . We no longer hear those familiar voices which from their high podiums and their editorial pages once claimed to speak in our name. . . . What part have they played in the rescue of a France now in mortal danger? . . . Bent beneath the weight of destiny, yielding to fear, they have grown quiet. . . . They have reneged on their commitments, failed at their tasks. Many have become traitors. . . .

The wind of defeat . . . swept away those supposed elites. France, abandoned by her guides, betrayed by her elites, harkened to her own heart. A few voices arose; month after month, they multiplied, grew strong. . . . They were the collective voice of the people, seeking in its own instincts and traditions the strength to cry out to the world that France was still France, that she had not been derelict, had not forfeited her honor, still claimed her rightful place in the struggle.

This voice is the voice of the Resistance. It arose from the cities and from the countryside until it drowned out the voice of treason. It is the voice of simple people, people without rank, who, without even knowing it, rescued the honor of our country. . . .

In the masses of this anonymous Resistance, men came to know themselves.

The ordeal made them grow, just as it cast down the falsely glorified.

France has passed judgment. . . . On the day after the Liberation France will ask of her sons, "In the hour of shame and misery, what did you do for me?" and according to their answers, regardless of their class, party or creed, she shall appoint those who will have the honor to represent her.

Why did Jean Moulin cling so stubbornly to this foolish project so contrary to the wishes of the entire Resistance? Later I was to learn that my reservations were shared and vehemently expressed by all the movements in both zones.

It was in April 1943 that Passy himself grasped this fact. What is

The Night Will End

all the more remarkable is that the most honored politicians were opposed to the reconstitution of their own parties. Here is how Passy sums up the opinion of the ex-president of the Senate, Jules Jeanneney*: "What remains of the old parties? Virtually nothing. They will assume an entirely new form after the victory." As for his opinion on the older leaders: "Herriot no longer meant a thing to me. . . . Léon Blum was forgotten. . . . As for Daladier, the less said the better. Paul Reynaud could never return to power. . . . Flandin was finished."

Even Jules Julien, who as Herriot's ex-minister and confidant was sure to express the opinion of his friend and mentor, had declared, "The parties? They no longer exist; their leaders no longer have any authority. . . . "

Why, then, did Jean Moulin, alone against everyone, suggest the creation of the C.N.R. to the general? I was not to understand why until several years after the war. For political reasons that were entirely personal and which I shall set forth at the end of this book, Moulin cleverly and methodically did everything in his power to get the Resistance movements under his thumb.

In late January 1943 our decision to merge the three movements was adopted. All we had to do was carry it out. The first question concerned the composition of the new directing committee and how its various tasks should be allotted among its members.

Of course D'Astier and Jean-Pierre Lévy demanded equal representation. This was clearly unjust. Impossible though it was to take a census of each movement, they were hardly ignorant of the fact that Combat was numerically larger than their two movements put together. The budget that Moulin allotted us rose in February 1943 to five million francs, while Libération received only one and a half million and Franc-Tireur only 950,000. These figures should by all rights have served as the proper ratio for equitable representation: six (Combat) to two (Libération) to one (Franc-Tireur). I immediately abandoned the idea of demanding the application of so strict a formula. Nonetheless, since Combat was already an amalgamation of two movements, and since we in Combat had been the

*Missions Secrètes en France, Plon, page 71.

The Maquis

leaders of the march toward unity, our representation should have been double that of the other two combined.

The discussion of this subject was particularly acrimonious. D'Astier and Lévy categorically rejected my proposal. My colleagues were prepared to accept nothing short of full equality. What could I do? If I refused this demand I might be scuttling the ship of unity just when she had finally sighted land. I presented the whole matter to the steering committee of Combat. It unhesitatingly declined to endorse my initial proposal. And so we decided to make the greatest of all sacrifices on the altar of unity.

These were to be the functions of the Coordinating Committee's several members: Jean Moulin would be chairman. D'Astier would be the *"commissaire* of political affairs" and I the *"commissaire* of military affairs" (that is, I would be responsible for the Secret Army). The representative of Franc-Tireur—alternately Lévy and Claudius Petit—would be the *commissaire* of information and materiel" and also responsible for our liaison with the POW movements. We clearly agreed, however, that all our decisions would be made collectively.

The organizational structure of Combat would be passed on to the new organization, which we decided to call the M.U.R. (Mouvements Unis de Résistance). This acronym had the right ring, for we were indeed the wall (*mur*) against which the enemy would be broken.

Each one of the original movements was to keep its separate press organ. At each level, and at the head of each service, a sole chief was to be appointed, assisted by two adjunct chiefs.

On March 8 a circular signed "Darthez," "Gilles," "Lefèvre" (D'Astier, J.-P. Lévy, Frenay) was addressed to the regions. It was to be passed around until it had been seen by even our humblest militants. It announced our fusion in tones of joy and victory.

At the end of this long, hard day, I returned, prey to conflicting emotions, to Charnay-lès-Mâcon where I now lived. I lay sleepless on my bed. Perhaps I was feverish; anyway, I had great difficulty in collecting my thoughts.

That day I had harvested the fruit of eighteen months of effort. I had carried out the mission entrusted to me by Combat's steering

The Night Will End

committee in our Saliès meeting. At last we were united behind De Gaulle. I remembered all the discussions in Paris, Lyons and London that had led up to this final result. This was what I had had to do, whatever the cost, and I had done it. Yet from it I derived no joy. I felt much as I had when, two years earlier, I had left the army. I was merely fulfilling a sad duty.

In my head I drew up a list of what we in Combat would be contributing to the M.U.R. These forces would be, in a sense, Combat's dowry, and they were impressive.

I wondered if the M.U.R. could be imbued with our high spirits and our dynamism. I feared lest we in Combat be subjected to more meddling, more maneuvers, right down to the regional and departmental levels.

Had we been right or wrong, I wondered, to have paid so high a price for unity?

What a question! Was not unity our law and our watchword? So I told myself as I went to bed that night.

Today, thirty years later, I believe we made a terrible mistake.

The Maquis

A UNITED FRONT

The time had come for me to leave Charnay-lès-Macon. I was living in Cluny now. After two days, despite a couple of long fireside chats, I could hardly claim to know my new hosts, M. and Mme. Gouze. I did notice that their faces seemed to shine with mutual tenderness and regard.

Both were teachers in their fifties. M. Gouze was a thin, silvery-haired man of average height who peered at you myopically through his spectacles. He was one of those schoolmasters who'd been trained before the First World War and who, though firm in his secular and republican convictions, practiced his profession with priestly piety. A Freemason, he'd been fired by Vichy from the headmastership of his high school. This was a wound that had refused to heal. Yet he spoke to me of it with unalloyed sorrow, for he was all gentleness, and I sensed that hatred was foreign to his soul.

Though inseparable, the two were physical opposites. Mme. Gouze was petite and rotund and wore her hair tightly drawn back. Attentive, intelligent and discreet, she was the very soul of the household.

Of their two daughters, the elder, Madeleine, worked in the Vichy administration—I didn't meet her until two months later—

while the younger, Danièle, then seventeen, lived at home. One of my most enjoyable relaxations in the weeks to come was to help her with her homework, especially her philosophy lessons. This pleasant and rather reserved girl later became Mme. François Mitterrand.

The whole Gouze family were at first unaware of my real activities and knew me only by the name of "Tavernier." Soon, with growing trust, I revealed to them my true name and my underground role. This apparently imprudent confidence was well founded, as later events were to bear out.

Their quiet house had a street entrance and an escape route through a rear garden. I was lodged in an adjoining wing, which, with its two rooms, had plenty of space for Berty, who was already insisting that she take her place by my side. And I sorely missed her intelligence and critical sense. Sure enough, she joined me in early March.

One day in early February 1943 I began to go through my letters with feverish apprehension. Somehow I was dead sure that one of them contained evil news. I opened a note from R.5: "'Joseph' arrested by Gestapo, Brive railway station, January 29. Incarcerated Limoges Prison."

My legs crumpled, my voice deserted me. Renouvin, my old friend, in the hands of the Gestapo! If they identified him, he was done for. Once again I had that sensation that always seized me when I heard of the arrest of some dear friend: a constriction in my throat verging on nausea, deep inner dejection, outward distress.

I immediately headed for the Buisson sisters' apartment in Lyons. Bénouville joined me. Both of us were weeping. The next day, "Bastos," Bénouville's assistant, also arrived. He told us that Renouvin had been transferred to Fresnes and that he, "Bastos," wanted to organize his escape with the help of ten volunteers dedicated to rescuing their beloved leader.

It was a mad enterprise and one that I myself probably wouldn't have ordered. But how could I have forbidden it? I hadn't the heart and probably not even the right. "Bastos" took off for Paris. His squad launched its operations; and, either through carelessness or betrayal, all its members were intercepted by the Gestapo. Reno-

A United Front

uvin was doomed. Deported, he died of extreme exhaustion in Matthausen. He never experienced the Liberation for which he'd given his life.

Shortly before his departure for London, Jean Moulin convened the directing committee. The date: February 21, 1943.

Once again—for it happened every time now—a yawning gulf appeared between Moulin and the movement chiefs concerning the Secret Army, especially in the provinces, and Moulin's own methods and conception of his role.

D'Astier and I for once championed the same views. A bitter, almost violent argument took place between us and Moulin. Some of our testiness, our outbursts—especially Moulin's and mine— could perhaps be imputed to the importance of the agenda.

In this meeting we all disclosed what we had heard from our regional services about the maquis. They were growing with unexpected rapidity. The four Alpine departments seemed to be the favorite refuge of the S.T.O. evaders, but maquis were also multiplying in the Massif Central (R.4, 5 and 6). Our regional chiefs found themselves beset with demands for arms, provisions and money. But what could we do? My report to London, with its list of requests, had never been answered.

Moulin thought that we should first get more precise information about the size and location of each maquis. We—Claudius Petit, D'Astier and I—upheld the strict duty of the M.U.R. to aid the maquisards immediately.

While Moulin and Delestraint were hesitant and circumspect toward the maquis, we were resolutely committed to them. Unable to infect Moulin and Delestraint with our own enthusiasm, we never dreamed that in their minds we were "attempting to turn the maquis into another Secret Army."

Such, in fact, was Moulin's opinion.* Yet he knew that the maquis were no creation of ours but the spontaneous reaction of thousands of young men to the S.T.O. Fleeing compulsory labor service and its enforcers in the gendarmerie, they'd abandoned their homes to seek refuge in sparsely inhabited areas. These little

*Henri Michel, *Jean Moulin l'unificateur.* Hachette, page 133.

The Night Will End

groups, without money, weapons or other resources, had no immediate intention of fighting. Soon bereft of all provisions, they'd sought the aid and protection of farmers and shepherds, who, in turn, had applied for help to the Resistance. This was the truth—and Moulin knew it.

How could we turn a deaf ear to their entreaties? Daily our newspapers and leaflets were urging these young men to disobey the authorities. Surely their legions would soon be giving young and vigorous blood to our Resistance.

It was plain that the maquisards were cold and hungry, that they were in danger of being tracked down, attacked and annihilated. Our duty was clear.

Once again we had disagreed with "Max," and once again, as the meeting broke up, I tried to explain my viewpoint. Aid to the maquis was a vital necessity. Not to provide it would destroy their faith in the Resistance. We could not afford to sit back and watch these men come down out of their mountain fastnesses and be deported to Germany. No, we needed more resources, resources to share with them. Most of all, we needed money.

"I'm sorry," said Moulin, "but I just can't help you. The funds at my disposal can't meet every single requirement. After all, there are so many."

" 'Max,' you don't seem to understand that aid to the maquis has now taken absolute priority. Why don't you join forces with us and help us to convince London? Together we'd make them understand."

"Of course I'll inform General de Gaulle—in a few days, I hope—but in the meantime I must tell you that I'm now obliged to reduce your budget."

"You've got to be kidding!"

"No, I'm not. In March Combat will get only three million francs."

"What! But last month we had a rough time making do with five million! The movement simply cannot sustain such budget slashes without disastrous results!"

"I understand your disappointment, but, believe me, I cannot do otherwise."

And so, just as our needs were skyrocketing, just as the maquis

A United Front

were desperately imploring our aid, this was all the sympathy I got from the emissary of Free France! How, in God's name, with a 40 percent budget cut, were we to feed and pay our underground comrades? These men had abandoned everything—their families, jobs and homes—to follow us.

Barely mastering my rising anger, I said, "Listen, 'Max,' up to now you've given us enough money to survive and fight on. If, for reasons I cannot understand, you refuse us the funds we need, we'll get them elsewhere—without you and, if need be, against your will. Goodbye, and *bon voyage!*"

We shook hands coldly and separated with averted eyes. Forty-eight hours later, Jean Moulin, accompanied by Delestraint, left for London, where he was to remain one month.

What were Jean Moulin's real motives? If he himself lacked funds, he should have told us. His own orders obligated him to reveal all his resources to the M.U.R.'s directing committee. Moreover, their allocation was to be made by joint decision. Yet not only had he not consulted the committee, but he had not even informed it of the budget slashes.

After the war I saw the figures he had kept from us.* They did indeed confirm that his own budget for March 1943 had dropped from that of the preceding month. Nonetheless, certain "important parties," unknown both to us and, I believe, to the B.C.R.A. and Liberation, had retained the full measure of their February allocations.

I also observed that although "Max" had refused us any subsidies for the maquis, there was one maquis that he himself was financing *sub rosa*. As embryonic as the others, this maquis received a budget equal to one third that of Combat! Its leader was Yves Farge, a personal friend of Moulin's. I shall speak again of this maquis, which, though born of a foolish gamble, was to become one of the loftiest symbols of the Resistance: the Vercors.

I wondered why "Max" refused to put his cards on the table as duty required. He seemed to be discriminating arbitrarily.

There is but one answer to all these questions: budget cuts were

*Colonel Passy, *Missions Secrètes en France*, Appendix XXII.

The Night Will End

the easiest way for "Max" to weaken our movement. These cuts prevented me from giving my full-time people the necessary funds for their subsistence. For instance, on May 7, 1943, "Max" wrote a letter to De Gaulle directed against me. Here he mentioned my people—the very body and soul of Combat—in the following terms:

He [Frenay] commands the allegiance only of those full-time militants whom he himself has cleverly placed and appointed (i.e., his immediate colleagues, regional chiefs, etc.).*

Thus, Berty Albrecht, Jean-Guy Bernard, André Bollier, Jacques Renouvin, Marcel Peck and so many others—not to mention those already captured and about to lose their lives—were serving at my side not because our struggle had united us in brotherhood but because I had "appointed" them!

Fate has often favored me. In the last fortnight of February, fate appeared in the shape of a man called Philippe Monod ("Martel"). He had replaced Claude Bourdet in the Alpes-Maritimes, and now he was asking to see me that we might talk over a certain highly important matter.

I asked him to join us in a meeting that was to include Bourdet, Aubry, Morin, Brault and Bénouville.

On the appointed day we gathered in Saint-Clair. Monod arrived in an excited state. His verbal delivery, choppy at best, attested to his feverish agitation. He told us that early last November in Cannes he had talked with an American, a very Parisianized fellow called Max Shoop, who for seven years had been Monod's supervisor in the Paris office of the large American law firm of Sullivan & Cromwell. He and Shoop trusted each other implicitly. Monod had explained his own activities to Shoop, noting the latter's interest in his disclosures. The very next day Shoop had departed for his new residence in Switzerland.

After three months of silence, Monod had received a message from Shoop.

*Passy, *op. cit.*, page 217.

A United Front

"Just as I thought," said Monod. "My old pal Shoop was no simple tourist. He obviously belongs to the American secret services. In fact, I now believe—given his own past and the message he sent me—that he's even something of a big shot. Mentioning our talks in Cannes, he promised us financial aid and requested that I provide him with a precise report on the Secret Army, the Groupes Francs and the maquis. In other words, he wanted to know what kind of military assistance we could offer the Allied cause."

"Monod," said Bénouville, "it's the good Lord himself who's sent you!"

The message received by Monod obviously reopened the whole question of our receiving money direct from the B.C.R.A. or other bodies. But this time we were not petitioning for a favor, and, moreover, Shoop's offer had arrived just when Moulin was refusing to finance us. It was the work of Providence! I said, "Listen, Monod old boy, now that you've initiated these discussions, why don't you yourself see them through? 'Lahire' here [Bénouville] can help you out. He has Swiss contacts and knows the frontier."

Bourdet added, "Initially your mission will be purely for information. We want to know if we can rely on the Americans for arms, money and good communications. That's the big question." Then, turning to Morin and Aubry, I said, "Well, you two are chief-of-staff and chief inspector of the Secret Army. Why don't you go ahead and draw up that report on the Secret Army the Americans want? I'll go over it when you're through. Bring it to me within forty-eight hours."

Our conversation took a euphoric turn. Monod was the hero of the day. We told him that in his talks with the Americans he should stress our allegiance to De Gaulle and our distrust of Giraud and the new Algiers authorities. He was to offer no political *quid pro quo* in exchange for American funds.

We split up, aglow with optimism.

Philippe Monod left for Switzerland in early March, bearing with him the hopes of our entire movement.

As I've mentioned, Berty had joined me in Cluny after a hiatus of ten months. She was much changed by her internment,

The Night Will End

imprisonment, confinement in the Bron mental ward and reclusive life in Toulouse. Her old zest for life was gone. Her eyes had lost their sparkle; they laughed no longer but glinted with cold determination. Her suffering had so marked her that the very evening of her return she said, "Henri, I can no longer accept the idea of being arrested. I won't go through that torture all over again. If they catch me again, I'll kill myself."

We never spoke of this again, but several months later her words were to haunt me pitilessly.

Since our Lyons and Marseilles intelligence had provided us with exact information on the schedules of German trains, I ordered the Groupes Francs of these regions to train six-men cells specializing in attacks on the railways. I encouraged them to move rapidly into open hostilities.

The sabotage of trackage, usually by means of explosives, became particularly widespread when Garnier ("Ledoux"), who had been arrested in February, was released from prison in June. The closest thing to a "professor of sabotage," he trained his own teams in both zones as well as making use of the Groupes Francs, to whom he taught the finer points of his inexhaustible technique. What Garnier alone destroyed could have filled a World's Fair!

For the moment I'll mention only his finest fireworks display. In honor of Renouvin and his methods, he organized a true "railway carnival": sixty strikes against the railways in one day! A series of derailments on the Lyons line prevented the members of the Légion des Combattants from attending their annual reunion and forced them to spend the entire day picnicking. At the same time, elsewhere, German troop trains were blown up.

Résistance-Rail soon completed a detailed final version of a D-Day attack plan, complete with pictures and maps. This was the famous "Green Plan" that we'll be hearing a lot more about later on.

Soon afterward, Soulage turned up. Like the rest of us, he was worried about the maquis. Our primary task, he believed, was to knit them together into a real war machine.

"Henri," he said, "I want to set up a training school for maquis

A United Front

officers. Believe me, I won't have any trouble finding 'students.' In less than a month I can turn them into guerrilla chieftains adept at underground combat and survival. Though I'd still be answerable to you, I'd like to teach them in my own way. Well, what do you say? Can you help me?"

"Listen, Robert, your maquis service could train the maquisards in close conjunction with our regional chiefs. If you succeed we shall have an infinitely precious reservoir of cadres. In other words, I'm with you. But as for helping you out, how can I? For the moment, we're penniless ourselves. Try to go it alone, and I'll get you some help as soon as possible—who knows, maybe tomorrow."

And go it alone he did, with stunning results. Aided only by his native ingenuity, he created a national service for maquis training schools, known to both us and London as "Périclès." He set up one such training school in the Massif de l'Oisans, a second in the Massif de Belledonne and still more in the Basses-Alpes and in Périgord. His men instantly recognized in him what I too loved so well: the idealist, the exemplary leader of men.

Less than eight days after his departure, Philippe Monod ("Martel") returned to Mâcon, accompanied by Pierre de Bénouville. I still remember Pierre waving at me from afar and calling, "Henri-boss! We've done it!"

Indeed, his mission had succeeded beyond my wildest hopes. His friend Shoop had taken him to Berne to see Allen Dulles, the mysterious Mr. "Scott" whom I'd met over eighteen months ago with General de La Laurencie.

Dulles was posing as an adviser to the American Embassy to Switzerland. In fact, he directed all the American secret services for Western Europe, known collectively as the O.S.S. (Office of Strategic Services).

The O.S.S. chief had cabled Washington to explain the situation, including our needs for weapons and money. He'd even gone over his lengthy cablegram to Washington with Monod. Optimistic about Washington's response to this request, Dulles had already offered us three million francs in specie.

"I could have brought them with me, but they would have been pretty cumbersome, Anyway, I wanted to report back first and get

The Night Will End

your okay on Allen's proposals. You see, we'll be able to communicate with De Gaulle and his B.C.R.A. via the embassy's radiocommunications service. In return, Dulles has asked us to share all our military intelligence reports with him. They'll be immediately radioed to London, where they'll be utilized as rapidly as possible. Lastly, he wants us to send a representative to Switzerland through whom he can maintain permanent relations with us. A secure liaison will then be set up between this representative and our Lyons center."

Gone were all our worries! Soulage would now have money for his training school, and the maquis would be armed by the Americans! Meanwhile we would have reliable radio contact with London.

"Henri," said Bénouville, "'Martel' and I have been talking on the way here, and we've come up with a proposition for you. The two of us will go to Switzerland. I myself shall organize the regular Geneva–Lyons communication line. On the other side of the frontier, the Deuxième Bureau of the Swiss Federal Army will help me out. 'Martel' will represent us there, at least for the time being. However, for a permanent representative we're going to need an older man, a man of recognized importance who can speak authoritatively to the Allies. I've been thinking about General Davet. He's an airman and an ex-militant from Action Française, like myself and poor Renouvin. He lives in Toulon, where he's chomping at the bit. I'm sure he'd be only too happy to help us."

"Hold your horses, 'Lahire.' As for your and 'Martel's' going to Geneva, that's fine with me; in fact, it's urgent. But as for this General Davet, we'll have to look into that later. In any case, I want to meet him first. When you get back from Switzerland you should bring him here.

"While you're in Switzerland, I'll bring the good tidings to the M.U.R.'s steering committee. By the way, 'Martel,' technically it's the M.U.R. you'll be representing in Geneva. Understand, what you'll be setting up in Switzerland will be a Resistance delegation. 'Lahire,' you'll be our 'foreign minister.' I guess you'll have to have a new alias, too, since you're such a godawful reactionary," I said, laughing, "We'll call you 'Barrès.'."

A few days later I told D'Astier and Jean-Pierre Lévy about the

A United Front

unhoped-for success of 'Martel's' mission. They were expecting to leave for London any day now and could fill in 'Max' and the B.C.R.A. on this new initiative. London eventually accepted the idea of an M.U.R. delegation to Switzerland, as well as Bénouville's new role. Soon Pierre returned from Geneva with a million francs and a report for the steering committee on the extraordinary facilities the Allies were now offering us.

I interviewed General Davet at length in Cluny, then designated him as the chief of our delegation.

Although Jean-Pierre Lévy (and, later, Claudius Petit, who spelled him during his absence) expressed reservations about the disclosure of our intelligence to the Allies, on the whole the bosses of Libération and Franc-Tireur appreciated the advantage of our promising new contact with the Americans. Nonetheless, I sensed in them an unmistakable frustration over Combat's new initiative. Yet their frustration was nothing compared to Moulin's on his return from London.

The Gestapo and the French police were now hitting us twice as hard as before. Henri Garnier was arrested and savagely tortured. On March 13, Marcel Peck was once again apprehended in Lyons. (Less than five days later he rang at the apartment of the Buisson sisters; a police inspector had facilitated his escape.)

At the same time my mail informed me of the simultaneous arrest of François Morin ("Forestier"), the Secret Army chief of staff, Kriegel-"Valrimont," and "Ravanel," the new head of the Groupes Francs. These men had been jailed in the prison of Saint-Paul in Lyons.

More arrests followed. Clearly our files had been copied and turned over to the German police. Once again we had to change our pseudonyms, codes and letterboxes.

Back from London, Moulin and Delestraint convened the steering committee. Pascal Copeau represented Libération, Claudius Petit Franc-Tireur. Of our many stormy meetings, this was the most tempestuous.

The stiff new directives brought back by Moulin were exactly what he'd sought: The Secret Army under Delestraint was to be

The Night Will End

removed from the jurisdiction of the steering committee, and a National Council of the Resistance (C.N.R.) was to be created, regrouping the old political parties and the Resistance movements. The C.N.R. was to head the Resistance as a whole.

Moulin had been named a member of the French National Committee—that is, in a sense, a minister—and his authority was to cover both zones.

In short, De Gaulle had followed Moulin's proposals to the letter. I wondered if D'Astier and Lévy, also in London, had ever been consulted. Yet, earlier, De Gaulle, Philip and Passy had promised that every important decision concerning the Resistance would be submitted to us for prior consideration. They had not kept their word.

I blew up, and, considering the circumstances, I didn't regret it. Never would we allow the Secret Army to be sealed off from the rest of the Resistance! Once again I had to shout my determination. If Moulin had ever bothered to get to know our cadres, if he had ever spoken with our head people in some town or village, he would have understood. But never, not once, had he made a thorough inspection tour. Our rank-and-file militants, their work, their inherent constraints and problems, were a complete mystery to him.

Even graver was the decision to create the C.N.R. Against the wishes of the entire Resistance, De Gaulle had settled the matter *ex cathedra*. He was resurrecting the political parties and placing them on an equal footing with ourselves. What a mockery!

I can still hear my own words at the end of our discussions: "'Max,'" I said, "as you know, I consider this decision a catastrophe. I've given you my reasons. I'm not going to dwell on them. In any case, I refuse to be associated with this rotten business. Never will I sit in your C.N.R.!"

Raising his voice, Moulin began to berate me: "'Charvet,' the C.N.R. shall be created whatever you say! You're free to join it or not to join it—as you wish. But you're *not* free to contact the Americans without notifying me—or to ask them for money, with God only knows what strings attached!"

"There were no strings attached! . . . Wait a minute, let me speak, and don't leap to conclusions before you know the facts."

A United Front

"I know plenty! The French National Committee has a representative in France who keeps us abreast of everything. We know how you've stabbed De Gaulle in the back!"

"How *dare* you say that! While you were trying to strangle us with budget cuts, the maquis were crying for help! We needed money!"

"Well, I'm going to ask the steering committee of the three movements if they're on my side or yours. Have you informed them of your shady deals with the Americans?"

A new gambit! Moulin knew perfectly well that the fusion of the three movements entailed *ipso facto* the dissolution of the old steering committees.

As I arrived in Cluny, Berty could tell at a glance that I'd had a bad day. I recounted to her the events of that sorry afternoon, just as I was later to recount them to Bourdet and others. Wearily I asked myself if it was necessary that we waste our energy fighting men in our own camp. It seemed that Moulin had presented us with the same options as the Germans—to capitulate or to resist. Of course it would have been much easier to capitulate—but how could I have faced my comrades?

I figured that tomorrow I'd be more clearheaded—on condition that I slept. My little viaticum from London was still in my bag. Two sleeping pills enabled me to get a long and good night's sleep.

The following day I regained my composure. But my biggest headache remained Moulin's intention of convening Combat's old steering committee.

To accept this ploy might well create a troublesome precedent. Soon we might be required to submit every decision of the M.U.R., either beforehand or afterward, to the steering committees of the three movements. That was utterly out of the question. Moulin's new demand did not square with the directive relative to the C.N.R. that he himself had brought back from London: "Its members shall be invested with the confidence of the groups they represent and shall possess sovereign and immediate decision-making power in the name of their constituencies."

Clearly, what went for the C.N.R. went *a fortiori* for the M.U.R., whose executive decisions were to be final.

The Night Will End

Moulin's subterfuge was obviously aimed at obtaining a disavowal of my position by Menthon, Teitgen and Bidault, all of whom he saw much more often than I did. It was they who directed the C.G.E. (Comité Général d'Etudes) and the B.I.P. (Bulletin d'Information et de Presse), both of which were directly answerable to him.

But there could be no question of my shirking a conflict. I had nothing to hide from my peers. After all, they were also my friends. Hence, the "dissolved" steering committee would have to meet to consider the question of my relations with the Americans in Switzerland.

Bourdet and Chevance, who had observed the Swiss business from the beginning to the end, staunchly defended it. Our comrades in Liberté, though hardly opposed to it, counseled prudence in view of what they called the "political risks" of our contacts with the O.S.S. In any case, Jean Moulin did not obtain the disavowal he'd been seeking either from Combat's steering committee or from the other two.

Thank God all news wasn't bad news. Jean Gemahling, the head of our intelligence and one of our earliest militants, who had been arrested in Marseilles early in the year, had recently escaped. The escape had been organized by the men of Combat, especially Benjamin Crémieux, the regional N.A.P. chief.

For a while Michel Brault had run Gemahling's intelligence arm. This hadn't lasted long, however, for soon Brault had taken command of the maquis service. Gemahling shortly resumed his activities and contacts in the southern zone. In several months he greatly expanded the M.U.R. intelligence.

Three branches of this intelligence arm had now developed. Besides military intelligence it now had political and counterespionage intelligence branches that worked in close cooperation with the N.A.P. Following the pattern established by so many other services in the past, military intelligence was soon removed from the hands of its founder. It was taken over in June by an emissary from London called Gorce ("Franklin").

The history of this service deserves to be written. Some figures confirmed after the war should show just how thorough our

A United Front

Gemahling was. Every ten days he provided us with 200 pages of intelligence reports along with regularly revised maps of the enemy's defenses along the Mediterranean. About 1,000 full- and part-time comrades worked for M.U.R. intelligence. Of these, 700 were officially acknowledged as ex-members of the network by the Ministry of War Veterans and Disabled Persons. Twenty-four had been shot and ninety-nine deported. Of the latter, twenty-six never came back.

We were now monitoring not only the BBC but Radio Algiers as well. By comparing its information with that of the Vichy press, we could get a pretty good picture of the situation in North Africa.

The military scene was promising. Toward late March the British Eighth Army had dislodged the Afrika Korps from the Mareth Line in Tunisia and forced it into full retreat. Two Free French brigades commanded by Larminat and Leclerc had participated brilliantly in the assault. Soon the juncture of the Eighth Army and the Americans under Eisenhower would be a reality. The enemy was undone. He surrendered at Cap Bon on May 13, 1943, leaving 250,000 prisoners and a gigantic arms complement in Allied hands.

On the other hand, since the death of Darlan last December the political situation had remained murky. General Giraud, now styling himself the "civil and military commander-in-chief," ruled in Algiers. The prisons and internment camps in Algeria were crammed with Vichy's political prisoners. De Gaulle was still in London.

Outside metropolitan France there were still two Frances in the war. We domestic combatants absolutely had to broadcast our will, especially because the English radio had recently announced a forthcoming Giraud–De Gaulle consultation. In our Coordinating Committee we decided that each of our three newspapers would publish an article on the confrontation between the two generals. A month later our position was vigorously endorsed by the C.N.R. in its first meeting. The Resistance would try to tip the scale in favor of the Free French leader.

Combat featured an article by me called "The People Have Chosen":

The Night Will End

France has reached a turning-point in her history. Sometime in the next few days, two generals will meet. . . .

The French people cannot forgive General Giraud for having resumed the struggle in the name of Marshal Pétain, the living symbol of capitulation and treason. Nor can they forgive him for having placed himself at Darlan's orders.

General de Gaulle, on the other hand, has never wavered. Nearly alone, he saved our honor by rescuing the flag which the cowards and traitors had abandoned.

All those who from the beginning have resisted Germany and dictatorial rule have chosen him as their leader and the symbol of their hopes. Those who, tomorrow, will be negotiating in Algiers must know this. Our Allies too must not forget it. Between De Gaulle and Giraud, the people have chosen De Gaulle. Such is their will.

For the first time I signed an article with my real name: Henri Frenay. To any statement on the De Gaulle–Giraud dichotomy I wanted to affix my own opinion and not that of a "Tavernier" or a "Gervais."

An unnecessary risk? Hardly. The Abwehr and the Gestapo had learned my identity long ago. They were hunting me already.

After the war, during an important trial that shook the entire former Resistance and which I shall discuss later, it happened that I was cited as a witness for the prosecution.

There were many of us in the antechamber waiting to be called. My friend Gastaldo, the head of the Secret Army's Deuxième Bureau and a deportation survivor, came over to me and said, "Henri, there's a man here who wants to meet you. Over there, the blond fellow by the window."

"Who is he?"

"Well, keep your shirt on. He was a big shot in the Gestapo."

"I've no desire whatever to meet your fine friend. I don't even know why you're asking me."

"Well, I *am* asking you. In fact, I insist. He's the one who interrogated me after my arrest in Paris. In fact, he was as courteous as his role allowed. He's very eager to meet you. Please

A United Front

help me pay off this moral debt. I really am indebted to him."

"Well, I guess I can't refuse. Bring your friend over."

In a moment Gastaldo was leading him toward me. He was a man of average height and with an angular profile. About forty years old, he was nondescriptly dressed. One might have mistaken him for an office worker in a ready-made suit. He bowed deeply to me, German-style, and said in excellent French, "Monsieur Frenay—*mon capitaine*—I've been wanting to meet you for a long time."

I did not shake his hand.

"I'm glad we're meeting today," I said, "and not in nineteen forty-three."

"Of course—I understand. Still, I'm delighted to make your acquaintance."

"May I ask why?"

"Of course. Listen. Early in nineteen forty-two, the agents whom we'd slipped in among you, and the interrogation of your arrested comrades, had conclusively proved that the leader of Combat was a certain Captain Frenay. All year long our intelligence helped us to trace the development of your organization, particularly its military arm. You yourself gradually emerged as our most dangerous adversary. At least, such was the opinion of the O.K.W. [Oberkommando der Wehrmacht]. As soon as we occupied the southern zone, the Gestapo and the Abwehr decided to do everything in their power to capture you."

This tale was getting more and more interesting! Despite the hubbub in the little room, Gastaldo and I weren't missing a word.

"The necessary condition for your capture was that all our intelligence reports about you, whatever their source, be centralized, cross-checked and put to use with maximum speed and precision. For this a special service was created, and its chief was the man whom you see before you."

With a smile he concluded, "Month after month I had one task and one task only: to capture you."

My interlocutor remained silent a moment to let me digest his revelation, then continued: "It was enthralling. Sometimes we would receive several intelligence reports a day that mentioned

The Night Will End

your name—files we'd seized, for instance, or interrogation reports. Your aliases gave us a lot of trouble."

"That was the idea."

"I remember 'Tavernier,' 'Molin,' 'Gervais'—right?"

"Yes, and many others too."

"I had to engage a co-worker. The two of us spoke of virtually nothing but you. Little by little you became a familiar figure to us, a kind of friend. When we lost track of you for a few days . . . well, silly as it may sound, the time dragged terribly."

We looked at each other and smiled. I felt the man was sincere. Don't hunters develop a special admiration for the most elusive game?

"We spared no efforts to catch you. If you evaded us, it was not our fault. Nonetheless, my colleague and I had to ask ourselves what we would do with you if you were to fall into our hands. Well, we planned to give your arrest enormous publicity—photos, radio, the works—so as to brand you as plainly as possible. Then we would have tried to organize your escape. Anyway, we never caught you—you got away. It was some time before we realized that you had departed for Algiers. Now maybe you understand why I wanted so badly to meet you. By the way, your photos were pretty poor likenesses."

There was a lull in the conversation; I felt I should say something.

"Well, what are you doing now?"

He looked at me and smiled again. "The same—for the Americans."

One day in April 1943 Claude Bourdet came to Cluny to see me. Berty, he and I were talking in my little bedroom.

"Henri," he said, "I'm just back from Cannes, where I saw 'Jérôme' [Michel Brault]. You know, he had a serious pulmonary congestion, but he's better now. He's in good enough shape to start working again. We thought that perhaps he should direct a general maquis service."

"Then we'd better set it up right away, otherwise we'll be snowed under with work. What did 'Jérôme' say?"

A United Front

"He was crazy about the idea. He said it would rejuvenate him."

"Jérôme" was almost an old man for us. He must have been all of forty-five! I talked with him at length in Villefranche about the weighty task he was about to shoulder. Then I spent several days drawing up a sort of military doctrine for the maquis. It treated of the choice of terrain, organization, command, discipline, arms and equipment, training and war operations.

My general idea, from which I'd never departed, was to form units of about thirty men that would harry the enemy ruthlessly without ever offering battle except on their own terms. Fluidity, rapidity and mobility were my three basic principles.

The Vercors maquis, as conceived by Yves Farge and endorsed by Jean Moulin, was the diametrical opposite. It was designed to be a sort of bastion harboring several thousand men who would not only send out hit-and-run teams but also defend their own positions. This conception struck me as dangerously wrong. I opposed it right from the start. It was obvious that no maquis, however strong, would ever be able to resist an assailant superior in numbers and possessing a complete range of modern weapons.

The Vercors bastion was set up anyway. Despite heroic resistance, it was crushed as soon as the Germans had enough free troops to storm it.

As the M.U.R.'s "*commissaire* of military affairs," I presented Brault's application to the committee. He was immediately ratified as national chief of the maquis.

He was soon assisted by Georges Rebattet ("Cheval"); Robert Soulage, who had already started recruitment for his training school; Albert Thomas ("Tricoire"), the ex-chief of the Secret Army in the Gard; and my precious secretary Lucette Pagel ("*Dominique*"), who, to my great regret, left me for her new role.

This team worked admirably well. Its first task was to take a census of the existing maquis, attach them to local commands, establish a complex system of liaisons and try to provide the maquisards with the necessary wherewithal for their survival and operations. "Jérôme," soon to become "Mézeray," was also to have several excellent regional maquis chiefs: Jaboulay ("Michelin") for

The Night Will End

R.1, Jean Monties ("Labarthe") for R.2, Sarda de Caumont ("Rosette") for R.4, and Dejussieu ("Pontcarral") for R.6.

The service entrusted to Bénouville had been well and rapidly organized. We had enough accomplices in the national railways and the customs to make frontier crossings possible several times a week. By early April our communications line was functioning perfectly.

In Geneva Philippe Monod was still negotiating with the O.S.S., who had proven extremely cooperative. They were shortly to give us 37 million francs.

The arms we needed could also now be provided in large quantities, and we were asked to find one hundred acceptable parachute-drop sites. Decidedly, our American friends went "all the way."

Allen Dulles was to perform many other services for us, including the delivery of photographic equipment, sabotage material, typewriters and other materiel.

Looking back, we saw how rapid our progress had been. We'd secured money and arms for the maquis, our intelligence reports were now being instantly put to use, and we had an open window on the world.

But our joy was short-lived. Philippe Monod soon informed us that the Interior *commissariat* in London had told the C.N.F.'s representative in Switzerland, Pierre de Leusse, to approach the U.S. Embassy in Berne with a request that they break off all contact with us. The aim of this tactic, said the message, was to forestall an "American takeover of the French Resistance."

This was too much! I practically wept with rage. Late that night, as we sat together in the Gouzes' dining room, I told Berty about this appalling new turn of events.

"London has now cut off our means of survival and refused us the right to seek them elsewhere. What the hell do they want us to do—drop dead?"

"Most likely they're afraid of some dissidence on your part, Henri. It's a misunderstanding. Why don't you go to London and straighten things out?"

A United Front

Berty was right: I had to go to London. Pierre agreed. Since he'd experienced the Swiss incident blow by blow, we decided that he should come too. We would leave as soon as possible. Our optimism returned.

Bénouville immediately went to Paris to meet with Moulin and ask him to arrange an air pick-up for us. With great difficulty he finally managed to pin Moulin down and get him to promise that we could leave shortly.

Plenty of Lysander operations took place that April of 1943, but none of them included us. It seemed that London wasn't any too eager to have us.

Shortly thereafter, Delestraint sent a memorandum to the regional Secret Army chiefs that was in open contradiction to his standing orders from us. "Forestier" intercepted it. The tension mounted.

In effect, Delestraint now proposed to put the Secret Army under the command of officers from the former Armistice Army. Clearly if the choice of such officers was not highly selective we were heading straight for a calamity. Many of these officers had remained Pétainistes; others had sought refuge behind the "Giraldist" formula. Virtually all were anti-Gaullists. Our boys would simply refuse to obey them.

The often stormy and always painful debate was resumed during several further sessions of the Coordinating Committee. To avoid losing my temper altogether, I addressed a letter to Delestraint containing a cool exposition of my viewpoint; then, on May 10, I sent a report to London.

In it I tried to explain the special nature of our troops, how they were really closer to the sans-culottes of the Revolution than to the soldiers of a conventional standing army. I also stressed the political nature of our struggle and the need for coordination among the leaderships of the movements. Finally, I offered several concrete proposals to help maintain the authority of the allied command over the Secret Army and to permit the Coordinating Committee of the M.U.R. to play a role of coordination and control.

Meanwhile De Gaulle himself had gotten a clearer picture of the

The Night Will End

situation. This was probably an upshot of a recent Passy–Brossolette mission to metropolitan France.

On May 21 De Gaulle sent General Delestraint a "secret and personal instruction" containing the following provisions:

Short-term operations are virtually always to be left to the initiative of the movements and their local organizations. . . . General Delestraint shall intervene in this domain only by means of broad directives fixed by accord with the Coordinating Committee. . . .

At the present time General Delestraint shall fulfill the duties of an inspector-general designated to take over active command only at the moment of the [Allied] landing. . . .

He shall verify the working order of the command organization system set up by the Coordinating Committee. . . .

In effect, Delestraint was no longer the commander of the Secret Army—merely an inspector general. De Gaulle had simply countermanded his orders of two months earlier.

My friends' and my own efforts to conceive, create and direct the Secret Army were not in vain. This was officially confirmed by the enemy himself, as we discovered after the war.

Of the tons of documents captured by the Allied authorities in Berlin, the Wilhelmstrasse papers were of special interest. Late in the summer of 1945 I received—from Admiral Barjot, I think—a document from Wilhelmstrasse entitled *Die Armée Secrète in Frankreich*. It bore the signature of Kaltenbrunner, the right arm of S.S. Reichsführer Heinrich Himmler, and was addressed to Von Ribbentrop, the Minister of Foreign Affairs. The latter had judged the document important enough to warrant its being shown to Hitler himself. At the top of the first page was the note "*Bei dem Führer vorgelegen*" ("reviewed by the Führer") and below it Hitler's signature stamp.

Dated May 27, 1943, it was a synthesis of all the intelligence gathered up to that date by the German special services. Though incomplete and at times erroneous—thank God for that—as a whole it gave a pretty good picture of our organization, though distinctly overestimating its size and armaments.

A United Front

When I first saw this report the war in Europe had been over for several months. I can't hide the fact that it made me feel rather proud. The report was accompanied by a commentary by General Seeherr that stated:

. . . The [Secret] Army will open hostilities only in the event of an [Allied] invasion. Up until that moment it will remain an invisible, unattainable and hence particularly dangerous force. . . .

It was with especial interest that I read the following words:

. . . The creation of the S.A., in its current form, is in large measure due to Captain FRESNAY [sic]. . . .

In January 1943 Captain Fresnay succeeded in placing the organizations known as Combat, Libération, and Franc-Tireur under a Coordinating Committee. . . .

Military affairs were placed under this same Fresnay, including the S.A. (the principal organization) and the Groupe Franc [sic] . . . an outfit of about 1,100 men, mostly explosives experts, who, by early March 1943, already had 150 operations to their credit.

The troop strength of the S.A. in the former free zone was placed at 80,000, with an overestimated arms complement and munitions dump. Our communications methods and our operational scenarios had received detailed study.

In the end Kaltenbrunner presented an analysis of the political position of the S.A.:

Captain Fresnay's political stance toward Germany may be summed up as follows:

Germany deserves exemplary chastening and should be rendered harmless for the indefinite future. The punishment should be brutal but short and should be inflicted solely upon the "Nazi authorities"—that is, upon a few score thousand individuals.

[He believes] it would be unwise to force the German people, as in 1918, to bear the burden of defeat. This would only sow the seeds of future conflict and might force the German people to revolt.

The partition of Germany should not be undertaken, and a unified

The Night Will End

Germany should be integrated into a united Europe. The economic unity of the world implies its political unity.

The abolition of political frontiers and the disappearance of such economic systems as make it impossible for some people to live decently will suffice to remove the deepest causes of war. At this point Europe will have to protect itself only against the recrudescence of nationalism, particularly in Germany.

Through the socialization of heavy industry and the creation of international armies the use of force will be rendered practically impossible.

The spring of 1943 came early. The air was chilly, but we enjoyed many fine days. Almost every morning I took the meandering narrow-gauge train to Mâcon or Villefranche.

Sometimes, to relax, Berty and I would stroll as far as La Cra, a town a few kilometers from Cluny where the Gouzes had a bungalow. Toward late April the first violets and primroses bloomed. The region was placid. We saw no Germans aside from an occasional truck convoy on the Montceau-les-Mines road. I'd have given anything to relax a bit, to go rambling in the budding groves, or maybe evern to angle for trout in one of the nearby streams, for the Mayflies would soon be hatched.

Once again Jean-Guy Bernard turned up with a downcast look. How well I knew that taut face, those clenched jaws. He had some new disaster to announce. Placing the mail on my table, he dropped into a chair.

"The Gestapo made two big new hauls. First, they nabbed Hyllaire and Ady-Brille, so R.5's bcen decapitated again. But the worst was in Marseilles: 'Barrioz,' 'Lunel' and 'Lamy' [Chevance, Multon and Crémieux] were all arrested, as well as others whose names we don't know yet."

Our big problem was Multon. As soon as he was arrested he started to "sing," and, worse still, he also offered the Gestapo his services. As Chevance's lieutenant he knew plenty of names and addresses. Dozens of arrests were made in R.2 before we were aware of his treason.

I ordered the Marseilles G.F. to execute him, but they couldn't

A United Front

find him. It took us some time to discover that he'd moved to Lyons, where he was pursuing his sinister work.

Despite our expectations Bénouville and I did not go to London during the April moon. It seemed that Lysander seats were hard to come by. Only one of us could go and only in the third quarter of the May moon. The pick-up was to take place in the Juras. It was decided that I'd be driven there from Lyons. Hence it was in Lyons that I awaited my coded message from the BBC.

Lyons was getting more dangerous by the day. If the Gestapo had your description—and they'd had mine for ages—it was very unhealthy to wander about. The railway station and all the city's bridges were under permanent full-time surveillance by German plainclothesmen.

I stayed on the left bank of the Rhône in Bénouville's little apartment on the Rue Tronchet. I went out as seldom as possible, never straying far from my new dwelling place. Only a few friends visited me.

Often Pierre and I chatted after dinner, not only about our daily concerns but also about the future.

Before the war, as a career officer, I'd abstained from political activity. Yet I had fervently supported the Popular Front, the Spanish loyalists and Haile Selassie's struggle against Mussolini's aggression. At that time Pierre had been not only an Action Française militant but also a *camelot du roi,* or member of Action's royalist shock troops. Our political views should by all rights have been diametrically opposed.

But they weren't. The fraternal nature of our struggle had made us friends. Distinctions that might have kept us apart in earlier days—in social origins, profession, wealth, age or politics— had melted away in the warmth of this friendship. We saw ourselves as we really were, with our faults, of course, but also with our virtues. For more than blind fate had brought us together. Though our motives for resisting varied widely, deep down we recognized a moral common denominator that overrode our differences.

It was our friendship that allowed us to broach all our problems

The Night Will End

with a common sympathy that quickly dispelled prejudices and preconceptions. In his heart of hearts, even Pierre, who yesterday would have been my political foe, nourished a deep desire for national renewal. This desire was, if I may venture to use the words, marvelously fresh and pure.

Pierre, my friend Pierre, who only a few months ago had been standing on church steps hawking right-wing newspapers, now understood that the elimination of frontiers, the unity of Europe, was one of our principal objectives.

Within us a revolution was taking place. Though as yet ill defined, each day its outlines became clearer. Our will to reconstruct our country now equaled our combative ardor.

The resurrection of the old political parties, which De Gaulle had imposed on a recalcitrant Resistance, was a mere contretemps. More than ever we now had to close ranks and march forward to our goal. This goal was in fact a sort of purified and rejuvenated socialism. André Hauriou was later to call it a "humanist socialism."

Berty, whom I'd seen briefly during a quick run back to Cluny, had asked me to help slip her daughter across to Switzerland, where some cousins could take her in.

"I'll no longer subject that poor child to the ups and downs of my existence," she said. "I haven't the right. What would become of her here in France if I were to disappear? No, this kind of life just won't do for her any more. Ask Bénouville to take her with him during his next trip."

Which he did. After the war Mireille told me that during their farewell her mother had said, "Mireille, I know I'll never see you again. Forgive me, my darling, for what I've put you through."

Alas, there was truth in that presentiment.

Back in Lyons, I was again assailed by problems connected with our delegation in Switzerland.

While showering us with protestations of friendship, Allen Dulles seemed very uneasy about the attitude of De Gaulle's services toward us. Yet our delegation never minced words concerning our staunch adherence to "Gaullism." Our military intelli-

A United Front

gence was transmitted to the O.S.S. in Berne a full forty-eight hours after its transmission to the London Gaullists.

As for money, the eight millions already contributed by Dulles were a mere drop of water compared to what he himself had promised. But Dulles's money rankled London so much that I wondered if we'd ever see it.

Not a day went by that I didn't receive an anguished entreaty from some maquis. The maquis' lack of weapons and money had reached a critical level. Our regional chiefs were either on the verge of despair or bitterly angry. As far as they were concerned, we and we alone were responsible.

We urged Moulin to increase our budget. Each maquisard needed about six hundred francs a month. Moulin replied that he had cabled London several times but had received no answer.

Fortunately, Bénouville and our delegation had by now perfected a system for the transfer of funds. They could be deposited at Baring Brothers in London and transferred to the Banque Lombard et Odier in Switzerland. The latter could then deliver them to different towns in France. This involved no risk of any kind.

Not only did Moulin fail to respond to this idea, but he began to foment new plots against us. In early May our delegation succeeded in intercepting an emissary sent by Moulin to ask Dulles to break off relations with us. Monod immediately sent him packing.

Through the Berne O.S.S. our delegation also learned that an important French labor leader had been received in the British Embassy to Switzerland. This person had apparently pointed out my "fascist streak" and my "dictatorial ambitions" and had advised the British to watch out for me and my "creatures" in the Resistance delegation. The fact that I had recently signed several newspaper articles in my own name was a publicity stunt signaling a forthcoming bid for total power!

A letter from Geneva, coded as always, confirmed that the American action on our behalf had been effectively blocked:

Max Shoop informed us yesterday that the . . . London French have deliberately torpedoed our endeavor. . . . Their mistrust, their dogged

The Night Will End

270

opposition and their attempts to discredit us have compromised our relations with the Americans.

The results of this policy are only too clear. The victims are the resisters, who have been awaiting the promised arms shipments for two months, and especially the unarmed Secret Army and the maquis, who still vainly entreat us for help. The London services, to spite us and to further their own ambitions, have committed what amounts to a crime against the Resistance. Yet all is not lost: We still have faith. . . .

Like our regional chiefs, I myself now felt unmanned, overcome by lassitude. I was drowning in revulsion at so much antipathy, perfidy and hostility. I remembered De Gaulle's words in the Savoy Hotel: "'Charvet,' it seems that France must choose between you and me."

Well, we hadn't quite broken off relations yet, but we were sore at heart.

By now I was actively preparing for my trip to England, devoting special care to three long reports that I intended to present to London—one on the Secret Army, another on our ties with our Allies in Switzerland and a third on the relations between Jean Moulin and the M.U.R.

Considering all the facts I'd packed into these three reports, I found it inconceivable that London would fail to understand me.

Illusions, illusions.

Late on the morning of May 27 there came a series of knocks on the door to Bénouville's apartment—our secret signal. It was Marcel Peck. An ominous sign.

"'Battesti'! *You* here? What's up?"

"'Victoire's' been nabbed by the Gestapo."

"Victoire" was Berty's current pseudonym. I went dizzy and my blood curdled.

"Tell me about it. What happened?"

"One of our boys from the Saône-et-Loire Secret Army came by this morning. His department chief had sent him. He gave me the message orally. It seems that the day before yesterday a note was slipped into your letterbox in Mâcon asking you to meet somebody the following day in the Hôtel de Bourgogne."

A United Front

"Who was this somebody?"

"We don't know. That same evening, in Cluny, 'Victoire' told the Gouzes that since you couldn't make it she'd go. Apparently she thought the meeting was urgent."

"But what did the message say?"

"Nobody knows that either. She arrived for the rendezvous on time. She never even made it into the hotel. Four men picked her up on the esplanade. She screamed for help. They forced her into the hotel. The hotel guests were forced to leave their rooms and were lined up against the dining-room wall at pistol point. One of the cops went down the line examining each man. Obviously he expected one of them to be you."

"Did anyone get a good look at that particular cop?"

"We got the usual vague descriptions. Average height, auburn hair, meaty face, glasses . . ."

"Stop right there! It was Multon, I just know it was! The bastard, the goddam bastard!"

But all my fury was of no avail. Berty was gone. Multon's perfidious note had been intended for me, and my poor dear Berty had been captured in my place!

"Well, then what happened?"

"They went out to the Gouzes' in Cluny. They burst into the place hollering, 'Where is he? Where is he?' Then they pushed the Gouzes into one room and ransacked the whole house, including the adjoining wing. They've confiscated all your and Berty's stuff. Your clothes, your typewriter, everything's gone."

Though interrogated at length, both together and separately, the Gouzes stubbornly feigned ignorance. They explained how the firing of M. Gouze had landed the family in a situation verging on dire poverty. To make ends meet, they'd rented out two rooms of the house. As for M. "Tavernier" and his secretary, they were just unobjectionable folks who seemed to do a lot of writing. They were polite but quiet.

"Madame, do you know whom you were harboring? The head of the French Resistance! Yes! Your unobjectionable M. 'Tavernier!'"

"But what did they do with Berty?" I asked.

The Night Will End

272

"Late that afternoon they took her to the Hôtel Terminus not far from the Mâcon railway station. She's still there."

The Hôtel Terminus in Mâcon, like its namesake in Lyons, was Gestapo headquarters. We hadn't a minute to lose! She would surely be transferred from Mâcon to Lyons, either to the Fort Montluc or to the Hôtel Terminus. The Gestapo always transported their prisoners by car. We would intercept that car!

"'Battesti,' you work this thing out. Cover the hotel with a surveillance unit. Then put a G.F. unit on the Lyons road and get them the description of that car as soon as it leaves Mâcon. They can figure out the rest themselves. I'm counting on you, Marcel. We've got to save Berty!"

Our people were deployed as ordered. A swollen-faced Berty was seen being forced out of the Hôtel Terminus and into a car. But this car, contrary to all our expectations, took the Paris road. Berty was lost.

From that moment on I remembered several times each day Berty's terrible words: "If they catch me again, I'll kill myself."

We waited. And waited. The thought of Berty haunted me.

I was now in a safe apartment on the Quai Saint-Vincent, not far from where I'd once collected intelligence reports from the Deuxième Bureau.

I didn't have a single suit left and not one change of shirts. The Gestapo had taken everything in Cluny. Pierre and his future wife, Georgie, took my measurements and sent word to Philippe Monod in Switzerland to buy me some inexpensive new clothes.

Then I got a brief note in the mail: "Vidal" and "Galibier" (General Delestraint and Captain Gastaldo) had been arrested in Paris on June 9. They had left for the northern zone to make contact with the movements there. It was a terrible blow to the Secret Army.

A few days earlier René Hardy had evaded Multon by the skin of his teeth. On the Lyons–Paris train he'd spotted him in his coach and leaped off onto the tracks not far from Chalon-sur-Saône.

René looked very different now. This last incident had made him

A United Front

visibly neurasthenic. He wore glasses and had dyed his hair, which now had unnatural bluish highlights.

We were getting tenser by the day. Fortunately the De Gaulle–Giraud conflict seemed to have simmered down. On Giraud's request De Gaulle had arrived in Algiers on May 30. A broadcast by Maurice Schumann, the radio spokesman for Free France, informed us of the delirious demonstration with which the Free French leader had been welcomed at the "forum" in Algiers. A few weeks afterward I learned that this demonstration had been organized by Combat–Algiers (René Capitant, Paul Coste-Floret, Fradin, etc.). Three days later the BBC announced that De Gaulle and Giraud had become co-presidents of the C.F.L.N.

Now I'd have to go, not to London but to Algiers. I had no doubt that it was De Gaulle, and De Gaulle alone, who could put an end to our problems,

Meanwhile Laval, after an interview with Hitler in the latter's HQ, had decreed the deportation to Germany of all men who had reached majority in 1941 and a large portion of those who had reached majority in 1942. The rumor circulated that they were to be incorporated into the Wehrmacht.

By hand I began to outline an article for *Combat*—my last before my departure.

The Saône was lolling lazily beneath my window. Before me was the basilica of Notre-Dame de Fourvière, perched, friendly as always, on the heights of Sainte-Foy. Each year of my childhood, on the Feast of the Virgin, Maman and Papa had taken me to the Place Bellecour to admire it. On that day, December 8, all Lyons was ablaze with light, and the basilica too, the town's own miniature Eiffel Tower, shone like a wondrous illuminated petit-point.

Maman! It was so long since I'd seen her! From time to time I sent her a postcard—just a few lines to tell her I was still alive—but she had no address for me. It was better that way, for twice she'd gotten police calls and been forced to submit to cross-examination.

And then Chilina. Not a word from her since January. Why? I'd hardly had any time to write her, and I felt terribly guilty about it. I cut short my reflections to scribble her the following short note:

The Night Will End

"Berty has been hospitalized. I'm very worried for her. 'Georges' [London] has invited me up and I'm going to spend a few months with him. I'll be off shortly. Love (etc.)."

Back to my article. It came out of me in one long avalanche:

On April 29, as if he were whistling for a dog, Hitler summoned Laval to his HQ. . . .

Laval promised Hitler 220,000 men, to be followed shortly by 180,000 more. Already Germany has begun to put them in uniform. . . .

We had thought that Laval had already reached the nadir of treason. But we had forgotten that he would be willing to sacrifice France herself to forestall the day of judgment. Laval, you are a bloodthirsty swine, and one day a dozen French gun muzzles, still smoking from the battles of our Liberation, will repay you for your crimes! . . .

Our boys, our faithful comrades, who, unlike you, are French to the marrow, know where their duty lies. By disobeying, they will serve their country. They know that in only a few months the French flag will float over our cities beside the flags of our Allies. They know that by then Vichy will be no more than a nightmare and you no more than a corpse. They know that in a few months they will have won. They shall not obey you!

Then, casting about for a title, I hit on "To Disobey Is to Serve."

The article was published on June 15, 1943, and it too bore my true name.

Forty-eight hours later, I left France. In my absence Claude Bourdet took my place in the M.U.R. and also directed Combat. Bénouville became responsible for military affairs. But not for long. I'd be back in, oh, about a month.

Or so I thought.

A United Front

DE GAULLE VS. GIRAUD

Less than a hundred meters overhead, a plane roared by. My companion turned to me and said in a hushed voice, "If the S.S. company in Saint-Laurent didn't hear *that*, we're pretty damn lucky!"

Once again I was on that same landing strip on the Saône north of Mâcon where D'Astier and I had waited three times in vain the previous year. Its code name was "Marguerite," and this evening of June 17, 1943, it was the scene of a world première. For the first time, a twin-engine machine, a Hudson, was being used for a night pick-up. Though a Hudson required a longer runway than a Lysander and one clear of obstacles along the sides, it could carry four to five times as many passengers.

That night there were at least eight of us crouching in the bushes in expectation of our departure. Several armed escort squads covered the nearby roads. The night was mild and redolent of new-mown hay.

We lit our beacons, and the plane circled overhead and landed impeccably. As it taxied toward us its cockpit door swung open and a man, then another, then two more clambered to the ground, followed by still others.

"You there," said a shadow, ex-

13

tending a helping hand from the cockpit, "let's go!"

One by one we were hoisted aboard. The door closed behind us. I felt the Hudson shudder. A few jolts, and we were off.

We sat on the floor, in total darkness, propped up against the fuselage wall. I held my overstuffed portfolio between my knees. It contained my toilet articles, a change of shirts, several reports that I'd drawn up for De Gaulle and his services, and, in two copies, Hardy's and "Harrel's" "Green Plan" for railway sabotage, which I intended to submit to the Allied Chiefs of Staff.

Nobody said a word. The engines droned on. Suddenly a clipped Parisian voice rose out of the total darkness: "We're making a detour around Lyons because of the Luftwaffe," it said. "Then we'll head down the Rhône Valley."

Wait a minute. *Down* the Rhône Valley? Then we were flying south. But what about London?

"No dice. The nights are too short now for us to make it to England, so we're taking you to Algeria instead."

What a break! Algeria! De Gaulle had been in Algiers for a month now. Today or tomorrow I could talk to him personally. I'd never thought things would move so fast.

It was dawn when I awoke. We were over the Mediterranean. I surveyed my fellow travelers. Who really were they, and what secrets were they bearing?

The African coast hove into view. In a moment we were in Algeria.

"Gentlemen," said Livry-Level, "we are now at Boufarik Air Base. You're requested not to leave the plane. We've orders to fuel up and take off again at once."

Of course this strange order couldn't possibly apply to me. After all, I'd already arranged to see De Gaulle, and De Gaulle was right here. I mentioned this to Livry-Level and then to the British officer in charge of the plane. No, they were sorry, but they couldn't waive their orders.

Well, I thought, maybe it was better that I see the B.C.R.A. first anyway. I'd be back here within a week.

We peered eagerly out of the aircraft at the bustling base with its brisk air traffic and its French soldiers in their shorts and summer uniforms. A few hours later we left Algiers.

De Gaulle Versus Giraud

We spent that night in Gibraltar. The following day, after a wide detour around the French Atlantic coast, we set down in England.

The Free French in London, with their eyes turned expectantly toward Algiers, had just celebrated the third anniversary of De Gaulle's June 18 appeal.

It was June 19, 1943.

Disappointment number one: Passy had just left for Algiers. I was told he wouldn't be away long, though, for the B.C.R.A. was still based in London. Only a small branch, directed by an assistant of Passy's called "Pélabon," had been moved to Algiers. I was informed that I'd better await Passy's return, because De Gaulle certainly wouldn't consider my business anyway until it had been screened by the appropriate services.

In Duke Street I talked with an officer called "Manuel" whom I'd met when he was on a mission to France the previous December. I agreed to bring him my heavy sheaf of reports the next day.

Alone in my room that evening I reread them one by one. "April 8, 1943," said one heading: "From 'Gervais' [me] to 'Valentin' [Delestraint] . . . April 8, 1943"—same date. Reading on, I saw myself back in Cluny typing this letter to Jean Moulin. "My dear 'Max' . . ." it started.

My dear "Max" . . . He'd never grasped, or cared to grasp, what I was trying to say. How irked he'd been when I'd told him that he knew nothing of the underground—how irked at the simple truth! How many times I'd asked him to pick a region, any region, and, going down the ladder rung by rung, to listen to its top cadres, then those of a typical department, then those of a typical town, right down to the humblest of our faithful. But he never did.

Yes, my relations with "Max" posed a difficult problem. What was really at stake was the rapport between London and our domestic resistance forces.

Granted, our actions had to be concerted, had to follow De Gaulle's guidelines; but the M.U.R. had to be free to apply them as it saw fit. Again, there was no denying that we should consult London before making any important decisions; but it was only fair that we have a representative to participate in London's delibera-

The Night Will End

tions. I also held that the C.N.F. delegate to France (i.e., Moulin) should not chair the M.U.R. meetings. He should simply see to it that London's directives were being properly followed.

The current malfunction had to be rectified as soon as possible, lest the rift between London and the Resistance grow steadily wider. At the present rate, that rift would soon be a gulf. My fears seemed well expressed in my report; no one, I thought, could fault my conclusions.

The next day I submitted my reports to the B.C.R.A. "Manuel" read them in silence. I searched his face in vain for some sign of approval or disapproval.

"I'll have them reproduced in a limited number of classified copies," he said. "They'll be passed around to the various desks involved—the general's staff in Algiers, the *commissariat* of the Interior and our departments here in Duke Street."

In the afternoon a cable from France was delivered. It was a bombshell. The previous day, June 21, Jean Moulin, along with several top people in the Secret Army, had been arrested by the Gestapo. Only several days later did we find out exactly what had happened.

They'd been meeting in Caluire to discuss what to do about the loss of Delestraint and Gastaldo. Among those present were Henri Aubry, Raymond Aubrac (from Libération) and René Hardy. Before the discussion had even got started the Gestapo burst in and arrested the lot of them. They were probably being interned in the Ecole de Santé Militaire in Lyons. Hardy, however, had managed to shake off his S.S. guard and get away, though not without being wounded by his pursuers' pistol shots.

Moulin arrested! The previous evening the very thought of him had galled me, but now, hearing this news, I broke out in a cold sweat. Did the Germans know whom they'd captured? And how had the Gestapo found out about the Caluire meeting? Through treachery? Through our sloppiness? By shadowing us? The identification of Moulin would put the entire Resistance in grave danger.

The arrest caused a tremendous commotion. In Algiers De Gaulle ordered that everything possible be done to rescue Moulin.

De Gaulle Versus Giraud

It was a hopeless task. Moulin was to suffer a long and terrible martyrdom. It was not until long after the war that we knew just what had befallen him.

Easily identified as the keeper of all the most important secrets of the Resistance, he was long and horribly tortured. Christian Pineau, who was then incarcerated in Fort Montluc in Lyons, glimpsed him once, flat on his back, disfigured and unable to speak. With a despairing, lackluster glance, "Max" conveyed that he'd recognized him.

A few weeks later he succumbed to his tortures without having breathed a single word about the Resistance. He died an authentic hero.

Soon afterward messages from several sources reached London accusing René Hardy of having "fingered" the Caluire meeting. The case against him seemed so strong that there had been an attempt to poison him. In the Antiquaille hospital, where his wounds were being treated, he'd received a jar of cyanide-laden jam from some M.U.R. people. His accusers claimed that he had wounded himself to escape suspicion.

Hardy a traitor to the Resistance, a Gestapo stoolie? His behavior at the head of our Sabotage-Rail had been a model of energy and efficiency. He'd already blown up countless German convoys. Why, he himself (along with his colleague "Harrel") was the author of the "Green Plan" which I had right here in my portfolio. He'd already served a long prison sentence in 1940 for resistance activity. Hardy was my comrade, my friend. There was no proof against him, and as long as there was none, I would defend him.

But the "Hardy Affair" had only just begun.

I hadn't forgotten how desperately our people needed funds, nor the cry of the maquis in their extremity.

Even before Passy got back from Algiers I gave the B.C.R.A. a memorandum I'd drafted on May 25, before leaving France, on "The Relations between the M.U.R. and the Allies in Switzerland." It too was reproduced and stamped "Top Secret and Confidential." It was still true, despite the polemics and passions that surrounded them, that our initiatives in Switzerland might well bring in a triple benefit for the Resistance: money, better communications and arms.

Nobody, least of all here in London, was unaware that Moulin's promises to D'Astier and me last November had not been kept. I knew this wasn't Passy's fault. The English were still playing their old game, and the maquis hardly fired their enthusiasm anyway. Hence these for us vital problems had gone unsolved. Now I, in the name of the M.U.R., would insist on their solution.

I talked with everyone I could, but I always ran into the same objections: to provide the Americans with intelligence was to undermine Free French bargaining power with the English; to accept American money was to fall willy-nilly under American influence; direct contact with the Anglo-Saxons would only divide the Resistance.

Vainly I repeated the arguments in my reports that had demolished this specious reasoning. Absolutely no one agreed with me. In fact, the more passionate my defense, the more suspect I became in the eyes of the Free French. They were beginning to regard me as a schismatic!

Yes, a schismatic—I who had done more than anyone to rally often recalcitrant men and movements to De Gaulle! Yet they still had no faith in our loyalty. They seemed unable to understand that we had established contact with the Americans only because the B.C.R.A. in London, and Moulin in France, couldn't or wouldn't give us money and arms.

We were ready to renounce these contacts if our French brothers would give us what we needed. But for them to refuse to help us, while forbidding us to procure help elsewhere, was to break our necks, to disarm us both materially and morally. This I could not accept!

It was a lovely July morning. The sun was beaming down on London as it rarely does. I was crying my eyes out. On my table was a message from France: Berty was dead. She had either been decapitated or shot by a firing squad—nobody was sure which. I was in despair.

For a long time I just sat there with my eyes closed. My legs seemed too weak to bear me.

De Gaulle Versus Giraud

I spent the morning communing with the Berty of my memories, recalling our sunny vacations in Beauvallon, the "phony war," our first steps together in the Resistance, her intelligence, humor, courage and efficiency. For the Resistance, for France, she had sacrificed everything—her comfort, her freedom, her family—and now her life.

In the next batch of mail I learned more.

Berty had been dead even before I left France. The Gestapo, without disclosing the cause of her death, had notified the Saône-et-Loire prefecture, which in turn had passed the news on to the Gouze family. The elder Gouze girl, Madeleine, had then informed Bénouville. After consulting with several other comrades, Pierre had decided to keep the tragedy secret from me so as not to weaken my morale at the very moment I was setting out for London.

From the depths of my memory a child's prayer rose in my heart, followed by the last words of the Mass of the Dead: "Give her, O Lord, eternal rest."

Passy was back in London. We met a few times, and he told me about what was happening in Algiers. I was chafing to go there. The situation there was still murky, but some progress had been made. There was now one central authority, the French Committee of National Liberation (C.F.L.N.), alternately presided over by De Gaulle and Giraud. The man in the street was a Gaullist, but the local bigwigs and a large part of the army were still pro-Pétain.

As for the problems that had brought me to London, Passy too was firmly opposed to direct contact between the Resistance and the Americans. However, he promised me that the possibility of financial aid to the M.U.R. via a bank transfer would be sympathetically reviewed.

Meanwhile, the situation of the maquis, now entirely bereft of arms and money, was rapidly deteriorating. Two desperate pleas for help arrived from Switzerland. Monod wrote:

The domestic situation of the Resistance is critical. Its captains, unable to provide their troops with the means of subsistence, have been discredited. Internal splits have taken place. The Secret Army and maquisards are

The Night Will End

on the verge of initiating armed attacks, some of them solely for the purpose of looting what they need to survive.

Jean Moulin had been provisionally replaced by Claude Sereules ("Sophie"), who was already in France at the time of the Caluire tragedy. One of De Gaulle's aides, he was still wet behind the ears as far as the underground was concerned. I wondered if he'd be able to accomplish anything.

The more I thought about it the more it seemed that I'd best see De Gaulle in Algiers. But if I got the green light from De Gaulle, would London follow through? Passy told me to go ahead and try but to remember that a great deal depended on the English and hence was out of his hands.

"In any case," he said, "you could do us a big favor by waiting until Giraud gets here. Right now he's in the U.S. talking with the Americans about how to arm the troops we're raising in the Empire. He's going to stop over in London on his way back to Algiers. It would be very helpful if the various Resistance chiefs here could meet him. He knows about you, and your opinion might carry a certain weight with him."

In July Giraud returned from the U.S., and a suite was reserved for him at the Ritz. A deputation of us Resistance leaders in London asked the general for an audience.

I remember a uniformed Giraud striding into the salon where we'd gathered. He was a tall man with lightly graying auburn hair, a long thick mustache and a totally impassive face.

Like a sergeant looking over a bunch of rookies, he asked us our names one by one, then shook our hands. Sitting very erect on the edge of an armchair, talking to everyone and to no one in particular, he said, "Gentlemen, you have requested to see me. Why?"

We told him how disappointed we were that De Gaulle had had to wait so long to go to Algiers. We pointed out that the C.N.R. resolution had stated that De Gaulle was to take over the provisional government and he, Giraud, only the high command of the armed forces. Moreover, we knew that he had gone to Washington to procure arms for the divisions being levied in North Africa.

De Gaulle Versus Giraud

Hence it seemed opportune to mention the scarcity of arms afflicting the Resistance.

"Arms, is it? Well, gentlemen, they're not indispensable, you know. One can get along without them."

We looked at one another dumfounded.

The general continued: "Gentlemen, what is of the essence in modern warfare? Of course! Air power. If you can neutralize enemy air power, you immediately have the upper hand. And what do you need to neutralize an airfield? Pebbles!"

We thought we'd heard wrong, but no, the general continued his oration: "To obstruct a hangar's sliding door and stop its aircraft from exiting all you need is a pebble. With another pebble you can block a plane's air shaft, causing it to turn over when it tries to land."

With the self-satisfaction of a nightclub magician Giraud rose and concluded: "You see, gentlemen, one can make war even without weapons!"

And this was the man who was going to command our armies!

The war news of July 1943 was reassuring. The Wehrmacht was fiercely resisting the Red Army's new offensive, but with its supply lines stretching hundreds of miles back west and subject to the constant harassment of Russian partisans, it was too hobbled to launch any new attacks.

In the Mediterranean theater, the Americans had landed in Sicily, and a *coup d'état* had toppled Mussolini. For over twenty years he had lorded it over Italy. Now he was behind bars.

I still couldn't understand why proper correspondence with France was so difficult to achieve. With one or two exceptions all my telegrams went unanswered. I wondered if my comrades were actually getting them. Their messages attested to a similar worry on their part. Maybe there was some sort of blockage, possibly intentional. I had no way of knowing.

One news item from France really warmed my heart. The unity already forged in the southern zone had been extended to the entirety of France. The steering committee of the M.U.R., now in

Paris, had been its architect. The underground was to be directed by an eight-member Central Committee (i.e., with one representative per movement).* What this really meant was that the movements had refused to bow to the C.N.R. They had opted to run their own affairs directly—just what I had always championed. The old political parties had been reduced to figurehead status.

But not for long.

Thanks to my communications with France and my contacts here, we'd been able to push through our own M.U.R. candidate to the high command of the Secret Army.

He was a Combat man, Dejussieu-"Pontcarral," the head of the Clermont-Ferrand Secret Army since its birth. A career officer become a dedicated resister, he had all the right qualifications for the job.

The situation in France was still deteriorating. I received several distress signals from Geneva. What could I answer—that I had received "numerous promises," that "the funding question was under review"? No, that was hardly what was expected of me!

I was beginning to wonder whether somebody wasn't blocking my trip to Algiers. Perhaps the counsel that I await Giraud in London had only been a ploy to hold up my departure. And now there was a new hitch. Oddly enough, the English just couldn't seem to come up with an open passage. The situation couldn't go on forever! Either I would ask to return immediately to France or I'd improvise some way to make it to Algiers without the B.C.R.A.'s help.

First I contacted Giraud's London representative. In forty-eight hours he got me a seat on an American plane. I was to leave for Algiers in a week.

Loyally, though, on a sarcastic note, I informed Passy of this fact. Sure enough, as if by some miraculous coincidence, his services "just happened" to get me a flight within twenty-four

*Three from the southern zone: Combat (Claude Bourdet), Libération (Pascal Copeau), Franc-Tireur (Jean-Pierre Lévy). Five from the northern zone: Libération-Nord (Ribière), the O.C.M. (Maxime Blocq-Mascart), C.D.L.R. (Jacques Lecompte-Boinet), C.D.L.L. (Lenormand), the National Front (Pierre Villon).

De Gaulle Versus Giraud

hours of the one I'd wangled out of the Giraldists! No spoilsport, I accepted his offer.

Only later—at the year's end—did I learn that André Philip, the Interior *Commissaire*, had sent the following telegram to De Gaulle:

1. Grave consequences if 'Charvet' [Frenay] goes back to France.
2. If his Algiers trip is turned down, we can still block his return to France.

Philip must have sent this telegram (which was totally out of character) at someone else's instigation. But whose? I had good reason to believe that he, like so many others, was under the spell of that charming and influential fellow Emmanuel D'Astier de la Vigerie.

After the war I found in the files of our delegation to Switzerland the text of a cablegram that Bourdet had tried to send me in late July 1943:

We have wind of a plan to restrain you there by force—stop—Beware! In this eventuality protest resignation from Resistance by me, "Barrès" [Bénouville], "Bresse" [Chevance], all chiefs of southern zone, several regional chiefs—stop—Initiative probably followed by several departmental chiefs—stop—We would launch big edition pamphlets attacking inadmissible procedure. Best, "Lorrain" [Bourdet].

Of course I never got that cable.

In the days directly before my departure, I summed up in my mind all that I'd observed, both positive and negative, of our relations with the London French and their envoy Moulin. I'd never before pondered this matter as a whole; I'd always reacted to individual events. Now I put all the facts together, and they told a very alarming story.

My differences with Moulin had not reflected mere personal rivalry. Everyone had backed him, including De Gaulle. Surely this support reflected some conscious policy.

The Night Will End

All at once *I understood.*

The rapid growth of the Resistance and of Combat in particular, though at first encouraged by the Free French, now alarmed them. Despite our proven loyalty, they were afraid that a new force was on the upswing in France, a force with a will of its own and capable of open contumacy toward De Gaulle.

In this view we were no longer friends but rivals—admissible rivals but rivals just the same. We were to be carefully watched and strictly controlled.

"France will choose between you and me," De Gaulle had told me last November. Now I saw that this was no joke. The possibility of serious rivalry had actually been considered in London. In this perspective, all was clear. Now I understood why Moulin and his operatives had monopolized our services, why the Secret Army had been sealed off, why a proper Resistance-London liaison had never been set up. Now I understood the reason for the cabals against our mission to Switzerland, the budget cuts and so on.

This was the only explanation for so much sheer antipathy and hostility. Yet it was so monstrous that I almost couldn't believe it.

Perhaps De Gaulle, in Algiers, could head off the onrushing thunderclouds.

My thoughts reverted to Lyons, to Mâcon, to our provincial regions. Before my eyes rose the faces of my comrades. If only they knew!

I grabbed my pen and dashed off the following indictment, which I intended to convey personally to De Gaulle:

While the French Resistance awaits the delivery of all its instruments of war from Fighting France, the latter merely tries to use it for its own political ends. . . .

The principle of "Divide and conquer" is being ruthlessly applied to [the Resistance]. If this goes on, nothing in France will be left to administer but ruins and corpses. . . .

The relations between Fighting France and the Resistance will improve only if a Resistance delegation is immediately set up in London to handle *all* the problems of the Resistance with the competent bodies. This

De Gaulle Versus Giraud

delegation, *and this delegation alone,* should speak in the name of the Resistance . . . and, conversely, it alone should inform the Resistance of what transpires in London.

We ardently desire to follow General de Gaulle—but with our eyes open.

Rereading my report, I concluded that it should not be a personal letter to De Gaulle but should be sent in duplicate to Passy, Philip and Boris as well. After all, I had nothing to hide from them.

To convince De Gaulle, who no doubt had been poisoned against me, would be no easy matter. But I had no other choice. If I could at least get his okay on the creation of an official Resistance delegation in London—some confirmation of our presence and our will—we would have made decisive progress.

It was with this hope in my heart that I took a train to Scotland in early August to board a plane for North Africa.

René Capitant, the head of Combat-Algiers, wasn't the sentimental type, but we fell into each other's arms at the Algiers airport. We hadn't seen each other since September 1942.

I spent my whole first day there with him. We spoke at length about our faraway friends, the fusion of the movements and the growth of our operations and propaganda. He didn't realize how much Moulin and I had been at loggerheads. He also found my revelations about the estrangement of London from the Resistance highly disturbing.

One problem overrode all others in the mind of Capitant and his comrades: the Giraud–De Gaulle duel. Since the American landing the Algerian Combat had unstintingly helped De Gaulle. However, contrary to what I'd thought, Combat had been carefully excluded from the preparations for the Anglo-American landings ("Operation Torch") of last November. Robert Murphy, the American diplomat behind these preparations, had requested his French outriders to conceal the whole operation from the Gaullists, including Capitant and his friends. The Americans found them overly hostile to Vichy and distrustful of Giraud.

However, as soon as the actual fighting and rioting had broken out, they had offered their help to the insurgents. Then Darlan had gone after them. After his assassination by Bonnier de la Chapelle, they had discreetly gone underground again, though many had been arrested and jailed in the prison of Barberousse. Eventually released, they were still being closely watched by the anti-Gaullist Admiral Muselier, now chief of police. *Combat,* though aboveground, was subject to heavy censorship.

It was Combat that had organized the impressive demonstration for De Gaulle's arrival in Algiers last May 30, including the large public meeting in the Majestic Cinema, where he had addressed the crowd and set forth his conception of the new French central authority. Thus De Gaulle had gained the adherence of much of public opinion both French and Muslim.

Capitant also told me about the persecution, now of course terminated, of persons wearing the Cross of Lorraine, which Giraud and his cronies considered a virtual badge of sedition.

On the other hand, men, officers and sometimes whole units, with their arms complement and field baggage, were deserting what they called "Giraud's army" to join up with the two divisions of Free French commanded by Generals Leclerc and Larminat. Of course Combat had encouraged these defections to the Gaullist camp.

My host promised to procure me an appointment with De Gaulle. In the meantime, I killed time by strolling about Algiers, which was now the working wartime capital of France. Here two worlds rubbed elbows. While the city streets swarmed with uniformed men, the eternally impassive Muslims looked out from the terraces of the Moorish cafés.

The Hotel Aletti was the big hotbed of local intrigues. In another hotel, the Saint-George, Eisenhower and his general staff had set up shop. Giraud himself now lived in the Moorish-style summer palace with its vast, semi-tropical grounds, once the residence of the French governors-general. A little villa called Les Glycines contained De Gaulle's offices, though he himself lived in another villa called Les Oliviers in the hilly residential quarter of El-Biar overlooking the city.

The port of Algiers couldn't possibly have berthed another vessel. On all the walls along the piers was written in large black letters the motto that Giraud had appropriated: "Only one goal—

De Gaulle Versus Giraud

victory." With this martial slogan the "civil and military commander-in-chief," deliberately ignoring all political problems, was ingratiating himself with Eisenhower and his political adviser, Robert Murphy.

De Gaulle, along with the few colleagues he had brought from London, worked in the unimposing Villa des Glycines.

Though Giraud had apparently planned to arrest him here a few months earlier, De Gaulle's security service, if indeed he had one, was showing no profile at all.

Gaston Palewski, his private secretary, ushered me into the general's tiny office.

As I entered, De Gaulle rose and extended his hand. He was in cotton fatigues. As usual, he wore a Cross of Lorraine set in a blue lozenge-shaped cameo.

"Well, then, 'Charvet,' here you are. You've been the butt of a lot of criticism lately. Sit down."

If he'd changed at all since last November, it was only to become a bit portlier. I also observed a tic of the eyelid I'd never before noticed.

"I know what you mean, *mon général*, and I've come here to talk about just those things. But if there's any criticism to be made, it shouldn't be laid at my doorstep. I think you'll be convinced if you hear me out."

"Well, I'm listening."

"I left France two months ago. I've come here because the relations between your services and the Resistance are very bad. A lot of suspicion has arisen between us, and we are just not receiving the wherewithal to keep on fighting."

"The wherewithal?"

"Yes. Money, arms, everything. Most of the maquis are in desparate straits. When we needed to double our budget for their sake, Jean Moulin slashed it without any valid explanation. He precipitated a crisis that's by no means over."

"I'm abreast of the situation. Before his disappearance, Moulin sent me a report on it. But I do not approve of *your* solution. You should not have gone knocking on the Americans' door. They

The Night Will End

290

welcomed you only because they believed they could circumvent De Gaulle."

"But, *mon général*, they haven't put any political pressure on us—probably because they knew that nothing would come of it. Besides, I've already provided the B.C.R.A. several memoranda on our relations with them and your envoys. I hope they reached you, because it's essential that you be aware of their contents."

De Gaulle answered with a grunt that I couldn't make out.

"You'll be here for a while. I'll read your papers and we'll discuss them, but you must realize that the important thing is for us to stay united. This place is pestilential. Vichy and the Americans are still toying with that poor devil Giraud. Your friend Capitant can fill you in on that story. We'll meet again soon. Check with my orderly on the way out to set up a lunch appointment."

A few days later—I think it was August 20—several Combat-Algiers comrades and I met in the garden of Les Oliviers. De Gaulle had decided to award me the Cross of the Liberation, which had been secretly granted me by decree last March. I was accompanied by Capitant and a few other comrades.

It was a radiant day. A young woman was also to receive the same honor in place of her husband, who had been killed in combat. She had brought along her son, who was about eight years old.

The ceremony was simple but dignified. A detachment of Algerian infantry did the honors. Two buglers sounded the "*Aux Champs.*" The general stepped forward and pronounced the official formula: "Henri Frenay, we recognize you as our companion in the Liberation of France, in honor and through victory."

Then he pinned the cross on the left side of my chest and embraced me. The ceremony was over. De Gaulle, all smiles now, chatted with the assembled company.

From the moment I'd snapped to attention before the general, my thoughts had strayed elsewhere, to France, to Berty, whom I'd recently proposed for the Cross of Liberation and who had also just been awarded it. I thought too of all my old comrades in Combat, for my citation had in fact recognized their valor even more than

De Gaulle Versus Giraud

my own. It was our entire movement, it was Combat itself, that was honored on that August day of 1943.

Four of us stayed for lunch: General and Mme. de Gaulle, Capitant and myself. As was the custom at De Gaulle's meals, politics were not discussed. However, from his recent trip to Morocco De Gaulle had received a reassuring impression. The sultan had broken off relations with Vichy. The general also believed Italy's surrender imminent. As far as he was concerned, the war was virtually won.

After coffee Mme. de Gaulle retired. De Gaulle chatted with us about the C.F.L.N. meetings. He himself was now presiding over them. Though the power remained divided, it was De Gaulle alone who was now responsible for seeing the committee's decisions through. He was—in fact, if not in law—the chief executive in all but the military sphere, which the supercilious and diffident Giraud retained as his personal fief. I tried to lead the conversation toward our problems in the Resistance—money, arms, the mission to Switzerland—but De Gaulle cut me short.

"If you don't mind, Frenay"—this was the first time he called me by my true name—"we'll discuss these problems in Les Glycines."

Everything now depended on the results of my upcoming and final interview with De Gaulle. It was set for September 2 at Les Glycines.

"Frenay," he said, "you're overdramatizing the whole business. Snags always come up. People live differently here than they do in France or in London. They can't possibly be expected to see things in the same way. They're only human."

"But, *mon général*, it's not simply a question of individual human beings. Is it normal that we cannot freely acquaint you with our viewpoint and learn yours without our messages being censored or blocked? Is it normal that I've never yet gotten my hands on a two-way radio when there are dozens in France?"

"You can look into the radio-communications business with Passy in London. Now—about that proposal in your second memorandum, the one where you ask for a permanent Resistance delegation here or in England. In fact, it would be useful to have such a body to consult."

The Night Will End

"Well, sir, I'm delighted. That's all I ask for. I think London would be the best place for our delegation, because that's where the B.C.R.A., the S.O.E. and the French section of the O.S.S. are."

"Agreed. I'll inform Philip of my decision. You tell Passy."

"What about money and arms, *mon général*? The situation was critical when I left, and it's getting steadily worse."

De Gaulle rarely showed his thoughts or feelings—I knew that—but his silences and facial expressions were highly significant. Now his chin was sticking out, and he was looking away from me toward the window.

"The total budget of the Resistance has been increased. I know that for a fact, though I don't know just how the money's being allocated. It's difficult to make everyone happy, and French banknotes are getting scarce. Maybe we can find some here in North Africa."

"Sir, why don't we use the clearinghouse system we developed in Switzerland?"

I told him about it in detail, adding, "As you can see, we have no need of French banknotes because the money can be delivered to the Resistance right inside France by French banking firms."

"I don't see anything wrong with that—on condition that these sums be subtracted from the total budget and that it be administered by my representatives. One thing, though. It seems that the English, for some unfathomable reason, can't stand the whole idea. Check that out with the B.C.R.A. too."

"One last thing, *mon général*. I must tell you about the underhanded campaign that's being waged against our delegation in Switzerland. You see, this delegation is indispensable to us. It's right in the heart of Europe, it's in almost daily physical contact with the Resistance, and it has secure radio communications with London and Algiers."

I told De Gaulle about the services already performed by our delegation, about Allen Dulles's promises and about the obstacles London had put in our path. I spoke—at least, so I believed—with emotion and conviction. De Gaulle heard me out without saying a word, though several times I had the feeling he was about to interrupt.

De Gaulle Versus Giraud

"'Charvet'"—again my pseudonym—"I don't like that delegation of yours. Whether you know it or not, it enables the Americans to get a wedge between us. You don't see what they're up to, but I do. Believe me, it's no thanks to them that I'm here in this office right now. Have you read the terms in which they recognized the C.F.L.N.?" (De Gaulle was alluding to the fact that a few days before Great Britain, the U.S. and the U.S.S.R. had "recognized" the C.F.L.N., each with its own formula.*) Believe me, if they could have used still more restrictive terms, they would have. As you can see, my faith in them is, well . . . And all your correspondence via them is 'in clear,' which is incredible! I don't deny that these contacts may be your lifebuoy, but obviously it's more important in these times for Frenchmen to stick together."

"But, sir, neither Allen Dulles nor Colonel Legge nor Max Shoop ever attached any strings to their aid. Their friendship and integrity cannot be faulted, especially in connection with Free France. If they'd wanted to divide us they could easily have financed and armed the Resistance without heeding the B.C.R.A.'s protests. Yet when they learned that their aid was provoking a crisis between Frenchmen, they suspended it. I'm sorry, but that is the proof of their perfect—and, to my mind, excessive—integrity. I say 'excessive' because it is not only principles that are at stake here but human lives."

"I repeat: I do not like your delegation, and you're harboring illusions about American disinterestedness. Let's stick together, 'Charvet!' Let's stick together!"

"Sir, unity is my motto, but it must embrace not only the Gaullist vanguard but also those honest people who were led astray by the Marshal's prestige and who have now rallied to our side. Sir, you must be generous. After all, it's much easier to play Joan of Arc than Richelieu or Henri IV."

*Washington considered the C.F.L.N. as "the administrator of those territories which recognize its authority," while Moscow stated that it represented "the interests of state of the French Republic." The British couched their formula in the same terms as the United States, with the addition of the highly significant clause ". . . the C.F.L.N. is the organism qualified to conduct the French war effort."

The Night Will End

De Gaulle looked at me without saying a word, then rose. The interview was over.

"You're going first to London, then to France. But is it wise of you to return there? Hasn't the Gestapo pretty much got your number?"

"*Mon général*, they've been on to me for at least two years, and they haven't caught me yet.

"Well, think about it. From now on the big decisions are going to be made right here in Algiers. Soon we're going to convene a representative assembly. Its composition and juridical status have already been worked out by Philip. There's a lot to be done here, an awful lot."

"I'm sure there is—in fact, recently I've become more and more aware of it. But there's a lot to be done in France, too, and my comrades await me!"

"It's up to you, 'Charvet.' Goodbye and good luck."

Two days later I said goodbye to my friends the Capitants. I was flown to Marrakech in an ancient army crate. Late in the same day I took off for London, where I landed in the usual cold drizzle. This inclement weather heralded the approach of the fifth autumn of world war.

I informed Passy, Boris and the B.C.R.A. of De Gaulle's ratification of the idea of a Resistance delegation in London. For the moment it would be composed solely of "Médéric" and myself.

"Médéric," who had arrived a few weeks earlier, represented the movements in the northern zone. He belonged to "Ceux de la Libération" (C.D.L.L.). Though this movement hadn't had the impact of the O.C.M., its special strength in Paris and its suburbs was an important factor. He was a florid fellow of about forty, a real force of nature. I figured we'd get along well.

André Philip (who was now shuttling back and forth between Algiers and London), "Médéric" and I soon laid down the role and powers of our delegation. They were to be formalized by a document conferring on us the status of "advisers" empowered to speak in the name of the Central Committee of the Resistance and

De Gaulle Versus Giraud

the eight movements that composed it. Overjoyed, we cabled the committee in France:

Starting to set up London French Resistance delegation to French and Allied services—stop—Delegation considers itself at orders of committees of two zones with following mission: inform committees by cables and mail situation London Algiers and international—stop—Acquaint entire world with Resistance via press-radio-lectures-pamphlets—stop—Serve as consultative organ in all decisions affecting Resistance—stop.

To carry out our mission properly request you address mail and cables directly to London delegation with all additional desiderata and notes on situation in France—stop.

Kindly acknowledge receipt immediately and send new delegates October indispensable mission is paramount—"Charvet-Médéric".

My aim was to set up the delegation with Médéric, cement relations with the Free French (and the concerned foreign services), and then—as soon as I'd found a good replacement for myself—to return to France.

It took us all September to set up shop in the offices for us at 19 Hill Street. Mmes. "Médéric" and Bloch served as our secretaries.

About September 10 we agreed with Passy that henceforth all incoming and outgoing mail deliveries of concern to the French Resistance (not including undercover espionage "rings") would be communicated to us. Naturally we were also to be allowed to correspond freely with our "constituency."

I was really in a wonderful mood. I was now convinced that a strong entente had been forged between London and the Resistance. To prepare for the revolution we bore within us, we had to make sure that London, Paris and Algiers were all on the same wave length. Our delegation would offer its own contribution.

And we were going to broadcast our message loud and clear.

Nonetheless, I wasn't harboring any illusions. I was sure that many letters, messages and cables both to and from France would elude us. Each day "Médéric" or I would go to Duke Street to check out the mail. Except in rare cases, we were given everything we asked for. Both in meetings and in memoranda we would formulate our opinions and/or proposals. Subsequent mail from France would at least theoretically enable us to see in what measure they were being acted on. Our conclusions we could forward in turn to our comrades in France.

It was with special interest that I read the reports sent by Claude Serreules and Jacques Bingen.* They had replaced Jean Moulin as De Gaulle's representatives, the former in the northern, the latter in the southern zone.

Passy had first made contact with the reality of the Resistance during its "Arquebuse–Brumaire" mission with Brossolette. Now Serreules and Bingen, following the same apprenticeship, were arriving at the same conclusions. They were those that I myself had long ago formed but had failed to impart to anyone else in London.

For instance, I had opposed the disastrous lack of communication between the movements and the officers in charge of parachute drops. London had to wait until Serreules' mission to hear (as he put it) that

. . . not a day goes by that I am not set upon by the chiefs of some organization who bitterly complain about their inability to arm their militants. . . .

The future delivery of large quantities of arms seems indispensable to me. This materiel, instead of being buried where it lands and then forgotten, should immediately be turned over to those organizations which can effectively use it.

Bingen also stressed the movements' lack of funds:

Please realize that the situation is tragic. It is no longer a matter of supporting official dignitaries . . . but of . . . rescuing from starvation and enemy bullets these young men to whom we have given our word in your name. . . .

It has been very difficult for us to transfer funds to the interior. . . . We would like to see you seriously review the transfer of funds via what I shall

*Jacques Bingen: A former director of the Free French merchant marine, he had recently joined the B.C.R.A.

De Gaulle Versus Giraud

call the "Lahire channel."* It is absolutely essential that a financial expert resolve this pressing question.

In July I had given Jacques Bingen a letter of introduction to Claude Bourdet. He had been warmly welcomed by our comrades, a reception for which he was later to thank me. A conscientious worker, he had already visited a region, inspected it in detail, then familiarized himself with a maquis selected at random. In other words, hc had automatically done what I had vainly beseeched Moulin to do for months on end. He had been very impressed with Michel Brault's performance at the head of the maquis and by Gemahling's intelligence-gathering. At last, thanks to Bingen, an entente between London and the Resistance was aborning in the southern zone.

Alas, Bingen was never to finish the work he'd so intelligently begun. Arrested by the Gestapo, he swallowed a cyanide pill.

A few weeks later Passy forwarded me a letter from Brossolette, who was just back from his own mission to France. Brossolette didn't mince his words:

. . . first, I'm going to get to the bottom of this mess [the shortage of weapons]. There's no doubt about it: the "Max–Vidal" [Moulin–Delestraint] military doctrine has royally wrecked the whole works. . . .

Then, speaking of the B.C.R.A.'s doctrine of sealing off the civilian from the military arm, he said:

. . . the biggest mistake was . . . the foolish illusion that decentralization can be decreed from on high. . . . That whole mishmash of . . . schemes and . . . war scenarios was insanity pure and simple. . . .

Our officers should first make contact with the heads of the movements in Paris; they are the ones who make the big decisions affecting the people in the provinces. . . .

The big problem, as you yourself observed, is the coordination of the civilian and military arms. . . . And this is precisely what the ingenious

*"Lahire" was Bénouville's pseudonym. The "Lahire channel" referred to the transfer of funds through Switzerland.

The Night Will End

mechanisms concocted by your services have made utterly impossible. Contrary to all instructions, that coordination is just what I'm going to try to effect. I'm sure that I'm on the right track.

For almost two years we'd been forced, despite all our warnings, to sever our paramilitary organizations from the rest of the Resistance. Now we were to glue the two pieces together again! Could anyone have possibly imagined a harsher verdict on the abstract rules that London, in its remoteness from reality, had tried to impose on us?

Meanwhile, Passy agreed that the study of the funding of the Resistance via Switzerland should be immediately resumed in accordance with Bingen's suggestion. Negotiations with the Exchequer would be initiated by Georges Boris, the *commissaire* of the Interior.

By early October of 1943 our delegation had become a magnet not only for French but also for other continental resisters. My own "European" views had not wavered. The Nazi occupation had inflicted the same ordeal on all the peoples of Europe. Now they were engaged in the same struggle for the same goal—freedom. Whenever I talked with a Pole, Belgian or Czech we would be struck by the similarity of our views.

I drew up a memorandum addressed to the C.F.L.N. and requesting that a "House of the European Resistance" be set up in London. Here resisters of all nations—men who would, after all, be playing important roles in their various countries after the Liberation—might exchange the fruits of their experience.

I also asked that a "medal of the European Resistance" be awarded by an international body after the war to the most noted resisters of all the occupied countries, thus symbolizing their unity in the war for liberation.

I submitted these two proposals again in early 1944. They were not adopted. Neither De Gaulle nor René Massigili, our *commissaire* for Foreign Affairs, were the kind of men likely to understand their value or meaning.

Hitler had tried to mobilize the peoples of the Continent to help Germany in the defense of Fortress Europe, *die Festung Europa.*

De Gaulle Versus Giraud

Not only had his appeal found no echo, but by this early autumn of 1943 the position of the Wehrmacht had considerably deteriorated. It had failed to blunt the Red Army's counteroffensive on the eastern front, and not one German soldier (prisoners excepted) was left in North Africa. Allied troops under Montgomery, the victor of El-Alamein, had landed in Salerno. Italy raised the white flag, and Marshal Badoglio, Mussolini's successor, was forced to accept a Draconian armistice.

Fired by the Italian surrender, Corsica revolted. Many of the Italian occupation troops swung over to the Corsican resisters, and together they ruthlessly beleaguered the German columns retreating to the north of the island. Our own shock troops under Gambiez decisively tipped the balance. In record time, Corsica was free. The liberation of this first French department clearly heralded the liberation of all France.

Though nobody yet knew whether the Liberation would come from the north or the south, measures for the seizure of state power were already being undertaken. By degrees London, Algiers and the C.N.R. worked out the composition and function of a new group of Liberation Committees.

To set up a central authority at the exact moment of Liberation would be difficult if not impossible. Obviously communications would be disrupted, and the enemy might stubbornly cling to certain portions of our territory.

Our Resistance delegation participated in the study of these questions. In a note ratified by the movement chiefs in London and sent to Algiers, I set forth our viewpoint on various subjects, including the so-called *commissaires* of the Republic. These *commissaires** were to play the role of "super-prefects" who would take over the administration of the various French regions upon the Liberation. In effect, they would be wielding temporary plenipotentiary power.

On September 17 a C.F.L.N. decree created the "Consultative

---

*Not to be confused with the *commissaires,* or proto-ministers, of the Provisional government.—Translator.

The Night Will End

Assembly" that De Gaulle had told me about during our last interview. It was to be convened in Algiers on November 3 and to comprise eighty-seven members. With forty delegates from metropolitan France and twelve from her overseas territories, the Resistance would form the Assembly's majority. The other delegates would be former legislators.

The organs of the Communist Party and its satellites (the National Front and the paramilitary F.T.P.) had recently revealed a significant and alarming shift of attitude: They were now trying to pass themselves off inside France as the one and only Resistance organization. In August 1943 a large number of leaflets, cleverly printed in widely separated departments, carried this statement:

. . . the National Front is recognized by the French Committee in London as the body that represents France on her home soil. . . .

Clearly these simultaneous claims followed some general design. The C.P. was also beginning to exhort its followers in a narrowly partisan way. In a tract that had appeared in France two months earlier, I read:

Everywhere we require resolute men to lead the masses. . . .
The development of the F.T.P. [Francs-Tireurs et Partisans] is of paramount importance to the Party. This organization shall provide an officer corps for the masses at the hour of national insurrection. . . .

Every day I asked myself if I shouldn't return directly to France. The B.C.R.A. told me it would be madness to go back. They had proof positive, they said, that the Gestapo would arrest me shortly after my return. I wondered how they could possibly have come by such information. Perhaps it was just a pretext to prevent me from assuming my role at the head of our organization.

Several times Bourdet and Bénouville cabled me insistently from France entreating me to return. Yet I had the feeling that our efforts here, and the results they'd already produced, were greatly

De Gaulle Versus Giraud

expanding our delegation's moral authority. Even in France this seemed to be understood, for soon Bourdet asked me to form a similar delegation to Algiers.

The consultative Assembly was to convene in Algiers on November 3. André Hauriou and "Ferrière" were eager for me to join with them in the first session. During my absence François Morin could replace me at the head of the London delegation.
On October 30 I took off for Marrakech and Algiers.

ALGERIAN INTERLUDE

Gaullism had gained
a lot of ground since my last trip
to Algiers. The Giraud–De Gaulle duumvirate was through. Henceforth the head of
Free France was also to be the unrivaled head of
the C.F.L.N. His leadership was soon decisively endorsed by the Resistance delegates to the Consultative Assembly.

On November 3 I made my way on foot along the seaside toward the Palace of the Algerian Assemblies, where the meetings
were being held. The Chamber of the Financial Delegations had
been redecorated and hung with flags. It was a semicircular amphi-
theater which, though smaller, was not unlike the Palais-
Bourbon. Here I found many old friends, including Cerf-
"Ferrière" and André Hauriou (the three of us were to represent
Combat), as well as Claudius Petit of Franc-Tireur, "Bordier"
of Libération, "Médéric" and many other Resistance comrades.

In the few minutes left before the session's opening, the lively and elated representatives gathered in the corridors.
Since many deputies hadn't been able to reach Algiers
yet, we were still only about fifty of the eighty-four
members who were to make up the full Assembly.
Though we'd been designated, not selected,
each of us was still the spokesman

14

for his comrades and implicitly bore their mandate. My thoughts drifted back to France—to Bourdet, Bénouville, Chevance and Jean-Guy Bernard. They knew we were meeting here today, and before I rejoined them I would clearly state what they expected of the government. The newsmen crowded in the galleries would convey my and my comrades' words to the entire world.

And so I participated, for the first time in my life, in a parliamentary meeting. The speech by Georges Buisson, the veteran leader of the C.G.T. and senior member of the Assembly, rang false to my ears. He spoke with the faded eloquence of the last century, hardly the language of our freedom fighters in the maquis. On the other hand, De Gaulle said exactly what I'd hoped he would:

. . . What we do . . . will have no value . . . unless we seek our inspiration in the ardent movement for renewal which secretly inspires the French nation. Those . . . who imagine that France, once liberated, will reassume the political, social and moral habits they know of old are grievously mistaken.

Yet afterward, in the corridors, not a word was exchanged about this profound renewal that De Gaulle so eagerly desired. Indeed, the main topic was the election of the Assembly's first president. The Resistance had nominated André Hauriou, a law professor and one of Combat's regional chiefs. He belonged to no party and seemed likely to pick up a lot of votes. Yet he was being opposed by Félix Gouin, a skilled Socialist wheeler-dealer. Already I could feel that the race was on between the old France and the new.

Two days later I again presented myself at Les Glycines. It was the scene of a great commotion. I was immediately ushered into De Gaulle's study.

"Good morning, Frenay. I noticed you in the Assembly. So you've decided to join us in Algiers?"

"Yes, *mon général*, but not for long. As soon as the Resistance has made its presence properly felt I'll be returning to France."

"Well, that's what I wanted to talk to you about."

The Night Will End

He offered me a cigarette, then went on: "The composition of the French National Committee does not correspond to the new situation created by the Algiers Assembly. In the next few days I want to reorganize it so that both the Resistance and the old political parties may take their rightful place in it. The Assembly must encompass men who—both inside and outside France—refused to kowtow to Vichy. The Communists, the Socialists, the centrist groups and the Resistance leaders must now cooperate with me by entering the C.F.L.N. In this context I thought of you who have played such an eminent role as the chief of Combat."

In fact, rumors of an impending cabinet shuffle had been circulating in Algiers. Apparently it was merely a way for De Gaulle to eliminate Giraud's cronies. Such a purge was no concern of mine, and I'd listened to the reports rather distractedly.

And now here was an offer for me to join the government! I was dumfounded.

De Gaulle continued: "I've made similar offers to Emmanuel D'Astier, René Capitant and Henri Queuille. Also Fernand Grenier* and Le Troquer.** There'll be still more when I've finished my consultations."

"Sir, I thank you for this unexpected offer. As the representative of Combat, I'm very grateful for the honor, but I'm wondering if this is really the place for me. My comrades in France await me. Isn't my true place with them?"

"I think not. You must understand that we are rapidly nearing the end of the war. Here is where the blueprints for the Liberation are going to be drawn up. Rest assured, Frenay, it's here that you can most effectively serve your comrades, and I have an important task to offer you. Listen: because of the war, several million Frenchmen have been wrenched from their homes. They are now prisoners, deportees, laborers in Germany, refugees and evictees from northern and eastern France. Their readaptation is an enormous task on which the moral and political health of France will depend. Well, there you are, Frenay. I'm sure you follow me.

*Fernand Grenier: a member of the Communist Party Central Committee, he had escaped from Châteaubriant prison and now represented his party to General De Gaulle.
**Le Troquer: Socialist deputy from the Seine.

Algerian Interlude

I'm asking you to devote yourself to this important national interest."

The more he talked the more embarrassed I got. Of course, he was right that the big decisions would be made here. And of course I wanted to influence those decisions. But for the official role he was offering me, I felt no inclination. We were still at war. It was inconceivable that a soldier like me should not serve at the front.

"General," I said, "I'm really not sure that I'm the right man for the job. May I ask what portfolios you envisage for D'Astier and Capitant?"

"D'Astier would be *commissaire* of the Interior, for in this post we need a man who's both firm and flexible and who's familiar with political matters. Capitant would take the portfolio for National Education."

The choice of D'Astier for the Interior struck me as sheer madness. I knew what D'Astier was like, and I had no trust in him whatsoever. Yet there was no sense in my trying to open De Gaulle's eyes. He'd think it was just more of the old Frenay–D'Astier rivalry.

"All things considered, General, I cannot accept your offer. Once again, I thank you. I hope I'm not wrong in thinking that my true place is in France. In two weeks I'll be home, and I shall not forget the faith you've shown in me."

De Gaulle began to pace up and down his office. Gradually his voice rose. "You're all the same—ungovernable! You're told to serve somewhere and immediately you rush off somewhere else. I've told you that I need you here. Doesn't that matter to you?"

He broke off. An uncomfortable silence intervened. Then he resumed: "Of course, you are a free man, Frenay."

"I'm terribly sorry to disappoint you, sir. Perhaps I'm wrong. Perhaps I *would* be more useful here. If I thought so, I'd surely stay. But right now, in all honesty, I believe it my duty to return."

"Well, Frenay, as I've said, you're a free man."

I was lost in thought as I walked back down from Les Glycines.

Had I done right? If I were to stay here it might still be possible for me to bring about a convergence of interests between the Resistance and the Provisional Government. Moreover, I'd be

The Night Will End

physically safe! But wasn't it my duty to join my comrades, to risk my life with them?

Still prey to these contradictory reflections, I entered the Brasserie Suisse for lunch. There, before a gathering of several friends—Hauriou, "Ferrière," Claudius Petit and "Médéric"—I recounted my interview with De Gaulle and its upshot, or lack of one.

"Listen, Henri," said Claudius, "I think you were wrong to turn down the general's proposal without consulting us. His offer concerns others besides you. In a sense, through you, he was offering the entire Resistance a portfolio. And it was for the Resistance to accept or refuse it. You see, to have one comrade more or less in the C.F.L.N. affects all of us. How about if I corral as many resisters as I can to discuss the matter?"

I yielded. That afternoon a dozen or so comrades and I gathered in a little room in the Palace of the Algerian Assemblies.

"Are you disposed to accept our decision?" asked Claudius.

"Yes—on condition that it's unanimous. If it isn't, I shall retain my own freedom to reject De Gaulle's offer."

In less than one hour they had arrived at a unanimous decision: I should accept the offer.

"Friends, I bow to your will. I ask you only to form a deputation to De Gaulle to underline our solidarity. Thus I shall enter the C.F.L.N. as a representative of the Resistance."

Of course De Gaulle brushed off this highly unorthodox deputation, and forty-eight hours later I became *commissaire* of Prisoners, Deportees and Refugees (P.D.R.).

Much later I wondered if I'd done well in yielding to my comrades' wishes. Perhaps some of them had ulterior motives; perhaps some of them were secretly glad that I couldn't return to France and take over Combat. At the time this idea didn't occur to me. A few years later, however, I was plagued by doubts.

The new C.F.L.N. had now been constituted. It sat in the Lycée Fromentin (a girls' high school) in the hilly part of Algiers. Each *commissaire* had a special place around the big table. Seven of them, including me, were participating for the first time in a government body, and only five had held elected office before the

Algerian Interlude

war. The Communists were not represented. They had tried to impose their own men on De Gaulle for the two portfolios reserved for them, but the general had discountenanced them.

In one corner of the hall sat the Secretary-general, Louis Joxe. He prepared the agenda, into which the *commissaires* wrote the subjects they wanted aired. De Gaulle gave all decisions their final verbal form, as well as approving the minutes and press communiqués.

My initial curiosity soon went stale. The protocol never changed. De Gaulle chaired each session in exactly the same way, granting one or another of us the floor with a "Monsieur the *commissaire* of——, you have requested to speak to us about——. Go ahead, please." Then this party would present a précis of his problem, which we usually knew all about anyway from a preliminary memo. Next, a discussion would take place. If the matter was very important, everybody would be invited to have his say. The general would put to us a few relevant questions, then sum up, though his conclusion did not necessarily reflect the majority opinion. We never voted.

It didn't take us long to realize that plenty of questions just weren't being aired in that pleasant girls' high school. Many a matter had already been decided at the Villa des Glycines before we ever got a chance to debate it. I also discovered that the general conducted his own "personal diplomacy" without consulting the bothersome Foreign Affairs people.

The Requisition Service provided me a small but nicely furnished house in Hussein-Dey, an Algiers suburb. I lived there ten months, served by a lady of venerable age who acted as both cook and housekeeper. Our humble style of life didn't fail to astonish many visitors accustomed to the ceremonious ways of the El-Biar district, where most of the *commissaires* lived.

I also had a chauffeur called Fernand Javel. A thirtyish *pied-noir* who ordinarily worked as a painting contractor, he was tall, athletic and endowed with a large dose of common sense. I often had recourse to the astute counsel of this taciturn but observant chap. His judgments on his fellow human beings were remarkably perceptive. In 1944 he began to pack a gun, for we *commissaires*

The Night Will End

308

had been warned that P.P.F. agents were about to be parachuted into Algeria to assassinate us. Javel probably would have made a crack bodyguard, but fortunately he never had to use his talents.

My new offices were right in the center of town, at 15a, Boulevard Saint-Saëns. For the time being my two rooms would probably be enough, for I alone constituted the entire *commissariat*. I didn't even have a secretary! I had to enlist my colleagues one by one, which was no easy task, for all males had been mobilized and most were already in active service.

My first night in Hussein-Dey was short enough, for I spent half of it trying to organize my work load. I had simultaneously to fulfill my government duties, build up my *commissariat* from scratch, enlist help for my comrades back home and prepare the future administration of a liberated France.

The Committee on Action in France comprised the army high command, the Interior, the director general of the Special Services and the secretary-general for National Defense—respectively, Giraud, D'Astier, Soustelle and Billotte. De Gaulle presided. Though ineligible for membership, I was frequently consulted.

That the *commissaire* for Prisoners, Deportees and Refugees could not by rights be a member of an action committee was logical enough, but nonetheless I was somewhat disappointed. After all, most of the cables arriving from France were addressed to either D'Astier or me. Actually my faith in D'Astier had sunk pretty low. Though I hadn't disclosed my feelings to anyone, I guessed that he'd had a hand in my exclusion from the Algiers-France circuit.*

Bénouville to D'Astier and Frenay: ". . . Received only 27 of the 65 million francs promised us for winter. . . . If urgent measures are not taken, the situation will be hopeless."

*My hunch was right. Many years later I was to read in Volume II of Soustelle's *Memoires* (page 325):

. . . D'Astier's natural atmosphere was one of intrigue . . . his desire for *sub rosa* contacts and personal secrets was transparent. . . . On several occasions I caught on to his maneuvers against Frenay."

Algerian Interlude

The November moon had disappeared too intermittently for aerial operations, and in December and January several attempted operations had failed. I joined forces with D'Astier to push through the implementation of the Geneva bank transfer system (the so-called "Lahire Channel").

Many meetings were devoted to this issue. We got nowhere. Over and over again we collided with the stubborn recalcitrance of our British counterparts in Algiers. These apostles of strict financial orthodoxy labeled the whole affair a "stinky business,"* for in their opinion it opened the door to the worst nightmares imaginable.

Eventually we forced them to admit that in principal the idea was valid. They agreed to use the Swiss circuit as a last resort for sums not to exceed 150 million francs.

Even today I can't explain their obstinate indifference to our tragic situation. Perhaps their refusal was politically inspired; perhaps they regarded the Resistance as an alien or even threatening force.

Fortunately, our services also managed to lay their hands on a large quantity of French banknotes in Tunisia. Much later, the C.F.L.N. issued coupons negotiable inside France against banknotes of small denominations.

We were as ill armed as we were ill financed, and again the key to the arms question was in London, for all parachute operations were based in England.

In concert with the B.C.R.A. I'd approached the British and American services several times in October. Before my departure to Algiers I'd passed the ball to François Morin. Each week he reported to me on his activities, and every other week he sent a solid report to the Central Committee of the Movements in France.

Several times our delegation in Switzerland sent us cables like the following:

The air raid on Annecy wreaked terrible havoc. . . . The planes overshot

*In English in the original.—Translator.

The Night Will End

the ball-bearing plant at an altitude of 5,000 meters. Civilian houses were destroyed. . . . Last week we sabotaged a number of transformers with explosives. . . . If you get us the arms, our groups will knock out any target you want. . . .

If you get us the materiel, we can guarantee you destruction of railways, harassment of troops, wiping out of locomotive depots. To leave our men unarmed is a grave political and military error.

Georges Rebattet, now national head of the maquis, telegraphed De Gaulle:

. . . Tragic situation for deportation-evaders; each week we lose 100 men. The Germans take no prisoners. . . . With your support and by means of incessant propaganda we have assumed the serious responsiblity of encouraging such evasion. Money, weapons and munitions must be immediately delivered, lest the evaders be forced into banditry or massacred.

Between November 1943 and February 1944 we received many such SOS appeals each month. Brandishing these cables, François Morin tirelessly harassed the British and American services. He tried to explain to the O.S.S. and the S.O.E. the vast savings in human lives and aircraft that would result from the proper arming of the Resistance. It was true: Military targets and industrial complexes could be more easily knocked out by ground sabotage than by air attack.

In Algiers, the entire Special Services Directorate, as well as D'Astier and I, maintained a constant parallel harassment of Eisenhower's general staff and the Allied special services. These conjoined actions actually bore some fruit. The Americans decided to match the British in the number of parachute operations inside France. Tripartite missions composed of a British, a French and an American officer were parachuted into each sub-region to ascertain its needs. In February 150 airlifts were flown, of which sixty were successful. In March, 370 were flown, of which 150 were successful, delivering for that month alone 100 tons of explosives, 20,000 machine guns and 15,000 pistols with ammo. Aid to the

Algerian Interlude

Resistance, though hardly satisfying all its needs, had been considerably increased.

During this period (November 1943 to March 1944) the situation in France deteriorated. Joseph Darnand, the head of Vichy's militia, was appointed Secretary of State for Public Order. His militia was beefed up and was hitting our maquis as hard as the Germans were. Vichy set up its own military kangaroo courts to try summarily those of our maquisards who managed to escape massacre on the field. Most of them were executed.

All our laborers in Germany were now in uniform, for the Nazi war machine was greedily devouring men. Laval broadened the S.T.O. to apply to all men between sixteen and fifty-five and all women between eighteen and forty-five.

Our underground press struck back. I echoed it over Radio Algiers (which was now heard in France):

. . . At the moment when the enemy is about to give account of his misdeeds before the court of the world, Vichy, on Hitler's orders, is decreeing the mobilization of France behind the already vanquished brigand. . . .

Gentlemen of Vichy: you are trying to slip over the head of France the noose which you already feel tightening around your own neck. . . .

One hundred and fifty years ago France presented to the world a Declaration of the Rights of Man. Every Frenchman knows the duty enjoined on him by this declaration: "When the government violates the people's rights, insurrection, for the people and for every portion of the people, becomes the most sacred right and the most pressing duty."

Comrades in France, behold the eleventh hour! We must stand fast and win. . . .

The repression was aimed not only at the maquis but at the entire Resistance. The Abwehr and the Gestapo cast and recast their nets, drawing them tighter each time. In November 1943 they arrested Marcel Peck. My dear friend, who had so marvelously organized R.1 and who had already thrice escaped, disappeared without a trace. What became of him we never knew.

Then Jean-Guy Bernard, my faithful companion, was arrested

The Night Will End

with his wife, Yvette, just as he was completing a number of decisive improvements in Resistance-Rail. Yvette later returned from deportation, but Jean-Guy, after being severely maltreated in Drancy, died in Auschwitz.

Often I found myself alone in the evening with my recollections, while the friendly and confident faces of my brothers and sisters rose before my eyes. I myself had recruited them and led them into battle, and now they had fallen! Marcel Peck had written me in November, Jean-Guy in January: Come back, Henri, come back! And I had not gone back. Now here I was alone, lost in sorrow.

I began to wonder if I shouldn't drop my duties here and join the survivors in France. I wrote a feverish letter to De Gaulle explaining my moral dilemma. A few days later he drew me aside as we were leaving a dinner at Les Oliviers.

"I got your letter, Frenay. I sympathize with you. Men are falling in battle, and as they fall their comrades and their captains suffer. But should they too die on this account? Frenay, listen to me. In France you're a marked man. You wouldn't last a month. Just try and picture what would happen if a member of the C.F.L.N. fell into enemy hands. The public interest requires that you continue the task you've assumed."

Well, there I was, *commissaire* of Prisoners, Deportees and Refugees. It was impossible to know even approximately who or how many they were. There were at least one and a half million POWs, some of them captured in May and June of 1940, but the majority of them merely seized in their barracks and packed off to prison camps where they'd been vegetating for over three years. I wondered what ravages Vichy's propaganda and the myth of the "national revolution" had made in the minds of these men so long deprived of news from abroad. They probably knew next to nothing about occupied France and the Resistance. The country they were about to rediscover would be a very different place from the one they had left. Their return might well be disappointing and upsetting. Moreover, their reaction might pose a serious political danger, for we in the government had already decided that municipal elections should be organized right after their repatriation. Their votes would weigh heavy in the urns.

Algerian Interlude

Then there were the deportees. In the first rank were those of the Resistance, from the earliest captives of 1941—such as our friends Anne-Marie Boumier and Anne Noury—to those who were being loaded onto trains each week, bound for the concentration camps whose names we were just beginning to learn: Buchenwald, Dachau, Bergen-Belsen, Neuengamme, Auschwitz. We knew that they had been mixed up with common criminals—thieves, pimps, black marketeers. Their number, though steadily rising, was totally unknown.

In Germany there were also several tens of thousands of workers who had heeded the slogans of the labor-conscription program. A few of them had no doubt actually believed that in so doing they were fulfilling their patriotic duty, but the majority had been lured by the carrot of personal gain. They had been joined in the Reich's factories by several hundred thousand men who had submitted to the S.T.O. and so followed, usually against their wishes, the orders of the Vichy regime.

And then the refugees. How many were there? From where? And where had they sought refuge? There were people from the "forbidden zone" in the north, from the east, where they had been supplanted by German settlers, and from Alsace-Lorraine, whence they had been expelled after the Reich's annexation of these provinces. I also had to try to help those of their countrymen who had been shanghaied into the Wehrmacht.

Altogether they were perhaps four million men and women, blown hither and thither by the gusts of war, often half drowning in misery. All of them had a claim on our compassion, however unequally they had served the nation. They, plus their kin, represented a fourth of the French population. In us rested their hopes. It was my duty that these hopes should not be blighted.

My task was twofold: First, to aid the prisoners. At this we did very well. Our services in Casablanca and Algiers, despite their relative penury, sent hundreds of thousands of parcels to the POW camps in Germany. We also established close ties with the International Red Cross.

Second, we had to prepare for the repatriation of displaced

The Night Will End

persons. They would obviously be liberated in unforeseeable conditions and in a zone of operations outside my authority. Therefore, we would have to set up welcome centers wherever the homecomers might appear, including seaports and possibly airports. I had to organize a whole administration and transport it to France as soon as possible. My motto was: speed, order and compassion.

And I was confronting this gigantic task without a single secretary! I had to create an entire administrative branch in a land where manpower was extremely scarce. One by one I recruited my first colleagues: Pierre Weibel, Jacques Honoré (my first staff secretary), Lucien Barnier (my information secretary), Raoul Jué (a Morocco-based industrialist who shut down his factories to serve by my side), Georges Ciosi (a teacher and my future brother-in-law) and Robert Guédon.

One day I learned that René Hardy had recently arrived in Gibraltar. Over him hung the terrible accusation of having "fingered" Jean Moulin and the entire Caluire meeting to the Gestapo. I had never credited these accusations, but I also thought that he should be relieved of the burden of doubt he'd borne for so long. Let him be cleared or forever damned! I had him escorted from Casablanca to my office in Algiers.

I beheld a changed man. Bony, nervous and shifty-eyed, he had dyed his hair a peculiar color. He was accompanied by a slender and very beautiful brunette with enormous eyes.

"Henri, I'd like you to meet my fiancée, Lydie Bastien."

That evening the three of us dined together. Lydie said nothing but occasionally threw me a long and almost provocative glance. Hardy recounted how he had been arrested along with Moulin in Caluire and how he had escaped from the Gestapo. I'd expected him to be outraged by the accusation that he'd "fingered" the Caluire meeting, but he spoke of it coolly, without anger of indignation. Now a marked man in France, he asked only that he be allowed to enlist in the army.

"René," I said, "first we've got to clear you of these allegations. As a witness to your performance in the Resistance, I don't believe

Algerian Interlude

a word of them. Still, I must ask you to present yourself to the military police and submit to a serious interrogation. Then and only then shall we discuss your future role in Algiers."

The next day I had him escorted to Paillole's police headquarters. There he was lengthily "grilled." Long afterward, I was to learn that Lydie had been utterly beside herself during her fiancé's questioning. She was even said to have confided in a girl friend that she "hoped to God he won't sing."

The following day I learned that the evidence against him had not warranted an indictment. Yet his enemies were not about to bury the hatchet, and it seemed best for all concerned that he just join the army. On second thought, however, I realized that his departure would probably be misinterpreted as evidence that I had spurned him. The man was a victim of calumnies. I was in desperate need of help. Why not take him into my *commissariat*?

Thus it was that René Hardy became one of the essential figures in the repatriation.

I devoted much thought to "my" French nationals in the Reich. Surely my first task was simply to understand them. The prisoners, inevitably, would have the mentality of defeated men. As for the civilians in the German war machine, we had to destroy their resignation, to rebuild their morale—maybe even to give them the spirit of fighting men.

Deciding to address them once a week on Radio Algiers, I inaugurated a long series of broadcasts on December 13, 1943. After blasting Vichy's specious rhetoric (i.e., the exaltation of resignation, repentance and work for Germany), I said:

I am a soldier, and as a soldier I address you. I shall preach neither resignation nor passivity, but the virtues of just anger and the struggle for freedom.

France, already engaged in the struggle for her life, is fighting on three fronts: the foreign front, where, side by side with the Allies, French soldiers make ready to storm your prisons; the home front . . . where everyday men and women are fighting in the underground; and lastly, the front inside Germany, your front, where you yourselves are fighting and must continue to fight.

The Night Will End

Each front has its own weapons: here, the battleship, the airplane, the tank; in France, the maquis, the irregular outfits, the clandestine press; in Germany, industrial sabotage, work slowdowns, the weapons of cleverness and guile. This war you have already begun, and I urge you to pursue it with all the means at your disposal. . . .

In France, as we have seen, two resistance movements had germinated among the repatriated prisoners. They were directed by Michel Caillau and François Mitterrand. The former was already in Algiers; now I heard that the latter too had arrived. I asked that he come by to see me as soon as possible.

I had many interviews with him during his brief stay, all revolving around two subjects: the necessity of merging the two ex-POW movements and the infiltration of those Vichy organisms dealing with matters of concern to my commissariat.

Not without difficulty we reached an agreement. In France itself the fusion of the two movements took place in March 1944. However, although I didn't know this at the time, it was not carried out according to the provisions we had laid down. Once back in France, François Mitterrand claimed that he had received instructions to bring into the unified movement a small group of militants whom I didn't know anything about. This group was actually an offshoot of the Communist Party. Naturally, Mitterrand's comrades bowed to what he presented as a C.F.L.N. directive. Of the five men on the directorate of the unified prisoners' movement, two were Communists.

This subterfuge, of which I remained ignorant until after the war, enabled the C.P. to infiltrate the world of the prisoners and deportees. It was to have, as we shall see, serious consequences.

I am reduced to guesswork as to why Mitterrand wanted thus to denature our accord. He was to remain out of France for three and a half months, most of which time he spent in London. In Algiers, he became acquainted with the Communist deputies to the Assembly and, in England, with the Communist Waldeck Rochet. I do not know whether he fell under their spell at this time or had already consciously opted to play ball with them.

In François Mitterrand himself I had discovered a man of

Algerian Interlude

lightning intelligence. Despite his secretive nature, I had no difficulty in discerning his calculating ambition. What I failed to perceive was his adeptness at intrigue, of which his political career was eventually to provide remarkable examples.

By late 1943 a great problem had begun to inflame the passions of the Free French community in Algiers—the problem of a general purge.

An October decree had created a Military Tribunal of the Army with jurisdiction over "crimes and offenses against the domestic and foreign security of the State committed by members of the *de facto* organism calling itself the government of the French State and by officers and members of antinational factions."

By virtue of this decree, General Berget and P.-E. Flandin, both former Vichy ministers, had been placed under house arrest. They had arrived in Algiers in the wake of Darlan (now dead) and Pucheu (of whom more later).

Another decree had set up a purge commission with jurisdiction over all other categories of citizens suspected of "having aided or abetted the enemy." This commission was really a sort of grand jury with the power to propose disciplinary sanctions and the opening of formal judicial hearings.

Alas, it was only too true that the enemy had found numerous collaborators in France and not only among the followers of Marcel Déat and Jacques Doriot. All of official Algiers believed that they should be ferreted out and severely punished. A few months earlier, before my putative return to France, I had left René Capitant an article on this subject to be published after my departure. It was entitled "Justice":

We have no intention of summarily condemning those masses of perfectly innocent people who were led astray by the false prestige of a man whose age and renown seemed a guarantee of his honesty and patriotism. We have followed the moral drama of France too closely not to sympathize with them and excuse their errors. . . .

But there are others whom we shall not pardon. . . . These are the men who knowingly played along with the Germans, who hunted down

The Night Will End

and betrayed our freedom fighters, who became slave merchants or dragomen for execution squads. . . .

France, our bleeding France, cannot abide that the latter escape our just retribution. . . .

The first debate that the Consultative Assembly inscribed in its agenda was the debate over the general purge. As we followed this torrent of rhetoric, both François de Menthon, now Commissioner of Justice, and I were dismayed by the tenor of certain speeches. Clearly, some men, even here in Algiers, had very few scruples about due process.

For several months the city was buffeted by gusts of perfervid emotion. In the antechambers of the Assembly, as in the popular Brasserie Suisse, almost every conversation was fueled by this great debate. The idea of a wholesale purge struck terror into the hearts of some while elevating others to maniacal exaltation. Certain men began to behave like latter-day Fouquier-Tinvilles.* By God, the Consultative Assembly would match the Reign of Terror! Already it was peopled by mini-Robespierres and -Saint-Justes, who were being avalanched with unsigned letters of denunciation. A dark cloud of suspicion enveloped the city.

The trial of Pierre Pucheu opened on March 4, 1944, before the Tribunal of the Army.

The ex-Minister of the Interior had resigned from the Vichy government after the occupation of the free zone by German troops and made his way to North Africa. Shortly thereafter he'd been arrested and jailed. In November he became a prime target of the C.F.L.N. decree aimed at ministers of the *"de facto* organism calling itself the government of the French State" and was removed to Algiers.

He engaged two attorneys to represent him, Mes Gouttebaron and Paul Buttin. The later, who was president of the Rabat Bar

---

*Antoine Quentin Fouquier-Tinville (1746–95) served as public prosecutor of Robespierre's revolutionary tribunal during the Reign of Terror, 1793–95.—Translator.

Algerian Interlude

Association, came to see me a few days later. He knew that in early 1942 I had met his client in Vichy when he was still Pétain's minister. I told him about our two interviews, and I agreed to provide him with written testimony to be read at the trial.

Of this trial the press furnished daily eyewitness reports. They were dramatic and intensely affecting. The trial had heavy political overtones, for Vichy itself was symbolically present in the dock.

The collaborators knew that the ex-minister's fate would in large measure prefigure their own; the Resistance expected and demanded an exemplary retribution. By cable the Central Committee of the movements informed us that it had condemned Pierre Pucheu to death *in absentia* as a "purveyor of human beings to prisons and firing squads and an accessory many times over in the crime of murder."

The history of this trial has been chronicled elsewhere.* It was, to say the least, rough sailing. Pucheu was vehemently accused of having personally selected the Communist hostages shot in Châteaubriant prison. And we resisters, in the Assembly and elsewhere, could not forget that he had been top dog in the police force that had so relentlessly tracked us.

In an atmosphere of vitriolic hostility, Mes Buttin and Gouttebaron asked that the trial be postponed until after the Liberation, for numerous witnesses for the defense were still in France. They also demanded that Rollin, the ex-head of the D.S.T. who had presented me to Pucheu in Vichy, be present to give testimony. In fact, this would have been fairly easy, for Rollin now lived in London. His anti-Nazi sentiments, which he'd never hidden from me, had led him to leave France soon after the invasion of the southern zone. Nonetheless, the court refused to grant this request.

Though showered with contumely all during his trial, the ex-minister gave proof of the great strength of character I thought I had discerned when visiting him in Vichy two years earlier. He knew his life was at stake.

*Paul Buttin, *Le Procès Pucheu*, Amiot-Dumont, 1947. Robert Aron, *Histoire de l'épuration*, Fayard, 1967.

The Night Will End

The verdict was returned on March 13. Pierre Pucheu was condemned to death.

Though the vast majority of the Assembly gloated over this sentence, I was not the only one in Algiers to be deeply distressed. In my heart of hearts I felt unable either to accept or to condemn the verdict.

If the charges against him were true, he deserved to die. But I wondered if they had been properly substantiated. Without certain missing pieces of evidence, the proofs advanced seemed insufficient. They constituted no more than grounds for the presumption of guilt.

On the other hand, we could not forget that a relentless struggle was still being waged in France. My own comrades had participated in the Central Committee's "sentencing" of Pucheu. They would see any clemency as a crime against the Resistance. Such clemency might well open a rift between us and them on the eve of the decisive battle.

A few days after the verdict, De Gaulle summoned me to his office. On his desk lay Pucheu's plea for a pardon.

"Frenay," he said, "you met Monsieur Pucheu twice in Vichy. Tell me what happened."

I recounted my two interviews in detail, mentioning the ex-minister's conception of the "double game" the government was supposedly playing. By his account, Vichy had merely been temporizing, trying to alleviate the burden of defeat, biding its time until the moment arrived to join the victors. I also told De Gaulle that in deliberately leaking secret conversations Pucheu had tried to divide and weaken the Resistance.

He listened quietly and attentively. After my last words he let a long silence elapse.

"This trial," he said, "is monstrous. The man is obviously not a traitor in the ordinary sense of the word. Maybe—probably, in fact—he thought he was serving his country in Vichy, but then the whole Vichy system was founded on dereliction of duty and could survive only through equivocation. In a sense, he was Vichy's first victim. In sentencing him, the Army Tribunal has condemned that system. There was no other way. And yet . . ."

Algerian Interlude

On March 20 Pierre Pucheu paid the supreme penalty. In order to spare a French officer the ordeal of commanding the execution squad, he asked to assume the responsibility himself. After shaking hands with each soldier, he himself gave the order to fire.

The justice of men had been done. But was it Justice? I think not. De Gaulle's hand had been forced by the inexorable law of "reason of state." For the first time in my life, horrified though I was, I understood that law.

The tide had now turned against the Axis. Italy, which had surrendered last September, had joined the Allies as a recognized cobelligerent. In January the German Gustav Line sustained a massive assault. Outflanked by the Americans at Anzio, crack German troops in Monte Cassino had repeatedly stemmed every assault on their positions, despite withering air strikes and the relentless softening-up rounds of powerful American batteries.

In late November 1943 Churchill, Roosevelt and Stalin met in Teheran. The C.F.L.N. had not yet been recognized as the representative of French state interests, and De Gaulle was not invited. Nonetheless, we knew that in the conference plans had been drawn up for the invasion, and hence the liberation, of France.

A few weeks later we learned that in Teheran the fate of Eastern Europe had also been decided. Great Britain and the U.S. had endorsed a Soviet plan to annex the three Baltic states of Latvia, Lithuania and Estonia, as well as a large part of Poland. (no doubt it was just as well that France, unrepresented, bore no moral responsibility for these annexations.) In exchange, Poland was to have East Prussia, Silesia and Pomerania, which would be severed from the dismembered Reich.

In February General Eisenhower was appointed commander-in-chief of the Allied forces for the liberation of Western Europe. He left Algiers to set up his GHQ in England and to prepare the Normandy landings ("Operation Overlord").

In Russia the Red Army under Stalin launched a massive offensive against the Dnieper. While Zhukov's vanguard crossed the Polish border, Koniev, striking south, pushed into Bessarabia.

The Night Will End

In the Far East the Japanese were in full retreat before the American onslaught in Burma. A few weeks later American troops overran the Marshall Islands.

The letters I got from France, plus the cables addressed to D'Astier and me, told of reshuffling of the Resistance leadership in view of a more efficient and coordinated action.

In late January the Committee for Immediate Action (C.A.I.) was replaced by a tighter body, the C.O.M.A.C. (Committee for Action), whose members could meet more easily. These members were: Chevance for the southern zone, Jean de Vogüe for the northern zone and Villon for the National Front. The following participated in its sessions as advisers: Jacques "Chaban"-Delmas, De Gaulle's appointee as national military delegate, and General Revers, the head of the Army Resistance Organization (O.R.A.).

The maquis were subject to ever more frequent attacks. As the Germans burned farms and executed hostages, our Groupes Francs and sabotage squads exacted an eye for an eye. In most issues of *Combat* a column now appeared called "The Resistance Front," which related these operations. For instance, here is an excerpt from *Combat*, No. 53:

In one month, from November 2 to December 2, 310 armed attacks and sabotage attempts were undertaken by the Groupes Francs and the Haute-Savoie contingent of the F.T.P. [Francs-Tireurs et Partisans—the military arm of the National Front], and sixty traitors were eliminated.

Near Folligny, an antiaircraft transport train with eight freight cars of heavy materiel was derailed and totally destroyed.

Near Maintenon a gasoline train was derailed and burned.

In the north, a convoy of forty-one trains destined for the Russian front was blocked for four days by means of four derailments on its intended route.

Near Fontaines-sur-Saône, a train of German troops on short leave was derailed. Sixty-seven Germans were killed and eight tank cars of gasoline were destroyed.

Algerian Interlude

In Aix-en-Provence, all four locomotives in the depot were seriously damaged.

In the eastern rail network, thirty-eight locomotives were destroyed on the one night of November 29–30.

In the Lyon-la-Mouche depot, all the reserve tanks of compressed air were exploded, immobilizing for fifteen days all machinery running on compressed air. . . .

In the Michelin complex at Clermont, a squad of thirty men subdued the depot watchman and seized most of the tire stocks, which it removed with five trucks.

In Royat, the German radio station was sabotaged.

Lastly, in Grenoble . . . on November 16, the gasometers and ammunition dumps of the test range were blown up. . . . The blowing-up of the depot was the work of a single man from our Groupes Francs. One man—against watchmen, sentries, and a whole detachment of guards!

As the end came into view the struggle became more bitter. In the hope both of conferring the international legal status of soldiers upon the domestic combatants and of unifying their command, we in Algiers passed a decree creating the French Forces of the Interior (F.F.I.) under General Koenig. But the repression continued unabated; the Gestapo struck relentlessly. Not a single letter arrived from France that did not announce fresh arrests.

Around this time the first signs of a power struggle surfaced in Algiers. As we have seen, the Assembly had chosen Félix Gouin over André Hauriou as president. Those members of the metropolitan Resistance group who had a prior political allegiance left us to rejoin their respective parties. Five out of the seven heads of *commissariats* were politicians left over from the Third Republic. Every day the danger of a rebirth of the Third Republic became clearer.

This danger alarmed not only me but also my comrades in France. They expressed their apprehension in strong terms:

. . . In France, there is no doubt that the old blocs are starting to ferment

The Night Will End

again as payday approaches. . . . But we are not going to exchange a rotten mess of Vichy pottage against another such mess which has been sitting in the pantry for three years. . . .

(Combat, No. 52)

. . . The Resistance militants would have preferred that De Gaulle not enter into association with the derelicts of the regime which led France into disaster and the Republic into the morass of Vichy.

(Combat, No. 53)

Claude Bourdet wrote me on February 8, 1944:

. . . "Max's" insensate politicization of the Resistance, which he initiated by creating the C.N.R. in the mold of the old parties . . . yields more catastrophic results each passing day. . . .

How delighted I was to realize that he was as opposed as I was to the resurrection of the Third Republic!

There was mounting pressure from the Communists in Algiers. As early as 1939, following the Nazi–Soviet Pact, the Daladier government had arrested and imprisoned many of the Party's leaders. Twenty-seven of them had been forced to spend three years in a prison camp in the Algerian Sahara.

General Giraud had released them in mid-1943. In conjunction with the clandestine C.P. Central Committee in Paris and Maurice Thorez in Moscow, they began to launch a heavy propaganda campaign.

With some of them—André Mercier, Fernand Grenier and Henri Pourtalet—I established cordial relations. Given the increasing importance of the C.P. in the underground battle, I deplored the fact that they were unrepresented in the C.F.L.N. For better or worse, the Communists had to be granted a share of the responsibility of power. In effect, they once again found themselves in the position they had occupied in 1936, when they had supported—though not participated in—the Popular Front government.

I found this issue so important that I wrote a letter to De Gaulle

Algerian Interlude

on March 27, 1944, insisting that they be brought into the committee, failing which I would tender my resignation. Many others, both in Algiers and in France, took the same position, and in early April Fernand Grenier became Air *commissaire* and François Billoux *commissaire* of state for Public Health.

The Communists' major concern in the spring of 1944 was to obtain the unobstructed passage to Algiers of Maurice Thorez, the Party's secretary-general, who had been in Moscow since late 1939. They besieged all the *commissariats* with this demand. It was André Mercier who approached me.

"Since June 21, 1941," I told him, "we've been fighting side by side in the underground. I understand and I approve your desire to have your secretary-general present, and I shall back your claim.

"But let it be clearly understood," I added, "that he, like all other Frenchmen, shall be subject to the laws of the Republic. In 1939, when the French army mobilized against the Nazi enemy, Maurice Thorez deserted. He should by all rights be imprisoned, but I'll enter an amnesty plea so that he may resume his place at the head of the Party."

The Communists were not exactly touched by this reply. It was something they never forgot.

In France, the National Front, with its strings still being yanked by the C.P., was stubbornly turning down all proposals to merge with other movements. By now the Front was competing openly with us. Its numerous clandestine pamphlets confirmed what I had long warned of—that the C.P.'s main goal was to steer the future national insurrection toward its own goals.

I was deeply disappointed. I'd long hoped that the C.P.'s role in our struggle would encourage it to forsake its Soviet sweetheart. It was increasingly clear that such was not the case.

Not only were the Communists jealously retaining exclusive control over their own forces, but they were also infiltrating our own organizations, within which their influence was steadily growing. Bourdet wrote me:

. . . "Salard" [Pascal Copeau, who had replaced D'Astier at the head of

The Night Will End

Libération] is philosophical about the growing predominance of the C.P., but I must admit that I view it with anxiety. Though I stand for close and loyal cooperation with the Reds, I refuse to be manipulated by them. . . .

Parliamentary politicking and Communist maneuvers—such indeed were the twin dangers for a true French renascence as I conceived it.

Many lacunas had been left in the Consultative Assembly by the "politicos" who had rejoined their various parties. Now the overseas Resistance, with which I was always in close touch, proposed to form a single bloc and obtain an absolute parliamentary majority. My friend Cerf-"Ferrière", the ex-editor-in-chief of the underground *Combat*, was elected president of this bloc. One of our major concerns was to extend our movement throughout all the French territories of Africa and Asia and concurrently to increase our newspaper's circulation. Calling ourselves "Combat-Overseas," by the month's end we counted fully three hundred chapters, many of them brand new, in Morocco, Tunisia, French West Africa, French Equatorial Africa, Djibouti and the French East Indian *Comptoirs*.

The directorate of Combat decided to convene an enormous congress on March 25–26 to consist of representatives of all the chapters of Combat-Overseas.

Several hundred militants filed into the great Pierre-Bordes auditorium. Among them were Menthon, Capitant and numerous delegates to the Consultative Assembly. Every chapter was represented, including Cayenne and Martinique. Capitant gave a résumé that enabled us to measure the rapid geographical spread of our movement.

To a silent and attentive audience I read a new manifesto that I'd prepared. It was titled "The Revolutionary Charter of Free Men" and it ended with an appeal to "all the men of the European Resistance" to meditate on "the ties that will bind the free peoples of tomorrow."

Algerian Interlude

The essential thing was to develop our strength and maintain our ties with our friends in France, especially Claude Bourdet, who had succeeded me in my former role as head of Combat.

It was then, early that April, that a cable arrived announcing Claude's arrest.

The Night Will End

THE LIBERATION OF PARIS

Bourdet's arrest was
one of a series. Later I was to receive a belated letter from him in which
he told of a wave of raids and massacres:

. . . Forain, our top man in Toulouse, was nabbed a few
months ago. We found him in a wood with his head blown off
by a grenade. . . . People of varying importance are being arrested
everywhere. The militia has assassinated Dr. Valois, whom I wanted
to make a regional chief, as well as his assistant, Bistozzi, a university
professor. At the same time they murdered Professor Gosse. We wiped
out his murderer a few days later and left his body at the same spot where
he'd killed Gosse. . . .

The maquis are being attacked from all directions and are daily losing
men and what few arms they have.

Claude also informed me of the Communist maneuvers in the
C.N.R. and the Action Committee. They were now waging
an implacable underhand struggle for the top positions in
the Resistance. Claude told me about a conversation he'd
had with Georges Bidault ("Bip"):

When I vehemently reproached "Bip" for his negative attitude toward the reds, he answered,

15

"The Communists are such disloyal double-dealers that I can't ever allow them the benefit of the doubt and must stay constantly ahead of them, as if in a race. The whole thing turns my stomach."

And Claude concluded:

. . . only the southern zone is still cohesively organized, and it has remained so because of the men you picked. The M.U.R. has never done anything but exploit the theories developed in Combat. . . .

If your voluptuous idleness hasn't utterly incapacitated you, you'll hop on the next plane for France—in secret, if necessary. We'll hide you, you'll hole up somewhere, but thank God we'll have you back. . . . As for me . . . you know I'm not cut out for this task. Now it's totally over my head. . . . I'm so tired. Oh, Henri, you should never have left us. I embrace you. "Lorrain."

Renouvin, Michelet, Berty, Marcel Peck, Jean-Guy and his wife Yvette—and now Claude! In my darkened room I saw them again as they had looked on various occasions. They seemed to be entreating me, saying, "You should never have left us!" Yes, I had been wrong. Nothing, nothing had been more important than to be with them and to share their dangers.

I went to bed but could not sleep. Hardly had I dozed off when I awakened with a start. Claude's words grew in my mind until they became a stifling burden of remorse. By sunrise my mind was made up: I would return to France!

Despite my insistence, it was several days before I obtained an audience with General De Gaulle. Two big problems had tied him up: the entry of the Communists into the C.F.L.N. and the attendant cabinet shuffle and the suppression of Giraud's supreme command. The latter deprived Giraud of all his duties save those of inspector-general of our armies; in other words, he'd been effectively cashiered. De Gaulle was now confronted with two tests of strength: first, to force the C.P. to accept his choice of *commissaires* (including those of C.P. provenance) and, second, to forestall any army strong-arm tactic prompted by Giraud's disgrace.

The Night Will End

Not surprisingly, when De Gaulle received me in Les Glycines he was very distracted. I tried to communicate my feelings to him, to make him understand that the arrest of Bourdet and so many others had virtually decapitated the Resistance. I wanted him to admit that my real duty was to go home.

"Frenay," he said, "it's easy to understand your anguish, but men don't make war with emotions. It's already a year since you were last in France."

"Not quite ten months—"

"All right, then, ten months! Since then the structures of the Resistance have greatly changed. You won't even have time to get in touch with your old contacts before the battle for the Liberation starts. What's the use of your going back now?"

"At least I'd ease my conscience and buoy the moral of my comrades—of those who survive, that is."

The general bore into me with his cold eyes. "What your conscience should be telling you, Frenay, is to stick with your job, to shoulder your responsibilities! To abandon your *commissariat* at this juncture would be a very bad move. People will say—and rightly too—that you failed your duty. I will not let you leave. Anyway, D'Astier already knows of your intentions. He's your brother-in-enmity, and just for that reason he'd never let you go back to France without him. He'd immediately request to return along with you. I cannot tolerate such disorderly behavior!"

His expression changed. I detected a certain gentleness. He rose and walked me to the door.

"Excuse me. I haven't the time to pursue this discussion." He clasped my hand rather longer than usual. "In a few days, when you've calmed down and can see things in perspective, I'm sure you'll agree with me."

Logically speaking, De Gaulle was right; but since when does logic alone dictate men's behavior?

Not a week went by before a telegram reached me from Spain: "In Madrid. Request you to have us flown to Algiers immediately. Best: 'Barrès' [Bénouville], 'Barrioz' [Chevance]."

How delighted I was! This was the elixir that would snap me out of my wretched mood. I did everything I could to speed the arrival of my two old pals. But now that they were out of France—and

The Liberation of Paris

what with Claude in enemy hands—I wondered who in the devil would direct our movement.

Who, indeed, was left?

Here I was at Boufarik Air Base again, bursting with impatience. A few moments later I was hugging Pierre de Bénouville and Maurice Chevance. Through them I felt a kind of physical contact with France and the Resistance. They too were thrilled to be with me again—I, their friend, their "Henri-boss," as Bénouville called me with that rusty voice of his. We all chattered at once. Our conversation was like a three-part invention in which intense joy over our successes alternated with fear for our daily disappearing comrades. The lack of arms, they said, was costing many lives. Rage against London and Algiers was mounting, for it was London and Algiers who had encouraged the maquisards to take to the hills and who were now letting them be decimated.

We talked for hours. From time to time, by a sort of tacit understanding, we would suddenly fall silent, take one another's hands and smile from the bottom of our hearts.

It was in those days that I met Antoine de Saint-Exupéry.

Until the spring of 1943 he'd been in the United States, where he'd written *Fighter Pilot, Letter to a Hostage* and *The Little Prince.* The fact that he had not belonged to Gaullist circles there was held against him in Algiers.

Now forty-three, he was too old, according to air-force regulations, to fly a Lightning (the high-speed, double-fuselage aircraft with which his unit was equipped). The author of *Man's Earth* and one of the pioneers of airmail service had become a "kiwi."

Permanently grounded, suspected of only lukewarm attachment to Gaullism and hence outcast from official circles, "Saint-Ex" wandered nostalgic and disconsolate through the streets of Algiers.

We saw each other frequently. Sometimes he'd come for dinner at my place in Hussein-Dey. I became his friend simply because I admired him and because his disgrace seemed so undeserved.

For his part, Saint-Ex loved to hear me talk about the underground, which he understood instinctually. He'd listen to me as

The Night Will End

wide-eyed as a child before of his first Christmas tree. There was an impish freshness, too, in his conversation and his laughter.

One day when we were at his place he said, "Bet you didn't know I was a musician! And I even do a bit of composing on the side."

He sat me down before the piano and began to play a melody whose genuine beauty was occasionally interrupted by exotic dissonances. He never glanced at the keyboard but gazed straight at me all the while in a sort of soulful, questioning way. Intrigued by this strange music, I rose and walked around behind him. With his open palms he was simply rolling two oranges about on the keys. He looked up at me with pure mischief in his eyes.

Yet all his mirth could not conceal a deep sadness that he had no place in the battle for France. So in early May I invited him to lunch with Fernand Grenier, the Communist who had just received the Air portfolio.

At my request, Grenier interceded with the Allied air commander in the Mediterranean theater on Saint-Exupéry's behalf. Regulations were waived, and he was once again allowed to fly. Toward mid-May he rejoined his unit, now based in Corsica.

Our friendship grew. Between his reconnaissance flights over France he would drop by at my place in Hussein-Dey—always with a bag of crayfish in hand—and tell me how blissful he felt when he looked down on the French countryside from his perch eight thousand yards up. He was a totally fulfilled man.

He took off for France on July 31, on a routine mission, never to return. Squadron Leader Antoine de Saint-Exupéry had disappeared forever.

I notified General De Gaulle of the arrival of Chevance and Bénouville, whom he received successively. Then I put them in contact with the principal members of the C.F.L.N. Three days after their arrival I invited Jacques Soustelle, then director-general of the Special Services, to lunch with the three of us.

At lunch Soustelle cold-shouldered me. At the time I thought that maybe he was put off by the fact that my two friends were harassing him about the arms question. The real reason, however, I learned only when I read his memoirs after the war.

The Liberation of Paris

It was this: For our first forty-eight hours together, Pierre, Maurice and I, virtually flying with the sheer joy of our reunion, had been trying nonstop to arrive at a synthesis of our information and views. It was this two-day truancy that Soustelle could never forgive:

. . . One day in the spring of '44 I learned that two Resistance chiefs had just arrived in Algiers and that Frenay, then Minister of Prisoners, had immediately *spirited them away** from our services. Frenay had never been able to overcome his infantile prejudices against us. . . . **

Again:

. . . I was all the more irked when I learned that Frenay had *kidnapped** these two resisters who had just arrived from France. . . . **

By this account, to welcome my two comrades, to put them up at my place, to chat with them awhile, was in fact to "spirit them away," to "kidnap" them! Soustelle really should have understood the Resistance a bit better. No doubt he thought that my two pals were his "agents," his underlings.

I believe that this incident, better than any other, reveals certain men's total incomprehension of the Resistance. People like Soustelle had never experienced our adventure and could never understand the simple friendship we shared.

Soon my two friends were roaring through the *commissariats*: If Chevance was a gale, Bénouville was a hurricane. With their impressive record they gained entry everywhere, jolting people out of their inertia, uprooting prejudices, sweeping away doubt and uncertainty. Their energy, enthusiasm and faith compelled the trust of others.

Soon installed in the offices of Diethelm, the war *commissaire*, they instigated the creation of the Forces Françaises de l'Intérieur (F.F.I.) and the decrees incorporating them into the French army.

*Italics mine.
***Envers et contre tout*, Vol. ll, page 365.

The Night Will End

Again, it was they who convinced the D.G.S.S. of the feasibility of liberating a poorly defended zone in the southwest. Lastly, it was they who reinforced the France-Algiers communication line (the "Brittany-Gascony liaison") which—as Soustelle himself has admitted—gave us enormous advantages during the last few months of the Resistance.

In August both men received government missions and were promoted to the rank of brigadier general. Chevance took over the F.F.I. in the southwest to harry the retreating German troops. Unfortunately, Bénouville was hurt in a car accident that kept him in bed for many months. However, this period afforded him the leisure to write the very best book on our Resistance, *Le Sacrifice du matin*.

On the morning of April 26 the Vercors maquis—that ill-conceived brainchild of Jean Moulin—was attacked by crack German units backed by French militiamen.

The maquisards had received a few airlifts, but they had almost no heavy weapons. For three weeks we in Algiers watched in anguish as the battle raged on. It was an unequal combat, just as I had warned Moulin that it would be. Our besieged brothers telegrammed us for help, but the C.F.L.N. simply did not command enough of the right kind of aircraft to provide the materiel they needed. In any case, the high command's concerns were elsewhere.

At this point—that is, sometime during the first half of May—the Communist Air *commissaire*, Fernand Grenier, without any advance notice to the cabinet, held an impromptu press conference. In it he pictured the heroic and unequal struggle of the maquisards, exalted the F.T.P., enumerated his own efforts on their behalf and deplored the indifference of the Allies and the Council of Ministers. Only the Communists were backing the Resistance. Only they were absolved of the responsibility for the rivers of blood.

Two days later, the C.F.L.N. was convened. A short time ago we'd started to meet in the Summer Palace, the fine Moorish-style residence once reserved for the French governor-general and occupied by General Giraud until his ouster.

The Liberation of Paris

De Gaulle opened the session, his face even more expressionless than usual.

"Gentlemen," he said, "before we tackle today's agenda we must settle an important problem. The day before yesterday, the Air *commissaire* held a press conference about aid to the Resistance. Here is how the newspapers reported his statements."

The general read some articles from the Algerian press.

"The worthy Air *commissaire* is as aware as anyone of the efforts that every one of us has made to try and provide the interior combatants with the means to live and fight. The worthy Air *commissaire* is as aware as anyone that the responsibility for the failure of these efforts must be laid at the door of those who actually have the required arms and the planes to transport them—that is, our Allies.

"To give out that you and you alone, Monsieur Grenier, have labored for the Resistance is pure prevarication. Your aim is clear: to fool the people into thinking that you and your party are the sole defenders of the Resistance. This base tactic also subverts the solidarity of the government. . . ."

The audience followed in utter silence. Where was De Gaulle heading? Now and then, Paul Giacobbi, the *commissaire* for Population and Provisionment, would nudge me with his elbow, murmuring, "Hear, hear!" François Billoux stared stubbornly at his papers, while Grenier squirmed and tried to interrupt De Gaulle.

"No, Monsieur Grenier, I've not finished yet! If you maintain your present attitude you will end by excluding yourself from the government. We shall take action, and public opinion shall be duly informed of the reason for your departure.

"On the other hand, you yourself may now see the necessity of retracting your statements. In that case, I shall ask you to draw up and sign a declaration that will be released to the press at the end of this session. Perhaps you desire a moment for reflection. The session is temporarily adjourned."

We went into the next room for a stretch. Grenier and Billoux were talking in low but animated tones. It took them a good quarter of an hour to make up their minds. Apparently it was not

The Night Will End

in the party's interests for them to leave the government. They decided to eat humble pie, and signed a retraction.

The Vichy radio, which our services monitored nonstop, announced that on April 26, for the first time since the Armistice, Marshal Pétain had obtained a German authorization to visit Paris. The capital had welcomed him enthusiastically. The cathedral of Notre Dame, where a solemn mass was celebrated, was jampacked with people.

To me nothing was more revealing of the state of France. On the very day that the Marshal's militia, in concert with German troops, began to storm the Vercors, and while his information minister, Philippe Henriot, vilified the Resistance over the radio, much of Paris gladly welcomed the old man. Yet those same men and women who wept to see him were suffering terribly under the occupation and longed truly for their liberation. Surely some of them were even aiding the resisters. There was no logic in their behavior, only emotion and vague hope. In four years they had not seen one French soldier in uniform, let alone the seven stars that gleamed on the Marshal's sleeve. In a sense, those crowds in the street were craning forward to get a glimpse of France herself.

Did this make them bad Frenchmen? In the coming months we were going to have to choose between begrudging them their old fervor for Pétain and inviting them to join in the national reconciliation proclaimed by De Gaulle. I wondered, though, if De Gaulle had ever realized that 95 percent of the French people had accepted the 1940 Armistice. For it was with this same majority that he proposed to rebuild a shattered France.

Meanwhile the Red Army had retaken Odessa and Sebastopol and liberated the entire Crimea. The German losses, both in men and materiel, were staggering. Every night the factories of the Reich were being pounded by English and American bombers. Hitler could not replace his destroyed and captured armor.

The battle of Monte Cassino finally ended with a resounding victory in which the young French army under General Juin won

The Liberation of Paris

the admiration of our Allies. We began to pursue the enemy northward.

In the Council of Ministers, De Gaulle, as the supreme commander of our armies, informed us that General Leclerc and his division would be transferred to England to participate in Operation Overlord—that is, the Normandy landings. General Koenig moved to London, where, assisted by Colonel Passy, he became the commander of the F.F.I. (Forces Françaises de l'Intérieur) General de Lattre was appointed to replace General Juin at the head of our troops in the Mediterranean theater.

None of us knew the exact date of the forthcoming assault on *die Festung Europa,* but it seemed imminent. Feverishly the *commissaires* began to submit to the council the administrative measures they had devised for the first French provinces to be liberated.

To set up a national administration was imperative, for the Americans were planning to assume this responsibility themselves. They had put together an administrative body, the A.M.G.O.T. (Allied Military Government of the Occupied Territories) that was to supplant the current authorities in all liberated lands, including France, which they planned to treat just like an enemy territory. To us this was intolerable. Only the C.F.L.N., backed by the C.N.R. and the Consultative Assembly, could represent France. It and it alone possessed the right and the duty to administer the liberated territories. Our rejection of the A.M.G.O.T. was a defense of our national sovereignty. Once again, with a kind of mulish stubbornness, the general fought this odious American project to a standstill.

Of course we had to replace Vichy—but how and with whom? This was the subject of an April 21 decree that we all signed. It ordained the provisional re-establishment of the municipal and general councils as they had existed before the declaration of war. The prefects were to be proposed by the Resistance and assisted by the departmental liberation committees (C.D.L.). After inspecting the electoral lists they would proceed as soon as possible to the election of new municipal and general councils. When all our territory was liberated, and as soon as circumstances permitted,

The Night Will End

general elections would be organized by a Constituent Assembly empowered to draft a Constitution.

To punish the quislings, the purveyors of the execution squads, the profiteers of the defeat was a national duty to be accomplished unskittishly. Yet in order to curtail the bloody settling of scores, the backlash of popular hatred, retribution had to be meted out speedily and in exemplary fashion.

The task was perilous. All the judges currently on the bench had taken an oath of allegiance to Pétain. It hardly seemed healthy for the nation, or conducive to respect for the judiciary, to ask them to don fresh gowns and start trying those whom only yesterday they had served. On the other hand, it was clearly impossible to replace the entire French judicial apparatus. Several sessions of the committee were devoted to just these problems.

On June 3, by order of the Consultative Assembly, the C.F.L.N. became the Provisional Government of the French Republic (G.P.R.F.) We were no longer *commissaires* but proper ministers. Actually, without the full recognition of the Allies, this didn't mean much in international politics. We just changed our identity cards and letterheads.

To acquaint public opinion with the plight of the POWs, I planned to organize a "Prisoners' and Deportees' Day" to be held all over the Empire and to be accompanied by speeches and a public fund-raising drive. In Algiers my ministry prepared an exposition called "The Barbed-Wire Front," and that evening I spoke at a large public meeting. That very same morning, May 21, De Gaulle paid an official visit to my ministry (now located in the Summer Palace).

On the steps, a detachment of spahis, drawn swords flashing, did the honors. The general, accompanied by his principal private secretary, Gaston Palewski, arrived punctually. The three of us were alone in my office.

"Well then, Frenay, let's hear how you've tackled your problem."

"Sir, it's a wilderness of unknown factors. I don't even know how

The Liberation of Paris

many French nationals I'm to look after. In fact, from the total figure I might give or take several hundreds of thousands. Now, we do know where the POW camps are, but we don't have any idea where the deportees and laborers are. They're probably all over the Reich, in factories, fields and forced-labor gangs. Also, there's no way for us to know how soon Germany will collapse after the landings. At present we know neither the fate of the big counteroffensive nor the amount of time we'll have to prepare for the absorption of our nationals."

"Are you in touch with the Allied command?"

"Of course. But they don't know any more than we do, and they refuse to countenance any plans based on hypotheses. Yet we have no idea of what state the railways will be in, or the degree of destruction of our public works. Hence, as you can see, we're obliged to set up an administration prepared for the worst eventuality. The most flexible and the fastest method would be repatriation by air, but the Allies won't hear of it, so we have to work on the assumption that we can only use roads and railways. We've already selected some twenty-seven sites for repatriation centers between Dunkerque and Annemasse. We'll still need time to build them, equip them and recruit staffs for them. Furthermore, since we cannot rule out the possibility of repatriation by ship, via the Baltic and the Black Seas, we're also planning a number of centers in Mediterranean and North Sea ports. By the way, I've called in one of my old pals from the École de Guerre, Captain Robert Guédon. I'd like you to hear what he's come up with."

We moved into an adjoining room, where Guédon was waiting with his colleagues by his side. He gave a short précis based on our three guidelines—order, speed and compassion. He also explained the organization of a typical repatriation center, where, in exactly seventy minutes, each homecoming French national would be "processed." This examination would include a papers check, a military-security check (to weed out criminals and undesirables), a physical, a deverminization, X rays, the filling out of a medical record, a shower, the dispensing of rations and transportation coupons and, lastly, a marks-to-francs exchange.

"At this point, sir," said Guédon, "the men may leave the centers free of any further bureaucratic formalities."

The Night Will End

"Tell me, Frenay," said De Gaulle, "can you estimate the length of the total repatriation period?"

"We're hoping," I said, "to complete the task in five months or one hundred and fifty days. In nineteen eighteen, for about a third the number of POWs we've got now, repatriation took a full year. Maybe I'm setting my sights too high, but, anyway, that's our target. And that's what I'm going to tell the press."

De Gaulle was clearly pleased with what he'd heard. As I escorted him back out to his car he said, "Now then, Frenay, where could you be of greater service than here? You're doing fine work and you've put together a first-rate staff."

As the war approached its end, I felt my responsibilities grow heavier by the day. The eyes of innumerable French families were upon me.

The "National Prisoners' and Deportees' Day" made a great impression on the public. The newspapers gave us heavy coverage, and guests flooded our exposition. That evening the huge Pierre-Bordes auditorium was mobbed.

Ever since I'd taken charge of the ministry a great fear had haunted me. Defeat and war had riven the French people both geographically and morally. The enemy's demarcation lines had partitioned our land. Our countrymen had followed diverging and sometimes hostile paths: resistance, passive wait-and-seeism and active collaboration. Among my charges were volunteers for German industry, deported resisters and soldiers, some captured in armed engagements, and others who'd let themselves be led like sheep from their rear-line barracks to German pens. It was tempting to mete out praise and blame. Yet, however just such words might be, they would only accentuate the rifts caused by the sorrows of war.

To me nothing seemed more important than the re-establishment of the moral unity of the French people. We had to erase, or at least blur, the differences that separated our countrymen and often incited them to internecine hostility. Henceforth, I decided, the workers in Germany would be euphemistically labeled "labor deportees" (rather than, say, "volunteers" or "S.T.O. men"). In this way, we could build a bridge between them and the

The Liberation of Paris

resisters, who would be called "political deportees." The POWs would be called the "combatants of the Interior German Front."

I set forth this unity theme before the almost two thousand people in the auditorium. My speech was broadcast live over Radio Algiers and could be heard in France.

Meanwhile, a grand strategy was being devised by the Communist Party—to take over the entire Resistance.

To seize the top positions at the national and departmental levels, the C.P. had to oust its opponents—especially the men of Combat. No holds were barred in their attempt to achieve this goal, including the most vicious sort of slander. An example:

Jacques Dhont, the M.U.R. regional chief in Toulouse, had just arrived in Algiers. He told me about the smear campaign that had recently been launched against him.

Vicious rumors had been circulated about him: He was untrustworthy, a right-winger, a henchman of the reaction. Soon a typewritten C.P. leaflet appeared declaring that he was a Gestapo agent disguised as a resister. A Groupes Francs squad actually received an order to kill him. Luckily, its chief, who knew and respected Jacques, let him know about this vile plot. Dhont demanded a confrontation with his accusers before a "court of honor." To this he attached one condition: If he were found guilty, he would abide by the verdict; if he were acquitted, his accusers would be executed. Of course they backed out, but the lies continued to circulate. Disgusted, exhausted and heartsick, Dhont resigned.

Before leaving Toulouse, Dhont sponsored as his successor a member of Libération, François Verdier. His choice was ratified by the M.U.R. directorate.

Immediately Verdier was subjected to the same smear campaign. He courageously stood his ground. A few months later he was arrested by the S.S., and later he was found in the Bouçonne forest, his body dismembered by a grenade.

At this point, "Ravanel," a crypto-Communist, took over the region.

Michel Brault, the national director of the maquis, met with a fate similar to Dhont's. Michel had really given his all to organize,

The Night Will End

supply and arm the S.T.O. evaders, first in the southern and then in the northern zone. Consequently he had assumed a growing importance.

He had to be gotten rid of.

Same story: The rumor spread like wildfire that he was an execrable "bourgeois" who hated and feared the people. For simply refusing to commit his men to hopelessly undermanned or ill-armed operations, he was accused of suspicious foot-dragging. Soon the campaign hit a more sinister note. "Joinville," the C.P. member who'd replaced Marcel Peck at the head of R.1 (Rhône-Alpes), accused Michel of being a henchman of Vichy's regional prefect. Brault went to London to clear himself. At this point Pascal Copeau, who'd become head of Libération-Sud, tele-grammed D'Astier (now Interior Minister) to ensure that Brault's re-entry into France be banned.

In similar fashion Sarda de Caumont, the head of the R.4 maquis, was ousted.

In Limoges, "Hinstin" and Ady-Brille (who had replaced Edmond Michelet after his arrest) were caught by the Gestapo and deported. Guingouin, a member of the Communist Party, took their place.

In Montpellier, "Cals," who'd been arrested and deported, was replaced by Gilbert de Chambrun. A young aristocrat who'd entered the diplomatic service several years before, he was related by marriage to Josée Laval, the quisling's daughter. Considering Chambrun's social origins, whoever would have guessed that he was one of those fellow travelers who were later to be dubbed "crypto-Communists"?

After Claude Bourdet's arrest, Marcel Degliame ("Dormoy") was appointed to the M.U.R. directorate. As it happened, "Dormoy," whom I'd put in charge of Workers' Action on account of his exceptional dynamism, was also a crypto-Communist. On April 19 Pascal Copeau wrote Emmanuel D'Astier:

. . . the appointment of "Dormoy" only a few weeks before the decisive hour . . . is a welcome guarantee of the solidity of our movement both now and in the future. . . .

The Liberation of Paris

Personally, my opposition to "Aubin" [Bourdet] was directly related to the issue of what policy to pursue toward the C.P. and the National Front. . . .

With "Dormoy" in place we shall have a thoroughgoing accord with them. . . .

To counteract the influence of Bénouville, Brault and Chevance in London, Copeau considered

. . . that the return of "Mézeray" [Michel Brault] would be a grave error. I shall request the directorate to forbid anyone in the interior to contact him. . . .

"Thuillier" [Chevance] left so precipitately that he would not have had a mandate from the action committee nor the M.L.N. directorate. . . . Though he is a very talented man, he is just not the type to whom one can entrust a political mission. . . .

The same goes for "Barrès" [Bénouville].

About the same time I got a letter from Pascal Copeau in answer to the one I'd addressed to the M.L.N. directorate. He wrote:

. . . You dwell on the twin dangers in Algiers: the Communist danger and the danger from Third Republic elements. . . .

In France itself we cannot deal with anything but the two big dangers *we* perceive: the German danger and the fascist danger. . . .

The political future of France depends upon our ability to induce the C.P., through its intermediary, the National Front, to join the new formation of democratic forces in France. . . .

This issue was to be resolved exactly as Copeau wished, for, in a few months, largely as a result of new arrests, departures, smear campaigns and various sordid connivances, the Communist and their allies gained control of the principal decision-making bodies of the Resistance. It was only then that I realized that Copeau was backing the C.P.

Toward late May I received a telegram from Rebattet [*"Cheval"*]:

The Night Will End

. . . I and all maquis and Secret Army cadres have been eliminated and replaced with political elements coming mostly from Workers' Action and Libération. . . .

This, then, was the current situation in the Resistance:

In preparation for pending military operations, the M.U.R. had set up an "executive authority" that wielded plenipotentiary power in the southern zone. Acting on its own, with no accountability to the directorate, it was composed of Pascal Copeau (political affairs), Marcel Degliame (Secret Army, maquis, Groupes Francs, Resistance-Rail) and Pierre Hervé (general secretariat). As the reader can see, this "authority" comprised two Communists and one fellow traveler.

After the arrest of Dejussieu ("Pontcarral") and the elimination of Rebattet, the action committee (C.O.M.A.C.), whose authority covered both zones, was composed of Villon, Kriegel-"Valrimont," "Joinville" and Vogüe. The first three were Communists.

The Central Committee of the Movements, in which the National Front had held only one out of eight seats, was gradually plowed under. As Pascal Copeau wrote me, ". . . the Central Committee having become a purely theoretical body, the permanent bureau of the C.N.R. is now the unchallenged central authority."

Now, as it happened, this bureau, though under the presidency of Georges Bidault, had also passed into the hands of the Communists and their sympathizers, including Villon (National Front), Saillant (C.G.T.) and Copeau. Only Maxime Blocq-Mascart, the head of the O.C.M., had managed to withstand their pressure.

The Communist Party had now all but obtained its long-sought objective.

What could we do to counter this subversion and infiltration?

I no longer had any personal contacts in France. My letters would have fallen into Copeau's hands anyway, since he was the M.L.N.'s top man in the southern zone.

To raise the matter before De Gaulle would have been so much wasted effort. Colonel Passy had recently directed his attention to

The Liberation of Paris

the highly suspect maneuvers of his Minister of the Interior, Emmanuel D'Astier. The general answered, "Passy, you forget yourself. Monsieur D'Astier is my Interior Minister." That was that. Passy was in semi-disgrace.

De Gaulle seemed unable to grasp the peril of entrusting the supervision of action in France to a man like D'Astier. In 1941–42 D'Astier had tried to lay a Socialist and labor-union foundation for Libération. However, when the socialists and the C.G.T. abandoned him to set up their own organization, he turned to the Communists. With his position as Interior Minister and his ties with Pascal Copeau, he was greatly to boost their enterprise.

People began to wake up only after the Liberation, when D'Astier became an avowedly pro-Communist Progressive deputy in the National Assembly. By them it was clear that his newspaper, *Libération*, was surviving on C.P. subsidies. The big eye-opener was when he became president of the National Movement for Peace, and the Soviet government kindly provided him with an apartment in Moscow.

All available evidence, especially the total break-off of communications between Algiers and London, indicated that Operation Overlord (the Normandy landings) would be launched at any moment. A dark and pregnant secrecy veiled the preparations for the Allied landings.

On the eastern front, the Soviet armies had reached the Vistula. At the approach of its would-be liberators, the people of Warsaw rose up with a single will. Only later did we learn of the final tragic act of this great drama. German troops were to crush General Bor and his heroic freedom fighters while Stalin stood by unmoved, refusing to give them the slightest help.

On June 3 De Gaulle convened his cabinet. A telegram from Churchill had invited him to London forthwith "in the interests of France." The Prime Minister had even sent him his personal plane.

"Gentlemen," said the general, "the landing is obviously at hand. I intend to leave this evening. In London I shall try to work out with the Allies the details of France's military participation and

The Night Will End

the administration of our liberated territories. Of course both my departure and the reasons for it must be kept top secret.

"The Minister of State, Henri Queuille, will serve as acting president. It is impossible for me to predict the speed of the operations and hence the exact date of my return. But I shall be in radio contact with you. I also request you to start preparing the transfer of your ministries to France."

Feverishly we began these preparations. For our combatants inside France the hour of truth was nigh. Anxiety gripped me. Would they be able to rise to the occasion, to implement our Green Plan for knocking out the railways, or our Violet Plan for destroying telecommunications? The German army was potent, its morale intact. We didn't even know if our men had yet received the arms and ammunition necessary for effective harassment. And what terrible ordeals awaited our towns and villages?

Morning, June 6. The Allied troops landed in Normandy. A narrow bridgehead was conquered between the Orne and the Vire. We prayed that it would hold.

By June 20 De Gaulle was back in Algiers. He furnished the cabinet a detailed account of what he'd experienced in the previous two weeks, especially his serious difficulties with the Anglo-American supreme command over the administration of the liberated French territories. Though the general spoke of these matters with apparent detachment, we could discern a sort of glacial hatred.

In any case, he'd agreed to go to Washington and confer with F.D.R. A simple exchange of views, he said. Not for anything in the world would De Gaulle have allowed himself to seem like a petitioner!

Less than a week before he'd entered France and inspected the liberated zone. What had impressed him most was the welcome of the liberated population. In every village people had hailed him with cries of *"Vive De Gaulle!"* and *"Vive la France!"* Sometimes simple folk would gather before their ruined houses, weeping and cheering as he passed by.

"Gentlemen," said De Gaulle, "I think the battle in Normandy

The Liberation of Paris

will last a few more weeks. You have time to prepare the return of this administration to France. The ministers should be among the first to arrive in Paris."

A few days later D'Astier and I lunched with De Gaulle at Les Glycines. De Gaulle jokingly related an anecdote from his brief stay in the liberated zone: "I was arriving by auto in a village. The people seemed forewarned of my arrival—how so, I have no idea. Anyway, the streets were mobbed. People were weeping and cheering. All of a sudden a woman holding a bunch of flowers clearly picked from her own garden rushed toward me, threw them on my lap and cried out '*Vive le Maréchal!*' Must have been force of habit, eh? Funny thing, I could tell she was a fine, upstanding Frenchwoman!"

It seemed that the general had finally understood that for many of our countrymen the cries of "*Vive le Maréchal!*" or "*Vive De Gaulle!*" meant simply "*Vive la France!*"

Even we in Algiers sensed something of the breathtaking speed of events in France. Bénouville and Chevance, though detained for several weeks, were now preparing to depart. We often got together in the evening in Hussein-Dey to discuss the current situation.

Our Special Services provided the government with daily information bulletins that we ourselves supplemented with frequent briefings from Soustelle, Paillole and their subordinates, who were getting dozens of telegrams from France each day.

In the former southern zone, entire towns had fallen to the Resistance. Apparently, hundreds upon hundreds of railway lines and telephone lines had been cut, considerably hindering troop movements. The Germans responded with bloody reprisals. In Normandy, three Wehrmacht armored divisions were beset day and night by our maquisards and Groupes Francs, losing two precious weeks during which the Allies beefed up their bridgeheads.

The American air strikes against Lyons, Chambéry and Saint-Etienne had failed miserably. The bombs, dropped from too high up, had missed their targets and killed thousands of people. The Resistance protested vehemently, once again demanding the con-

The Night Will End

siderably cheaper wherewithal to knock out the same targets from the ground.

SOS calls kept coming in from the Vercors maquis, which had been continuously besieged since late April. D'Astier, Bénouville and Chevance stepped up their pleas for parachute drops. Meanwhile, during late June and the first three weeks of July, the final battle raged on that high plateau. Hundreds of men fought heroically to the bitter end. Some managed to escape through loopholes in the ever-tightening net. Most of the prisoners and wounded were simply massacred. They paid with their lives for the terrible error of those who had thought to turn their redoubt into an "impregnable bastion."

In late June the Vichy radio announced that despite a reinforced guard Philippe Henriot had been assassinated by a "band of terrorists" in his ministerial offices on the Rue de Solférino. This remarkable punitive operation had been executed by one of the M.U.R.'s Groupes Francs, and it put a just end to the man who had so ruthlessly devoted his intelligence, talent and faith to the enemy's designs.

Bénouville had left one week ago. After three fruitless attempts he'd finally made it to France. He'd hardly arrived when he was badly hurt in a car accident. From his hospital bed in Marvejols he'd made contact with the Resistance, especially with Rebattet and Pascal Copeau. He'd also managed to install a radio transmitter in the Aubrac maquis.

He sent me a stream of long telegrams insisting that I, followed by the entire government, come and set up shop in the Massif Central, which was now three-quarters liberated. He depicted a confused and disturbing political situation: "The Departmental Liberation Committees," he said, "are behaving like petty tyrants . . . requisitioning and taxing without restraint." He concluded:

. . . the psychological shock of the government's arrival is needed to crystallize popular enthusiasm and establish proper authority. . . .

Then Maurice Chevance left for Toulouse. Fernand Grenier, the Air Minister, had opposed his departure simply because the

The Liberation of Paris

Communists had preponderant power in Toulouse. Paradoxically, Grenier had no desire whatsoever to see the government—whose representative, after all, he was—take the situation in hand. Only through the greatest cunning had my friend managed to hop a plane and eventually assume command of the Free French forces in the southwest of France. There he soon broke the enemy's grip and captured 25,000 prisoners.

On August 1 Leclerc landed his Second Armored Division on the Normandy coast. Day by day it expanded its bridgehead. The Resistance too struck fiercely all over France. On August 15, General de Lattre de Tassigny and his First Army landed in force between Saint-Raphaël and Hyères, investing Toulon and pressing on toward Marseilles.

A fever descended on Algiers. Everyone was dying to know how the new authorities were functioning in France. The key thing was to insure a minimum of order, without which the military operations might be compromised and the Allies intervene in the administration of the country.

On August 18 the Provisional Government made an appeal to the people:

. . . You must know that disorder, destruction and useless pillage only impoverish the nation. . . . The maintenance of public order is in everyone's interest and the people must be vigilant in seeing that order is preserved.

This appeal was diametrically opposed to the wishes of the Communists, who were dead set on taking advantage of the confusion of the Liberation. Forty-eight hours later, on August 20, each minister received a letter signed by the eleven Communist deputies in Algiers. It was an out-and-out attack on the government:

. . . Yes, in a sense [the workers] are presently engaging in "pillaging." They loot the enemy's arms and ammunition dumps, they plunder the munitions of those assassins, the militia . . . all because you never gave them what they asked for. . . . There is no doubt that they are attacking

The Night Will End

"the forces of public order," for the order which holds sway in Paris is Hitler's order, the order defended by traitors whose hands are still dripping with French blood. . . .

It was under this same pretext, the maintenance of public order, that the French government of June 1940 . . . decided to deliver France to the enemy. . . .

It would have been far more sensible to have advertised the measures already adopted by the C.N.R., especially those relying upon the intermediary of the Liberation Committees, to assure the maintenance of democratic and patriotic public order. . . .

The letter ended with an urgent demand on the part of the eleven deputies to be conveyed as soon as possible to the capital, which was now on the verge of insurrection. They wished, of course, to place themselves at the forefront of the uprising.

The Anglo-American forces were converging on Paris. Yet the enemy was still retreating in orderly fashion, defending his positions bitterly as he withdrew.

August 17. De Gaulle addressed the cabinet:

Gentlemen, tomorrow I shall go to Britain, and I hope to be in France shortly thereafter. The liberation of Paris is in sight. Our national interest requires that General Leclerc and his division be the first to enter the capital—and I with them. I hope that General Eisenhower will understand. Naturally, I shall keep the government abreast of the operations, and I ask each one of you to make ready to join me immediately upon receiving word. Nothing is more important than the establishment of the government in Paris in the hours following its liberation.

De Gaulle left the next day. Forty-eight hours later he was in France and in radio contact with us.

Late on August 23 Louis Joxe informed us of a telegram from De Gaulle that disclosed that Leclerc had been ordered by Eisenhower to press forward to Paris. General Koenig was to become the city's military governor. D'Astier, Giaccobi and Tixier (respectively, the ministers of the Interior, Provisionment and Social Affairs) were to rejoin the general immediately.

The Liberation of Paris

In the mid-afternoon of August 24, Henri Queuille convened the cabinet on short notice.

"Gentlemen," he said, "at noon I received a telegram from General de Gaulle. It was sent from Rambouillet this morning. Let me read it to you:

Today Leclerc's division enters Paris. I plan on being there tonight. . . .
Contrary to rumor, the capital is in good condition.
The Germans still hold certain points, but their position is hopeless.
I request all members of the government to rejoin me immediately in Paris.
The Le Mans airstrip is usable."

Then Queuille continued: "I've asked the secretariat-general to convey the government to France. The air channels are unsafe. The minister of the navy has proposed that we embark on the training cruiser *Jeanne D'Arc*. Since the Atlantic ports are still in German hands, the *Jeanne* will take us all the way to Cherbourg. From there we'll proceed by auto to Paris. We shall leave on August 27. The exact date of sailing will be announced sometime tomorrow."

That evening, as I packed my bags, I tried to sum up my experiences in my ten months in Algiers. Until the arrest of Claude Bourdet and the arrival of Bénouville and Chevance in Algiers, we in Algeria had been on the same wave length as our comrades in France. Our concerns, projects and objectives had been the same. Our actions had been complementary and hence of guaranteed utility.

Those days were over. Men whom I only half knew had succeeded my old friends.

The struggle for the reconstruction of France had only just begun; nobody had won the upper hand. It was in the coming months that we would win or lose the battle for the France of our hopes.

France! In a few days we'd be home!

The Night Will End

Of course we'd been expecting it—it was only a matter of days—but now that the blazing headline had appeared, I wept with sheer joy.

Paris was free!

We were itching to know all the details. And yet we knew only that the people of Paris had taken an active part in the city's liberation and that Leclerc, now joined by De Gaulle, had been one of the first to enter the city. The capital was intact. By some miracle the retreating German troops had not devastated it in their wake.

Telegrams began to pour in from all over the world. In South America, especially in Montevideo, hundreds of thousands of men and women swarmed joyfully into the streets. It seemed that for humble folk the world over Paris was a second capital. How moving were these signs of sympathy and tenderness that flowed toward France!

August 28. The *Jeanne d'Arc* weighed anchor in the Algiers roadsteads. Never before had she seen such passengers: The entire government* (with the exception of De Gaulle, D'Astier and Le Troquer, who were already in France, and Jean Monnet, who was in the United States) was on board, including Félix Gouin, the president of the Consultative Assembly, and Louis Joxe, its secretary-general. Each of us had a cabin.

We took meals in the skipper's dining room. Shortly after we rounded Gibraltar the sea became rough, and the ship began to roll. The chairs around the long luncheon table were not fastened to the deck, with the result that one row of jolly parliamentarians would be pressed tight against the table, while the other row, still aligned as if in some comical military review, would glide smoothly backward into the far bulkhead. An instant later the rolling would return the later gents to their proper places before their lurching lunches, while the first row would slide backward in turn. The

*François Billoux, Henri Bonnèt, René Capitant, Paul Giacobbi, Fernand Grenier, Louis Jacquinot, René Mayer, François de Menthon, Pierre Mendès-France, Henri Queuille, Adrien Tixier.

The Liberation of Paris

scene went on for over an hour; cabinet ministers turned into schoolboys!

At some two or three hundred miles from the English coast, a Catalina seaplane specially equipped for anti-submarine warfare appeared in the skies to protect us. The following days were unmarred by a single alert.

On the morning of September 1 we stood off the French coast. With tears in our eyes my colleagues and I gazed at the landfall. At about ten o'clock we docked in Cherbourg harbor—exactly one year, two months and thirteen days after I'd left France.

The Night Will End

Debout contre l'esclavage!

FRANÇAIS!

Laval, sur ordre d'Hitler, mobilise la jeunesse.
Ce n'est pas pour travailler en France ou pour la France, c'est pour " relever " les morts Allemands tombés sur les charniers de Stalingrad ou du Caucase.

Le " Service du Travail Obligatoire " pour tes enfants :
— c'est l'éloignement de leur pays, de leur foyer.
— c'est la honte de travailler pour l'ennemi.
— c'est la mort sous les bombardements justiciers de la R.A.F.
La défaite, pour Laval, c'est le poteau. Pour retarder l'heure notre vengeance, c'est toute la France martyre que par morcea il livre à son maître

HIER : Les Alsaciens et Lorrains. Les ouvriers de la relève.
AUJOURD'HUI : Ceux de la Déportation, puis toute notre jeun
DEMAIN : Les hommes de 20 à 31 ans, déjà recensés, puis t
les autres...

contre l'esclavage,
pour la liberté de nos enfants,
Français, tous debout!

JEUNES,
A la veille de la Victoire, vous ne serez pas les esclaves du vaincu.
Lacérez les affiches.
Ne répondez pas aux convocations.
Vieillissez-vous de 2, 3, 4 ans sur vos cartes d'identité, d'alimentation, scolaires.
Si vous le pouvez, quittez votre domicile.
Si vous ne le pouvez pas, entendez-vous avec vos amis, vos voisins. Résistez par tous les moyens, au besoin par la force, à votre arrestation.

DÉSOBÉIR A LAVAL, c'est OBÉIR A LA FRANCE!

FEMMES et MÈRES, exhortez vos maris et vos enfants à montrer leur courage.
S'ils sont arrêtés, accompagnez-les avec vos enfants, vos parents, vos amis jusqu'à la gendarmerie.
Manifestez aux cris de
Liberté — Mort à Laval — La police avec nous

MÉDECINS, "recalez" le plus possible de jeunes à la visite.

POLICIERS et GENDARMES, ne soyez pas les fossoyeurs de la jeunesse française.

PEUPLE DE FRANCE, tu es tout-puissant si tu le veux!
Hitler chancelle, Laval tremble, l'Europe attend ton exemple.

TOUS DEBOUT!

Dans chaque ville, dans chaque village, secourez nos jeunes, cachez-les, ravitaillez-les, embauchez-les.
S'ils sont arrêtés, formez-vous en bandes, manifestez, réclamez-les, faites-les évader...

ALLONS, ENFAN S DE LA PATRIE!

Édité et diffusé par COMBAT

Tract que j'ai rédigé coute le travail obligatoire en Allemagne

One of Combat's anti-deportation posters.

Some of Combat's publications. (Author's Collection)

Men of the maquis. (Photo Seeberger)
Old Norman woman saluting General de Gaulle. (Photo Keystone)

General de Gaulle awarding the Croix de la Libération to the author (August 1943). (Photo Combat)

Paris revolts (August 1944). (Photo Keystone)

Generals Leclerc and De Gaulle enter the capital. (Photo Associated Press)

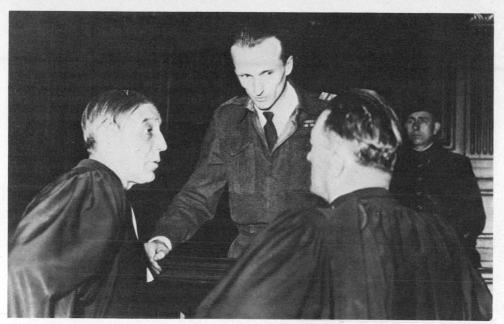

René Hardy, head of Résistance-Rail. (Photo Keystone)
André Bollier, head of printing and distribution of Combat's underground press.
(Author's Collection)

Strasbourg liberated. (Photo E.C.P. Armées)

François Mitterrand, head of the M.N.P.G.D. (National Movement for POWs and Deportees). (Photo Keystone)

M.L.N. poster. (B.N., Paris)

Marshal Pétain in the dock. (Photo Keystone)

The author in Prague with Jan Masaryk. (Author's Collection)

"Despite all obstacles, you were able to achieve this great task: the homecoming, the welcome and the resettlement of our most sorely tried compatriots."
—General de Gaulle to the author, November 24, 1945. (Photo Keystone)

General de Gaulle and the author at the Tomb of the Unknown Soldier, November 11, 1945. (Author's Collection)

DAWN

The piers of Cher-
bourg were already piled high
with war materiel, crates and vehicles.
There were lots of American soldiers about,
some English, and a sprinkling of French.
It took us two hours to reclaim our baggage and take
our seats in the long row of Dodges awaiting us. The local
authorities counseled against our taking the direct road to
Paris, which was still unsafe in stretches. We'd do best to head
southwest first, they said, and stop over at Le Mans, where the prefecture could be instructed in advance to find us a night's lodging.
How lovely the Norman countryside was, and how sweet-
scented! Yet only a few weeks before it had been the scene of a
bitter battle. The signs of war were everywhere: burned-out tanks,
overturned vehicles by the road, blasted bridges, wooden crosses in
the meadows, fresh rubble beside the hastily cleared streets of the
villages. Yet life went on, invincible. Cattle browsed contentedly in
the pastures, swallows wheeled overhead, and people turned
with soothed and smiling eyes and waved to us as we
passed by.
The following day, after hours on the road, we
reached the capital's suburbs. Boulogne, the
Porte de Saint-Cloud, the Avenue de
Versailles, the Seine, the Eiffel Tower.

Improvised flags, often showing the Cross of Lorraine, still hung from the windows. We passed several detachments of F.F.I., recognizable from their armbands; some had rifles slung over their shoulders.

Suddenly I felt myself transported three years back into the past. I pictured the swastikas that had so disheartened me when I'd first seen them floating over the capital. Now Paris was free again! Yes, I was at last in a liberated Paris. And in a Paris that, by some miracle, had been spared devastation.

What I didn't yet know was that Paris owed her miraculous survival to a German, General von Choltitz, who had disobeyed the Führer and risked his own life to save the capital of France.

I and most of the other ministers stayed in the Hôtel Claridge on the Champs-Elysées while waiting to be allocated official apartments. Ministerial departments had already been set up by secretaries-general named several months ago by the government. I had asked and obtained that my own department be headed by François Mitterrand.

He had installed our offices in the Paris seat of the General *Commissariat* for Prisoners of War at 3, Rue Meyerbeer, right off the Place de l'Opéra. During the Paris insurrection he and his men had stormed the premises, driven out their occupants and opened fire on the enemy from inside.

Mitterrand must have been about twenty-five then. He had already learned to master his youthful spontaneity. Though I was glad to see him again, he didn't seem to reciprocate my feelings. Apparently he'd hoped that by then I'd be elsewhere and that he'd be minister of prisoners. If such was his desire, he must have been very disappointed. I still wanted his services, though, because he'd put together a solid staff and wielded wide influence.

I asked him to stay on with me as secretary-general. In this key job, he'd have headed my entire administration with its six subdirectorates. He would have been at the apex of the pyramid. I thought my offer attractive, a wonderful break for a man of his youth and relative inexperience. Yet his ambitions already overreached it, and he declined it. Dreaming of a career in politics,

The Night Will End

burning to show what he could do, he was simply using the P.D.R. as a steppingstone to bigger things.

De Gaulle had not moved into the Elysée or the Matignon. By living and working on the Rue Saint-Dominique, he wanted to draw attention to the absolute priority of the French war effort. He called his first cabinet meeting in liberated Paris late on our very first afternoon.

"Gentlemen, great tasks await the government. We must actively contribute to the war and the complete liberation of France, we must feed the people, we must re-establish communication with the provinces, and we must restore the authority of the state wherever necessary. All this will require many months of sustained effort. We shall also need a government that represents more accurately than has hitherto been the case all the forces of the Resistance. In order that I may form this government, I must request each of you to tender his resignation. All of you have shouldered heavy responsibilities in a trying period of our history. Your help has been precious to me. Allow me to offer you my heartfelt gratitude."

On September 9 the list of the new government was released to the press. It included ten new ministers. Six former ministers were let go. I was relieved to notice that D'Astier (Interior) was one of them. In fact, he wasn't even in the new government. He had been replaced on the Place Beauveau by Adrien Tixier, a candid, straightforward Socialist who'd lost an arm in the First World War.

De Gaulle had not overemphasized the complexity of the tasks now confronting the government. Before the war we'd had 12,000 locomotives; now we had only 3,000. Three thousand one hundred public works had been destroyed. Our navigable rivers and canals were blocked by wreckage and collapsed bridges. Entire areas had been mined by the retreating German troops and had to be cordoned off. Coal and electricity were running cruelly short. Two and a half million of our men in Germany, and manpower was lacking.

Lyons had just been liberated, but all its bridges were shattered

Dawn

hulks. Burgundy, the Juras, the Vosges and Alsace-Lorraine were still occupied. The Allies had only just entered Belgium. To block the necessary foodstuffs and materiel from arriving from America, Hitler had left garrisons in all our Atlantic ports and in Dunkirk. These troops were sacrificing themselves solely to prevent the provisioning of the desperate French population.

We had almost no contact with the liberated zones, so vast had been the underground's destruction of telecommunications. Adrien Tixier, the new interior minister, had no choice but to send envoys to the provincial *commissaires* of the Republic and the prefects.

Their regular reports back to the cabinet were highly alarming. Apparently the Departmental Liberation Committees, most of which had been set up by Pascal Copeau or his minions, were refusing to recognize the prefects' authority. They defied them at every step. Some of them were even levying their own taxes, raising salaries and arresting or interning people.

In several cities armed F.F.I. and F.T.P. bands had extorted large sums of money from banks. The total sum, according to Aimé Leperq, our new finance minister, came to several hundred million francs.

The F.F.I. and F.T.P. had also set up so-called "popular tribunals" (sometimes dubbed "military courts"). They tried, sentenced and often executed people, usually in total disregard for due process and frequently in the most appalling fashion. Apparently a real reign of terror had descended on Haute-Vienne.

Things were bad everywhere, but unequally bad. Much depended on the charisma of the local prefect and *commissaire* of the Republic. Nowhere, however, did the proper authorities command the means of constraint necessary to re-establish republican law and order, for most of our troops and F.F.I. outfits were at the front, and the police, who only yesterday had hung on Vichy's lips, often felt stripped of the moral authority necessary to confront armed bands claiming to be resisters.

Indeed, the number of resisters had suddenly jumped. In July and August, thousands of temporizers and just plain cowards who hadn't dared lift a finger in four years suddenly jumped on the bandwagon. How heroic they looked in their improvised F.F.I.

The Night Will End

armbands! Some of them—no doubt to make up for their earlier gutlessness—suddenly began to see themselves as latter-day Saint-Justes.

These "September resisters"—the epithet soon stuck—like those of the preceding months, had been welcomed into the National Front with open arms. Mixed in with genuine resisters and officered by Party militants, they were organized into "patriotic militias." When trained and armed they posed a serious threat of anti-government insurrection.

Not long afterward I went to Fresnes penitentiary in the hope of finding some trace of Berty's death. The warden showed me the register for the spring of 1943. I was in luck. There was a page for each internee comprising his or her civil-status information and prison record. I read:

> Berty Albrecht.
> Deceased: May 28, 1943.
> Reason: Unknown.

Now this word "unknown" had been written over some earlier word that had been erased. The erasure was somewhat longer than the word "unknown" and was obviously the real explanation of her death. Farther down the page I found this invaluable piece of information: "Interment: Fresnes Cemetery, No. 26."

The exhumation was carried out several days later in the presence of Dr. Wolfsohn, an old friend of Berty's and mine. We discovered that Berty had not, as had previously been stated, been decapitated. On her neck were obvious strangulation marks.

Of course it was highly unlikely that the Gestapo had strangled her. It had every reason to keep her alive, to make her talk.

Then I remembered what she had told me in Cluny after her escape from the Bron mental ward: "Henri, if they catch me again, I'll kill myself."

I am virtually certain that Berty Albrecht hanged herself.

For me, life went on, I left the Claridge for a pleasant residence hotel on the Avenue Léopold II in the XVIth Arrondissement. All

Dawn

September long I received dinner guests every evening, including my old colleagues from Algiers, Combat men who'd managed to escape from the Germans and various members of the present government.

My job had not really changed since my Algiers days. I had to participate in the Government decisions, fulfill my ministerial duties and help the Resistance (especially the M.L.N.) to advance its great cause—the renewal of the Republic.

My ministry took priority. Though victory seemed nigh we had nothing but blueprints for the enormous task of "processing" the imminent flood of homecomers. Over four million men—with their families, one quarter of the French population—were now looking hopefully to my young ministry. Among them were old comrades from Combat who had been deported to Germany. All were counting on me.

All the traditional ministries were now relocated in their customary prewar *palais* and *hôtels*, but the P.D.R. (Prisoners, Deportees and Refugees), as mine was called, was fittingly homeless. Eventually we set up shop in the Gestapo's old offices on the Avenue Foch and the Square du Bois. Ah, sweet revenge! The first of my colleagues to enter our new premises were greeted by the explosion of a time bomb. Fortunately, they emerged unscathed. By late September we had the ball rolling smoothly.

Now we had a home but no staffers. I decided to use any Vichy officials I could find who had not acted in a blameworthy way. But they hardly sufficed. I needed a large number of envoys to be dispatched to the Allied armies. Following in the wake of the advancing troops, they could contact the deportees and POWs and implement our repatriation plans. Alas, this project entirely depended on the Anglo-American Joint Chiefs of Staff, since it was the latter who had all the authority and materiel in the combat zone.

The "repatriation centers" in our ports and bordertowns were each outfitted to "process," if necessary, no fewer than 20,000 people a day, for we couldn't count on being able to apportion the refugees equally among these centers.

The Night Will End

In the departments themselves, placement desks were set up to help solve the legal, professional, social and family problems sure to afflict men who had been away from home for over four years. In fact, we'd mobilized a whole army of legal experts and arbitrators. Lastly. to run this vast organization we needed a 20,000-man strong central administration to be recruited in the shortest possible time.

It was not only in Germany that the repatriation process was totally dependent on the Allied High Command. The same was true in France itself. Not only had my ministry no proper means of its own, but it also served as a tributary to the other administrations. Yet France now had only 300,000 cars and trucks, or about one tenth of its prewar total. Both tires and fuel were scarce. Raw materials were hardly to be had at all, for our industries were still operating at 20 percent of capacity. None of the ministries could satisfy their basic requirements, and only an implausible altruism could have led them to make way for the P.D.R. Interministerial quarrels simmered and often boiled over, requiring the arbitration of the chief of state. Once, in March 1945, I even resigned, but De Gaulle refused to accept my resignation.

In early September we were hit by the refugee problem. There were over 2,500,000 refugees, of whom 900,000 were national disaster cases. While waiting to return to their villages they had to be fed, lodged and (hardest of all) provided with living allowances. The latter eventually totaled ten thousand million francs, or a quarter of my budget.

Through the Red Cross International Committee, an agreement was reached for the evacuation of 170,000 persons living on the verge of famine in the German-occupied pockets along the Atlantic. They too had to be lodged elsewhere in the nation.

The retreating Wehrmacht had left over 100,000 foreigners behind in France. They were men and women of forty-two different nationalities, including Todt laborers,* remnants of

---

*The Todt administration, named for the engineer who directed it, was responsible for many big fortifications, including the "Atlantic wall."

Dawn

Vlassov's Army** and Polish agricultural laborers forced to work in our northeastern farmlands. It was no easy task to sort out these masses of humanity, take a census of them and provide them with decent living conditions.

The Russians alone totaled 40,000. When I mentioned them to Bogomolov, the Soviet Ambassador, I got this reaction: "Those men are prisoners of war, which means they failed to fight to the death. They do not interest me. Do what you will with them."

Very different from the spirit of the nation as a whole was the gladness that reigned on that festive evening when the C.N.R. formally received De Gaulle in the Palais de Chaillot. I can still hear the ovation that greeted the general as he appeared on the stage where the C.N.R. and cabinet awaited him. His speech still rings in my ears. At the end, a moving "Marseillaise" was joyfully sung by the 3,000 spectators; they were joined by the thousands of Parisians who had gathered in the capital's squares to hear a live relay broadcast of the ceremony.

Yet the elation that had momentarily infected many citizens after the Liberation had by now disappeared. The hostility between the public authorities and the forces born of the Resistance became stronger with each passing day.

At each cabinet meeting, the interior minister gave a report on the domestic situation. Here a prefect had been defied, there armed bands had broken into jails and slaughtered suspects. In the Rhône Valley, a group of departmental Liberation Committees had even "notified the government" of a set of local *diktats*.

The C.O.M.A.C., headed by Villon and his cronies Joinville and Kriegel-"Valrimont," now wielded an authority paralleling that of the war minister, André Diethelm. This unlawful shadow authority often received the allegiance of the F.F.I., who frequently disputed the war ministry's directives. Everywhere in the former southern zone, and even in Paris, the "patriotic militias" paraded in the streets—often armed to the teeth—in a show of force.

**Vlassov was a Russian turncoat general who had recruited several thousand of his fellow POWs into the Wehrmacht.

The Night Will End

The government had to impose its will—firmly but delicately. It didn't have the strength to force a showdown. Given our international position, the government was unwilling to withdraw two divisions from the front and commit them to problems of law and order at home.

The Communists wanted a revolution. So did we. But, as Georges Bidault had said at the Palais de Chaillot on September 12, we wanted a "revolution by law."

Between his first steps on French soil and his triumphal march down the Champs-Elysées, De Gaulle had discovered how immensely popular he was. The real aim behind the series of trips to the provinces that he began on September 14 was to build this popularity into a sort of dike to hold back the surging forces of disruption at large in the land. He visited Lyons, Marseilles, Bordeaux, Toulouse and Normandy. Everywhere the crowds went wild, everywhere tens and thousands of rapt citizens joined him in the "Marseillaise." It became very difficult for the F.F.I. chiefs to oppose him openly. Only rare verbal *outrances* marred the triumph of this man whom the nation as a whole now fervently followed.

Between these trips De Gaulle would give his impressions to the cabinet. "My travels through France have convinced me that she is behind her government and that she respects its justice and authority. There are and will be abuses, but the nation as a whole reproves those who commit them and wishes to join us in an orderly march forward."

As for the F.F.I., he felt that it was regrettable but understandable that they should have some difficulties in emerging from underground. They needed a helping hand.

A helping hand? For De Gaulle, that surely meant the government's hand—the hand of the law.

The first decree disbanded all F.F.I. outfits who failed to contract to serve till the end of the war. Those who did were sent to the front, where in fact they gave a brilliant account of themselves. The others were informed that if they did not surrender their arms they would be committing an unlawful act.

Dawn

The "patriotic militias" required more radical action. They had been created from scratch *after* the Liberation by the Communist Party, which also officered them. They had to be disarmed and dissolved.

Such a move would necessarily involve a bluff on De Gaulle's part. Yet the *commissaires* of the Republic were divided as to the advisability of such a bluff. The interior minister, Adrien Tixier, believed that the risk should be taken only if it reflected a collective government decision. Hence the whole affair was laid before the cabinet.

The subject was aired before the Council of Ministers in late October. The agenda itself made no explicit mention of the matter but referred obscurely to a "communication from the Minister of the Interior." It was in fact Tixier who broached the subject. He had prepared a detailed statement that had probably obtained De Gaulle's prior approval.

First it reviewed the situation in late August, then gave an account of the most perilous phase of the insurrection. In passing it offered homage to the F.F.I. and to the Resistance in general, while enumerating the measures enacted for a general purge. It also explained the functions of the special courts of justice and the gradual return to republican order, which the *commissaires* of the Republic and the prefects were now in a position to guarantee. In such conditions, the militias, which might have had a certain use if the local authorities had been threatened by subversion, had no further *raison d'être*. In any case, the Republic traditionally suffered the existence of no other armed forces than those constituted by the state. Tixier concluded that all such forces must be dissolved.

As I surveyed that hushed Council of Ministers my eyes continually reverted to De Gaulle and to my two Communist colleagues, François Billoux (Public Health) and Charles Tillon (Air).

The general stared at the ceiling and husbanded his eternal cigarette in sovereign indifference. Occasionally his glance raked the table. As his eyes lit on Tixier he would smile faintly, furtively, as if in complicity. Billoux's eyes were glued to the pad on which he

The Night Will End

was taking notes. Tillon, his jaws clenched, stared intently at Tixier, only occasionally seeking Billoux's eyes, which, however, remained hooded.

De Gaulle said, "Gentlemen, you have heard the report of the minister of the interior. I shall now ask each one of you if you agree with his conclusions."

Each of us in turn expressed his views. All the non-Communist ministers backed Tixier.

Then Billoux, in relaxed and almost bantering tones, explained why such a decision would be mistaken. He felt that the risks of subversion had not subsided, that there were many signs that the opposite was true. The people must be made to feel supported, not feared.

Tillon, by contrast, was curt, imperious, and barely able to conceal his vexation. He echoed his colleague's words about "the fear of the people," then went on to recommend that a democracy should not so lightly cast aside the cooperation of elements that it might soon find indispensable.

After we had thus gone round the table, De Gaulle summed up Tixier's arguments, concluding, "Gentlemen, I have noticed with satisfaction though without surprise that each one of you is as attached as I am to the principle of law and order. After the ordeals from which France has just emerged, it was natural and inevitable that some troubles would occur. However, the moment is here to fully restore republican order. Such is our duty.

"Republican order is founded on the predominance of the state. The state must have but one judiciary, one army, one police force. That is why we support the propositions of the minister of the interior."

His glance circled the table again. Utter silence reigned (De Gaulle's cabinet never voted).

That was that. We went on to the next point on the agenda.

The C.N.R., which had theoretical control over the "patriotic militias," and the C.O.M.A.C., which had them directly under its wing, were each in turn forced to yield to the general. In the end such was also the fate of their string-puller, the Communist Party, whose hostility to De Gaulle and his government immediately rose

Dawn

365

sharply. Henceforth that hostility was to be very openly expressed.

I was still friendly with Bidault, Menthon and Teitgen, all like myself ex-members of Combat's steering committee. But ever since early 1943, when the M.U.R. had been created, our meetings had become more and more infrequent, for our interests had diverged.

Georges Bidault had replaced Jean Moulin at the head of the C.N.R., while the others, as active members of the C.G.E. (Comité Générale d'Etudes), had devoted their time to studying the problems of postwar France. Having matured in the same spiritual family, they had all gradually become convinced between 1943 and 1944 that France needed a large political bloc based on Christian principles but also resolutely democratic.

During their later years in the underground they had periodically gathered their friends together—most of them were ex-militants from Action Catholique—to prepare the advent of this movement. In fact, *L'Aube*, which Bidault had edited before the war, was the first paper to appear above ground after the Liberation (though now edited by André Colin and Francisque Gay). The new Mouvement Républicain Populaire (M.R.P.) rapidly gained a following in the provinces, especially in the north and west, and soon won the adherence of many brilliant people. Among them was Maurice Schumann, who had already made himself a worldwide reputation during his four years in London as the official spokesman for Fighting France.

I believed that the creation of this movement was a serious mistake. In hindsight I may add that many subsequent political ills may be attributed to it.

If they had done nothing else, the war and the Resistance had finally buried the ancient problem of "established religion." For years Christians, atheists, Jews and Freemasons had marched together in the great underground struggle. In the light of what was happening, they had finally realized how petty their old quarrels were.

I feared and believed that to create a party led exclusively by known Catholic militants would be to revive the old quarrels that

The Night Will End

had sown so much discord among Frenchmen. I didn't hesitate to tell this to my friends, and, though a practicing Catholic, I never joined their movement.

I continued to harbor the burning conviction that the Resistance should give birth to a great revolutionary party based on a marriage of the Socialist tradition (stripped of its narrower Marxian side) and Christian humanism.

In early June the M.L.N. took over the entire building at 10, Rue des Pyramides. Since Claude Bourdet's arrest, the M.L.N. party apparatus had fallen into the hands of the Communists and their friends. During the Liberation Pascal Copeau had become the movement's secretary-general. Emmanuel D'Astier, now freed from his ministerial duties, ran its political bureau. They were assisted by Pierre Hervé, Kriegel-"Valrimont," Victor Leduc, "Joinville," *et al.*—a young and ardent team that was unquestionably devoted to the C.P.

With the help of some of the *commissaires* of the Republic, they had placed their men in most of the regions and departments of the southern zone. Such was definitely the case in Lyons, with Yves Farges, and in Marseilles, with Raymond Aubrac. However, though they had found the levers of power, most of the rank-and-file were not behind them. It was only fair that the real majority, as represented by the militants of our old movements (Libération excepted), take its rightful place as the true constituency of the M.L.N. Such a restitution had to precede all political action within the movement.

Yet I had few illusions about the likelihood of such a restitution, for, alas, most of my old friends from Combat were no longer there to help me in this difficult hour.

Berty, Billon and André Bollier were all dead. Renouvin, Michelet, Dejussieu, Bourdet, Jean-Guy Bernard and Jean-Guy's sister, Jacqueline, and his wife, Yvette, had all disappeared. Chevance was still fighting in the southwest; Soulage and Rebattet had signed up under De Lattre de Tassigny. Henri Ingrand and Jean Mairey (Peck's assistant) were now *commissaires* of the Republic. Bénouville had recently arrived in Paris, but his leg needed another operation. Both Michel Brault and Jacques,

Dawn

disheartened by the underhand maneuvers that had led to their ouster, had forsworn politics. The only people in the M.L.N. with the will to fight on were Jacques Baumel, Léo Hamon and Claude Raynal. I had cordial relations with all of them but not the sort of confidential intimacy that I had once shared with my absent friends.

I felt terribly alone.

On November 9, in the presence of the government, De Gaulle addressed the National Assembly in the Palais du Luxembourg, emphasizing the nature and importance of its role and its exclusive responsibility:

. . . to carry on the war, to restore the . . . authority of the state in all domains, to insure that justice is done, to reassume our proper role in the concert of the great powers. . . .

This last role France was already beginning to reassume. After years of equivocation the Allies had finally officially recognized De Gaulle's government. Proof was offered by the appearance of Winston Churchill and Anthony Eden in Paris on November 11, 1944.

A splendid autumn sun beamed down on the Champs-Elysées that day. A joyous, noisy crowd packed both sides of the avenue. Now and then a brightly colored balloon would float skyward.

Churchill, in blue-gray RAF battledress, accompanied De Gaulle to lay a wreath on the Tomb of the Unknown Soldier. On the official platform we ministers awaited their return.

A great cry arose and drifted toward us. As the spectators reached a pitch of enthusiasm, I caught sight of the Prime Minister standing beside De Gaulle in an open convertible. He greeted the crowd with his celebrated "V for victory" hand signal.

"Vive Churchill! Vive De Gaulle!" shouted the crowd, almost breaking through the police cordons.

Then came a parade of French and Allied troops.

Immense joy welled up in my breast. This procession, under this perfect sky, in the presence of these two great statesmen and in the

The Night Will End

midst of this sea of Parisians, was a fitting crown to our years of struggle.

I slept a little later than usual that morning of November 25. It was almost eight when I suddenly heard a nearby belfry begin to ring a full peal. Soon another peal echoed it, then another and another. As I threw open my window I saw windows opening everywhere.

All the bells of Paris were ringing, joined, as I later learned, by all the bells of every city and every town and every hamlet in the land. Leclerc's troops had just liberated Strasbourg. All France carilloned her thanksgiving and her joy.

Dawn

THE RETURN OF THE PRISONERS AND DEPORTEES

It was in Algiers, both in cabinet meetings and elsewhere, that I'd first heard the general discuss the guarantees that our country would need to live in peace. He believed that France's future security depended on our presence in the Rhine Valley, either in force by or means of a Rhenish buffer state independent of the Reich. The latter, he thought, should include not only the west bank of the river but also part of the east bank, and it should be economically and perhaps even politically attached to the West.

Since 1870 most thinking Frenchmen had been virtually obsessed with Germany. This was particularly true of the general's generation—that is, of men who had been just over twenty in 1914. This obsession had only been deepened by the terrible ordeal that Germany had inflicted on the world. Hence De Gaulle's major preoccupation was to prevent a reoccurrence of German aggression. By December 1944, when Germany's doom was a foregone conclusion, De Gaulle began to speak of this burning question on every available public occasion.

On January 25, for example, he declared to two hundred newsmen:

The Rhine is France's future security.

17

. . . Germany has repeatedly invaded France, and each time France has almost perished. Thus France wishes to have a solid presence the entire length of this natural frontier.

It was ostensibly to obtain a mutual assistance accord with the U.S.S.R. that De Gaulle flew to Moscow on November 27. Yet as we watched De Gaulle, General Juin and Georges Bidault board their plane that day, we were well aware of how happy he would be to see his Russian trip shake loose the grip in which the Anglo-Saxons had held him for four straight years. He was boldly reasserting the independence of French foreign policy.

We welcomed him back in Orly Airport two weeks later. Both his expression and Bidault's smile amply confirmed their deep satisfaction over the "Treaty of Alliance and Mutual Assistance" which the foreign ministers of the two countries had just initialed.

Though the treaty's role in international politics seemed rather obscure, it had tremendous repercussions on domestic affairs. Maurice Thorez, the secretary-general of the French Communist Party, who himself had also recently returned from Moscow, addressed the Central Committee of the Party on January 23, 1945, in terms that astounded his audience even more than it did French public opinion:

Public safety must be maintained by regular police forces which are constituted with this express function. The civil guards, and generally speaking all irregular armed groups [i.e., the "patriotic militias"] should be disbanded.

Concerning the Liberation Committee, he added:

. . . The local and departmental Liberation Committees must no longer try to supplant the proper municipal and departmental administrations. . . . Their task is not to administer but merely to aid those who do administer.

The militias disbanded and turned over their weapons (most of their weapons, anyway) with virtually no resistance. This abrupt curtailment of the unlawful activities of these various C.P. fronts

The Return of the Prisoners and Deportees

was not always to their members' liking, but they obeyed the Central Committee anyway. Thanks to the Moscow accords, the government now had a precious ally in—of all people—Maurice Thorez.

Shortly after my arrival in Paris I engaged Madeleine Gouze (the elder daughter of the Gouzes with whom Berty and I had stayed in Cluny during the spring of 1943) as my personal secretary.

Madeleine greeted me with a distressed look as I arrived in my office on December 12.

"Did you hear what happened this morning? It's René Hardy. He's been arrested!"*

"Arrested! Wait a minute. What happened?"

"Shortly after he checked in at the ministry this morning, some D.S.T. inspectors arrived with a warrant and took him away."

"Didn't he protest or demand some sort of explanation?"

"No, he just seemed weary and resigned."

I immediately rang Wybot, the director of the D.S.T.

"Frenay," he said, "we found a document in the files of the Marseilles Gestapo that proves they arrested Hardy on June 7, 1943, and that he immediately went over to them. The details of the document in question leave very little doubt concerning Hardy's guilt. The case is about to be opened, and it will involve an investigation of his alleged denunciation of General Delestraint and Jean Moulin. It seems virtually certain that he did denounce them."

I was totally crushed. Hardy a Gestapo agent? True, he'd almost been caught by the traitor "Multon" in a Paris-bound train. Two days later he'd told Bénouville that he'd escaped by jumping onto the tracks. But then what was that "document" in Marseilles?

I went to see Bénouville. I also rang Jacques Dhont and René La Combe. None of us could accept Hardy's guilt. Bénouville had observed him in prison in Toulon for an entire year, and nowhere can one judge a man better than in jail.

"I saw him right *after* the Gestapo was supposed to have caught

---

*Hardy, whom I had taken in my ministry in Algiers, had continued to work for me in Paris.

The Night Will End

him," said Bénouville, "and he said nothing to me about having been captured. If he'd become one of their agents, he would have informed on us at some point. That allegation is unfounded!"

Everybody from Combat agreed. As long as there was no conclusive evidence of his guilt, we would all defend him.

So began the notorious "Hardy Affair," which was to arouse public opinion and cause division in Resistance circles for many years thereafter. It was also to be thoroughly exploited by the Communist Party.

I was soon to become "the stoolpigeon's protector" and "the man who brought the traitor into his ministry."

Hardy's mistress, Lydie Bastien, lived only a few steps from me on the Avenue Léopold—II.

From time to time she came to see me. She was eager to fill me in on her many overtures to obtain testimony in Hardy's favor. With this aim she rushed about in an oddly febrile way.

Already in Algiers Hardy's passion for her had been plain to see. He'd seemed humble in her presence, while she'd treated him with a casual disdain that shocked me.

Now, strangely, his imprisonment seemed to have awakened her passionate devotion. She labored day and night in his cause.

She was an unnerving woman. In truth, she was *too* beautiful. Tall, slender and leggy, she "came on" in an offhand but really very studied way. She dressed elegantly if a bit too showily, and she loved to fasten her enormous, languid eyes on men in a kind of gentle but insistent provocation.

If worse came to worst, if Hardy were really proven guilty, it would mean that he'd gone over to the S.S. immediately after being caught—that is, without suffering any maltreatment whatever. This was unimaginable. Unless . . .

Unless the Germans had had some irresistible means of pressure at their disposal.

Such as, for example, a woman whom he utterly adored.

How was it that he had met her, anyway? Yes, he had met her *by accident*, in the Brasserie des Archers in Lyons. Probably he'd been overwhelmed by her sheer physical beauty. They'd become

The Return of the Prisoners and Deportees

lovers. Yet he knew nothing about her, nothing about her past or any of her doings.

Slowly a hypothesis grew in my mind: If Lydie, unbeknownst to René, had already been working for the Gestapo, everything could easily be explained.

Here was my scenario: *Hardy is arrested. The Germans inform him that his mistress is one of their agents. If he does not consent to work for them, they'll denounce her to the Resistance.*

This hypothesis (for which I of course had no proof at all) very neatly explained why Hardy, plunged into despair by this revelation and unable to bear the thought of Lydie's execution by the Resistance, might have accepted the Gestapo's offer. Thereafter she too would have been bound to him by their terrible secret.

One day Lydie invited me over for lunch. We were alone. She told me about various trips she'd made to Marseilles, Lyons and the Gard. She told me that she had found witnesses who could prove that from June 9 to 12 René Hardy had not been in the Gestapo's hands. I listened attentively, now and then asking her some brief question and generally creating a feeling of trust. She seemed delighted by the general turn in our conversation. Then, suddenly, with my eyes fixed on hers, I said, "Lydie, I'm convinced that if anyone is guilty in this business, it's you!"

Her eyes widened with horror. One by one great tears rolled down her cheeks. She did not protest. She did not even answer.

Without a word, I got up and left.

For two years René Hardy remained in prison awaiting the outcome of an endless judicial inquiry. For counsel he had retained M\ua^e Maurice Garçon, a young lion of the Paris bar and a future academician. All France awaited the impending trial with baited breath. It opened in the Seine department courthouse in January 1947. All the papers devoted long features to it. *L'Humanité, Libération, Action* and all the other pro-Communist organs insisted on his guilt and called for a death sentence.

We grieved to see our old comrade again, his eyes aflame and his emaciated body swimming in his old colonel's battledress.

Bénouville, La Combe and I were successively called to the witness stand by the defense. I said simply that I had observed Hardy's attitude toward Vichy and Nazi Germany from July 1940

The Night Will End

to June 1943. During these three years he had been a model of courage, ardor and efficiency. First in Combat, then in the M.U.R., he had created and then directed the Resistance railway-sabotage operations, dealing the enemy many a deadly blow. As long as no proof of his treason could be presented, I would refuse to believe in it.

My comrades said substantially the same thing.

Maurice Garçon, with his extraordinary gifts as a courtroom orator, gave a marvelous defense plea. There was no corroboration of the evidence of Hardy's arrest; thus, there was no proof that he'd ever gone over to the Gestapo. Garçon's argument was water-tight. On January 24, 1947, his client was acquitted. Cries of protest arose in the courtroom, but they were drowned out by thunderous applause.

But why, why had Lydie Bastien never been called to the witness stand?

Several days later, René, without Lydie, joined us for dinner. We'd laid a cheerful fire in the hearth. During the meal itself René spoke mostly of his latest prison experience and of his reflections on war, friendship and love. After dinner Chilina (now my wife) discreetly retired. We sat there alone, gazing thoughtfully at the flickering fire.

"René," I said, "we suffered from those accusations too. You know how overjoyed we were when you were acquitted. Yet for me this joy is not unalloyed. Certain points remain obscure. Maybe it's on this account that I don't feel that we've quite recaptured our old intimacy. There are two things I think you should explain. First, how does Lydie Bastien tie in to your story? Second, please tell me who, in your opinion, *did* denounce the Caluire meeting?"

Hardy fixed his gaze on the flaming logs and held out his palms for warmth. Then he looked deeply into my eyes and said, "You're right, Henri. But I can't talk now. I shall though. Soon."

Two months went by. Hardy never showed up.

He was again arrested by the D.S.T. on March 24, 1947. In the archives of the national sleeping-car firm a report dated January 8, 1943, had been found. It had been filed by the conductor on the

The Return of the Prisoners and Deportees

375

arrival of the Paris–Lyons train. It said that two travelers occupying the same compartment had been apprehended by the German police, who had escorted them off the train at Châlon-sur-Sâone. One of them was named René Hardy.

A lightning bolt struck me. It was all clear now. In that short, unaccounted-for interval of a few days, René Hardy had been captured by the Gestapo. He had not been roughed up, for he bore no traces of maltreatment. Then, saying nothing, he had recemented his ties with us. During the war so monstrous a lie would have entailed his execution.

And when he came to Algiers, then too he had lied! And when I brought him into my ministry, he had again lied! To his lawyer, Me Garçon, to the judges at his trial, to everyone he had lied! Worse still, he had written a four-column front-page article a few weeks ago for *Ce Matin* saying, "I jumped off the Paris–Lyons train en route," and for this abominable tissue of lies he'd been handsomely paid.

Before me, his boss, before his comrades, before all of us, he was guilty of the most execrable breach of faith that any human being could imagine!

Eventually, when the tumult of my emotions had died down, an infinite sorrow welled up in my breast. A deep friendship had been betrayed and cheapened and reduced to ashes.

Naturally *L'Humanité*, with the rest of the Communist papers in tow, vitriolically attacked those who had hitherto refused to accept Hardy's guilt—especially me:

The Communist Party has an especial right to accuse the contemptible stoolpigeon Hardy and all those who still back him for reasons of class hatred or personal interest.

(3/28/1947)

L'Humanité of April 6–7, 1947, ran the headline "TO THE DEFENDERS OF HARDY THE STOOLPIGEON: WE DEMAND AN EXPLANATION."

René Hardy was to remain in prison three years and two months. Just before Christmas in 1947 I got a phone call from a

The Night Will End

very distinguished-sounding woman. She rattled off her name, title and professional address.

"Monsieur, I have been a penitentiary visitress for twenty years. Before, during and after the war I have been able to alleviate the anguish of many convicts. For several months now I have been making weekly visits to a certain René Hardy, who is, I believe, a friend of yours."

"*Was*, Madame."

"Well, in any case, he gave me your name and address, and he seems especially attached to you. Since his incarceration he has been living in a moral hell. He feels abandoned by all his friends. He doesn't even know if he'll ever be tried, if a judicial inquiry will ever be opened or how long he'll be interned. I believe that some gesture or word from you would do him more good than all my visits. That's why I'm appealing to you now to help me."

"Madame, your words touch me. However, it is not for me to make a gesture but for René Hardy himself. I'm going to ask you to give him an oral message.

"In 1943 he concealed his arrest by the Gestapo. Not only has this fact rendered him highly suspect, but it also means that he failed in his duty to me, his boss. At the same time, he betrayed a noble friendship.

"Kindly remind him of the two questions I asked him last March after his release from Fresnes. Let him write me the answer on a scrap of paper. There's only one way for him to regain his comrades' friendship: to come clean."

Weeks, months passed. No sign from Hardy. I rang the prison visitress and asked her if she had passed on my message to him.

"Yes," she replied, "I did. He's writing a long memorandum for you which he has not yet finished."

"Madame," I said, "please tell him to spare himself the trouble. I'm not a judge, and I don't want a defense plea—just the simple truth in one or two pages."

I never got an answer.

Hardy was tried again in May 1950. Again Maurice Garçon was his defense counsel. Again I was called to the witness stand but this time for the prosecution. On the stand I repeated what I had already said during Hardy's first trial about the great services he

The Return of the Prisoners and Deportees

had performed, but this time I added, "In covering up his arrest by the Gestapo, Hardy betrayed our friendship and trust. He must be held accountable for a serious misdeed that leaves him open to the direst speculations. Nothing that I know can either explain or condone his failure to come clean."

Once again, Garçon got him off. In my eyes, however, his acquittal proved nothing.

Every Frenchman who followed that trial has his own convictions. I have mine. I have fully expressed them already and will do so again, if necessary, by refusing to shake hands with René Hardy.

December 1944. The war was still raging, and France was shouldering an ever-growing part of the war effort. General Billotte's division was now combat-ready, and three others, composed of an amalgam of F.F.I. troops and regulars, were awaiting marching orders. Strasbourg and part of the Bas-Rhin were already enjoying their new-found freedom.

On November 17, the very day on which we awaited De Gaulle's return from Moscow, the press announced a German offensive in the Ardennes. This forest was exactly where the Wehrmacht had so easily broken through our defenses in 1940, thus prefiguring our total defeat. The news grew daily more alarming.

As Christmas approached the general calmly informed us that Marshal von Rundstädt's offensive had hurled back its American adversaries and advanced several dozen miles west. The battle hung in the balance. Everything depended on the amount of time necessary to commit Allied strategic reserves. Nobody knew how long they would be in coming.

A new cloud of defeatism descended on Paris. Some spontaneous evacuation was noted. Rumors spread. People said there were no defense lines between Rundstädt's armor and the capital.

It was in this heavy and almost anguished spirit of foreboding that the year 1944 drew to a close.

De Gaulle now informed the Council of Ministers that General De Lattre, the field commander of the First French Army, had received an order from the American General Devers, the commander of the larger army group in the Alsace sector, to fall back

The Night Will End

into the Vosges. This would entail the evacuation of Strasbourg, leaving the Alsatian capital open to German occupation.

"Gentlemen," said De Gaulle, "the Americans regard this measure as necessary because they fear being attacked from the rear if the Germans swing south. I understand this fear, but there are better options than abandoning Alsace. The population cannot be evacuated. Only a few weeks ago it overwhelmingly demonstrated its attachment to France. It would be subjected to pitiless reprisals. No, France must defend Strasbourg with all her might! That is the order that I shall give De Lattre."

"Sir," I said, "I'm sure we all share your wish to see Alsace defended. On the other hand, General De Lattre must answer to the Allied High Command. He has received his orders. His failure to carry them out may be interpreted not only as a break-off of the alliance but also as a danger to the entire Allied troop build-up. It might even hold up the end of the war."

We debated the question for a while. It was clear that our decision would be momentous.

"Gentlemen," the general concluded, "it was the French government that attached General De Lattre to General Eisenhower in the first place. If an overriding national interest requires it, we can also withdraw him. However, I frankly don't think it will ever come to that. Both Churchill and I are scheduled to meet Eisenhower together in his GHQ. I'm sure that my view will prevail."

The cabinet meeting was adjourned. We hoped that De Gaulle could find a proper solution acceptable to all.

He did. Eisenhower countermanded his orders and changed his strategy. He managed to stem the German offensive anyway. Strasbourg was never evacuated.

In early February Colmar was liberated. On March 7, the first Allied troops forded the Rhine.

The winter of 1944–45 was harsh indeed. Coal was scarce. Our administrative offices were unheated. An Arctic cold reigned in my enormous office on the Avenue Foch. My colleagues and I worked with our coats and scarves on. When I had to write a note by hand

The Return of the Prisoners and Deportees

I would defrost my fingers before a little electric heater on my desk.

Our problem, though purely psychological, seemed highly important to me.

Our POWs, deportees and workers in Germany had been out of the nation for a long time now—the POWs for over four years. During their absence the country had changed enormously on moral, political and material levels. De Gaulle had replaced Pétain; France was once again at war; provisions were inadequate; communications were precarious; many towns and villages were half in ruins.

The prisoners and deportees had suffered and reflected in captivity. They had greatly changed, and so might find a changed homeland all the more distressing. Families would be welcoming home men who were quite different from those they had once known. We had to devote ourselves to promoting their mutual understanding.

Late in the year I called in my old friend Robert Soulage and offered him a new job. He was to acquaint the homecomers with the changed face of France.

In a few weeks he and his colleagues organized a daily evening radio broadcast for the French radio and the BBC. They also put out a newspaper of four tabloid pages called *Votre France* that was printed in England at 500,000 copies an issue and dropped over the camps each week by air. Fourteen issues came out, followed by a pamphlet on the occupation and the Resistance that was handed out to each ex-prisoner during the repatriation process. (Such activities were bound to have a big influence on the ex-prisoners' mentality, a fact that was not lost on the C.P. Soulage's service was soon packed with Communist infiltrators.)

With the government's blessing and the cooperation of all the POW associations and the labor unions, my ministry organized a "Week of the Absent One." Its aim was to prompt all France to devote some sincere thought to those whose homecoming we were preparing.

On December 31, General De Gaulle, accompanied by the diplomatic corps, inaugurated an exposition at the Grand Palais in Paris called "The Barbed-Wire Front." I explained its purpose in a brief address:

The Night Will End

. . . To those who have never known the monotony of those endless days and hopeless months, to those who have not witnessed the prodigious moral reawakening which took place in the camps, it is necessary to show what the life of these men was like and what sort of spirit has now arisen in them.

In this sense, it is the soul of the camps that we have tried to bring you in these exhibition halls. . . .

In the silence of those camps, through the ordeals suffered there, men's souls have been enriched. . . .

After their return, they will contribute their enormous moral strength to France. . . .

In our thoughts, we must associate the POWs, the deportees and the forced laborers . . . with special reverence for our comrades of the Resistance, who fell . . . after willingly confronting torture and death.

A magnificent spirit of solidarity swept through France. Responding to a union-originated appeal, the workers contributed a day's worth of salaries to the remaining captives. A billion francs were collected.

At the same time 432 centers were created to focus the efforts of the many volunteer organizations that had vowed to help us.

By March 1945 the nation was psychologically prepared to welcome its sons home.

The departmental Liberation Committees were increasingly hostile to the government, especially in the former southern zone. They accused it of not carrying out the purge with the necessary speed and firmness. No doubt they mourned the passing of the popular tribunals and improvised military courts.

By late 1944 "special courts" were functioning in every French department. Their much-reproached foot-dragging was really just the natural consequence of their respect for due process of law. In several departments, however, suspects had been kidnapped and even executed by lynch mobs.

To help out the judiciary, the cabinet—at the instigation of the Keeper of the Seals—approved the constitution of a number of "magistrates' courts" attached to the regular courts. They had provisional or first-instance jurisdiction over minor felonies. These

The Return of the Prisoners and Deportees

"magistrates' courts" were empowered to put the prisoners, once convicted, in a state of "national contempt"—*indignité nationale,* as it was called—entailing their forfeiture of civil rights and exclusion from certain public offices and professions. Lastly, a special high court was set up to try Vichy's ex-ministers.

In reality, the southern Liberation Committees' beef against the government was entirely unfounded. In late December, François de Menthon reported to the cabinet on the functioning of the courts. Almost 20,000 cases were under review, and 24,000 verdicts had been rendered, of which 300 had resulted in death sentences and 500 in forced-labor sentences.

Of course every big daily had put together a team of court reporters who dared not be caught napping. Every morning in *Combat* I would read the accounts of the current trials.

Yet as the months went by, and as the occupation and its horrors receded into the past, I reacted with growing skittishness to the announcements of trials and executions in the press. Two years earlier, in the heat of battle, I would gladly have gunned down the big collaborators with my own hand. Now they were merely disarmed opponents, men brought to their knees. Still, they were not prisoners of war. Some were bloodthirsty criminals who, if they had won, would have turned France into a Nazi fief and hunted us down like rabbits. Others had morally armed our torturers with their writings and public addresses. Again I saw the grave faces of Berty Albrecht and Claudius Billon and the youthful smile of André Bollier.

Sometimes echoes reached us from the prisons and execution squads. Some of the condemned called for national reconciliation and fell with dignity and courage. Justice must be done; it was a terrible and inexorable law. Yet I couldn't stop myself from pitying these men in their suffering, their humiliation and their occasional courage before death. Whatever their crimes, they were still human beings.

They were still my brothers.

We were working now hand in glove with the Red Cross. My relations with its delegate, M. Pradervand, were excellent. He was

The Night Will End

a distinguished Swiss diplomat who spoke several languages fluently and wrote French and German equally well. He was also a dogged worker. His services and mine collaborated cordially and efficiently. This was a real windfall, for it was precisely at this time that the condition of our POWs and deportees became highly alarming.

We had undertaken very delicate negotiations with the German government. To my relief they ended successfully between January and March.

In France, we managed to assemble 425 freight cars that could henceforth be used inside the Reich for the provisionment of the camps. However, the state of the German railways rendered their use problematical. Hence my ministry also obtained one hundred new trucks from Renault, and the Allies added almost four hundred more. The International Committee of the Red Cross received permission to drive them into Germany.

In columns of four to fifteen vehicles, loaded with food stores, medicine and medical personnel, these trucks began to wind their way into Germany. As it happened, just at this moment the advancing Allies began to liberate the deportee camps, and their ex-inmates were flocking west and north.

Painted white to protect them from air attack, our trucks soon overtook long and heart-rending columns of deportees. Our medics fed the able-bodied, treated the lame, footsore and wounded and tried to ease the agonies of the dying. Several postwar testimonials by deportees proved that our "white trucks" had saved thousands of lives.

The Red Cross worked on indefatigably. We gave them our okay on a rather unusual project: an attempt to exchange German civilians detained in France against French deportees in Germany, starting with women and old men.

Direct negotiations with Heinrich Himmler, the supreme commander of the S.S. and overlord of the camps, were initiated in late January. They were arduous indeed. The Germans wanted a simple one-to-one exchange, a principle that obviously worked against us, for we held only a few hundred German women (not civilians, actually, but Wehrmacht auxiliary corpswomen, or "gray

The Return of the Prisoners and Deportees

rats," as they were called). In the end, however, an accord was reached: We released all the German women, and all the Frenchwomen were returned to us.

It was in late March, six weeks before the Armistice, that the first convoy of Frenchwomen left Mauthausen. Count Bernadotte, the president of the Swedish Red Cross, obtained the repatriation of the women interned in Ravensbrück via Lübeck to Denmark and Sweden. As the hostilities in Europe ground to a halt, ten convoys arrived in the free zone.

Neither I nor any of the others who were there that day will ever forget the arrival of the first train of homecoming women in the Gare de Lyons. We shall never forget those emaciated faces at the compartment windows, some numb or spellbound, others full of frantic joy.

Rooted to the platform, half choked, our eyes smarting with tears, we were making our first contact with the sinister reality of the holocaust. The coming days and months were to unveil it in all its horror.

About February 10 we learned that President Roosevelt, Marshal Stalin and Prime Minister Winston Churchill had met secretly somewhere at Yalta. Here the conclusion of the war was broadly determined. The battle was to be waged until Germany had unconditionally surrendered. Her territory was to be occupied by the three Great Powers and by France. A Charter of Europe based on accepted democratic principles was to legitimize the partition of Europe into two spheres of influence. The Allies were also to send representatives to San Francisco in April to lay the foundation for the United Nations.

For De Gaulle, France's failure to receive an invitation to Yalta was an affront. Though she was in no way bound by decisions made in her absence, these decisions must be fully known. Only after receiving a detailed transcript would we issue our own communiqué.

As for Roosevelt's subsequent invitation to meet him in Algiers, De Gaulle rejected it out of hand. The general found it unseemly that the French chief of state had been "invited" to the French city of Algiers by a foreign chief of state. Furthermore, such a meeting

The Night Will End

would give the false impression that France subscribed to the Yalta accords. As for us ministers, never had it been clearer that we were mere extras in this drama. De Gaulle was *not* going to Algiers. That was that.

In the days that followed, his attitude was judged scandalous by most of the French and world press. But De Gaulle was hardly scandal-shy. I doubt that even F.D.R.'s death a few weeks later led him to regret his intransigence.

In late January the National Front, the M.L.N., the Communists and the Socialists all caucused. Already everyone was talking about the municipal elections, the first real test of all political blocs, both old and new. A long armed vigil had begun.

Then, just before the congress, De Gaulle said offhandedly to his cabinet: "Gentlemen, I'm sure you agree that it would be undignified if members of the government were publicly to oppose one another. The nation would get rather a wretched picture of its leaders. I have no objection to your attending your party caucuses. However, I shall demand of you that you refrain from taking the floor."

I was silenced, silenced in a decisive moment for the Resistance! How terribly disappointed I was—yet I had to admit that the general had a point.

I had my speech mimeoed, for I wanted it distributed to each delegate. Alas, the written word was a poor substitute for the podium, for from experience I knew that I could command an audience's attention.

Five hundred delegates arrived from all corners of France. There were also two or three hundred observers and journalists. The great hall of the Mutualité was buzzing like a beehive. Speech followed speech: the stentorian voice and close reasoning of André Philip, the subtle dialectic and disarming smile of Emmanuel D'Astier, the anti-government harangues of Pierre Hervé and finally the incantatory grandiloquence of André Malraux, who tried vainly to "rise above the melee" and proclaim an exalted goal to "electrify the masses." (With some surprise I finally realized that this visionary's proposals actually boiled down to a plea for the nationalization of credit!)

The Return of the Prisoners and Deportees

Claudius Petit presented a long political report. It was serious, dense, well thought out and had a distinctly "laborite" orientation. In fact, this was the first time that the expression "laborite"— *travailliste*—was publicly used in France.

Yet one could feel that the congress's true concerns lay elsewhere. Everyone was obsessed by the question of which faction would rule the M.L.N. of tomorrow. This was the question I too had discussed in my "written speech." After attacking the "September resisters," I once again tackled the issue of sectarianism:

. . . each one of us knows men and women, and sometimes members of his own family, who, though unquestionably patriotic, followed a road that was not our own . . . The enemy's triumph will be total if fine Frenchmen who were victims of propaganda are ostracized from the national community . . .

This led me to the problem of the national purge:

. . . One must boldly and publicly proclaim that if traitors, profiteers and collaborationist officials must and shall be punished, the nation as a whole, including those who never joined our ranks, has no vengeance to fear from the Resistance and shall even be encouraged by us to help in the reconstruction. . . .

The purge that threatens everyone, the false image we have assumed as a result of the eleventh-hour joiners who are more eager to exact vengeance than to serve their country, and the excesses of a few so-called "resisters," have brought about a rift that may well result in our estrangement from the nation. . . .

Then I explained why a merger of the M.L.N. and the National Front would doom us either to political paralysis or to becoming a C.P. satellite. I recommended our

. . . adherence to the "laborite" bloc consisting of the O.C.M. and Libération-Nord—that is, of groups with Socialist and labor majorities. This union, reinforced by our own group, should invite the Socialist Party and the M.R.P. to join it. . . .

The Night Will End

Thus a large bloc could be put together representing over half the French people. . . .

It is no exaggeration to say that together we can work out a . . . formula that will both ally and transcend the two forms of socialism—the Marxian, and the Christian—which, in their universalism, are characteristic of the French mainstream. . . .

Clarity is indispensable . . . even if at the price of scission, which I believe preferable to slow disintegration. . . .

The debates both public and private went on for five days in an atmosphere of emotionalism and occasionally of hatred. Two motions were submitted: Pierre Hervé (seconded by D'Astier, Degliame, Albert Bayet and Kriegel-"Valrimont") called for the fusion of the M.L.N. and the National Front, while Philip and Baumel (seconded by Claudius Petit, Malraux, Leenhardt, Morandat and Viannay) rejected not only this merger but also *any* merger "tending to induce factionalization"—i.e., including the one I'd recommended. It also called for a "creation of a national federation of all [Resistance] movements without exception."

On January 26, at 3:00 A.M., the anti-merger motion was passed by a large majority: 250 aye's to 115 no's.

The worst had been avoided, but the M.L.N. had still failed to set itself any concrete goals, and time was passing swiftly. Perhaps the new directorate, in which the D'Astier–Copeau clique was now a weak minority, would be able to stop equivocating. Perhaps it would even be able to build that "labor movement" (*mouvement travailliste*) that the Communists so terribly feared.

The municipal elections were to be held all over France on April 29, with the runoffs on May 13.

I'd opposed this decision in the Council of Ministers, for I believed it a mistake to hold elections before the return of the POWs and deportees. Now they would have no representation in the municipal councils.

I had other reasons for opposing the elections. What I could not say openly before the Council of Ministers was that the M.L.N. plenary congress had still not chosen a political platform. Its internal rifts certainly could not be mended before the opening of

The Return of the Prisoners and Deportees

the election campaign on April 14. Things might even be aggravated by some National Front ploy in the communes.

The National Front caucus had convened, as if by accident, several days after our own and had voted to effect a merger with the M.L.N. on the commune level—against our plenary congress's express will. Obviously the National Front wanted to put forward electoral lists representing a bogus "national unanimity." This subterfuge would win the Communists preponderancy in the municipal councils.

Then Jacques Duclos, representing the C.P. to the National Front congress, declared:

. . . the Communist Party shall fight side by side with all Frenchmen and Frenchwomen of good will, without inquiring into their past.

In effect, anybody who wanted his role in the occupation forgotten, especially if he had collaborated, would be attracted by this promise to leave his past unturned. Such people would make especially docile C.P. militants, for they could be kept in line through implicit blackmail. They'd soon be made to understand that any deviation on their part would lead to the revelation of their shady past.

In the short time left before the elections we had both to warn the public against this deceit and to put together a coherent M.L.N. program. The task seemed impossible unless De Gaulle himself publicly endorsed the M.L.N. Actually, I had few illusions that the general would accept our offer. But I had to try anyway.

A relaxed De Gaulle received me in his office. I reminded him of the deep desire for national renewal that had animated the Resistance under the occupation and which could not be satisfied by the old parties. Then I drew his attention to the methods employed by the Communists and their allies to paralyze our efforts.

"Sir, if our 'labor movement' does not make an open bid for electoral support right now, it will never get another chance. Its place on the political chessboard will be usurped by the old parties, especially the C.P. There is only one way of exorcizing this

The Night Will End

danger—that you yourself call upon the nation to join in our movement of reunification, that you yourself champion it."

De Gaulle followed me without interrupting, moving his head from left to right and sticking out his lower jaw the way he often did. Then he answered, "No, Frenay, I shall not do it. It's not my role. I understand your fears, and I know that the current mayhem in the Consultative Assembly and elsewhere isn't likely to appease them. But believe me, men like you have only one option: to enter the parties and to change them from inside. Everything else is an illusion."

The future was to prove that De Gaulle was simply not the right man to take up this challenge. When the war was at its height, he had, under pressure from such men as Christian Pineau, openly declared himself the resolute enemy of the oligarchies, the big money, the vested interests. At the time I had thought—and I wasn't the only one—that he was expressing Socialist or at least proto-Socialist convictions. But I was wrong. He was merely following his *étatiste* instincts. We had thought he was Proudhon when he was simply Richelieu.

The Allied troops broke into Germany on March 7. Except for the "Atlantic pockets," all our territory had now been liberated. I made an inspection tour of our repatriation centers from the North Sea to the Swiss border. On the whole I was favorably impressed. Up north Raoul Jué had done a fine job. His centers were ready and waiting. On the other hand, our centers in the Ardennes, which had just been finished at the price of tremendous efforts, had been occupied by American troops and left in a shambles. There was a gaping hole between Givet and Strasbourg, for here fierce battles had taken place only three weeks earlier. Between Strasbourg and the Swiss border, however, our centers were growing steadily.

In passing I tried of course to accelerate the whole process. In fact, a remarkable job was about to be completed in record time. Bases were set up to provision the centers, each one containing four days of food stores per homecomer.

The Return of the Prisoners and Deportees

It was distressing that SHAEF (Supreme Headquarters of the Allied European Forces) still refused to countenance the idea of aerial repatriation. Brigadier General Lee, the sympathetic British liaison officer attached to my ministry, had failed to swing the Allied Chiefs of Staff. How much simpler it would have been to prepare repatriation centers well inside France and away from the combat zones!

The military repatriation corps now comprised over 10,000 persons. Since most of them had to work inside the theater of operations, these noncombatants were accorded "relative military rank" according to the importance of their jobs. Diplomatic missions were eventually sent to all those countries where our captives had been detained or had sought refuge: Sweden, Denmark, the Soviet Union, Yugoslavia, Hungary, Italy and Austria.

In France I tried to coordinate my own work with that of all the other organizations representing our displaced nationals. Twice a week they conferred with me in the framework of a so-called "Council of the Absent One." They were eventually to shoulder much of the burden of welcoming the homecomers and reintegrating them into their families and the nation as a whole. For this program (which we called "the return to life") I raised large subsidies. One group, the National Federation of Prisoners of War, was allocated fully 570 million francs in 1945.

Hardly had I returned from my border tour when an aide burst into my office. "*Monsieur le ministre*! Last night the Longuyon center received the first group of displaced persons!"

The Great Return had begun.

Germany was now caught in a vice. A total offensive had been unleashed from both east and west. The Luftwaffe had virtually disappeared from the skies. Yet despite the overwhelming physical superiority of the Allies the Wehrmacht fought on undaunted.

As the Anglo-American troops advanced they began to liberate POWs and forced laborers. Scores of thousands of these ex-prisoners were now clogging the roads, blocking troop movement and supply lines. Soon they might even jeopardize the battle's outcome.

At this point the Allied field commanders began to load them on

The Night Will End

the empty supply trucks that were heading toward the rear. Within three weeks almost 200,000 men who had been penned up in the Rhineland were shunted back into France.

Our national railway company (S.N.C.F.) soon informed me that their evacuation had become highly irregular. The logistics of the situation demanded that they be conveyed not to the repatriation centers we had so laboriously set up but to Paris! On March 30 I gave the railway people my okay, though I was very worried about the pressing new need to equip our already overcrowded capital with the equipment and manpower to "process" between 5,000 and 10,000 men per day.

A few days later, on the morning of April 11, Brigadier General Lee and his American counterpart entered my office looking very embarrassed.

"Mr. Minister," they said, "we've got good news for you. SHAEF has consented to let its planes be used for repatriation purposes."

"Well, I'm utterly delighted. When does SHAEF want to get started?"

"Er, well . . . it's been decided that the first aircraft will land in about forty-eight hours."

"Forty-eight hours! How in God's name can I prepare for them in forty-eight hours? And just how many men are you going to be flying in per day?"

"Orders are to transport eight thousand men per day."

"Eight thousand men! Good Lord—that's about three whole regiments! Gentlemen, you've saddled me with a horrendous problem. However, I think we can manage it—on one condition: that I myself can specify the destinations of the transport planes and farm the men out to various centers."

"We're terribly sorry, sir, but the planes must land on the airstrips where the food and materiel for the front-line troops are located. And . . . well . . . those airstrips are all in the Greater Paris area."

"Gentlemen, that's impossible! Paris is overcrowded as it is. I have a standing order to keep my operations out of the capital."

If these thousands of air passengers were to be added to the already arriving trainloads we would soon have 15,000 men per day

The Return of the Prisoners and Deportees

swarming into Paris! What could I do? I had pretty good reasons for refusing the offer; the situation was our allies' fault anyway. On the other hand, I would have felt bad about condemning tens of thousands of impatient men to a near desperate situation in Germany.

If I were to accept, we'd have to improvise the equivalent of two frontier centers in two days. Moreover, we'd have to feed and "process" an enormous floodtide of human beings in which ex-militiamen, S.S. and enemy agents would surely try to hide.

Well, so what! I would accept the challenge!

After an on-the-spot interministerial conference we decided to equip the Gare d'Orsay as a frontier center. Five hundred workers in three daily eight-hour shifts finished the job in the record time of seventeen days.

I also requisitioned the Reuilly barracks, the Vélodrome d'Hiver and the warehouses of the Saint-Martin riverlocks and converted them into shelters. The Gaumont Palace and Rex cinemas (with respectively 3,000 and 2,000 seats) also became transit centers.

The Hôtel Lutétia on the Left Bank, then occupied by general staff officers, was also requisitioned for the deportees. (I'd finally convinced the Allies to give the deportees priority in the repatriation process.)

Lastly, to deal with a possible mass deluge of prisoners, a large Parisian circus was turned into a mobile repatriation center.

This extraordinary effort was accomplished by my ministry in concert with the POW associations, the French Red Cross and other groups such as the service of Etienne Ader, a government appraiser who became the director of repatriation in the capital. All of them gave of their time unsparingly, and many caught no sleep for days on end. We proved that in exceptional circumstances our national solidarity was no myth.

By the end of April we had repatriated 330,000 ex-captives.

While we were facing up to our onerous responsibilities day and night, and often almost collapsing under the strain, the Communists and their allies launched a violent campaign against me personally. It was to last several months.

They were afraid of the influence I might wield over these

The Night Will End

millions of returning Frenchmen who were bound to have a big say in the future. The C.P. had not forgotten my oft-repeated pledge that these homecomers would one day actively join in the renewal of our nation. Hence they decided to cast a slur on me in the eyes of these men and, if possible, to stir up their hatred. They pursued their goal relentlessly.

The signal for this general offensive was given as I was presenting my ministerial budget to the Assembly in late March. Raymond Guyot and "Philippe Dechartre" (who then headed the P.D.R. subcommittee) expressed themselves in particularly venomous terms whose obvious immoderacy did not in fact serve their purposes. Of course I fired back with a denunciation of their demagoguery. The entire Communist press, from *L'Humanité* to the humblest neighborhood newsletter, broadcast the same attacks and slogans. In this way they hoped to work up the families of all the "absent ones" against me.

Each morning I'd thumb through the dozens of clippings in the "Press" tray on my desk. An example:

. . . The work [of the P.D.R. minister] shows zero net results—below zero as far as repatriation and absorption are concerned. . . ."

(Raymond Guyot, *L'Humanité*, 2/28/45)

Several times the Communist papers noted that my representatives had not shown up for the arrival of such and such a train in such and such a Paris railway station. This is true. Mysterious calls, supposedly coming from my ministry, would sometimes "inform" the welcoming teams that the expected train had been held up for several hours and that they could catch a short breather. Lies, of course. The train would arrive on time, at which point M.N.P.G.D. people would mingle among the homecomers and point out the callousness of the minister of prisoners. The Communist press went wild:

. . . Monsieur Frenay's plans include the bottling-up of the prisoners in their camps for a period of up to eight months after the Liberation. . . .

(*La Voix du Peuple*, Lyons, March 6, 1945)

The Return of the Prisoners and Deportees

Never before had I been exposed to a full-scale smear campaign. I won't try to hide that I suffered terribly. What I didn't know was that the mud-slinging had only just started.

The war was drawing to a close. F.D.R. was never to see the victory toward which he had so intelligently and so tenaciously led his people. On April 12 the American President died of the disease whose ravages his face had plainly revealed for many months.

His successor was a virtual unknown. Harry Truman had been all but hidden behind his gigantic predecessor. Yet it was he who would have to make and preserve the peace. Maybe he was another Wilson—maybe just a small-town politico in a big pair of boots.

The American and Russian troops were converging. On the 25th they met on the Elbe. War correspondents took photos of GIs and Soviet infantrymen embracing one another. Hundreds of thousands of German prisoners had been taken, among them beardless youths of fifteen and men of sixty years and more.

Then General De Larminat stormed the "Atlantic pockets" with French troops. By late May, all France was free.

André Favereau, the head of my staff, walked into my office smiling broadly and holding out a letter written in pencil. My eye went straight to the signature—Claude Bourdet!

Dear old Claude was alive! But what condition was he in?

Each day we learned more horrible details about the state in which the Americans had found the camps: the gaschambers, the charnel houses, the appalling physical state of the survivors, the rampant typhus epidemic. The tales of the first inmates to be set free gradually enabled the press to acquaint an at first incredulous and then appalled public with the terrible treatment of the deportees.

Though we did all we could to speed up the repatriation, our officers were seldom authorized by the Allies to enter the camps. The return journeys of the deportees were often pure pandemonium, and priority was all too frequently given to various grandees instead of to the seriously ailing or to the freedom fighters of the Resistance.

The Night Will End

Claude was emaciated now. Yet he still had the same brilliant eyes and the same sly smile that I knew so well. On April 27 he addressed the nation over the radio:

. . . to live among one's own kind, to be free on a free soil . . . to hear French voices speaking freely and to read a free press. . . . These are the things we really notice on our return. There's still much to do, but we have waited and hoped so long that hope has become our very nature. . . .

Do not try to share your worries or problems all at once with the deportees. . . . Let them see things for themselves. Their way of seeing will never be quite the same as yours. Share with them the joys and simple hopes of the early days of the Liberation. . . . For the Liberation has opened up new horizons. Nothing is finished, everything has just begun.

In effect, Claude felt—as I did—that the role of us resisters was by no means over. He too wanted to militate within the M.L.N. But first he needed some rest.

Everything had just begun. Those were his words. In fact, "everything" had begun a few months ago but not exactly as we'd planned. It didn't take him long to realize it.

By rail and air the repatriation process went on. Each time that I was informed of the imminent arrival of some old friend I would go to welcome him or her home.

But the others! Where were they? Where were Jacques Renouvin, Marcel Peck and Jean-Guy Bernard? Where was poor General Delestraint? Weeks, months passed. Little by little we were forced to admit the terrible truth. We would never see them again.

Hitler and Goebbels were no longer to be heard on the German radio. Although we didn't know it, they had already committed suicide in their bunker. Admiral Doenitz was now responsible for an occupied and ruined Germany, bled white by a merciless war. The end was at hand.

Early in the afternoon of May 7 the interministerial phone rang.

The Return of the Prisoners and Deportees

A few hours ago the Germans had surrendered. The capitulation had been signed simultaneously in Paris and in Berlin. The nightmare of Europe was over.

In vain I struggled to feel properly overjoyed. I could not, perhaps because my comrades who had not lived to witness the victory were still with me in spirit.

The evening newspapers and the radio brought the great news to the country at large. May 8 became "V-E Day." It and the following day were declared state holidays. I mingled in the crowds on the boulevards and in the Champs-Elysées. Yes, joy was surely in the air; the streets were thronged with revelers. Impromptu parades wended their way toward the Arc de Triomphe. Motorists honked and passengers waved home-made flags.

That afternoon all the bells of Paris were pealing. Artillery salvos echoed from the outskirts of town. Yet I had the feeling that there was something forced about these manifestations of joy. They certainly couldn't stand comparison with the collective delirium that had come over Lyons on November 11, 1918.

I was thirteen years old then, but the picture had remained firmly etched in my memory: the crowds cheering with abandon, the strangers kissing in the streets, the spontaneous circle dances, the roman candles shooting upward from nowhere and the awkwardly improvised tricolors floating from windows as far as the eye could see.

That day France had been the great victor. Today, each one of these men and women walking beside me was aware that our role in the victory had been small indeed and that far away in the antipodes the war was raging on. That evening there were *bals populaires* and dancing in the streets, but something was missing.

Apparently it was a different story in Moscow and New York. There V-E Day had been the triumph that France had only feigned to celebrate.

Exactly one week later in the Consultative Assembly De Gaulle gave a wonderful address. As is well known, he had a knack for doing this in exceptional circumstances:

As a state, as a power, as a doctrine, the Reich has been totally destroyed. . . .

The Night Will End

He reminded the nation of the condition of France on her entry into the war in 1939, of the defeatism of Vichy and of the birth and development of the Resistance:

. . . before our goal could be attained, a national action was needed, a single-minded, independent and sovereign action embracing both the interior and the exterior, an action that would refuse to abdicate any of the rights of the state before anyone. . . .

Our effort had at all costs to be undivided. Only thus could France be indivisible. . . .

In honor of the dead, both civilian and military, he said:

. . . The thought of you rendered yesterday's grieving sadly sweet. Your sacrifice is today the reason for our pride. Your glory shall always be the companion of our hopes. . . .

And, turning toward the future, he concluded:

. . . The end of the war is not a completion. For the Fourth Republic it is only a beginning. Forward, then, forward to the great task of work, unity and renewal! May our victory also mark a new leap forward!

The audience listened with baited breath to the general's speech, occasionally breaking into unanimous and enthusiastic applause. Joy and pride swelled within me. Never before—even in the Chaillot last year—had I heard a "Marseillaise" as grand, as beautiful and as powerful as that which we joined De Gaulle in singing, as with a single voice, on that May 15, 1945.

The Return of the Prisoners and Deportees

THE MYSTIQUE OF UNITY

The mystique of unity—including union with the Communists—was as powerful as ever.

The Communist Party had succeeded in convincing many people that "anticommunism is the beginning of fascism," thus casting suspicion on anyone opposed to the Communists and their tactics.

Albert Bayet, a commentator who did not even belong to the C.P., went so far as to write in the newspaper *Action* that "non-communism leads to fascism," surely a record-setting dictum in the annals of intellectual extravagance!

Certain regional groups succeeded in blocking all bulletins of the political bureau's directives, thereby inciting the departmental organizations to revolt against the M.L.N.'s apparent inaction.

Minority cabals also proliferated within the F.L.N. (Women of the National Liberation) and the J.L.N. (Youth of the National Liberation). Here too the minority wing instilled division and confusion, thus disheartening even the staunchest of our militants.

The minority wing also wielded great influence over those newspapers theoretically connected with the M.L.N. Eventually each paper began to adopt its own editorial position in total disregard for directives from the na-

18

tional leadership.

It was clear that the Communist Party, through the agency of a few M.L.N. members, was trying to paralyze and to divide the entire Resistance movement.

Internal friction prevented the M.L.N. from forming—without union or compromise with the C.P.—a genuine rally of democratic and Socialist forces. The outcome of this total disorder was that in the municipal elections of April 29 and May 13 not one non-Communist Resistance candidate was slated anywhere in France. Bereft of precise directives, the various regional M.L.N. sections adopted totally contradictory positions. As a bloc, the Resistance had revealed just how impotent it really was. The election returns confirmed this impotence, while at the same time sanctifying the resurrection of the old political parties.

In late May the chestnut trees on the Avenue Foch blossomed. Perhaps because the European war was finally over, the spring seemed more limpid and lovely and sweet-scented than ever before. Had it not been for the jeering chorus beneath my office windows I would have been entirely satisfied with the manner in which the repatriation had taken place.

Every day the C.P. put together a deputation of a few dozen carefully monitored men who would camp until evening on the front lawn, chanting "Frenay, our clothes!" or "Frenay, our discharge pay!" or "Frenay, resign!" Naturally they were hoping that I'd call in the police, that there would be a scuffle with a few casualties to serve as "the victims of the sinister Frenay, Pucheu's protégé." I certainly preferred their raucous serenade to the trap that had been set for me.

One day, while I was in conference, a highly distressed Madeleine Gouze stuck her head through the doorway to my office. As she had standing orders not to bother me at such moments, I made her an urgent gesture to leave me alone.

Hardly had the visitor left my office when she rushed in, holding out a request slip for an audience.

"Look at this," she said. "You won't believe it."

I read, "Lunel, known as 'Multon.'"

"Multon"! The traitor, the man who'd gone over to the Gestapo,

The Mystique of Unity

who'd had dozens of our comrades, among them Chevance—
"Bertin," arrested in Marseilles and who'd laid the ambush in
which Berty had been caught—"Multon" had actually come to see
me!

I immediately rang Wybot, the D.S.T. chief, informed him of
"Multon's" incredible visit and gave him his address.

"My dear Wybot," I said, "I want that man apprehended by this
evening at the latest. In any case, whenever you get him, no
matter how late, ring me here or at home."

The next morning at about 6:30 the phone rang.

"Roger Wybot here. Sir, we arrested 'Multon' less than an hour
ago."

"Good! Where is he now?"

"At my headquarters in the Rue des Saussaies."

"Tell your people I'll be over before eight."

I dressed absent-mindedly, lost in thought. Obviously "Multon"
had indeed given Madeleine his true address. What could he want
of me?

I found him sitting in the corner of a small room in D.S.T.
headquarters. As I entered he rose hesitantly. I wondered if he'd
have the nerve to extend his hand. No, he merely let his head
droop, silent, expectant. But what in God's name was he expecting?

"'Multon,' you came to see me yesterday afternoon in my office.
You are fully aware that I know of your crimes and that I'm alive
today only in spite of your efforts. Yet you still want to speak to me.
Well, what is it?"

He raised his head. His face was as round and meaty as ever. His
eyes, beneath his thick glasses, seemed swollen with sorrow.

"I'll tell you the whole story. Then maybe you'll understand why
I came to see you—you, Henri Frenay, 'Tavernier,' 'Gervais,' you,
my old chief."

And so he told me how he'd consented to become a Gestapo
agent on the very day of his arrest.

"I was afraid. It was Dungler* himself who questioned and
threatened me. To avoid being tortured I told him I would work for

*Dungler, known as "Delage," was the Gestapo chief for Marseilles.

The Night Will End

him, with the secret hope that I would escape shortly. But they were stronger than me. I was tailed everywhere, forced to finger one, two, then ten comrades. You see, they held my whole family in the Poitou as hostages. So I just went on and on. Oh, I was a coward!"

"But what about Berty? Did you *have* to inform on her?"

"It was you they wanted, it was you the trap was set for. But you didn't show."

"All right, go on. Then what?"

"I had only one desire in life—to slip out of their clutches. In early nineteen forty-four I gladly agreed to perform a mission for them in North Africa, figuring that over there I could escape. And I did. I even landed in Provence at the head of an army unit, happy, in a way, that I had ransomed my honor—at least in my own eyes. I fought all winter long in the Vosges, and I even received a commendation for valor. I hadn't been so happy in years.

"I also managed to get in touch with my family, though in secret, for I was sure that the French police had not forgotten me. Sure enough, my family was under surveillance. It was impossible for me to pick up where I'd left off.

"I started to reconsider my situation. I couldn't live forever under a false name. I couldn't hide from everyone. And I couldn't stand being an outcast anymore. For that's what I am—a pariah."

Then, humbly raising his eyes to mine, he concluded: "You were my chief, you were the head of Combat, in which, after all, I served a very long time. My only way out was to turn myself in to you. That's why I came here yesterday."

His confession, though delivered in a monotone, had by degrees distressed and then overwhelmed me. I have never been able to hate, and this downcast man aroused my pity more than my aversion.

If, like millions of his countrymen, he had stayed at home in moral hibernation he would never have run the risk of being a coward. He might even have become a brilliant F.F.I. fighter in August 1944.

For all that, I knew that this man, however pitiful, was still responsible for an appalling amount of agony and death.

The Mystique of Unity

"'Multon', you say that you have come to put your fate in my hands, but only Justice can decide that fate. I think you know what the verdict will be."

"Multon" was soon brought to trial, and, several months later, he was shot.

Meanwhile, the headlines blazed with the story of an important trial about to open in Dijon. Several dozen Frenchmen accused of being Abwehr agents were to be arraigned. Distractedly I ran through the list of names, then caught my breath.

Jean-Paul Lien!

It was not a common name. This had to be the same fellow I'd recruited in 1941 and sent to Toulouse to organize our movement there. Time had revealed him to be a very mediocre organizer. Yet, early in 1942, he'd been the first to warn us of Devillers' treasons, which had cost us so dearly. It seemed highly unlikely to me that Lien had been an enemy agent.

Yet nothing could have been truer. While the trial was still making headlines I was called to the witness stand. It was then that I learned that though Lien had informed us of Devillers' activities, and thus tried to save us, he himself had also been working for the enemy.

Early in the war, and without our knowledge, he had been arrested and offered large sums by the Germans to collaborate with them. An Alsatian refugee in the free zone, uprooted, penniless and weak in character, he had accepted the terrible bargain.

As his interrogation eventually proved, after the Devillers affair Lien had entered the Resistance network known as Alliance. In this undercover "ring" (which was commanded first by an army officer called Faye and then by Marie-Madeleine Fourcade), he'd managed to gain his comrades' trust and had even reached the apex of the organization. His tip-offs had resulted in the arrest and death of Faye himself and of many other members of the "ring." A gambler and a despoiler by temperament, he had done it all for lucre. And here he was now, sitting in the prisoners' dock with a big number on his chest to distinguish him from his co-defendants. The shades of his victims seemed to hover over him.

Called by the defense, I mounted the witness stand with

The Night Will End

contradictory emotions in my breast. A witness must report what he has seen and heard. I knew that Lien had wanted to save us. I was obliged to report that fact, and I did. Why had he helped us? Nothing in his position had constrained him to. Probably he still bore some sympathy toward those who had been his companions. Perhaps this deed had counterbalanced his sense of his ignominy and so salved his conscience.

I wondered if I should tell only what I personally knew and leave it to the others to present the positive evidence against him. No, such an attitude, I decided, might lead the court to conclude that I was indifferent to those of his crimes that had not affected myself or my movement. That was out of the question.

Hence I also gave my opinion of his crimes, insisting that they had been neither erased nor mitigated by his denunciation of Devillers.

Barely able to master my emotions as I spoke, I noticed that Lien's eyes were riveted on me. As I passed the dock on my way out of the court, I distinctly heard him say, "You bastard!"

Lien was sentenced to death and shot. Was there any other way?

Then it happened—just what I'd least expected.

On the morning of April 27, Marshal Pétain and his wife, en route from Germany to France, were arrested at the Franco-Swiss frontier station of Vallorbe. De Gaulle and the Keeper of the Seals, though surely abreast of the situation, breathed not a word about it—not even to the cabinet. The former chief of state and his wife were immediately incarcerated in the Fort de Montrouge.

What was to become of him?

"I alone am responsible," he had said. "History will judge me." Well, whatever history might decide, it was we ourselves, his contemporaries, who were about to judge him, for he was soon to appear before the High Court of Justice, empowered to try all of Vichy's former ministers and residents- and governors-general. It had already condemned Admiral Estéva, the former resident-general in Tunisia, to life imprisonment, and General Dentz, the former high commissioner in the Levant, to death.

A few days later I learned that the Marshal, hearing that he was to be tried *in absentia*, had seen fit to turn himself in to French

The Mystique of Unity

justice. His trial was now inevitable, but, given the current circumstances, I wasn't the only one to have serious reservations about it. To pass judgment on the Marshal, and thus on Vichy in general, would require solemn reflection, while in fact the passions engendered by the occupation were still raging. It would be important for us as a nation to distinguish between Vichy's foul crimes, which we in the Resistance had fought and denounced, and various other quite unreprehensible deeds. In our present state, I doubted that we had the time, the legal apparatus or the men necessary to open a truly valuable judicial inquiry leading to an indictment of such breadth and significance.

Five judges and twenty-five jurymen, presided over by the chief justice of the High Court of Appeals, M. Mongibeau, composed the special High Court of Justice. Twelve of the jurymen were former parliamentarians who had voted against Pétain's reception of plenipotentiary power on July 10, 1940. Twelve others, all former resisters, had been designated by the Consultative Assembly. I wondered if they would be able to contain their rancor and desire for vengeance, to stand fast against the ragings of public opinion; for true justice is a matter of conscience alone.

The previous July, when I was still in Algeria, several of us resisters had deliberated on what Pétain's just fate should be. At that time he had envisaged turning himself in to Henri Ingrand, the regional chief of R.6.

We had all agreed that he should be tried, but we were divided as to which court he should appear before and what the most fitting punishment would be.

I had thought, and I still did, that he should not be deprived of his liberty. It would serve no good and only irritate the public sensibility to make an eternal martyr of this old man so lately adulated by millions. To be truly exemplary, in the loftiest sense of the word, his retribution had to be sought in a purely moral realm.

We had to affirm before all future generations that a French field marshal, whatever his intentions, cannot, without forfeiting his honor, collaborate with the enemy. Had he not personally led millions of Frenchmen astray, had he not encouraged many of them to serve Hitler and his henchmen? Was he not responsible

The Night Will End

for the harvest of retribution, with its many death sentences, which they were now reaping? If he had been heeded and followed, it was precisely because of his great moral authority as a French field marshal.

Here, then, was the solution I had devised for this grave problem: Marshal Pétain would be condemned to death, immediately pardoned and publicly cashiered before the Tomb of the Unknown Soldier in front of a parade, in full review order, of the veterans of Keren, Koufra, Bir-Hakeim and other battles. Then the old man would be sent to his villa in Villeneuve-Loubet to live out his last days.

Pétain's trial, which opened in the courtroom of the first hall of the Court of Appeals of the Palace of Justice on July 23, has been amply chronicled. To justify his policies, Pétain read a declaration stressing the gravity of his responsibilities. Though fundamentally unacceptable, it lacked neither firmness nor dignity. Then he withdrew into a stubborn silence from which the provocations of the public prosecutor, General Mornet, altogether failed to draw him out.

On October 15, by a vote of 14 to 13, he was condemned to death. De Gaulle immediately pardoned him, commuting his sentence to life imprisonment. He was interned in the Fort du Pourtalet, where he himself had once locked up so many men of the Third Republic, and then in the Isle of Yeu. Six years later, in 1951, he died, still a prisoner, at the age of ninety-five.

The tide of repatriation was rising rapidly. By V-E Day 500,000 French POWs and deportees were already home. Most of our centers were working twenty-four hours a day. On the one day of May 13, 1945, 40,000 ex-captives were "processed" and sent homeward. Many had taken only three days to make the circuit from Germany to their home villages.

Sometimes we ran afoul of the Allies. Such was the case with my vain attempts to raise the quarantine they'd clamped on certain concentration camps, especially Dachau and Bergen-Belsen. In general, however, our relations were cordial. Toward mid-May De Gaulle passed on to me a letter from General Eisenhower praising the military repatriation corps:

The Mystique of Unity

. . . The aid and cooperation of the French authorities . . . have been a source of great satisfaction to me, and the work of the French personnel in the field has been first-rate. . . .

Overwhelmed by the sudden flood of liberated prisoners, the SHAEF often directed convoys of Frenchmen into foreign countries. They were very hospitably received in Sweden, Switzerland and Holland, where we had also set up functioning missions.

With the aim of showing the nation the results of the repatriation process, Robert Soulage's services organized a sort of festival on June 1 for the millionth homecomer.

He turned out to be a big blond fellow of about twenty-five by the name of Caron. I welcomed him back to France with an embrace at the Gare de l'Est. Then, alone and rather nonplussed in the back of a vast convertible limousine, he was driven across Paris to the acclaim of a large and good-natured crowd. He was to be hailed from station to station all the way home to his birthplace in the Hautes-Alpes, where his family still dwelt.

A radiant French people was joyfully gathering in its scattered sons.

By mid-June the only Frenchmen in West Germany were the seriously ill and a number of men who had decided to remain there. The repatriation of our captives in the Anglo-American zone had been achieved in less than a hundred days—just the target I had set for our services one year ago in Algiers. However, the homecoming from the Russian zone had only just begun. Many prisoners and deportees were still concentrated in Poland, Czechoslovakia and East Germany. Their return was mired in serious difficulties. I decided that I had best intercede personally on their behalf.

We were shivering in the cockpit. It was an unusually overcast day in July 1945, and the military plane taking me to Poland was skimming over Germany at a low altitude. Occasionally, perhaps to satisfy his own curiosity, the pilot would drop to 1,000 meters.

I gazed through the window at this land from which so much misery had been unleashed on the world. It was a desolate spectacle; villages and often whole towns were in ruins. Sometimes

The Night Will End

the bombing raids had razed every single wall in sight. What had once been bustling neighborhoods had been blasted level with the ground. I asked the pilot to circle a few times over Berlin. Sadly I scanned that immense city, searching in vain for a single undamaged house.

What a dreadful holocaust Hitler had inflicted on his people! And what a lesson for Germany! I wondered if these ruins, the millions buried under them and the survivors who wandered forlornly among them had really been necessary to convince her that war is never "lovely" or "redeeming" and that it is mortal folly to entrust one's fate to any man who claims to be the incarnation of Providence.

Yes, the men and women who were trying to survive in the wasteland beneath us had surely understood! It had been a dreadful lesson but a salutary one. And to us French too, I thought, the 1940 defeat, the occupation and the war had brought home a few truths. Our two peoples had somehow been reconciled by their sorrows. Perhaps the unity of our sad old continent was no longer an idle dream.

Roger Garreau, the French Ambassador to Poland, was awaiting me at the airport. At my request, our car drove unusually slowly through the streets of Warsaw on the way to my hotel.

They offered a heart-rending spectacle.

The city had been totally destroyed. Many streets had not even been cleared yet. Though it was noontime, a heavy silence hung over the hulking ruins, broken only by the occasional appearance of a jeepful of Soviet soldiers. Life itself seemed to have deserted forever the great metropolis by the Vistula.

Here and there, however, we began to make out the survivors. Most of them were still living underground, as they had during the insurrection. Others—very few indeed, it seemed—had re-emerged into the open. With planks, sheet metal and blocks of stone they had built rudimentary shelters from which smoke rose wispily. At several intersections I noticed that a statue of the Virgin had been rescued from the debris and enshrined on a makeshift pedestal. Beside Her a few candles would flicker, while at Her feet knelt praying women.

The Mystique of Unity

In the Soviet zone prisoners of war of all nationalities had been herded into a vast number of D.P. camps whose names had not even been given us. The first thing I did in Poland was to obtain a list of these camps and an authorization for the officers of the French mission to enter them. Thus could we take a census of our countrymen and organize their return.

In Russia, Mme. Catroux, the wife of our Ambassador to Moscow, General Catroux, kindly offered me her assistance. An awe-inspiring major-domo of a woman, she could put the fear of God into the Russians themselves. In uniform, her generous bosom clinking with medals, Queen Margot, as she had been known for the past twenty years, tyrannized her underlings and dumfounded all those who came to see her, but she also got results. The services she performed for my ministry amounted to little short of a miracle.

One of the tasks incumbent on me preoccupied all France. The inhabitants of Alsace-Lorraine had been regarded by the Reich as German citizens and many had been incorporated into the Wehrmacht. Some had been killed in combat, but a great number were now among the German POWs in Russian hands. Like the German prisoners, they were being very harshly treated.

In a center not far from Warsaw I met and comforted ten of these men who had been identified before my arrival. All in all, I figured that there must have been about 150,000 such captives. Despite our repeated overtures to the Moscow authorities and to the Soviet Embassy to Poland, I never received permission for my officers to enter the camps where they were detained.

At the request of the Soviet government, we took a census of all males absent from the towns and villages of Alsace-Lorraine, listing their names in alphabetical order and by Wehrmacht unit. This took us many months, but eventually we gave these lists to the Soviet authorities, who, unescorted by us, conducted a search and roundup of our men in their POW camps.

Similar problems faced me in Prague.
Unlike Warsaw, the Czech capital still rose intact out of its

The Night Will End

beautiful surroundings. Jan Masaryk, the foreign minister and the son of the founder of the Czechoslovak Republic, received me twice in his ministry. Tall and dark-skinned, he was the spitting image of Raimu, the popular Provençal actor. With his superb French, he even conversed like a man from our Midi, making his hands work overtime.

Eduard Beneš, the President of the Republic, also expressed a desire to see me. We'd met over a year previously when he'd visited De Gaulle in Algiers. At that time he had asked me to describe the Resistance to him in detail. He was especially interested in hearing about the French Communists and our relations with them. I had not concealed from him my apprehension that the Communist organizations had retained total autonomy, with the aim of seizing power.

Beneš seemed tinier than ever in his immense office. He immediately resumed our Algiers conversation as if we had broken it off only yesterday.

"So you see, Monsieur Frenay, all your fears about the Communists were unfounded. The liberation of France has taken place without civil conflict and the Communists are participating in the government alongside the other parties. I suppose the return of Maurice Thorez induced a kind of social peace you hadn't even hoped for."

"What you say is true enough, Your Excellency. Law and order do reign in France today, but only because of exceptional circumstances. First, our liberators were American, not Russian; second, we have De Gaulle and his extraordinary prestige; and, lastly, the government is shielded, so to speak, by the Franco-Soviet Pact. Elsewhere, where circumstances are different—in Poland, Rumania, Hungary and even here—the Communists may well find the temptation to seize power irresistible."

"Monsieur, I can speak only for my own country. By geography, language and customs, we are at the crossroads of the Slavic and Germano-Latin worlds. In the past we have witnessed only conflict between these two civilizations. Today, however, we may have the chance to serve as a bridge between them.

"The destiny of Czechoslovakia is to build just such a bridge between East and West Europe. My ambition is to be the architect

The Mystique of Unity

of this policy. Already I have excellent relations with Stalin, Churchill and General De Gaulle. I hope, and I believe, that I shall succeed."

Alas, the old statesman's optimism soon proved unwarranted. Stalin's iron curtain was to fall right on the western border of Bohemia. A tiny Communist minority was to seize power in Prague. Beneš was to die, and Masaryk was to hurl himself—or be hurled—from the balcony of the very office in which he'd received me.

The acceleration of the repatriation process had not silenced my Communist foes. Quite the contrary. Each and every morning I spent a full hour going through articles in the Parisian and provincial Communist press blasting me and my ministry.

In these columns bogus news, vicious insinuations, insults and slander were inextricably mixed. I was attacked for every imaginable misdeed: for underhandedly recruiting Vichystes and *cagoulards*, for slipping copies of Philippe Henriot's collected speeches into parcels destined for the POWs, for trying to slow down the repatriation process and thus prevent the ex-prisoners from voting in the upcoming elections, for abetting the burglarizing of our storehouses and, of course, for the criminal negligence and scandalous inefficiency of my administration. Subtly they conveyed that the *real* repatriation was being accomplished *despite* my ministry and even *against its will* by various popular organizations.

The walls of Paris and the provinces were plastered with posters denouncing me. All over France meetings were organized to indoctrinate our exiles as they arrived home and to escalate their demands for garments (of which I disposed of only a very small store), bonuses and discharge pay.

On June 12 several thousand militants, many of them Communist ex-deputies, gathered in the Salle Pleyel in Paris in the presence of the C.P. politburo. Jacques Duclos called on all the ex-POWs and deportees to back the Party's campaign or, better still, to join its ranks. André Marty, reiterating the charges against my ministry, enumerated the many demands that it had allegedly

The Night Will End

failed to satisfy and, to wild applause, vitriolically denounced "Henri Frenay, the man who hides his name."*

The Communists were obviously hell-bent on characterizing me as a horrid aristocrat, a wicked counterrevolutionary, an enemy of the people. This campaign was so well orchestrated that two years later new acquaintances still sometimes asked me what my real name was!

It was not surprising that this campaign had a big effect on the returning captives. In July, 20,000 to 25,000 ex-prisoners marched beneath my windows, clamoring for clothes, discharge pay and another wholesale purge. These familiar demands were interspersed with chants of "Frenay, resign!" and occasionally even "Frenay against the wall!"

It was, of course, the Communists who were in the vanguard, but I was rather surprised, and not a little hurt, to see among them the familiar face of François Mitterrand.

One day around May 20—that is, well before this huge demonstration—I got home exhausted from a very taxing day. After dinner I went to bed, but after several hours of sheep-counting I was still wide awake.

The incessant Communist-inspired attacks were a major factor in my fatigue. Never had any man in French politics been subjected to so long and so foul a smear campaign. I was alone, terribly alone, in a flood of filth. Discouraged to the point of nausea, I was almost in total despair. Though the M.L.N. had tried a few times to rein in its Communist minority, I could now clearly feel that people were abandoning me out of fear of becoming targets themselves. Some of my "comrades" were clearly not at all unhappy to see me so furiously attacked and, as they hoped, cast down.

Where now were all my old friends from that warm and well-knit team of Combat? Our old ethos of comradeship and fraternity had disappeared as the movement had become diluted in the M.U.R.

*This expression of contempt originated during the Reign of Terror, when aristocrats "hid their names."—Translator.

The Mystique of Unity

and later the M.L.N. And then, so many of my old friends had disappeared forever!

Alone, totally alone, I was invaded by successive waves of rage and disgust. Yet I was still morally obliged to present an untroubled façade to my colleagues in the government, to my political allies, to my friends.

In my staff it was my friend Raoul de Ricci who had the task of collecting and sorting out the many attacks on me that appeared in the press. One evening I took a bundle home with me. From this mud pile I selected two particularly foul examples.

The first one clearly intimated that I had delivered to General Franco, and hence to certain death, a number of Spanish political refugees in France. In the second, a certain Marie-Louise Baron claimed that I had refused to endorse the grant of asylum to 1,000 foreign Jewish children, thereby withholding "a signature that would have saved the lives of these 1,000 little martyrs." The article ended on this note:

. . . This endorsement has been refused, one suspects, for reasons of xenophobia and anti-Semitism, two words that alarmingly recall Vichy and its masters in Berlin.

I decided to sue *L'Humanité* for libel.

Oh, I harbored no illusions of easy victory. I knew that the trial would be long and that my opponents would use every possible subterfuge to retard the day of judgment. Too, in attacking only one newspaper (albeit my principal adversary) I could not silence the others. The slanders would go on to the end of the repatriation process; the evil would be done. Hundreds of thousands of decent Frenchmen would forever know me only as the Communists had depicted me.

Yet justice was my only weapon.

As I expected, the hearing before the criminal court of the Seine was postponed first to October, then to November. The president of the bar, Maurice Ribet, was my counsel. The hearing created a

The Night Will End

sensation, but, to the stupefaction of the public, my suit was dismissed.

Because of temporary adjustments in the judiciary, criminal cases of the first instance were at that time tried not by three but by only one judge. Given the reigning political atmosphere, as well as the awe and fear the Communist bosses then inspired, that particular judge would have had to be a hero to pass a verdict of guilty on Marcel Cachin, the editor of *L'Humanité.*

Of course, I appealed.

On June 26, 1946, the case was brought before a court composed, this time, of three judges. Cachin was sentenced for libel to pay a fine of 15,000 francs and to publish the sentence in his newspaper.

As for the preventive effect of this conviction, it was, so I was told, the twenty-seventh the old Communist leader had earned for the same offense!

When, in late May, I'd filed suit against *L'Humanité,* I had been well aware that several months would go by before the case was opened. In the meantime to acquaint the public with the truth, I had only one mouthpiece: *Combat.*

I wrote a series of four articles in which, having demolished my enemies' slander, I raised the debate to the level of political morality. Democracy, I insisted, required that public information be kept truthful and honest; slander and untruth could only poison public opinion and undermine democracy. Consequently, all forms of public prevarication should be swiftly punished, not with symbolic convictions but with the full rigor of the law.

Pascal Pia shook his head as I showed him my articles in *Combat's* head offices on the Rue Réaumur.

"Listen, Henri, I can't take it upon myself to publish these articles. Any direct attack on the C.P. would create dreadful problems for me. Let me talk to the editorial staff first. That'll take about twenty-four hours. I hope you won't hold it against me that I can't give you a yes-or-no answer immediately."

The answer that I got the next day, though couched in the friendliest of terms, was a flat no.

The Mystique of Unity

I immediately began to wonder who it was, after all, that really owned and ran *Combat*. Upon my return to Paris last September I had of course considered settling this question with the editorial staff, which had just then emerged from underground. It was only now that I saw how wrong I'd been to table this matter. At the time, however, my ministerial schedule had been heavy, and I'd had full confidence anyway in my friends on *Combat*'s staff.

As it happened, Claude Bourdet had just returned to Paris after a month of recuperation. After I had left France, it was Claude who had become *Combat*'s boss and written many of its editorials. The two of us agreed that Pia's and his colleagues' attitude was indefensible, especially considering that I myself, along with Menthon, had founded the newspaper in Grenoble in October 1941. In fact I myself had chosen its title and even designed its letterhead!

There could be no question of taking old Resistance comrades to court. The only solution was an arbitration between Bourdet and me on the one hand and Pia and his colleagues on the other. They agreed.

So began an interminable process in the midst of which we discovered that shortly after the Liberation Jean Bloch-Michel, the head of the company that managed *Combat* (which had itself been formed without our knowledge) had taken out a registered trademark on the newspaper's title.

There's no point in my going into the several years of legal pettifoggery that ensued. In brief, the Pascal Pia staff disappeared, largely as a result of poor management, to be succeeded by Henry Smadja, who, with his millions, was probably the only man capable of rescuing the nearly bankrupt paper.

In 1954 we tried a new and final tack. By now our sole aim was to retain the title *Combat*, the name under which we had fought and which was, in a sense, our banner. A new arbitration commission was set up, with Georges Izard and Pierre Mendès-France as arbitrators. This arbitration too was eventually broken off. Not only could my friends and I no longer afford such a procedure, but Pierre Mendès-France himself had meanwhile become president of the Council of Ministers and was obliged to resign from the commission.

The Night Will End

And that is why, until his death in May 1974, Henry Smadja retained control of the newspaper we had founded.

Most of the politicians of the Third Republic had returned to France around V-E Day. Imprisoned by Pétain after the Riom trial, they had been apprehended by the Gestapo in the days following the invasion of the free zone and subsequently deported to Germany.

Though interned by the Germans, they had been civilly treated. Because of the high offices they had formerly occupied, their American liberators had immediately escorted them back into France by plane and private car.

Léon Blum, the great Socialist leader who had been president of the council in 1936, returned to France at this time, accompanied by his wife. His captivity had in no way altered his fine physical and mental condition.

After spending a week in the new France, he addressed the secretaries of all the departmental sections of the S.F.I.O., who had assembled in the Montrouge town hall. The next day's papers fully covered his speech. I was delighted by what I read. His thoughts seemed so close to mine that I decided to meet him as soon as possible. In any case, the Montrouge meeting had proved that Léon Blum was still the undisputed and respected leader of his party. Perhaps an entente between Blum and the non-Communist Resistance could lead to the birth of a French "labor movement."

By now I'd moved to 15, Rue Raynouard, where I had a pleasant apartment with a good view of the Seine and the Left Bank. It was there, in very early June, that I first met Léon Blum. He and his wife kindly accepted an invitation to dine with me. I also invited Léo Hamon. (The latter, the former top man in the Toulouse section of our Workers' Action, had become a member of the C.D.L.R.* directorate and, like myself, belonged to the majority wing of the M.L.N.)

The first thing that struck me about Léon Blum was his exquisite courtesy. He had nothing of the "tribune of the people" about him

---

Ceux de la Résistance, those of the Resistance. One of the two major organizations in the occupied zone.

The Mystique of Unity

in speech or bearing. His voice, when unamplified, must barely have carried to the back row of an auditorium.

His recollections of his internment did not seem particularly bitter. In fact, he had shared his captivity with the rightist ex-chief of state, Paul Reynaud, and, though they had become close in a way, they still tiffed regularly over politics. His forced leisure had also given him the opportunity to do a lot of thinking and writing. Though convinced that socialism would emerge tempered to greater strength by the forge of war, he believed that it would still have to adapt to totally new postwar conditions.

"My dear President," I said, "you could never guess how delighted I am to hear this coming from you. Léo and I are quite representative of Resistance circles. Léo here, though originally a Communist, did not find in the C.P. the spirit of liberty he was seeking. As for myself, I'm a son of the old Lyons middle class, though I confess I never found in it much generosity or sense of justice to complement my own. It was in the Resistance that Léo and I and so many others first met. Our daily struggle against Nazism and Vichy conservatism, as well as our reflections and experiments, turned most of us into socialists. That would be obvious from a cursory glance at any back issue of *Combat* or any of our manifestoes."

"Sir," said Léo, "the masses of the resisters already lean to the left, and they yearn to help build a better society. However, they have no political experience. This is both an advantage and a serious drawback. Though they fairly beg to have their enthusiasm channeled in a positive direction, they are also very vulnerable to the rhetoric and obfuscations of the Communists."

We went on to describe in detail the factional struggles within the M.L.N. and the C.P.'s attempt to absorb or, failing that, to paralyze the movements begotten of the Resistance.

"And how did my friends in the M.L.N. react?" asked the old Socialist leader.

"Well, André Philip, 'Lionel' [Francis Leenhardt] and Max Juvénal are on our side, but even they hesitate to take a strong stand in favor of fusion with the Socialist Party, for fear, I think, of destroying what remains of M.L.N. unity. And by the way, we

The Night Will End

416

haven't found your secretary-general, Daniel Mayer, very sympathetic. In fact, he actually seems anxious over the contribution the Resistance might offer the S.F.I.O. Maybe he wants to keep the party hermetically sealed. If so, he's making a big mistake."

"Of course I can't say much about the M.L.N.'s strategy," said Blum. "For one thing, I don't really know your situation. But I can tell you that cooperation between the Resistance forces—that is, the truly democratic ones—and my own party is an idea that I find very compelling. Your people may well provide the new blood we need, for we've just eliminated many of our less qualified cadres. Believe me, I consider the Resistance a salient political phenomenon, and I use the word 'political' advisedly. Your movement has a marvelous potential that must be harnessed."

"The Communists agree with you there," I said, "but they want to do all the harnessing themselves."

"Well, then, we'll just have to be more convincing than they are," insisted Blum. "Of course, they're using crooked tactics against you, but that doesn't surprise me one bit. Remember what I went through? Here's the important thing: Don't *you*, under any pretext, start using the same tactics. Loyalty and honesty always triumph in the end—even in politics."

Our guest and his wife stayed on rather late; it must have been past midnight when they left.

Léo and I were thrilled: Blum was with us! We had just made a very powerful new ally. I was certain that he would be able to convince his party to accept our offer.

I walked Léo to the Place du Trocadéro.

"You know," I said, "I think we're really getting somewhere now."

"Well, I hope so," he answered, "but don't underestimate the sheer inertia of any big party apparatus."

It was a shrewd insight, as the future was soon to prove.

At last! The M.L.N. leadership had finally taken serious steps against the cabals of the Communist-led minority wing. The Federation of the Rhône was kicked out for having fused with the National Front, and, in the directorate, Claudius Petit pushed

The Mystique of Unity

through a motion calling for common action with the S.F.I.O. and Young Republic.* The Communists and their fellow travelers had lost the battle for our party. They shortly exited en masse and founded their own M.U.R.F. (United Movement for the French Resistance).

We ourselves soon became a full-fledged political party under the name U.D.S.R. (Democratic and Socialist Union of the Resistance). Léo and I drew up its first manifesto, stressing the themes dearest to me. Preliminary overtures were immediately made to the S.F.I.O. In truth, we had lost a lot of time. The enthusiasm of the Liberation had already subsided, but perhaps it was still not too late to capture the public's allegiance.

At any rate, I enjoyed watching *L'Humanité*'s editorialists boil over with helpless rage as they denounced "Frenay the minister's divisive maneuvers within the M.L.N."

On the other side of the globe the United States was bearing the brunt of the war against Japan. How far away it seemed! The truth was that this war was no longer ours. The man in the street read the headlines but did not feel involved. And yet the conquest of each Pacific island required a furious battle that usually terminated in hand-to-hand combat, for the Japanese never surrendered. Each day the war correspondents told of another savage struggle on some remote island whose very name had been unknown to us the day before. The Empire of the Rising Sun was clearly lost, but how many years would it take the Americans to occupy the whole of the Japanese archipelago and strike down its last defender?

As the war raged on, the structures of the new peace were also being elaborated. Since late April the foreign ministers of the Allied and nonbelligerent countries had been conferring in San Francisco to draft a United Nations Charter. Our own delegation was directed by Georges Bidault. Before its departure, the cabinet had deliberated the position that France should take toward the proposed charter, which had already been sketched out in her absence at the Yalta and Dumbarton Oaks conferences.

*Young Republic was a prewar political group of left-wing Christian persuasion and inspired by Marc Sangnier's movement, Sillon.

The Night Will End

Recalling the impotence of the League of Nations, several of us recommended that veto power be proscribed from the future organization. Our delegation did not of course receive a mandate to support this essential provision. Although it would have stood little or no chance of being accepted by the foreign powers, I believe that France would have distinguished herself by submitting it. Anyway, De Gaulle was too concerned with regaining full national sovereignty to consider abdicating even a jot of it to an international organization.

By the end of the conference, in late June, France had received the satisfaction of sitting beside the Big Four and being considered, like them, a permanent member of the Security Council. Each of those five powers received the right to exercise a veto, a right that was to paralyze the UN and render it ridiculous during the major confrontations of the postwar period.

And now yet another conference took place, and yet again we were not invited. This time it was a summit meeting in Potsdam. We could only speculate whether its purpose was simply to settle Germany's status or to prepare some more portentous design.

Roosevelt was dead; the United States was represented by his still obscure successor. Then, right in the middle of the conference, Winston Churchill was obliged to withdraw as the representative of the British Empire. The Tories had lost the British general elections to Labor. To the utter stupefaction of the French public, the great statesman and war chieftain, who, during the darkest hour, had so brilliantly incarnated the placid but indomitable British character, had been swept out of office. Ingratitude, they say, is a characteristic of strong peoples.

Churchill was replaced at Potsdam by the new Prime Minister, Clement Attlee. I'd talked with him privately twice in 1942 and 1943, when he was still serving the War Office. He'd impressed me as being very like a solid junior employee in some big office. Perhaps in those days he was simply eclipsed by the solar brilliance of Winston Churchill.

Harry Truman and Clement Attlee: did they have the combined weight to counterbalance the monolithic Stalin?

Europe was juridically at peace, but there was no peace at the

The Mystique of Unity

Potsdam conference table, for the Soviets' imperialist aims were by now a clear and present danger. Appalling news had begun to reach us from the Soviet zone. The democratic freedoms promised at Yalta had been snuffed out, and tiny Communist minorities were seizing power everywhere.

I remember General Juin telling me in the Matignon one day that he considered war between America and Russia inevitable. I believe that he was expressing not only his own thoughts but also De Gaulle's.

Despite France's absence from Potsdam De Gaulle succeeded in obtaining what he believed to be a priceless short-term advantage for France. We were to have our own zone of occupation in Germany, and our representatives were to sit in the Berlin Armistice Commission on an equal footing with those of our three great allies.

Was it really necessary for France to become an occupying power? I think not. First, occupation is only justified as a means to prevent the vanquished from seeking revenge, and anybody who had seen the extent of Germany's devastation knew that revenge was out of the question. Still more important, the mutual good will of our two peoples would hardly be nurtured by such an occupation, however justifiable. By not taking part in Germany's occupation, by leaving this task to the English and the Americans, France could, I believed, create a solid psychological foundation for an entente with Germany.

One day in early June I happened to be in De Gaulle's office in the Matignon over a legislative matter relating to our POWs. I mentioned to him my negative reaction to the idea of a French occupation force in Germany, though without the slightest hope, of course, that he would come to share my view.

"Frenay," he said, "you are a child. Haven't you learned yet that policy, especially foreign policy, is not made with noble sentiments? Do you think that Roosevelt, Churchill or Stalin indulge in noble sentiments? Of course not. They ruthlessly defend the interests of their nations. Such is their duty. *My* duty is to defend the interests of France, which, as far as Germany is

The Night Will End

concerned, begin with our presence on the east bank of the Rhine."

I was unconvinced. I persisted in believing that between nations, as between individuals, all solid and lasting relationships are based on a *quid pro quo*. The only alternative is an unstable balance of power in which each nation constantly jockeys for the upper hand.

Every single debate in the Council of Ministers widened the abyss that separated De Gaulle's notions from my own:

. . . If France does not invest the Rhine, her international position will be seriously weakened, because she will be constrained to conclude alliances for which she would not otherwise opt. . . .

France has a vital interest in drawing to her all the territories on the east bank of the Rhine. They constitute a geographical, strategic and economic complement of our country. . . .

We must strive at all costs to prevent the emergence of a sovereign German Reich, for Germany's tendency to unity is the essence of her will to power. . . .

This statement is only one of the many to which I objected on the spot. If De Gaulle had in fact been able to impose his will—if France had in fact "drawn to her" the east bank of the Rhine—he would have created a source of conflict between us and our neighbors for centuries to come.

How odd that De Gaulle is today so commonly portrayed as the architect of Franco-German *rapprochement!* An overly flattering portrait, I think, and one that history is unlikely to accept.

On the morning of August 7 my chauffeur was awaiting me as usual behind the steering wheel of my car. As I got in he handed me a copy of *Combat*.

A headline, followed by several columns of text, announced that on the previous day an atomic bomb had been dropped on Hiroshima. According to all available information, the city had been entirely destroyed by the explosion and resultant firestorm.

More than thirty years have passed since that summer day of 1945, yet I can still feel the horror that invaded me when I saw that headline.

The Mystique of Unity

Oh yes, I know: all wars have their atrocities; war is hell. But by 1945 the world had adopted conventions governing the use of arms. The collective conscience of man had even prevented the use of gas and bacteriological warfare after the 1914–18 war. In dim remembrance, perhaps, of the old days of chivalry, man had framed laws even for war and insisted on their being accepted and respected. True, they had often been infringed, but they were still the law of nations. Had they not provided the touchstone for Allied preparations to try the major Nazi leaders as "war criminals"?

"Woe betide him," says the Holy Writ, "who setteth an evil example unto others," and lo, the very land that had led the crusade for freedom and human rights had set the evilest of examples.

In late May the government had announced its intention of holding elections before the end of the year. In so doing, De Gaulle had kept the promise, made back in London in 1942, that he would "return France's destiny to her people."

The parties, movements and newspapers of France all caught campaign fever. Not only was this election to be exceptionally important, but it would also allow us to answer several crucial questions. How had the electorate evolved since 1939? And what would be the impact of female suffrage? Women would now be voting for the first time in French history, and nobody knew if they would be a stabilizing or a polarizing force.

It was also very likely that France would soon have a new Constitution, for, with the exception of a few conservatives and Radical Socialists, everybody considered the 1875 Constitution outdated.

Journalists, law professors and politicians all advanced their own solutions for the manifold issues of constitutional reform: the number of chambers in the legislature, election procedure and the powers and tenure of the current Assembly and its relation to the provisional government.

De Gaulle made it known that he wanted the new Constitution approved by popular referendum, but opposition to this procedure was quasi-universal. For various and opposing reasons, almost everyone in politics now distrusted the chief of state. Many feared

The Night Will End

that he would turn the referendum into a dubious plebiscite of the sort used by the Little Napoleon.

By the time we met on that blistering July 9 in the gilded chambers of the Matignon, the constitutional reform campaign that raged in the nation's newspapers and meeting halls had relegated all else to comparative insignificance.

De Gaulle had clearly worked long and hard on the précis with which he opened that ministerial conference. He had just ended a series of private talks with all the important political personalities of the day, including Albert Lebrun, the ex-President of the Third Republic.

It was his custom, both in public and before the Assembly, to speak purely from memory, but today he read a prepared statement, removing his glasses at each salient point to look up and scan his audience. It must have been rather difficult for him to judge our reaction, however, for we ourselves were all busily absorbed in taking notes.

As was always the case on any decisive occasion, De Gaulle's arguments were measured and masterful—on the condition that you bought his premises.

He called to mind the merits and defects of the various constitutions under which France had lived since 1789. Focussing on the 1875 Constitution, he dwelt at length on the weaknesses of the Third Republic, including the paralysis of the executive and legislative branches, the succession of forty-five presidents of the Council of Ministers and the total discredit into which the regime had fallen in 1940.

Already ill-adapted to our prewar needs, this Constitution had become a positive albatross. The interdependence of nations, the tempo of modern life and the greater role of economics in public policy required sweeping adjustments. However, some aspects of the old Constitution were worth saving. We needed a creative synthesis of tradition and innovation.

The tone of the public campaign for constitutional reform, continued the general, was utterly deplorable. Among the various solutions put forward was one that he categorically rejected: the proposal for a unicameral legislature with both full legislative and constituent powers. Such a chamber could make and unmake

The Mystique of Unity

governments according to its good pleasure; in a sense, they would be no more than its executive commissions.

"Gentlemen," he concluded, "such an assembly would be pure folly. Subject to powerful internal and external pressure groups, it would very likely succumb to one of them, in which case our freedom, and perhaps even our independence, might perish. I cannot accept France's exposure to such risks.

"Perhaps a unicameral assembly will do, but in that case its mandate must be carefully delimited in advance. We shall decide if this is possible. If not, we must return to the Constitution that Vichy destroyed."

Then each one of us was requested to offer his opinion. As a rule, depending on the subject under debate, this procedure was chaired either by the foreign minister or the Keeper of the Seals. Oddly enough, today the honor devolved on one of the two Communist ministers, François Billoux.

Of course he too had a prepared statement—prepared, that is, by the C.P. Bravely defying the general, he repeated word for word what Maurice Thorez had said to a recent Party Congress: France needed a unicameral assembly that was at once sovereign, legislative and constituent. Its members should be chosen by direct popular vote and proportional representation. To accept any other formula would be to capitulate to the "fear of the people."

In the midst of the long argument that ensued it was René Capitant who cast a brilliant ray of light. He insisted that to ward off the anarchy the general so justly feared our national institutions had to be carefully regulated until the new Constitution became the law of the land. Only the people, in whom sovereignty resided, could impose such regulations. By the same token, only the people could accept or reject the new Constitution. Hence, the people had to be consulted by referendum on *two* questions.

After our fourth hour of discussion we took a breather, strolling about the harmonious gardens of the Matignon in little groups. The general spoke first with Capitant, then with the interior minister, Tixier, and finally with Billoux. After a few minutes we re-entered the building and the council was again called to order.

The Night Will End

The debate resumed with the general taking up Capitant's theme: "These two referenda," he said, "must constitute a true manifestation of the national will. If they threaten to turn into manipulative plebiscites I shall refuse to accept them."

To our general surprise, we managed to agree unanimously on a press communiqué. The two Communist ministers had obviously received a directive to avoid a cabinet crisis.

Our communiqué was read to a record-breaking number of newsmen. The legislative elections, it announced, were to take place in October after the cantonal elections. The nation would decide by referendum if the Assembly should or should not be constituent. If the answer were affirmative, the Constitution would be submitted to the Assembly for approval.

All the political blocs, including the U.D.S.R., were dissatisfied with this project. Referred to the Consultative Assembly in late July, it was resoundingly rejected by 210 to 19 votes, despite De Gaulle's personal appearance in its defense.

The recalcitrance of the Consultative Assembly left the government with only one option, a resolution sponsored by Vincent Auriole and Claude Bourdet that had received over a hundred votes. This resolution endorsed the principle of the double referendum, with the proviso that the government could be unseated by a no-confidence vote in the Assembly.

Later, in August, a government decree set October 21 as the date for the elections and also provided the exact text of the two questions to be referred on that date to the people's will.

The Consultative Assembly convened for the last time on August 3, after which most of its members left to canvass their putative constituencies.

One day, perhaps, historians will arrive at a final estimate of the Assembly's achievements. They were, I believe, pretty slim. Moreover, the delegates' attitude toward De Gaulle and the government in the last few months grievously distressed me.

Parliamentary opposition is necessary, even salutary; but when it becomes a form of continual and systematic harassment it forfeits its claim to represent the public interest. Such was the case with the Consultative Assembly.

The Mystique of Unity

By late August I was in dire need of three or four days' rest, and I went to visit my brother and his family at Chambon-sur-Lignon in the Haute-Loire.

One morning I arose before dawn to enjoy that peaceful highland landscape. I gazed in delight at its meadows, its fir trees, its rushing stream where yesterday, for the first time in five years, I'd gone angling for trout. Yet despite the scenery my thoughts were still tethered to the upcoming political contest.

Only two years earlier my "Revolutionary Charter of Free Men" had been enthusiastically approved by the congress of Combat-Overseas:

. . . We desire that the government's authority . . . though subject to the control of popular representatives, be such as to enable it to fulfill its duties to the nation. . . .

Then, as my mind drifted still further into the past, I saw myself sitting with André Hauriou and Claude Bourdet in that little café on the Place du Capitole in Toulouse in 1942, putting the finishing touches on our manifesto, "Combat and Revolution." ". . . The Republic for which we yearn shall be strong, stable, and modern. . . ."

How disappointed I was now! Well, perhaps our fine sentiments had only reflected our naïveté about politics and human nature.

As for my personal future, logic seemed to dictate that I run for the Assembly in October. Several friends had suggested that I take a crack at Lyons, my birthplace and the cradle of our underground movement. Others had mentioned the Alpes-Maritimes and Ariège. I'd put them off, saying I wanted time to reflect. And here I was now, doing just that in the clear air of this mountain village.

By the time the U.D.S.R. had been born we'd already lost ten months quarreling ourselves hoarse in the M.L.N. The position on the political chessboard that should have been ours had been seized, as the municipal elections conclusively proved, by the old parties and the M.R.P. The political wind had turned against us; it would be rough sailing from now on. Our last hope was to form a compact, homogeneous and dynamic bloc with the Socialist Party. Unfortunately, such a bloc did not seem in the offing. In the

The Night Will End

S.F.I.O.'s Thirtieth Congress, which had ended ten days ago, Léon Blum's words had fulfilled all my expectations and had clearly reflected our June conversation:

. . . I've staked my reputation . . . on the entente between the Socialist Party and the Resistance movements. . . .

When I was far from you I became convinced of the need for a renewal of our party, and now that I am here I feel it even more strongly. . . . In the Resistance movements I saw a great potential for such a renewal. . . .

Have no fear, I adjure you, of contact with these fresh forces. . . .

The Socialist congress approved, by a vote of 6,100 to 2,700, the implementation of a unity program with the U.D.S.R., while at the same time almost unanimously rejecting an alternative plan for organic unity with the C.P.

Nonetheless, I knew that more than a few men in the S.F.I.O. were terribly afraid of our "fresh forces."

Claudius Petit and I received the U.D.S.R.'s authorization to initiate discussions with the Socialists. We contacted its secretary-general, Daniel Mayer, and the chief editor of *Le Populaire*, Robert Verdier. Highly suspicious of the proposed entente, they responded to us in a reserved, finical and rather patronizing fashion. This reception only fueled my apprehension about the rapidly approaching moment of truth when we and the Socialists would have to pick our common candidates for the upcoming elections.

It was then, for the first time, that an important question suddenly occurred to me: Was I really cut out for politics?

If somebody had asked me this question when I was in the underground and still far removed from the reality of a political career, I would have immediately answered yes. But by now I'd had some experience of life in politics, and it had proved very unlike my fancies. I smiled at myself as I recalled with what simplicity (a result, no doubt, of my military background) I'd conceived of that life. On one side I'd ranged the enemy and his confessed or unconfessed allies; on the other, myself and my comrades, united in the struggle against a common adversary.

The Mystique of Unity

In politics, if a strong personality emerges, the Lilliputians gather in the shadows to topple him. I'd already seen this happen several times—in the M.L.N., the U.D.S.R. and other parties. I now knew that to speak openly, to confide in others, is pure folly, for the slightest word or allusion may one day be used against you. In political life you have to be universally mistrustful, doubly so in the presence of political "friends."

Not so long ago I'd believed that politics were really only the above-ground equivalent of our underground struggle, that I'd find in politics the same *esprit de corps*, the same unshakable solidarity that had bound us together in the Resistance. What an illusion! Any politician who "wants to win," as they say, must be secretive, impenetrable, unmoved by expressions of feeling. He must carefully weigh his words, carefully construct his silences and never, never trust anyone.

Was I that sort of man? No, I had to admit that I wasn't—not by a long shot. I didn't feel superior to politicians, but I knew I wasn't one myself. Of course I too wanted to get to the top—that's where you can really put across your ideas—but not at *any* price.

I was pushing forty now, and there was one thing I knew I'd learned from life: that friendship is a great treasure. It was friendship that had brought me my greatest joy, the joy of sharing my feelings unguardedly and unreservedly with others. I clearly saw that if I ever approached the summit of political power, I would have colleagues aplenty but no true friends.

No, I could never forgo the warmth of friendship, especially not for a game whose harsh rules I was by nature incapable of playing.

My mind was made up. I would not run for office, but I would continue to militate within the U.D.S.R. and thus prove to all and sundry that I was not a rival and so could remain a friend.

Upon making this decision I immediately felt soothed, unburdened. Of course it was bound to disappoint some of my comrades, especially those who had openheartedly joined my camp and who believed that I should play an eminent role in the new Republic. Well, I would take them aside and explain my position to them. They knew me well and would surely understand.

What was I to do for a living? I had no idea. Taking advantage of a recent law reducing the number of officers in the army, I'd

The Night Will End

retired from its ranks for good. What would the army be like tomorrow? That was none of my concern for the moment. The important thing was that on this day I'd decided not to pursue a political career.

I returned to Paris in early September. In the first cabinet meeting I attended De Gaulle incidentally expressed his wish that the forthcoming November 11 ceremonies assume an especial gravity. They were to be our first celebration of Armistice Day, of the victory of 1918, since the collapse of the Nazi regime.

Such commemorations are usually the war minister's concern, but on that day De Gaulle asked the entire cabinet for suggestions. Intrigued, I devoted much thought to these ceremonies.

I came to the conclusion that they should be an occasion for solemn meditation, for reflection on the war that had just ended and that was so different from that of 1914–18. The sacrifice of a million and a half Frenchmen in the 1914–18 war was simply but grandly symbolized by a faceless and nameless soldier who lay in eternal repose and anonymous glory under the Arc de Triomphe.

It was the very grandeur of this symbol that led me to feel that its use for the 1939–45 war would be inappropriate. Moreover, what single Unknown Soldier could truly represent all those who had fought and died in this last war? Should he be a soldier of the 1940 campaign or a clandestine freedom fighter? A firing-squad victim or a gassed deportee? A Free French regular killed at Bir-Hakeim or Monte Cassino, or a maquisard from the Vercors or Mont Mouchet? Surely no one of these alone could evoke all those sons of France who, for five years, in uniform and in mufti, in France, Africa, Asia and the prison camps of Germany, had died for the liberation of their homeland.

Little by little, as the days went by, an idea took shape in my mind as to how that unity might be fittingly expressed.

The ten or fifteen different categories of war dead might each be represented by the mortal remains of at least one comrade. Far from being unknown, his name, chosen by lot, would be made public.

Arranged into several processions, these mortal remains would be escorted into the capital on the evening of November 10,

The Mystique of Unity

starting at the entrances in the city's old fortifications. The coffins would arrive at the Hôtel des Invalides at precisely the same moment, there to be disposed about the tomb of the Emperor. All through the night the old companions of each hero would keep a silent vigil for their dead comrade.

The following day, in one great cortège, our slain heroes would be borne in honor to the Etoile, where the coffins would be placed on high catafalques around the Arc de Triomphe. Thus the fighters of 1939–45 would rejoin their elders of 1914–18.

After De Gaulle and the government had offered their homage, the coffins would be transported to a temporary sepulcher. The permanent sepulcher I saw as a great lighthouse erected on the summit of Mont Valérien, where so many resisters had been slain. Their bodies would be placed in a crypt, and, that the capital's inhabitants would forever remember them, the lighthouse would nightly beam forth a luminous V for victory.

One day, in the general's office in the Rue Saint-Dominique, I suggested my project to De Gaulle.

"Frenay," he said, "I find your idea . . . well . . . deeply moving. I'd like you to develop it in a memorandum that you may submit to the Council of Ministers."

The Council approved my memorandum without reserve and charged me to direct a cabinet commission for the November 11 ceremonies.

Few tasks have given me so much satisfaction.

With the cantonal elections coming up in late September, to be followed on October 21 by the legislative elections and the constitutional referendum, all France was devoured by campaign fever.

As Capitant had suggested, the referendum was to comprise two questions:

(1) Do you the voter wish that the Assembly elected today shall be constituent?
(2) If the electorate answers the above question in the affirmative, do you approve that the public authorities selected to govern in the interim

before the new Constitution becomes law be organized in conformity with the provisions of the bill on the overleaf of this ballot?

The latter bill stated that the Constituent Assembly's tenure would be limited to seven months and that it would elect the head of the government, who would be accountable to it. It was also to have both legislative and budgetary authority.

Despite their importance, the cantonal elections of September 23 and 30 received little public attention. It was the legislative elections and the constitutional referendum of October 21 that aroused the people's interest. The government, of course, expected a yes answer to both questions on the ballot.

We in the U.D.S.R., despite a dissenting faction, campaigned for a double yes, as did the Socialists and the M.R.P. The Communists, the M.U.R.F. and the C.G.T. championed a yes-no answer and the Radical Party a no-no answer. The cacophony of yes-yeses, yes-nos, no-yeses and no-nos assumed an increasingly maddening rhythm, dumfounding the public and utterly delighting our satirical songsters.

The Communist Party bared its fangs. Having been unable to merge with the Socialist Party, it attacked the Socialists ruthlessly, especially Léon Blum, who at that time wrote a daily morning column for *Le Populaire*. The M.R.P. took a few blows too, becoming, in the current Red Propaganda, "the Great Pétainiste Reprocessing Machine." Though now out of the race, I myself was frequently lashed by the Communist press, a reprisal, no doubt, for my lawsuit against *L'Humanité*, scheduled to be heard that month before the 17th Criminal Court of First Instance of the Seine.

As I'd expected the U.D.S.R.'s discussions with the Socialist Party for the slating of common candidates proved highly trying. Though in the Seine we easily arrived at an equitable agreement, such was by no means the case in many other departments, where we failed to obtain the S.F.I.O.'s approval of the candidacy of many outstanding Resistance comrades. Often the latter were forced to yield to confirmed mediocrities whose principal virtue

The Mystique of Unity

was to have owned a party membership card for the past twenty-five years. Occasionally, for lack of agreement, the two parties offered separate slates.

I can hardly claim that I was surprised by the elections. The most cursory reading of the big dailies would have been enough to convince me beforehand that we were in for a bad time.

Nor was I surprised that the right was routed in the cantonal elections and that the Socialists, Communists and Christian Democrats (M.R.P.) scored big victories. The U.D.S.R., with its forty-four councilors-general, cut a pretty poor figure next to the Socialist Party, with its 810.

On October 21 the people voted overwhelmingly yes-yes, largely because De Gaulle had delivered a radio speech in favor of this position. Ninety-six percent answered yes to the first question, 66 percent answered yes to the second. The former Vichy zone, heavily canvassed since March 1944 by the Communists and their allies, provided the biggest contingent of yes-nos. For all that, the Communists as a whole had sustained a serious reverse.

Though the U.D.S.R. had won few enough seats in the Constituent Assembly, it was our percentage of the electoral vote that really revealed our weakness. While the M.R.P. had racked up 24 percent of the electoral vote, followed by the C.P.–M.U.R.F. with 22.3 percent and the Socialist Party with 18 percent, we of the U.D.S.R. (counting both our own slates *and* those we shared with the Socialists) had won a paltry 7.1 percent.

The elections signaled the demise of the Resistance as a political force. How right I had been, a week or so earlier, to write in a report to the U.D.S.R. political bureau that

. . . the way things are going, it's likely that within a few months the U.D.S.R. will be only a memory, and our representatives in the Constituent Assembly will be the last men to bear its label. . . .

The renascence of the old parties, who . . . represent nothing even remotely approaching a radical renewal, are slowly reconstituting the prewar political structure of the nation.

After proposing some urgent measures for greater party cohesion, I concluded:

The Night Will End

To continue to work under current conditions is to certify the prompt demise of the U.D.S.R. It is necessary that the political bureau—especially its top men—decide just what it wants and how best to get it.

If it cannot find a direction, we must prepare to toll the death knell of that Resistance which we will have buried with our own hands.

Perhaps it is unfair to say that the U.D.S.R., the last political hope of the Resistance, had already expired in the elections, but there is no doubt that it had entered its death throes.

In the first two weeks of November events followed one another at a furious pace. First there was the publication of the programs of the various political parties, then, in the Palais Bourbon, the initial session of the Constituent Assembly, which, restored to primacy, had rediscovered its true destiny in the lackluster person of Félix Gouin.

As soon as Gouin assumed the presidency of the Assembly De Gaulle tendered to him the resignation of the entire government.

Now if De Gaulle had remained permanently benched it would have been no skin off the backs of the Radicals and the minority wing of the S.F.I.O. On the other hand, the Socialist Party majority wing, headed by Léon Blum, as well as the M.R.P., the U.D.S.R. and all the moderates, hoped that the general could be persuaded to form a new government. In two meetings of several hours each the latter parties concluded an agreement backing De Gaulle.

As for the Communists, they initially demanded majority status in a new Popular Front, but, countered by De Gaulle, they backed down and agreed to accept his proposal for a national unity government. Their one condition was that they receive one of the three key portfolios of the Interior, National Defense or Foreign Affairs.

The upshot was a full-blown crisis. De Gaulle addressed the nation over the radio on November 17:

. . . because of the specific demands of one party, I now find it impossible to form, as I had wished, a government of national unity . . . and thus I am constrained to return to the nation's representatives the mandate which they entrusted to me. . . .

The Mystique of Unity

On November 21 the Assembly renewed that mandate by a vote of 555 to 0. De Gaulle formed his new government.

The Provisional Government was now a thing of the past. It had lasted exactly two years and fifteen days.

Two weeks had passed since the first session of the Constituent Assembly, two weeks that had left ashes in my mouth.

Our politicians, so lately under De Gaulle's thumb, were blatantly gloating over the fact that they at last had him at their mercy. Now they could exact their revenge.

Oh, I'd had my scrapes with the general all right, and his ideas certainly weren't my own, but how pathetic and alarming it would be if a Cuttoli or a Gouin were to be chosen over a man of his stature! Yet such, perhaps, was the way of democracy.

Is democracy necessarily the triumph of the mediocre over the excellent? Could our democracy not find a place for her great men, could she not be strong and confident enough to accept their services without fear?

No, today our democracy had neither that strength nor that confidence. And I shuddered to think of tomorrow.

November 11 was to be for me, as for most Frenchmen, a day of solace and joy.

For the past two months we of the Interministerial Commission had been drawing up plans for the ceremonies approved by the Council of Ministers.

On Monday, October 29, in the Hall of the Flags in the Hôtel des Invalides, the cabinet, the joint chiefs of staff and the representatives of the C.N.R. and the Veterans, Deportees and POWs gathered for a brief and solemn ceremony. We proceeded to select by lot the names of those heroes whose mortal remains would be honored by the nation. They were to include veterans of the 1940 campaign, Free French, resisters, deportees, prisoners and fighters from our overseas empire.

Was it chance or the hand of Providence that drew the name of Mme. Berty Albrecht out of the urn? I myself have never really believed in chance, and in truth who better than my dear old

The Night Will End

friend could have represented the heroic Frenchwomen of the Resistance?

On November 3 French and foreign newsmen jammed my office for a press conference. Through them, through the news media, the public was informed of the ceremonies' program and meaning. In every town and village of France, in Algeria, Morocco and the entire Empire, other, more modest ceremonies were organized to coincide exactly with those to take place in the capital.

A national committee had been formed to proceed with plans for a monument on Mont Valérien. It was presided over by De Gaulle and composed of the members of the Government and the most distinguished Frenchmen of the day. A national subscription was launched so that this monument might embody the gratitude of our entire people.

Everything was ready down to the tiniest detail. Nonetheless, I couldn't help worrying a bit. Would the ceremony go according to plan?

After nightfall I went incognito to the Colonnes du Trône whence one of the three processions was to depart.

That evening all theaters, cinemas and cabarets were closed. Along the prescribed route from the Place de la Nation to the Invalides the streetlights had been extinguished. A large and solemn crowd, more felt than seen in the darkness, filled the sidewalks, while the bells of Notre-Dame, echoed by those of all the churches in Paris, tolled in honor of the dead. From the Atlantic to the Rhine, from the North Sea to the Mediterranean and beyond the seas as well, churchbells rang solemnly in reply to those of the capital. In mourning and in silence, in meditation and in prayer, our nation mourned its fallen sons and daughters.

The coffins were placed on trucks that, escorted by motorcyclists and preceded and followed by two squadrons of torch-bearing cavalry, advanced slowly through the streets. A silent crowd solemnly fell in behind the cortège and accompanied the dead homeward. In the darkness one could hear only the hoofs of the horses, the shuffle of the crowd, the echo of artillery salutes

The Mystique of Unity

somewhere to the south and the mournful throbbing of the death knell.

I returned home to spend the evening alone with the memory of my dead friends. I hoped that at that moment every Frenchman and Frenchwomen felt in some way the warm presence of the brother, husband, son or friend who had never returned.

Toward 3:00 A.M. I walked through a silent Paris to the Invalides.

The fifteen coffins had been draped with flags and laid in the alveolas of the dome above the Emperor's crypt. Beside each one four persons, both men and women and most of them in uniform, mounted a guard of honor.

November 11 dawned bright and chilly. I had slept only three hours. Dressing quickly, at exactly 9:40 I joined the other members of the provisional government—the government whose last public appearance this would be—on the Place de l'Etoile. It was already packed with people. De Gaulle, himself no longer the chief of state but looking taller than ever in the company of the president of the Constituent Assembly, Félix Gouin, arrived about ten minutes later.

Then came a cavalry squadron, followed by the marching band of the Republican Guard, and then an infantry unit, heading toward us at a funeral pace and with lowered arms and escorting in its midst the caissons bearing the fifteen coffins. Another cavalry squadron brought up the rear.

One by one, clearly visible to the public on their high catafalques, the coffins were placed around the Arc de Triomphe. I started as a nearby cannon suddenly fired a salute.

De Gaulle advanced and ceremonially fed the flame. This ritual had been so often performed that I thought it had lost all meaning; yet now, as the bugles sounded the *Aux Morts*, I clenched my jaws and felt tears rising into my eyes.

Then the general delivered a brief address:

Disposed about the soldier whose name only God knows, and escorted by the shades of all those who, for two thousand years, have given their lives to defend the body and soul of our homeland—behold these, our

The Night Will End

gathered dead! They are symbolic of the many others who chose the path of glory with the same humbleness.

While this procession brings tears to our eyes and pride into our hearts, we the living sons and daughters of France must also understand the lesson which the dead have bequeathed us. . . .

We must agree to unite in brotherhood and heal our wounded France. Yes, in brotherhood! And that means that we must forget our foolish quarrels and take the same road together, at the same measured pace and with the same song on our lips! . . .

While these our dead rest here a moment before arriving at the shrine where they shall forever watch over our capital, let us, as one great and reunited people, raise our eyes and our hearts toward the future.

Long live France!

Yes, it was indeed that France might live that you fell along the way to victory: you, Berty, whose coffin is still before my eyes, and you, the slaughtered heroes of Cologne, and you, Jacques Renouvin, Marcel Peck, Jean-Guy Bernard, Claudius Billon, and you, all of you, my comrades in Combat, my friends both known and unknown.

At last we had arrived, we the survivors, before the gates of destiny.

Unity in combat was our law. This great ceremony, conceived in your honor, served all France as a reminder of that law.

For, thanks to you, the night had come to an end.

Tomorrow, as I well knew, was dark with foreboding.

But tomorrow was the future, and the future belongs to God.

The Mystique of Unity

EPILOGUE

More than thirty years have passed since that day in July 1940 when I drafted my first manifesto. Yet, in the course of writing this book and of summoning my memories of five years of war, I have felt the emotions of these years stir within me and reawaken, as if in the meantime they had only lightly slumbered.

I discovered, still fresh and unfaded, the moral tone of those first two years, that term of despair when, though we had all to lose and nothing to gain, our faith bested our reason.

Then men and women came to us with a rare offering, a quality unwitnessed in daily life but which, in my eyes, was their truest measure: a consonance of conviction, word and deed, which remained unbroken even by loss of liberty and the threat of death.

Each one of us sensed this common treasure in his fellows, and so it was that all of us, companions of the first hour, drew together in a warm and well-knit brotherhood, where rivalry, baseness and guile were unknown.

We were, I believe, truly fulfilled—first, in the accomplishment of our freely accepted task, but also in the exaltation of working side by side within a community so strongly cemented by the sheer selflessness of its members.

Most of us were young. Thus, we were not only happy but joyous too. There could be no falser picture of the resisters than as clench-jawed, hawk-eyed skulkers along walls.

True, there were times of tension and fear. The hardest ordeal was the disclosure that this or that comrade had fallen into Gestapo hands. Aside from such moments, which, thank God, were the exception, how many times did we not gaily gather to savor the wit of some friend or the tall tales of another?

What a contrast with the life that awaited us after the war! It was the same old chilly and formalistic democracy, in which the individual, lost in a faceless crowd, feels desperately alone. Nothing, nobody calls him to a noble task in which he can outdo himself. He lives as an atom with no organic function in any communal effort. Condemned by society to live in narrow egoism, he is unfulfilled. He has lost a limb of his being.

How different it was during the war, the first two years especially, when we felt so fully realized! Each one of us, with his brotherly warmth, with what he achieved in concert with others, gave the best part of himself to the group and its goals, harvesting in return the certainty that he was doing a man's work.

We never built the new, open and generous society of our dreams, whose picture, little by little, we had put together in many a discussion and many a white night. But was it not a mere castle in Spain, a romantic chimera, a city visioned in a fever? Was not France inevitably doomed to disinter those ways of the past which we had so unremittingly denounced?

No! Even after so much time gone by and so much reflection, I still stand by my old belief that most of the objective conditions for the revolution were present. For those of my readers under forty and for the short of memory, let me review a few essential facts behind the spiritual trauma of 1940.

We French had convinced ourselves not only that we were the cleverest and wittiest of peoples but also that we were the strongest and that our Maginot Line was impregnable. Had we not trounced Germany in 1918? Indeed, in 1940 Paul Reynard was still insisting that "we shall win because we are the strongest."

The Night Will End

Then, in a matter of weeks, the Wehrmacht, reborn only seven years earlier and commanded by a lowly Corporal Hitler, routed our armies and our war-college generalissimos, swept across our land, and sent two million men into captivity.

A dumfounded people tried to grasp what had happened. A culprit had to be found, and that culprit was, of course, the regime that had neither foreseen nor averted the catastrophe. In the twinkling of an eye, political edifices that had required seventy-five years to build were pulverized by our defeat. The leaders of the Third Republic disappeared in the quagmire of public discredit. Out of this apparent vacuum emerged, one by one, we, the men of the Resistance.

By degrees, the dangers and ordeals of underground action created between us a deep solidarity, a warm comradeship, an unshakable faith. This ethos enabled us sincerely to compare our opinions and verbalize our experiences and to peer together, with no thought unshared or dissembled, into the dim future.

Month by month, year by year, ideas and personalities cross-fertilized one another. Though it would be absurd to claim that we all had the same views or that conflicts based on class origin or personal interests had totally disappeared, we were still overjoyed to discover that our views, with a few exceptions, were very close indeed and that they united us more than they divided us.

So great was our unity that most of the political initiatives conceived during the Resistance were similarly inspired and aimed at similar goals. If this political kinship had not existed or if it had been a mere chimera hatched in the generous spirit of a few visionaries, there could be no explaining the fact that the profoundly innovative—and in some ways revolutionary—program of the C.N.R. was endorsed by every one of its members, including men as representative of French conservatism as Joseph Laniel and Louis Marin, not to mention the holdovers from the Third Republic.

Yes, the France of 1944–45 was ready and willing to embrace a society founded, as we desired, on socialism and individual freedom. Yet that society was not to be. Why?

There are many answers to this question, but they are all rooted

Epilogue

in one basic psychological fact: General De Gaulle utterly failed to understand the new phenomenon of the Resistance.

As the war recedes deeper into the past, the French public seems less and less to question the myth that the germ of defiance was planted by De Gaulle's appeal of June 18. Any reader of the general's *Memoirs* would naturally conclude that it was he who inspired, organized and directed the Resistance. Thus it may seem absurd or shocking of me to insist that he never even understood it.

Such, however, is the simple truth. Certain historians have in retrospect divined this truth, but the public as a whole remains ignorant of it. The wall between London and us, far from crumbling with the approach of victory, grew constantly broader and higher, and, by the spring of 1943, when reasonable men like Passy, their eyes opened by missions to the interior, began to see the light, it was already too late. For by then this wall of incomprehension and mistrust already towered between us, and nobody and nothing could breach it.

For almost two years De Gaulle and his crew remained incapable of conceiving any but military operations under the occupation, first and foremost intelligence but also sabotage. They ignored all the other kinds of action that our experience, especially in the free zone, had led us to adopt, unless such action became frankly political, in which case it only aroused their suspicions.

When, in the spring of 1942, one of the leaders of a big resistance movement in the northern zone arrived in London, Passy made no attempt to harness the potential political energy of this movement. Quite the contrary, he incited this leader, Christian Pineau, to forsake his movement and to build something that he, Passy, regarded as infinitely more important—an intelligence "ring." The same Christian Pineau was to exhaust himself wrangling out of De Gaulle a political declaration addressed to the nation and in whose implications the general showed no interest whatever.

For two long years it was military action alone that interested him. And efficiency required that it be directed, of course, from London, the seat of the Allied general staff, with whom targets

The Night Will End

could be fixed and from whom money and arms could be obtained.

In 1942 De Gaulle still thought that the Resistance should take orders from whatever agent he designated to represent him. The logical result was that the latter, and the latter alone, received control of the only real handles of power in our clandestine war—first, money; later, communications; and, finally, arms.

This plenipotentiary agency was bad in itself, regardless of the man chosen to embody it. Its powers were so broad as to make him absolute lord and master of the Resistance. Instead of opening new channels to that ardent and protean force, De Gaulle personally jammed up the already existing ones. Henceforth our messages, appeals and suggestions could be transmitted, accepted, modified, distorted or even blocked by De Gaulle's agent—whatever his good pleasure dictated.

De Gaulle thus pushed aside those captains who, during eighteen months without contact with him, had levied the legions of the Resistance. In so doing he refused these men, who knew the Resistance so well and who exercised such unquestioned authority over it, the right and the channels to communicate directly with him.

De Gaulle had condemned himself and, consequently, his services to see and hear only through the eyes and ears of one man.

That man was Jean Moulin.

In January 1942 De Gaulle entrusted him with "building a cohesive organization out of all those who resist the enemy and his collaborators in the free zone." In granting him such broad powers, De Gaulle incurred a very heavy responsibility. In the use he was to make of them and by the influence he in turn exerted on De Gaulle, Moulin himself incurred a still heavier and more political responsibility.

In criticizing him I do not mean to begrudge Moulin his exceptional and proven qualities—his piercing intelligence, his staunchness in action and the courage that eventually made him one of the great heroes of the war. I was among those Companions

Epilogue

of the Liberation who stood on the steps of the Panthéon on December 19, 1964, when his ashes were conveyed into the temple of glory. Yes, I was there, despite our differences, despite what I am going to say now and what I already then knew.

I was required a certain distance to understand that our mutual opposition, far from being a string of random altercations, was the inevitable consequence of a great blueprint that was undeniably political and had precise aims.

What satisfactory explanation can there be for the behavior toward the Resistance of a man as intelligent, reflective and pertinacious as Jean Moulin? What could his underlying motivation have been, a motivation that would answer every question that my comrades and I ever asked ourselves about him? Questions such as:

Why did he perpetually insist on removing numerous functions from the resistance movements and discharging them himself, thus diminishing their strength and augmenting his own?

Why did he systematically play the movements one against the other, with the particular aim of weakening the two biggest ones, Combat in the southern zone and the O.C.M. in the northern zone?

Why did he deliberately refuse to implement his standing order to amalgamate all the groups in the southern zone under the M.U.R. umbrella, and why did he favor certain independent groups by financing them instead of merging them with us?

Why, just when we had to fight back against stepped-up forced-labor deportation, did he slash our budgets while continuing to fund *sub rosa* various maquis that should by all rights have been attached to us?

Why did he favor the reconstitution of certain political parties, especially the Socialist Party, when he had received clear written instructions to the contrary?

Why, despite the opposition of all the movements, did he do his utmost to obtain De Gaulle's authorization to set up the National Council of the Resistance (C.N.R.)?

To these questions, which already plagued me during the war, I added several others after the war on obtaining further information:

The Night Will End

444

Why, in violation of directives received,* and concealing his acts from both London and the Resistance movements, did he send an envoy into the northern zone in 1942, and why did he select a Communist for this mission?

Why, without telling us anything, did he urge Georges Bidault to join the National Front?

Why did he sponsor as secretary of the C.N.R. directorate Annie Hervé, a Communist militant and the wife of Pierre Hervé, a future editorialist for *L'Humanité*?

Why were all his principal political assistants—Manhès, Meunier, Chambeyron—eminent members, or future eminent members, of the Communist Party?

There is but one satisfactory though purely hypothetical answer to all these questions, an answer that reflects my own deep convictions: Jean Moulin was the Communists' man.

I do not mean to imply that he was a card-carrying member of the C.P. but simply that he played their game and that all his actions—at least, all that I knew of—directly or indirectly served Party interests.

The fact, for example, that Moulin was Pierre Cot's protégé and staff secretary in the Air Ministry in 1936 is highly suggestive. In effect, since the beginning of the Popular Front, Pierre Cot has not once diverged from the C.P. line. For thirty-six years he had been, and remains today, a model crypto-Communist.**

As it happened, Moulin's own favorites—Manhès, whom he secretly dispatched into the occupied zone to prepare his subsequent actions there; Meunier, whom he elevated to the C.N.R. secretariat; Yves Farge; and Chambeyron—had all served under him on Pierre Cot's staff. It was they, and they alone, whom he chose to assist him in his political endeavors.

That Jean Moulin was a crypto-Communist is the only satisfactory answer to my questions. If we adopt this hypothesis, suddenly all is clear.

---

*These directives, signed by De Gaulle, strictly limited his authority to the southern zone.

**As a young student, Pierre Cot belonged to the royalist faction of the French Right. In the early Thirties he joined the Radical Socialist Party and was rewarded for his efforts with the Air portfolio in the 1936 Popular Front cabinet.

Epilogue

After patiently laboring all during 1942 to curtail the importance of the resistance movements for his own advantage, Jean Moulin killed two birds with one stone by creating the C.N.R. First, he humbled the movements, to the great profit of the remnants of the Third Republic; second, he offered the C.P. an exceptional opportunity.

The latter, legitimately suspect and isolated because of its attitude prior to June 21, 1941, had been unable to make any headway in the land. Still dynamic, well organized and disciplined, it discovered in the C.N.R. a perfect instrument with which to infiltrate the Resistance. For this reason the Communists, so sparing of praise to any but their own, have always glorified the memory of Jean Moulin.

I would not even dismiss the hypothesis that Moulin first went to London in 1941 with the blessing of the Communist Party.

In light of these facts we can see how gravely De Gaulle blundered in interposing an agent between himself and France. Worst of all, he chose as his agent a political partisan whom he had mistaken for a disinterested servant of the state.

The interposition of Moulin, though of course the general's own doing, eventually worked against him.

As the events of 1940 receded into the past, the Resistance grew apace and also became conscious of its own strength. I believe that De Gaulle feared the power and prestige of a Resistance claiming to represent France.

Is there any other explanation of his sudden outburst in the Savoy Hotel in November 1942 when he reproved me with the strange words, "'Charvet,' France must choose between you and me"? What can explain, if not the fear of a potential rival—a Richelieu's reflex—his constant desire to place his own men, men whose destiny depended on his good graces alone, over the Resistance?

De Gaulle had a certain tendency to enlist the aid of any man who suited his own purposes, supremely confident that he could eventually cancel the inconvenient side effects of that man's personal convictions or political ideas. It was thus, for example, that he entrusted the Interior portfolio to D'Astier. However, it

The Night Will End

was his choice of Moulin that had especially sinister consequences for France, for D'Astier in his capacity as interior minister only inherited the role already carved out by Moulin. Like his predecessor, D'Astier—along with his counterpart in France, Pascal Copeau—frustrated the political renewal we desired and winked at the C.P.'s infiltration of our organization.

Although it is true that De Gaulle's prestige and authority were the country's only serious defenses—aside from the American troops—against a Communist takeover after the Liberation, it was his own bad choice of men, and his own misbegotten relationship with the Resistance, that had paved their way in the first place.

The Gestapo did the rest. Very few of my companions of 1940–41 were to arrive at the end of the road.

Decimated by arrests and executions, mired in the machinations of the old parties, subverted by the Communists, by the summer of 1944 our movements no longer had the strength and autonomy necessary to initiate the revolution we bore within us.

However, it is likely that De Gaulle would have curbed such a revolution anyway. Fortified by a prestige he owed largely to the Resistance, the De Gaulle of the post-Liberation period allowed nothing to happen without him, much less against his will.

De Gaulle's encomiasts have tried to picture him as a great precursor, a visionary. The De Gaulle of the June 18 appeal was indeed such a visionary, but the man who in 1943 had the Lebanese President thrown in jail, who in 1944 publically advocated the balkanization of Germany and the attachment of the entire Rhenish corridor to France, who in 1945 installed Admiral d'Argenlieu in Saigon and who in 1959 assumed responsibility for the break-off of the Melun talks—thus ensuring that Algeria would become the den not of Ferhat Abbas but of Houari Boumedienne—this man was in no way, as his old guard would have us believe, the great "European," the archetypal statesman of the future.

True, in his public life he did advocate a measure of liberal reform, but only when buffeted by external events and always against his own inclination. Only after long years of war did he grant Algeria her independence; only after the events of May 1968 did he introduce a measure of participatory democracy into

Epilogue

France. Besides, who ever heard of De Gaulle himself practicing participatory democracy in state affairs?

In fact, De Gaulle probably would have been a giant in the era that ended in August 1914. It does not diminish him to say that he was in fact a sort of French Bismarck—a paternalistic and authoritarian nationalist.

Decidedly he was not the man to have encouraged the Socialist humanism, the society based on labor principles, that we were so eager to construct.

Lastly, for us to have achieved our political objectives, the directorate of the Socialist Party, and especially Daniel Mayer, would have had to rediscover the lucidity and intelligence of its old leader, Léon Blum, the man who had so enthusiastically welcomed the alliance of the Resistance and the S.F.I.O. Such a marriage, I believe, would have begotten a leader of the stamp of Jean Jaurès; instead, the S.F.I.O., squinting myopically at the immediate future—that is, the 1945 elections—eventually fathered Guy Mollet.

All our disappointed nation ever received was a pathetic caricature of the Third Republic.

Politically, we had failed.

In the moral realm, however, as in the military realm, I believe that we accomplished our task as we had conceived it in 1940. However great the valor of the Free French, it would not have been enough to save the honor of France. France needed a vast popular movement rooted in her national soil and commanding an ever-growing number of men and women ready to sacrifice themselves for her liberation.

"Liberty or death" was the motto of the sans-culottes. It was also implicitly our own. For in that land of ours, so sorrily abused by the Marshal's prestige and so abysmally deceived by a servile press and radio, it was we who showed the way, who nourished hope, who instilled courage and, finally, who led the battle for the Liberation. Yes, for those five years it was the Resistance that maintained the dignity of France.

There is a dark side to this picture. It was inevitable, and largely necessary, that numerous eleventh-hour joiners swell our ranks.

The Night Will End

They were numerous indeed, and many jumped on our bandwagon only in the thirteenth hour. These were the sort of people who always rush to rescue a drowning man just as he manages to reach the shore. Unfortunately, they often imparted a false image to the Resistance.

I have one bitter regret about that entire period—namely, that the government of which I was a member was unable to oppose this small minority of bandits and self-appointed executioners who, falsely taking the name of the Resistance, slaked their own thirst for blood and perpetrated misdeeds and even crimes.

The period was highly emotional, our authority precarious; it was impossible to quench these excesses. We could, however, have condemned them. This we failed to do. Even the true Resistance, I admit, was tarnished by our weakness.

After I had left France, and as the Allied landings drew near, I wondered with increasing anxiety how our military organizations—whose men we had recruited, organized and armed, alas, so meagerly—would perform if they would really spring out of the shadows on D-Day and strike at the enemy's jugular. How efficient would they be, how much punch would they pack? In a word, would the Resistance play an honorable part in the liberation of the country?

These questions have been answered by the historians and also by General Eisenhower. Without the maquis, the Groupes Francs, the N.A.P., Sabotage-Rail and the F.T.P.—in a word, without the French Resistance—the Allied landing would have been neither so complete nor so swift. It is even plausible that without the Resistance's having considerably slowed down the German armored divisions sent as reinforcements by the O.K.W., the Allied troops would have been thrown back into the sea. It is certain that they would have been in great peril.

I turned forty late in 1945. What was I to do with my future?

I could, of course, have re-entered the army. It had given me a first-rate background and one that I was grateful for. But I would now have found its earlier rewards and pleasures cloying, and after my last five adventuresome years any uniform would have pinched a bit, even if studded with stars or draped with yards of gold braid.

Epilogue

As for politics, I'd already rejected further government or parliamentary service, for I believed the Fourth Republic doomed to sterility. To be a stock minister in administration after ephemeral administration, to wield a political power bereft of any great objectives—in a word, to be a career politician—held no attraction for me.

Six months later the U.D.S.R., or its remnant, merged with the Radical Party, the very party that symbolized the defects of the regime that had abdicated in 1940 and that we had so assiduously denounced. I regarded this merger as politically dishonorable. Along with several friends I resigned from the U.D.S.R., banishing forever the thought of any further militancy in France.

It was then that I turned toward Europe, whose unity, after the last cannon shot, seemed not only necessary but an already existing fact. Victors and vanquished alike lived in ruins, bemoaning the loss of their loved ones and their hard-won possessions, shivering with cold and hunger. Europe, the mother of civilization, had become a pathetic and vulnerable invalid to be protected and nursed back to life by its muscular child, America.

During the war we had already sighted our great objective: the unity of the peoples of Western Europe in a federation, an authentically all-European power. Only this could save us from the tyranny of Stalinism or eternal dependence on the United States.

I believed that this federation should include those nations that had begun to realize that their sovereignty was a hollow concept, a fiction of international law that might even serve to veil their gradual deliverance into servitude.

In the framework of the socialist movement for the United States of Europe, and then in the European Union of Federalists, I devoted ten years of my life to the cause of European unity.

Here too my job was arduous but inspiring. I traveled all over Europe, held out my hand to the same Germans whom yesterday I had been fighting and participated in innumerable congresses, meetings and lecture sessions. Many people embraced our gospel with alacrity. It was youth especially that responded to the call of Europe.

The Night Will End

As in 1940, our greatest stumbling block was the "reasonable" people—that is, the fainthearted and the skeptical—and, again as in 1940, they looked down on us with that special pity people reserve for visionaries and dreamers.

During the summer of 1954 the Common European Defense Treaty was rejected by our National Assembly. The great ardor which, in the war's wake, had swept Europe's peoples toward unity had sputtered out. A new phase had begun in which a world-weary public opinion was to play no part. Europe had fallen into the hands of the diplomats, the technocrats, the experts, who for the most part represented only selfish national interests.

Yet all our efforts had not been in vain. Look at what we accomplished in less than a quarter-century! For over three hundred years the nations of Europe had ceaselessly torn each other apart. Today a European war is unthinkable. In 1945–46 our idea of European unity brought a smile to the lips of "sophisticated" people. Today, all Frenchmen proclaim themselves Europeans. The most diehard jingoists would feel silly unfurling their flags. They too tag along in the great forward march, though of course at a slyly lame pace.

I and my old friends in the European Union of Federalists (U.E.F.) know that from 1945–55 we helped give the European cause a powerful *élan*, a large audience and maybe even a deeper and livelier spirit.

I could not, of course, play the man for all seasons. With the rejection of the C.E.D., a season ended. The hour had come for me to withdraw. As in a relay race, I passed the torch of witness to others.

In 1958, despite my opposition to General De Gaulle, his return to power seemed to me necessary to quash the threat of civil war, to reform our decadent institutions and to resolve the Algerian problem. I also had a score to settle with the Communist Party. For these reasons I yielded to the friendly insistence of two old comrades and agreed to run for the legislature in Montreuil, then the fief of the Communist bigwig Jacques Duclos. Endorsed by the S.F.I.O., of which I was a member, and listed as a "left Gaullist," I was no unconditional minion of the general's, and the Gaullists knew it well. Thus the U.N.R. decided to run against me a man

Epilogue

who, though a perfectly decent fellow, was kept on a short leash. The rising Gaullist tide of 1958 carried him into the Palais-Bourbon.

This was, I believe, the best that could have happened. I was not, of course, elected, but the 10,400 ballots that bore my name ensured the defeat of Jacques Duclos. That goal, at least, had been achieved.

The years have flowed by, peaceful and serene. We have been troubled only once, by the word of De Gaulle's death. In one instant, as if by a miracle, everything in him that had once provoked my opposition, my intense irritation and even my disgust vanished from my soul. In one instant I forgot his immense vainglory, his cold ingratitude toward so many of his old companions, his Machiavellism. In one instant something huge and indefinable thawed in my heart, leaving a great emptiness for which reason could not account.

Perhaps it was that same feeling of emptiness that compelled the four of us, though so seemingly dissimilar in temperament—Pierre de Bénouville, Marcel Degliame, Colonel Passy and myself—to speed together toward the Colombey-les-Deux-Eglises that evening of December 11.

Though it was reason that had guided us toward De Gaulle in 1940–41, it was, I believe, a sort of unsuspected tenderness that had bound us to him. This man had bodied forth before the eyes of the world our army of shadows, had spoken—and with what brilliance!—for us the silent ones. If our tenderness had often been disappointed, it had never, as I now realized, been diminished.

How strangely moved I was, next day, in that little church of Colombey, to see that throng of old companions gathered from the remotest quarters around his great bier. Among them were, of course, the veterans of Free France but also the men of the Resistance, including many who had been his bitter political opponents. Yet there we stood, with lumps in our throats and tears in our eyes, wordless as statues before the grandeur of this farewell.

REQUIEM AETERNAM DONA EIS DOMINE . . . As the coffin disappeared in the crowd, carried by the young men of the village, we turned the last page of a chapter of our lives, indeed the noblest

The Night Will End

and most beautiful chapter. We knew that a man of rare stamp had just departed from our midst. The world knew it too, for the world mourned with us.

As I conclude this book, I am also ending a long voyage into the past. Like every one who has had the courage to act, I have known both success and failure, both hope and disappointment, both joy and sorrow. All in all, I have been deeply gratified by life, for my own has been varied, impassioned and exalting. I also believe it has been useful.

I now enter the winter of that life, and I can truthfully say that I would change nothing in it. As I lay aside this manuscript, my soul would sing a hymn of thanksgiving.

Porto-Vecchio, July 1971
Neuilly, September 1972.

Epilogue

ABBREVIATIONS

A.S..: *Armée Secrète.* Secret Army.

B.C.R.A.: *Bureau Central des Renseignements et d'Action,* Central Bureau for Information and Action. The Free French secret service in London.

B.I.P.: *Bureau d'Information et de Presse.* Information and Press Bureau. Underground organ directed by Georges Bidault.

B.O.A.: *Bureau des Opérations Aériennes.* Bureau of Aerial Operations. For clandestine airlifts.

B.R.A.L.: *Bureau de Renseignements et d'Action de Londres.* Successor to the B.C.R.A.

C.A.I. *Comité d'Action Immédiate.* Immediate Action Committee. Created in 1943 as an organ of movements in both northern and southern zones.

C.A.S.: *Comitéal'Action Socialiste.* Committee of Socialist Action. The underground French Socialist Party.

C.D.L.: *Comités Départementaux de Lib-*

ération. Departmental Liberation Committees. Created by the C.F.L.N.

C.D.L.L.: *Ceux de la Libération.* Those of the Liberation. Resistance movement in the northern (occupied) zone.

C.D.L.R.: *Ceux de la Résistance.* Those of the Resistance. Resistance movement in the northern (occupied) zone.

C.F.L.N.: *Comité Français de Libération Nationale.* French Committee of National Liberation. Immediate predecessor of the G.P.R.F.

C.G.E.: *Comité Général d'Etudes.* General Committee for Studies. Underground group for political studies created by Jean Moulin.

C.G.T. *Confédération Général du Travail.* General Federation of Labor. France's largest organization of labor unions. Communist-dominated.

C.I.C.R. *Comité International de la Croix-Rouge.* Red Cross International Committee.

C.L.D.: *Centre de Liaison et de Documentation.* Center for Liaison and Documentation. A secret service created in late 1944 for communication with French POWs in Germany.

C.N.F.: *Comité National Français.* French National Committee. De Gaulle's directorate of the Free French in London.

C.N.R.: *Conseil National de la Résistance.* National Council of the Resistance. Coordinating organ of all Resistance groups, labor unions and former political parties in both the northern and southern zones of France.

C.O.M.A.C.: *Comité d'Action.* Action Committee. Military directorate of the Resistance located in France.

D.G.S.S.: *Direction Générale des Services Spéciaux.* General Directorate of Special Services. Under De Gaulle's aide Jacques Soustelle. Successor to the B.C.R.A. in Algiers.

The Night Will End

F.F.C.: *Forces Française Combattantes.* Fighting French. The totality of all Allied French forces both in and outside metropolitan France.

F.F.C.M.: *Forces Françaises Combattantes Métropolitaines.* Metropolitan Fighting French. The armed forces of the metropolitan Resistance.

F.F.I.: *Forces Françaises de l'Intérieur.* French Forces of the Interior. Created by the C.F.L.N. with the aim of conferring the international juridical status of combatant on the metropolitan resisters.

F.F.L.: *Forces Françaises Libres.* Free French. Name for all French people who rallied to De Gaulle following his Appeal of June 18, 1940.

F.N.: *Front National.* National Front. Communist-led Resistance organization.

F.P.: *Faux Papers.* False Papers. Combat's service for providing counterfeit identity papers.

F.T.P.: *Francs Tireurs et Partisans.* Irregulars and Partisans. The military arm of the National Front.

G.F.: *Groupes Francs.* Irregular Groups. Combat's shock troops.

G.P.R.F.: *Gouvernement Provisoire de la République Française.* Provisional Government of the French Republic (under De Gaulle).

M.L.N.: *Mouvement de Libération Nationale.* Movement of National Liberation. The umbrella organization (and later political party) representing the French metropolitan Resistance.

M.N.P.G.D.: *Mouvement National des Prisonniers de Guerre et Déportés.* National Movement of POWS and Departees. (Underground.)

M.R.L.: *Mouvement Républicain de Libération.* Republican Liberation Movement. Group representing the Christian democratic elements in the Resistance. After the war became the M.R.P.

Abbreviations

M.R.P.: *Mouvement Républicain Populaire*. Republican Popular Movement. Christian Democratic political party founded after the Liberation. Recruited militants from the Resistance.

M.U.R.: *Mouvements Unis de Résistance*. United Resistance Movements. Created in early 1943 through the merger of Combat, Libération and Franc-Tireur.

N.A.P.: *Noyautage des Administrations Publiques*. Infiltration of Public Administrations. A Combat special service designed to subvert the Vichy hierachy.

O.C.M.: *Organisation Civile et Militaire*. Civil and Military Organization. A Resistance movement in the northern (occupied) zone.

O.K.W.: *Oberkommando der Wehrmacht*. German general staff.

O.R.A.: *Organisation de Résistance de l'Armée*. Army Resistance Organization. Created by army officers after the dissolution of the French Armistice Army in late 1943.

O.S.S.: Office of Strategic Services. The U.S. Secret services.

C.P.: Communist Party.

P.P.F.: *Parti Populaire Français*. French Popular Party. Pro-Nazi political party founded before the war by Jacques Doriot. Later became a major collaborationist force and an element in the extreme right-wing opposition to Pétain.

P.S.F.: *Parti Social Français*. French Social Party. Ultraconservative prewar political party founded by Colonel de La Rocque.

R.1: The Rhône-Alpes region of the French Resistance shadow administration. Center: Lyons.

R.2: The Provence–Côte d'Azur region. Center: Marseilles.

R.3: The Languedoc–Roussillon region. Center: Montpellier.

The Night Will End

R.4: The Sud-Ouest region. Center: Toulouse.

R.5: The Limoges region. Center: Brive-la-Gaillarde.

R.6: The Auvergne region. Center: Clermont-Ferrand.

R.P.F.: *Rassemblement du Peuple Français*. Rally of the French People. Short-lived political party founded by De Gaulle in 1947.

S.F.I.O.: *Section Française de L'Internationale Ouvrière*. French Section of the Workers' International. Formal title of the French Socialist Party.

S.H.A.E.F.: Supreme Headquarters of Allied Expeditionary Forces. The high command of the Allied troops in all European theaters.

S.O.A.M.: *Services des Opérations Aériennes et Maritimes*. Service for Air and Sea Operations. Predecessor to the B.O.A.

S.O.E.: Special Operations Executive. The European branch of Britain's secret services.

S.O.L.: *Service d'Ordre Légionnaire*. Legionary Public Order Service. The military arm of the Legion Française des Combattants, a Vichy veterans' organization.

S.T.O.: *Service du Travail Obligatoire*. Compulsory Labor Service (also called *la relève*.) Forced labor draft of French workers for German industry. Masterminded by Pierre Laval.

U.D.S.R.: *Union Démocratique et Socialiste de la Résistance*. Democratic and Socialist Union of the Resistance. Formal title of the political movement based on the non-Communist Resistance elements in the M.L.N.

Abbreviations

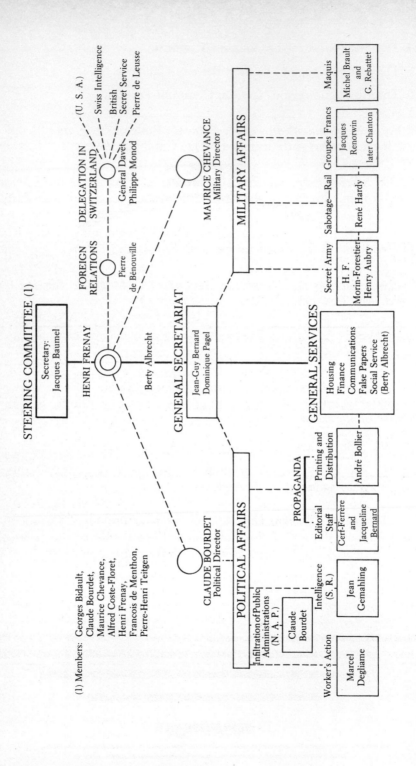

INDEX

Index

Index

Index

Index

Index

Index

Index

Index